THE REBEL
ON THE BRIDGE

GLYNN BARRATT

THE REBEL ON THE BRIDGE

A Life of the Decembrist Baron Andrey Rozen
(1800–84)

PAUL ELEK : LONDON

First published in Great Britain in 1975
by Elek Books Limited
54–58 Caledonian Road
London N1 9RN

ISBN 0 236 31015 1

Printed in Great Britain
by Ebenezer Baylis and Son Limited
The Trinity Press, Worcester, and London

For Halina

CONTENTS

LIST OF ILLUSTRATIONS

The jacket design is based on a water-colour by K. I. Kol'man (Shown in reverse) depicting the Decembrist Uprising (see below)

Between pages 70 and 71

The manor-house at Roosna-Alliku early this century (from Heinz Pirans, *Das baltische Herrenhaus*, Riga, 1928)

The fifteenth-century Munkadetagune Tower, Tallinn (photo by E. Raykyul)

The Senate Square, St Petersburg on December 14, 1825; water-colour by K. I. Kol'man, *c.* 1830 (Istoricheskiy Muzey, Moscow)

Andrey Yevgen'yevich Rozen, *c.* 1825; water-colour by N. A. Bestuzhev, 1832

Medallion showing Anna Rozen, *c.* 1824 (property of her descendant, V. N. Vladimirov; photo by B. Karsonov)

St Isaac's Bridge, St Petersburg, where Rozen halted his troops on December 14, 1825; as it appeared in the 1840s (oil painting by Bishbois; photo by B. Karsonov)

Between pages 182 and 183

Cells in the Crownwork Curtain of Peter-and-Paul Fortress (from *Petropavlovskaya krepost'*, Khudozhnik RSFSR, Leningrad, 1971)

Exterior of the Curtain (from *Petropavlovskaya krepost'*)

Decembrists in Chita. *Above:* Annenkov (*extreme left*), Lorer, Baryatinsky (*right*); water-colour by N. P. Repin (photo by B. Karsonov). *Below:* Repin, Rozen, Yakushkin, Fonvizin, Obolensky; sketch in Historical Museum, Moscow (photo by B. Karsonov)

The siege of an aoul by Russian troops (from Lesley Blanch, *The Sabres of Paradise*, John Murray, 1960)

The manor-house of Edise (Ets), as it appeared in 1972 (photo provided by Eve Peets)

Rozen as an Arbitrator of the Peace, *c.* 1862 (photo provided by Pushkinskiy Dom, Leningrad)

Maps

AUTHOR'S NOTE

I take this opportunity gratefully to acknowledge all the help I received in the writing of this book. Thanks are due, first, to Eve Peets of the Estonian State Historical Museum (Eesti N.S.V. Riiklik Ajaloomuuseum), Tallinn, for opening the archives of the State Museum to me, and for arranging to have photographs sent to me from the Library of the Academy of Sciences of the Estonian S.S.R. (Eesti N.S.V. Teaduste Akadeemia Teaduslik Raamatukogu); to Sirje Annist who, although officially on leave, returned to Tallinn and escorted me through those archives; to the Director of the Tallinn Municipal Museum (Tallinna Linnamuuseum) for information on the Rozen manuscripts in Tartu; and to Dr Waldemar Miller, Chief Archivist of the Academy of Sciences of the Estonian S.S.R., whose kindness and whose learning are familiar to all who have visited his province by the Lenin Boulevard.

My gratitude is also due to the Director of the Manuscript Division (Rukopisnyy Otdel), Saltykov-Shchedrin Public Library, Leningrad, for permission to work on materials kept under reference *fond* 124 (the former P. L. Vaksel' collection); to I. F. Grigor'yeva, Chief of the International Exchange Section of that Library, for making available microfilm of Rozen estate papers (1846–75) and family correspondence (1824–25); and to Irina Yevgen'yevna Grudninina, of the Workroom (Rabochaya komnata) of the Institute of Russian Literature of the Academy of Sciences of the U.S.S.R. (Pushkinskiy Dom), for providing illustrations of A. E. and A. V. Rozen (1824 and 1869).

I would also like to thank those connected with the newly-instituted Decembrist museum (in the former Rozen house) in Kurgan, Western Siberia: August Martin, now of Kokhtla-Yarva, Estonian S.S.R., and Boris Nikolayevich Karsonov of Kurgan.

Next, a word of thanks is due to Mr Wolf von Kleist, editor-in-chief of *Baltische Briefe*, for putting me in touch with the Rosenscher Familienverband, that is, the modern family association of the House of Rosen. In particular, gratitude is here acknowledged to two members of the Rosen family: Baron Friedrich of Vienna, and Baron Kersten of Flensburg, West Germany, who made available to me the *Nachrichtenblatt des rosenschen Familienverbandes* for 1956 and 1959—booklets containing information on the subject of this book by Hans von Grocholin and Ingeborg von Rosen; Baron Kersten also entrusted me with unpublished materials, notably a letter from A. E. Rozen to his father, Eugen, of early August, 1832.

Finally, mention must be made of scholars in the West who have given me support and encouragement throughout the writing of this book: Professors Anatole Mazour, late of Stanford University, and Gleb Struve of the University of California; Isobel de Madariaga and Georgette Donchin of the School of Slavonic and East European Studies, London; Peter Squire of Cambridge University; Geir Kjetsaa of Oslo; and J. Koit of the Estonian Learned Society in Sweden.

On two technical matters: I have referred to "Ests", and not "Estonians", wherever A. E. Rozen does so. Since *estonets* was in common use by 1850, his choice, though archaic perhaps, was deliberate. So too, with "Revel'". "Revel'" seems more appropriate than "Reval" in an overall Russian context, the context of this book, and since Rozen himself commonly spoke of "Revel'" the matter is sealed. On the question of spelling: with regiment and surname endings, I adhere to the modern British rule, which is to break the rule: -sky, not -skiy. Individuals in the Russian service but of German origin are generally referred to by their Russian forms, e.g. Shteyngel', not Steinheil, Benkendorf, not Benckendorff. In a nineteenth-century Russian setting, the Rosens become Rozens: before 1800, they are left in peace.

Ottawa, 1975

SYNONYMOUS GERMAN AND ESTONIAN PLACE-NAMES

Dorpat	Tartu
Ets	Edise
Fellin	Vil'jandi
Garrien	Harjumaa
Gapsal	Haapsalu
Ievve	Jõhvi
Mehntack	Maëtaguse
Neuhausen	Vastseliina
Oesel	Saaremaa
Pernau	Pärnu
Sónorm	Roosna–Alliku
Valk	Valga
Veisenstein	Paide
Venden (Wenden)	Tsesis
Verro (Vyru)	Vora
Vezenberg	Rakvere
Worms	Vormsi

INTRODUCTION

1975 sees the one hundred and fiftieth anniversary of the Decembrist rising in St Petersburg. This study is designed, in part, to mark that bleak but seminal occasion. It is also designed to provoke a somewhat greater interest than has been in evidence among historians, either in the Soviet Union or in the West, in the important, non-Slavic Decembrist, Baron Andrey (Andreas) Yevgen'yevich Rozen (Rosen) (November 3, 1800–April 19, 1884). Baron Andrey Rozen was in three respects unique among the well-born constitutionalists, republicans, and would-be regicides who attempted a revolution in St Petersburg on December 14, 1825, and who thus came to be known as the Decembrists. First, alone of the adherents to the Severnoye Obshchestvo (the Northern Society)— a secret, politically-motivated group based in the capital—he was brought to a complete halt within sight and sound of the revolt on Senate Square, between the Senate and the Admiralty, by perfectly divided loyalties: on the one hand, to his concept of the honour and duty of a Russian officer, on the other to the liberals, his comrades. Secondly, he alone of the Decembrists was sufficiently aware throughout his life of his non-Slavic origins to give expression to that consciousness in articles and essays. Ethnically, and emotionally, his links were with the Baltic German Province of Estonia (Esthland), not with Great Russia; it was a consciousness that was to give him special interest in, and insight into, what is now referred to as "the question of the nationalities". Thirdly, he was viewed by his companions in revolt, as by his fellow-exiles in Siberia and contemporaries in 1870, as the individual who, by producing an authoritatively accurate account of the entire Decembrist movement, from its first stage to its last, provoked the minor avalanche of reminiscences, memoirs and notes published on or by ageing Decembrists between 1870 and 1885. Certainly, Rozen's memoirs are of very special value to historians in their account of the period and of the rise of Russian liberal thought at the time. Incomparably accurate and factual, yet pervaded by a pleasant sense of balance, they were first published in a non-Slavic language—German, Rozen's native tongue—and so were accessible from the start to wide German, French and English readerships.

To amplify on these three points: Rozen was descended from the Rosens of Bohemia who, as Knights of the Order of the Sword, had held lands and exercised great influence in Estonia since the thirteenth century. It was an ancient family, with military traditions and a strong sense of honour of which

Rozen was highly conscious. Awareness of that code promised him, by 1825, a career in the Imperial Russian Army of some note: the Grand Duke Nicholas had noticed him, and liked him. Yet, by the same token, loyalty to his companions who refused to swear an oath of allegiance to Nicholas on the ill-fated morning of December 14, 1825 (and it was right to refuse, he saw; allegiance had been sworn to Constantine two weeks before), brought his career down in ruins. Torn by that conflicting understanding of his duty and by utterly divided loyalties, he simply stood, midway across St Isaac's Bridge on the Nevá, three hundred yards from the embattled carré of the rebels, and looked on. From his vantage-point, he saw the grim unfolding of a scene in the long tragi-comedy of Russian liberalism: the arrival of the Tsar and of his seven-year-old son; the manœuvring of horseguards over icy cobblestones; the gestures of grand dukes, priests, mounted officers; and, finally, as dusk approached, the swift, bloody finale as canister swept everyone from the Square, killing at least one hundred onlookers. Small wonder that his account of that day is among the most reliable and lucid that we have.

Sentenced to ten years' hard labour and then perpetual exile in Siberia by a special supreme court on July 10, 1826 (a sentence shortened, later, to six years), Rozen left for Chita, in Transbaikalia. Four years later his wife Anna joined him, and together with his growing family State convict Rozen passed two years in Petrovsky Zavod, east of Lake Baykal, then two more years in Georgia where, despite a fractured leg, he was officially required to serve as a private soldier. For "those gentlemen", Nicholas is reported to have told his heir, who had himself seen several of the Decembrists in Kurgan in 1837 in the course of his grand tour of Siberia, the way home to European Russia "could lie only through the Caucasus".

But for Rozen, Russia proper was not home, nor had he any wish to live in Moscow or St Petersburg. And in Georgia, where the Government was introducing an emphatic policy of swift russification of all newly-conquered southern peoples, Baron Rozen grew even more conscious of his German origins, and of his special Germanness as one of the *Herrenvolk* of the Province of Estonia. The pressure on new subjects of the Emperor to profess Orthodox Christianity and to speak Russian, not Georgian, Circassian or Armenian, which Rozen felt in the vicinity of Tiflis (Tbilisi) in the late 1830s, was unpleasantly familiar— and would become far more so. He could not usefully protest against infringements of the Georgians' rights to be free to live their national life within the Empire. He himself had been stripped of title, rank and property. Returning to Estonia in 1839, however, he immediately saw that he could still wield influence, both in the region in which he settled and, through relatives, elsewhere.

Installed in Ets (Edise), then in Bol'sháya Sóldina (Suure Soldina), five miles south-west of Narva, Rozen once again took up his earlier occupations and main interests—interests which had deepened in his thirteen years of exile: scientific farming, the abolition of *corvée* in favour of some form of quit-rent leasing to the peasantry, and history, specifically the history of Estonia. He did everything he could to ease the peasants' lot. Educating four young sons, caring for an estate, corresponding with his comrades in Siberia and the south, years passed. Finally, in 1855, it became necessary to move to the Province of Khar'kov. His eldest son, Yevgeniy, was unwell. The Malinovsky lands, part of which his wife Anna now owned, had to be managed. The Rozens left Estonia, but only physically. Emotionally, the Decembrist never lost his ties with his "dear native land".

Increasingly during the sixth decade of the nineteenth century and more especially after the granting of Imperial amnesty to the Decembrists by the Emperor Alexander II, in August 1856, Rozen became aware of his connections —psychological, social, and even intellectual—with his former fellow-exiles. By corresponding, he maintained contact with many; on brief visits to Moscow and the provinces of European Russia between 1856 and 1862, he met others. Not that he now lived in the past—on the contrary. After emancipation, he served two three-year terms as an Arbitrator of the Peace (*Mirnyy Posrednik*) in the district of Izyum, Province of Khar'kov, and performed his duties diligently. He opened a school for the local peasant children, and a bank, using his own limited funds. He read widely. But now, immediate issues could not touch him as they had. The Crimean War struck him as pointless, and British gunfire in the Baltic sounded less impressive than the cannon which, some thirty years before, had opened Nicholas's reign with bloodshed. He reread old notes and started to arrange them consequentially. Finally, in the 1860s, he began to write the memoirs which appeared in German in 1869.

Rozen's memoirs provoked great interest in Russia and the West alike. In Russia, they were seized upon by liberals of a younger generation, happy, like Nekrasov, to glorify the rebels of 1825—martyrs to the cause of liberty. In the West they were translated into English, and regarded as the best available account of the Decembrist tragedy. And so, indeed, they were: always Rozen strove for factual accuracy, struggling to avoid personal bias. Nowhere, perhaps, is this trait more evident than in the seven finely-drawn biographies or, more properly, obituaries of his friends and fellow-exiles that are spaced throughout the memoirs. A military historian by temperament, Rozen respected fact, and did his best (a rather different matter) to treat it in a way and tone conducive to expression of the truth; to that end, he cultivated balance. Statement, one is reminded by his work, implies omission; and omission can be conscious. But all is not fact in his articles and memoirs, though precise, factual statements form their spines; there is also a sense of movement and of colour in his writings. In Siberia and Georgia, he was quite alive to the exotic, but no less conscious of the dignity and worth of, for example, the life of Old Believers in Tarbagatay, or of mountain tribesmen in the area of Belyy Klyuch. To be sure, Rozen deplored the dirtiness and paganism of the Buriats; he was a conscientious Lutheran. He also disliked the idleness so prevalent among the Greeks whom he had watched in Georgia, the superstitious piety of peasants in Voronezh, and the cool manipulation of the peasants around Vil'no by the local Catholic clergy. But never did antipathy lead to distortion. For the anthropologist and social scientist as well as for the cultural historian, Rozen's accurate descriptions of Siberian life during the 1830s, of its climate and geography, peoples, commerce, industry, priests and customs, are of real and lasting value.

Yet, in his last years, Rozen increasingly ran counter to the mood of far younger liberals—a mood inclined to celebrate the grand Decembrist myth created, twenty years before, by A. I. Herzen, who was not disposed to praise the quest for simple truth. The Decembrist message had been blurred, even deliberately changed or misinterpreted. How better, since he was alive still and could easily refute would-be distorters, to serve his former comrades' memories by presenting future Russians with a faithful, full account of the whole movement. So he came to see his rôle in his last years; and his comrades were in general willing to accept his view. Rozen's articles, dealing with individual Decembrists, the Decembrists in the Caucasus, his own experiences as Arbitrator of the Peace, his attitude towards Estonian problems in the 1860s, are of as much value today as ever. Surely there is no greater compliment to any memoirist than the fact that his reminiscences are taken by successive generations—and, in the main, most justifiably—at face value. No eye-witness account of the Decembrist tragedy is more deserving of our confidence; few others are more elegant, lucid, or controlled in tone and style. Primary sources for all subsequent accounts of "what actually happened" on the Senate Square, in Peter-and-Paul Fortress and in the Winter Palace, in Siberian imprisonment and southern purgatory, the memoirs of Decembrists have an obvious and undeniable importance to all students of the period. They are the bricks that all later historians use; they are the vital records that a dozen generations have interpreted, reread and weighed. But even this is not their whole charm or significance: because there are no less than twenty-seven different accounts of the events of 1825–36, by Decembrists, all may very well be left to prove their worth and to establish their validity as factually accurate. Each one supports another—or fails to do so; thus, by comparing various texts, we are nudged towards the truth. By comparing Rozen's account of, say, the journey to Siberia in 1827 with those of other memoirists, we may test Rozen. Again, by placing his descriptions of Siberian life beside those of contemporary Western visitors—Erman, Haxthausen, Cottrell—we may verify his picture. Suffice it to observe here that however carefully one scrutinizes Rozen's statements on a wide spectrum of issues, and on happenings that cover fifty years, one is brought to the conclusion that, of all Decembrist memoirs, his most merit confidence. If only for this reason, they deserve respect and wider use.

Clearly, no book as short as this can hope to deal exhaustively with any individual's life. No biography, perhaps, can more than hint at the main traits and interests of men or women never seen, never addressed; the flesh is gone, and with it the reality. For this reason, I have chosen to place emphasis on facets of A. E. Rozen's work and life that interest me most: his consciousness of being an Estonian or, rather, a German-speaking officer born in Estonia, serving the Russians; his conduct on December 14, 1825; his interest in history; and, lastly, his awareness of becoming the annalist *par excellence* of the Decembrist movement. It is hoped, however, that these facets, which lie side by side, may be seen together with others to form a sound and sympathetic whole.

Farewell, garden of Taara, flowering banks of Emajŏgi; farewell, dear hills, forests, fields of the fatherland. The child becomes a stranger to its mother's breast, and the man must tear himself out of Love's arms.

Kalevipoeg, V.

I

THE ROZENS IN ESTONIA

The Rosens of Ets, Sónorm (Roosna-Alliku), and Mehntack (Maëtaguse, Maëtaga) in Estonia, were the senior Baltic branch of a great international family whose history covered a thousand years. Theirs was, indeed, among the longest of all Baltic-German lineages, and the family of Baron Andrey Yevgen'yevich Rozen, the Decembrist (1800–84), the most ancient of those deeply implicated in the rising of December 14, 1825, in St Petersburg. Several Decembrists could boast of mediaeval lineage: the Murav'yovs, Ivashevs and Yakushkins had been boyars and had wielded influence in Muscovy during the sixteenth century. Prince Sergey Trubetskoy, elected and supposed to lead the rebels in the capital but absent at the crucial hour, was descended from the royal Lithuanian House of Gedymin, of the fourteenth century.[1] But these, compared with Rozen's antecedents, were the brief records of upstart clans.

Commonly regarded as the founder of his house, members of which flourished in the Polish, Swedish, French and Russian services and every part of Europe, Count Robert Rosen of Slavnik in Bohemia in A.D. 991 married Maria, sister of the German Emperor Henry II. So the Decembrist proudly tells us in his *Skizze zu einer Familien-Geschichte der Freiherren und Grafen von Rosen, 992–1876*,[2] a work of his old age but, in the main, a valuable source of biographical and other information. From the first, it is apparent, the Rosen knights had prospered by the sword, not by any diplomatic skills or amiable qualities of character. For land or influence, they had hired their services to any prince and had acquired great power throughout that territory known as Estonia after its native populace of Saxon times, as well as in Livonia to the south.

Waldemar von Rosen, who was prominent in Riga between 1282 and 1290 when he held various posts of an administrative/military kind, is now generally regarded as having founded the first line (*die erste Stammereihe*) of the Baltic House of Rosen which flourished in the region to the north and east of Riga. Others of the family, with Otto Robert at their head, fought with Erik Menwed at Jutland in 1290–91 and also knew the fruits of power. In 1452, the fifth generation divided into two with two ill-assorted brothers, Hans and Jurgen. From the elder brother, Hans, sprang the second Baltic line. The father of the subject of this book, Baron Eugen Octave August (1759–January 26, 1834), who himself founded the seventh Baltic line (Rozen of Mehntack), represented in direct male line the sixteenth generation from Count Waldemar, the twenty-third from Robert, Count of Slavnik. Andrey Yevgen'yevich, it cannot be too greatly stressed, sprang from an ancient, alien line of feudal lords.

But Estonia, his martial forebears had at once seen, was no land of milk and honey, but "an inhospitable land, with little natural wealth . . . peopled with heathens who lived on a tribal basis scattered about their gloomy forests, heaths and marshes".[3] In most parts of the country there were sombre woods and marshes, and the Rosens themselves, if not quite heathen, were more than slightly inhospitable. They quickly consolidated their new power in stone and mortar. From strongholds in Livonia, Gross-Roop (1263), Klein-Roop (1272)[4] and Hoch-Rosen (1275), they terrorized those very peasants who had built them, laying waste the lands of all who dared oppose their will. From 1290 to 1310 they asserted their position in the Danish lands. They were members of a ruling class and race—Knights of the Sword who once, as Knights Templar, had fought the Turks in Christ's name, but who now grew famous only for feats of cruelty against unarmed, oppressed Estonians. A conquering nobility, a *Herrenvolk*, these were the violent German forebears of the Baltic-German barons.

In theory, the Rosens of Estonia, like their fellow knights, were vassals of the ruling King of Denmark. In practice, they were virtually autonomous and ruled their huge estates like petty sovereigns. In Estonia, as a modern writer has remarked, the Germans found a veritable conquerors' paradise;[5] and Rosens played their full part in eliminating any sign of dissidence on the part of an Estonian peasantry which, by 1300 at the latest, had been reduced to a state of serfdom far more absolute than that in Bohemia or Saxony, whence many of the German conquerors came. But the desperate Ests would not sullenly accept their fate, as had their southern neighbours in the future Latvia. Revolt followed revolt despite most horrible and sanguinary reprisals.

After the massive peasant rising of April 23, 1343—the "St George's Eve insurrection"—it was apparent to the Danish king and knights that such authority as Denmark had once exercised over Estonia no longer existed. On the eve of St George, more than ten thousand peasants had marched stolidly from the district of Harju, in the north-west of Estonia, to the fortress-town of Tallinn (Revel'), and there, in one long day, murdered and maimed some eighteen hundred Germans, including several Rosens. The Knights of the Sword ordered reprisals and the population of Harju was destroyed to the last infant, dog and pig. In 1346, the Danish king sold his "title" to the sovereignty of northern Estonia to the knights—but to the Teutonic Knights, not the Knights of the Sword. The latter were unable to pay 19,000 silver marks. In its turn, the Order of Teutonic Knights resold the "title" to the military force of the Archbishopric of Terra Mariana (Riga), the Livonian Order. The Danes withdrew, more Germans came, some went. But such royal contracts and high dealings mattered little to the Rosens. They were members of all orders in the Baltic, for their family was large and forward-looking; besides, they held great castles, so could not be sent away unceremoniously. They remained, and spread their influence.

It was indeed, as J. H. Jackson has it,

> a strange colony that the Germans established on the far Baltic shores. Historians at a loss for a parallel have compared the Teutonic invasion of Estonia with the Norman conquest of England, on the slender ground that both invaders came as Crusaders with the blessing of the Pope and that each remained minute minorities in the conquered country. But whereas the Normans established central government, whereas they intermarried with the natives so that a fusion of the two races took place, whereas they allowed the written as well as the spoken language to become that of the conquered English, the Germans never attempted any centralized government and always held themselves apart from the natives, forbidding mixed marriages under pain of direst punishment, insisting on the use of their own language in all written transactions . . .[6]

Nothing, perhaps, was more indicative of the Germans' consciousness of racial superiority than this, the linguistic bar. Estonians were forbidden to speak German, lest they presume to false equality with nobles. Protestant pastors in a later century, by the same token, always preached in the Estonian tongue and, incidentally, through various translations of the Bible, hymnbooks, calendars and almanacs, went far to guarantee that the Estonian language would not perish. "If we must play the game of historical parallels," continues Jackson wearily, "the nearest approach is certainly the conquest of Ireland by Norman barons. It occurred about the same time, and there is much in common between the Meyendorffs, Tiesenhausens, Rosens and Uxkülls . . . and the Fitzgeralds and de Burghs."

Necessarily, given their circumstances in their newly-conquered land, the Rosens, like all other German lords and petty princes, were acutely conscious of belonging to a special class, a race, as Dr A. Bilmanis puts it, "predestined to be Paladins of Germanism on Germany's northern and eastern borders".[7] They were rulers of their own domains, and owed obedience to no king. Yet, at the same time, they were never truly independent lords; such was the price the former knights paid for neglecting to centralize their power in the fourteenth century when they could easily have done so.

In the long term, the Rosens could survive and keep their influence intact only by following a policy of full co-operation with whichever power was paramount throughout the area at any given time. As the Grand Princes of Moscow were, from 1330 onwards, prospering through politic servility towards the Tartar khans, so the Rosens, in their smaller but no less deliberate way, strengthened their position in Estonia by appeasing first the Poles and Lithuanians (Klein-Roop was near the Polish sphere of influence in the later Middle Ages), then the Swedes, and finally the Russians. Not that the Rosens were particularly servile; to the contrary, they were proud. But they were also shrewd and, as a house, well able to pursue a policy that called for stamina and some persistence. One feckless Rosen, it was plain, could totally destroy the family's joint efforts to remain on amicable terms with the chief power of the day. But, happily for them, they were a systematic, patient family. By 1560, when Estonia became part of the Swedish Baltic empire, their position was no weaker than it had been in the time of Waldemar, three centuries before. The way in which they used the rise of Swedish power to bolster and extend their own is in itself instructive of the slow but subtle working of the family's entire approach to foreigners, that is, its foreign policy, throughout the Middle Ages.

In 1558, turning aside from the Crimea and the ancient Turkish threat as, in his turn and in the same spirit Peter I would do in 1699, Ivan IV sent a large army west towards the Baltic coast. The Russians reached Livonia in January. They turned north towards the Rosen lands and captured Ets, soon to become part of the extensive Rosen patrimony. On May 11, they bombarded, burnt and, towards sunset, seized the fort of Narva. The booty included 230 fine brass cannon.[8] The days of the German orders were plainly numbered on the Baltic littoral. For the lords of the Teutonic Order, possibly, some hope remained. Since their great defeat at Tannenberg (1410), the knights had formed a duchy, embraced Protestantism, and edged towards the core of modern Prussia. But what would happen to the erstwhile Knights of the Sword, who held that portion of the Baltic coast that was both economically and politically essential to a growing Muscovy? The danger was apparent; the knights, including a Rosen, appealed to the Emperor Charles V to prevent the passage to Moscow of European scholars and, above all, of military officers. It was, they urged, a question of inheritance. But Sweden felt her claim stronger than Muscovy's.

The Russians captured many fortresses in 1558. In July they took Tartu, and with it massive stores of grain and 552 more cannon. But Sweden's power was also growing, and the Rosens had to decide whether to throw their lot in with the Russians, or calculate on ultimate Swedish control over Estonia. Their solution to the problem was to help both parties in a guarded way, and always to keep several options open. It was, *par excellence*, the Rosen policy, and the family adhered to it until the final outcome was apparent. No Baron Rosen fought the Russian infantry at Narva, or aided Kettler in Livonia; noting the fact, Ivan did not reduce their local influence or confiscate their lands while he was able. Again, one Reinhold Rosen did his best in 1571 to capture Tartu for the Poles (the Russian star then being on the wane throughout the Baltic, since an army of Crimean tartars 120,000 strong had briefly captured Moscow); how could the Poles not view the Rosens' claims with favour? Yet by 1581 Ivan had lost Polotsk, Wenden and Narva, and the Swedes were well entrenched again in Tallinn and throughout northern Estonia. By that year, it seems entirely natural, the Rosens were in Sweden's pay, their position, wealth and influence unshaken by long international turmoil and a decade of intrigue.

Like Boleslaw of Poland and Waldemar of Denmark, Charles X of Sweden had a Rosen in his suite. So the Rosens went from strength to strength. In the Niguliste Church in Tallinn, which was shelled in World War II, there was a handsome epitaph in the baroque style to Count Bogislaus Rosen (1572–1658). He was, so the inscription read, Swedish Vice-Regent in Ingermanland and loyal servant of the Swedish Crown.[9] Other members of the family, too, held posts in the new Swedish Baltic territories. In acknowledgement of their joint services the Swedish Crown granted to them, in perpetuity, the estate of Sónorm thirty miles north-east of Paide and a mere day's ride from Tallinn. The mansion that they built there was inhabited continuously by the heads of the Estonian branch of the family until 1764.[10]

One member of the family especially, Gustav Friedrich (1688–1769), earned the deep gratitude of Charles XII. Born in Tallinn, this young Rosen joined the Swedish cavalry at the age of seventeen, fought the Russians at Poltava and fled with Charles to Turkey. He was made Governor of Karlskrona in 1717, became a Swedish baron in 1731, and for six years served as the Swedish Governor-General of Finland.[11] Among Gustav Friedrich's numerous descendants were many senior officers, four senators, at least one military historian (Karl von Rosen), and one first-rate national painter (Count Georg von Rosen, Director of the Royal Swedish Academy of Arts in 1881–87).[12]

But what do we know of the forty generations of landowning Rosens in Estonia whose descendant, the Decembrist, would join a movement with the stated object of reducing the prerogatives of his, and their, class? (For character, as Hesketh Pearson has so well observed, is perhaps no less determined by a man's "myriad ancestors" than by his parents.[13]) Little, sadly enough, except what Rozen has himself told us in the work already named. All seems to conspire in silence. For the period of the Teutonic and the other German orders, and for the eighteenth century, we have records—those of the orders themselves, and of the Imperial Russian archives in St Petersburg. Over the intervening centuries, roughly from 1550 until 1710, a pall hangs which few records and still fewer memoirs or contemporary accounts help us to disperse. Even gravestones are little help. The Rosens were buried in at least three different vaults, in Ievve (Jŏhvi), near Ets Castle, in Klein-Roop and in Sónorm, but nothing visible remains of any one of them. Records of births, marriages and deaths do survive, but they tell us nothing about how men conducted their lives, what characters they had, what gifts and vices.

The Rosens, it seems, lived longer than most men. Many reached the age of seventy, and some four-score. They were, without exception, landowners or soldiers, often both. Apparently they did not think writing a fitting or profitable pastime. Few private letters have survived. No scholars passed their childhood at Sónorm, or, if they did, their works remained unwritten or have perished. It was not until much later, in the nineteenth century, that the family produced writers and orientalists, students of art and amateur musicians. The Rosens were a military family. They were, Rozen informs us, impassive, lean men for

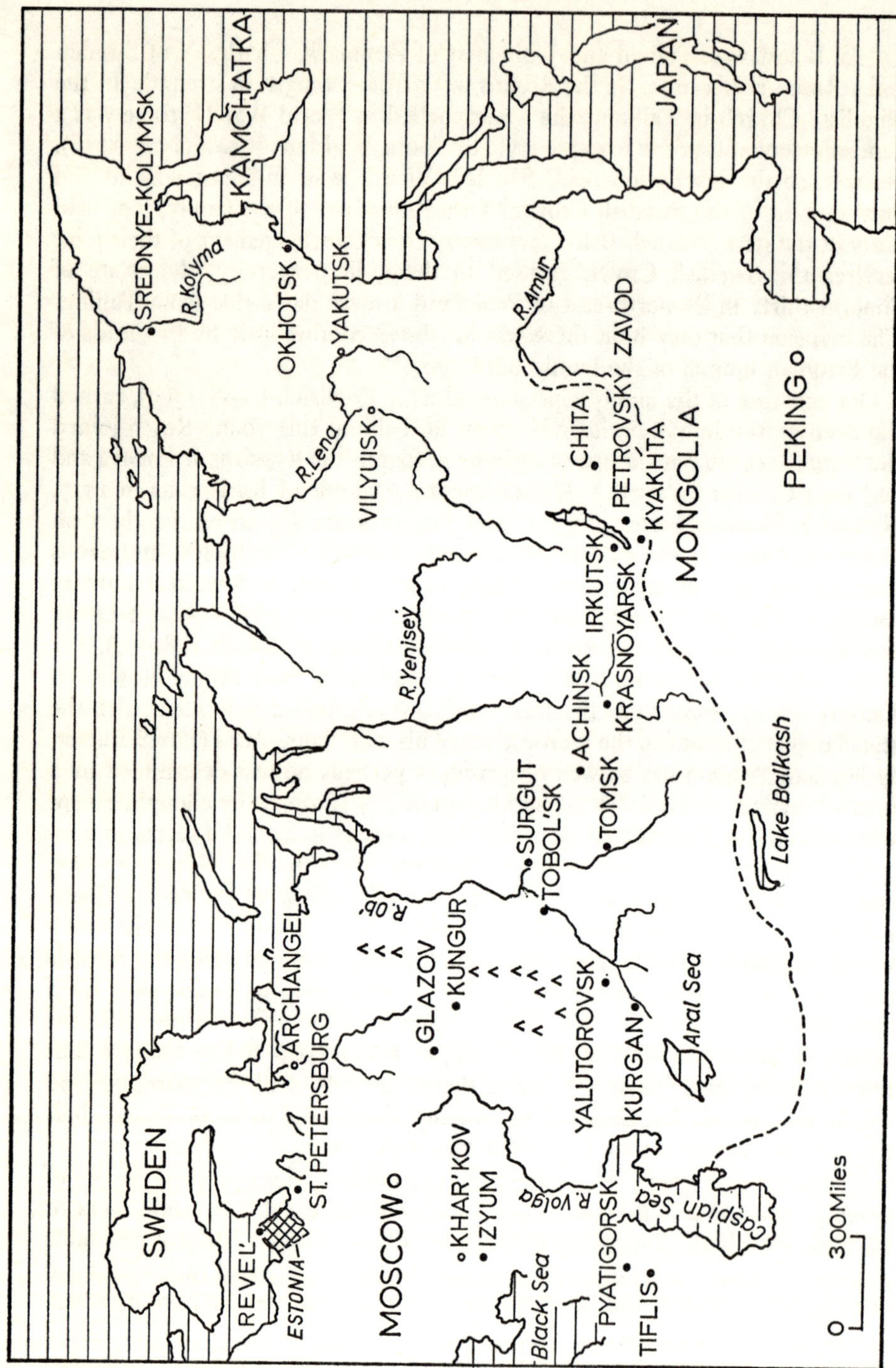

The Russian Empire: Rozen connections

the most part, and they held their heads unusually high (in a physical sense). They were patient, conducted their affairs methodically and weathered their misfortunes stoically, and yet they had in their make-up "a certain element of thoughtlessness" (*nekotoraya dolya legkomysliya*).[14] They were also, like most Baltic-German families long settled in Estonia, prolific. Of course, Rozen could only judge by later eighteenth-century relatives, but it seems likely that the Rosens had been tall, lean and impassive in the previous century as well. We see from several Barons Rosen of the seventeenth and sixteenth centuries, all of them soldiers, landowners and members of a ruling class, that the more apparent vices of such castes—pride, narrowness of vision and indifference to the suffering of inferiors—were well developed in them. But in none were savageness and sheer persistence more arresting to contemporaries than in Konrad Fabian von Rosen (1628–1715), Marshal of France and second most distinguished of his almost countless family of soldiers (that Andrey Yevgen'yevich was the most distinguished, notwithstanding his disgrace, few surely would dispute).

Konrad was a restless youth. When he was sixteen he joined a squad of Swedish cavalry passing through Riga. Having lost everything on cards, wandered through northern Germany, been near to destitution and seen active service twice, he entered the French military service at the age of twenty-three (1651). He embarked upon a brilliant career. The king, Louis XIV, thought highly of him, and his loyalty and courage were rewarded. By 1687 he stood high at Court and held the post of Governor of Languedoc. Next year, he was appointed Governor of Roussillon. He enjoyed Louis's full trust, but it was James II, and not Louis, who was to guarantee that Rosen's name would long survive his brothers'.

James II launched his brief Irish adventure in 1688. The French, we may recall, agreed to aid him in his struggle against William and the Protestants. Rosen, now *Lieutenant du Roi* and Commander-in-Chief of all French troops in Ireland, sailed for Kinsale from Brest with 10,000 seasick men on the morning of March 12. On June 19 he arrived outside the walls of Londonderry and took over command from Richard Hamilton. What followed has been told, with a flamboyancy of style that throws as much light on the author's prejudices as the grim facts of the case, by Thomas Babington Macaulay. Here, we see one of the Decembrist's martial ancestors in action:

Rosen arrived at the headquarters of the besieging army on the nineteenth of June. At first he attempted to undermine the walls; but his plan was discovered; and he was compelled to abandon it after a sharp fight, in which more than a hundred of his men were slain. Then his fury rose to a strange pitch. He, an old soldier, a Marshal of France in expectancy, trained in the school of the greatest generals, to be baffled by a mob of country gentlemen, farmers, shopkeepers, who were protected only by a wall which any good engineer would at once have pronounced untenable! He raved, he blasphemed, in a language of his own, made up of all the dialects spoken from the Baltic to the Atlantic. He would raze the city to the ground: he would spare no living thing; no, not the young girls, not the babies at the breast. As to the leaders, death was too light a punishment for them: he would roast them alive . . .[15]

This Rosen did his best to do, until James himself, shocked by the savageness of his "half-wild" general's tactics, had him sent to Dublin. But "the barbarous Muscovite", as the king referred to him, lived on to see more bloody sieges, and was indeed created Marshal. He died, a man of almost eighty-eight, in 1715. His tomb was opened and despoiled during the revolutionary disturbances of 1789. The bones found in the grave were smashed and widely scattered on the ground.[16]

But to return to the Estonian branch: the Marshal's brother, Georg, was a less adventurous, more prudent nobleman. Sensing the slow decline of Swedish power, at least where the Rosens now held sway, he chose to serve the interests of Muscovy. His son and grandson, on the other hand, ill-advisedly favoured the Swedish-Baltic claims which they thought more likely to prevail. And so it came about, in the long Russo-Swedish war of 1702–21 (the Great Northern War), that members of the family fought each other. One youthful Rosen, Georg's nephew Otto Fabian (1679–1764), even went so far as to collaborate with Menshikov, actively furthering the Russian cause, while Georg's grandson died in Moscow of a wound sustained from Russians in 1709. It was, by all the standards of the family, a wholly undesirable situation. Never before had matters been so sorrily arranged. The Rosens, after all, had always prospered through alliances with conquering kings, not with defeated champions like Charles XII. The correct approach was obvious: Baron Otto Fabian at once severed connections with his relative, General-Major Gustav Friedrich of the Swedish branch (who, however, flourished in the service of his king). It was the ancient, proven Rosen policy, and once again it worked. Peter I looked kindly on those German families who, sensing the decline of Charles's fortunes in Livonia and Estonia even by 1701, had paid their court to him. Once more, the Rosens were secure. Now, and for two centuries, their private history was to be linked with that of Peter's town, St Petersburg, the Russian city soon to rise less than a hundred miles from their possessions in Estonia, and where once Rosens had ruled in Sweden's name.[17] Before briefly considering the family's fortunes in the eighteenth century, the position of the Germans in the Baltic area in its entirety at the time of Peter's triumph and, indeed, until the time of Nicholas, may usefully be scanned.

In the eighteenth century, as in the nineteenth, Baltic Germans accounted for less than one per cent of the whole population of Estonia, Livonia and Courland. Yet they held all the political and economic power, under the aegis first of Sweden, then of Russia. Writing in 1842, the German scientist and traveller, Johann Georg Kohl (1808–78), could make the following remarks on the great influence of German Balts throughout the Empire, while justly emphasizing their insignificance in numerical terms:

There are at present in Russia about 400,000 Germans . . . Of these, about
100,000 are settled in the Baltic provinces; 250,000 of the Germans who are
scattered over various parts of Russia are agricultural colonists; and the different
cities of Russia contain about 50,000 German artists, mechanics, etc. . . . Esthonia
contains 15,000 Germans, among whom it may be estimated that there are 1,500
nobles. The whole of the nobility of the Baltic provinces, so exceedingly important
and influential to Russia, constitute only a small population of about 8,000
souls . . .[18]

Kohl then expands upon his chosen themes, the diligence and intellectual
acumen of Germans, with pardonable relish:

For the military service they have a decided predilection . . . And in Russia, which
so readily assimilates to herself all that is foreign, we find . . . Englishmen in the
Navy and in the commerce of the north; Frenchmen in the Army and in the
corps of schoolmasters and tutors; Italians as artists, etc. But there is no private
employment or public service in which the Germans do not act an important
part . . .

How did this come about? Kohl supplies a reasonable, if simple, explanation
of the German and, specifically, the Baltic-German dominance of Russia's
military, civil and court services:

The development of Russia as a European power, as exemplified in her rapid
advancement since the time of Peter the Great, is mainly attributable to Germany,
and has been worked out under German auspices. The organization of the
Russian army, the improvement of the laws, the custom-house and tax regulations, the ranking of the classes of the nobility, even the rules of Court etiquette,
all have been transferred from Germany, or partially imitated from German
models. The Russian monarchs were frequently in the habit of travelling into
Germany . . .; and, during the last century, the princes of the Russian imperial
family have married German princesses . . . By the Petersburg Court Calendar,
for the year 1837, it appears that of 600 of the highest posts in the Empire, from
ministers and field-marshals downwards, no fewer than 130 were filled by German
names. Here, therefore, the German element stands in the proportion of one to $4\frac{1}{2}$
of the Russian. Reckoning the whole population of the Empire to be 62 millions,
it follows that the 400,000 Germans furnish as many individuals to fill the highest
posts as 14 millions of the non-German population . . . None of the German
provinces of Russia furnishes the State with more able servants (especially in the
military profession) than does Esthonia. The nobility of that province are poor,
and most of them have numerous families. Their sons for the most part devote
themselves to the public service.

Further to emphasize the numerical insignificance of these same nobles in
proportion to the power that they wielded on their lands and in the Russian
Empire as a whole, let us consider certain statistics adduced, on the basis of a
census of the province in 1839, by the Latvian historian A. Svābe. In 1839,

we find that in the whole Baltic area—Estonia, Livonia, and Courland with Semigallia—there were no more than 685 hereditary noble German families.[19] Of these, 225 were in Estonia. (Collating Svābe's statistics with Kohl's earlier remarks, it would seem that each noble Estonian family had approximately seven members. The Rozens of Estonia were thus typical. The Decembrist had three brothers and two sisters; he himself had five sons and two daughters, of whom one girl and four boys reached maturity.[20]) Like other noble families in the Baltic region, (two of whom, the Swedish-based Igel'stroms or Ygelströms and the Livonian Tizengauzens or Tiesenhausens, would also produce rebels against Nicholas I), the Rosens felt some pressure to succeed in the Imperial Russian service. Their estate, though of some fourteen hectares, was not so large or prosperous as to support large, idle gatherings of sons.

Next, let us turn our attention to the question of the Baltic Germans' *right* to rule over the native populations of Estonia, Livonia, and Courland. The Rosens felt convinced that they enjoyed just such a right, in perpetuity, as is made evident enough by the behaviour of their heads during the reign of Waldemar II, for example in 1858 when Baron Julius von Rozen, "acting-Governor . . . was waiting for the revolted peasants of Mahtra in Tallinn, and had them arrested, dragged to the market-place and beaten, some of them to death. The sentences to Siberia and to the lash that followed each of these incidents shocked even the German burghers of Tallinn."[21] Theirs was, of course, the *ius belli*: their forebears had themselves carved out their rights over their land.

But what of their less demonstrable rights over the peasants, who resisted them decade after decade? Less savage times required more polished arguments. The Rosens, like their fellow *Herrenvolk*, developed a less brutal set of claims to their hereditary power of life and death over the serfs in their domains. There was, it seemed, an ancient document, which King Sigismund II of Poland had signed in 1561. On this, the so-called *Privilegium Sigismundi Augusti*, the Rosens took their stand (not that lawyers dared to question them, of course; such an impertinence would be reserved for the days of the Estonian Republic). The Polish king never signed such a document; even if he had, Poland had never held effective sway over Estonia, and possessed no right to allocate northern Estonian lands to any foreigner.

One king, however, had signed a directive that related to the German Balts' traditional prerogatives and power. In 1650, as the Soviet historian M. V. Nechkina remarks,

the Swedish *Riksdag*, or Diet, had taken steps to bring about "a reduction", that is, a return to the state of landed estates which had at one time or another been granted by the king to private persons. In 1655 the *Riksdag* definitely approved the process of "reduction", which was extended to the Baltic provinces of Sweden in 1680. "Reduction" had a double aim—to rectify the disordered state finances and to undermine the power of the feudal aristocracy.[22]

The Rosens, to be sure, had nothing to be apprehensive of: Sónorm, as we have seen, had been granted to the family in 1561 by the Swedish king himself. Still, such developments were rather disturbing. Not unnaturally the Rosens, together with the other German landlords of Estonia and Livonia, did their best to make the Russians undertake simply to cancel the whole process of "reduction" in return for their unqualified support of Peter's army. And in Article XI of the Treaty of Nystadt (1721), they at last acquired a concrete set of privileges with which to lend some lustre, if not legal plausibility, to their continuing power. Not only did that article annul all Swedish findings where land titles were concerned, it also promised that the sovereigns of Russia would perpetually "maintain all . . . nobles . . . in all the privileges, customs, and prerogatives which they enjoyed under the dominion of the kings of Sweden".[23] On these foundations there began the period of co-operation between Baltic-German barons and Imperial autocracy that was to last until the present century.

For the peasants of Estonia a new era of slavery was dawning. Sweden's defeat, it quickly grew apparent, had not only ended Sweden's rule as a major power; "at the same time it cut short all progressive economic and cultural development in Estonia implemented by the Swedish Government. Estonian territory was devastated, its population decimated, and part of the inhabitants driven into Russian slavery . . . The social structure of the provinces remained upon foundations which became more and more antiquated as time passed."[24] The peasants were officially accepted as belonging, soul and body, to their Baltic-German overlords.

Like their class and caste in its entirety, the Decembrist's ancestors regarded their Estonian serfs as chattels to be bought, sold, flogged or banished at will. On the Rosen territories of Sónorm and Ets there began a time of *jacqueries*, reprisals, fires, famines and even murders by the knout of a ferocity unparalleled since 1343.

In August 1739, a certain wealthy miller named Jaana (John), of the settlement of Vohnja, complained that one Heinrich von Baer, a landowner, had stolen property belonging to Jaana himself. The case has been well summarized by Evald Uustalu and its conclusion gives us an example of the Rosens' view of serfs:

The ancestors of John the Miller had managed this mill without interruption for 150 years. After the Great Northern War, the Swedish landowner had not returned, and the estate went to von Baer, who at once began to demand more services from the mill than had been customary. John's father Anton, who was in possession at the time, sued von Baer in the local court, which decided in his favour. Von Baer flouted the court's decision and used corporal punishment to exact even more services from Anton, and finally began to confiscate Anton's cattle and produce. When Anton dared to protest he was so severely flogged that he remained an invalid . . . In 1737, von Baer confiscated the mill together with the fields belonging to it. John now went to St Petersburg to lay his woes at the feet of the Empress Anna Ivanovna herself. For two months he waited in vain for an audience, and then, on the advice of a Baltic nobleman, he returned to Tallinn to try his luck once more with the Governor. But instead of redressing his grievances, the Governor cast John into prison . . . After lying a whole year in prison, John escaped and again reached St Petersburg, and in 1739 he filed a formal suit against von Baer.

The Russian Imperial Cabinet requested the College of Justice for Baltic Affairs [*sic*] to examine the case and pronounce a final verdict . . . and they referred the inquiry to the College of Councillors of the Livonian Nobility [*Landratskollegium*], who now had the satisfaction of interpreting their own privileges . . .

The interpretation was given, in the *Landrat*'s name, by Baron Otto Fabian von Rosen (1679–1764), of Sónorm:

1st: the *Dominium* of the nobles was established at the first conquest of the country. Since that period the peasants have always been part and parcel of the Demesne as *homines proprii*. In virtue of this status it follows that they can be made objects of bequests, acts of alienation and of session by sale.

2nd: the *Dominium* of nobles is not confined to the person of the peasants, but also extends to his goods, which are accessory to his person. The right of nobles to the goods of peasants has never been restricted.

3rd: the nobility has the power to augment or to diminish the share of the peasants' goods which may be retained by him.

4th: the nobility formerly had the right of life and death over the peasant, but voluntarily renounced this right to the State, retaining only the power of correction and of discipline, including corporal punishment—a retention on which the peasants themselves insisted.[25]

Comment seems superfluous. Miller Jaana's children rose in desperate rebellion against Rozen's great-grandfather. They were scourged, branded and banished to Siberia. Unorganized, reduced to the extremities of misery, illiterate and ignorant of German as of Russian, they were treated like unruly animals. Rozen had much to learn from his own family history, and he learnt it well. In the districts of Sónorm (now in Yarvaskiy *uyezd*) and Mehntack (Vyruskiy *uyezd*), the latter bought by Otto Fabian in 1736, inherited by his first son, Vladimir, and so by Rozen's father, Eugen Octave (1759–1834), there were minor peasant outbreaks in the 1750s, 1770s and 1780s, 1830s and 1860s. Nothing but forced labour on a grand scale, as J. H. Jackson notes,[26] could have put back into even half-production those estates burned or abandoned in the war against the Russians; and the methods of the 'thirties lingered on into the 'eighties. Systematically exploited, worn down by famine (worst in 1781–84, 1802 and 1808, when Rozen was a boy of eight and could appreciate the grim reality), oppressed by an iniquitous taxation, the Rosen serfs had reason, by the time of the *Aufklärung*, to hate their overlords.

Such, then, were the conditions in Estonia in the years immediately pre-

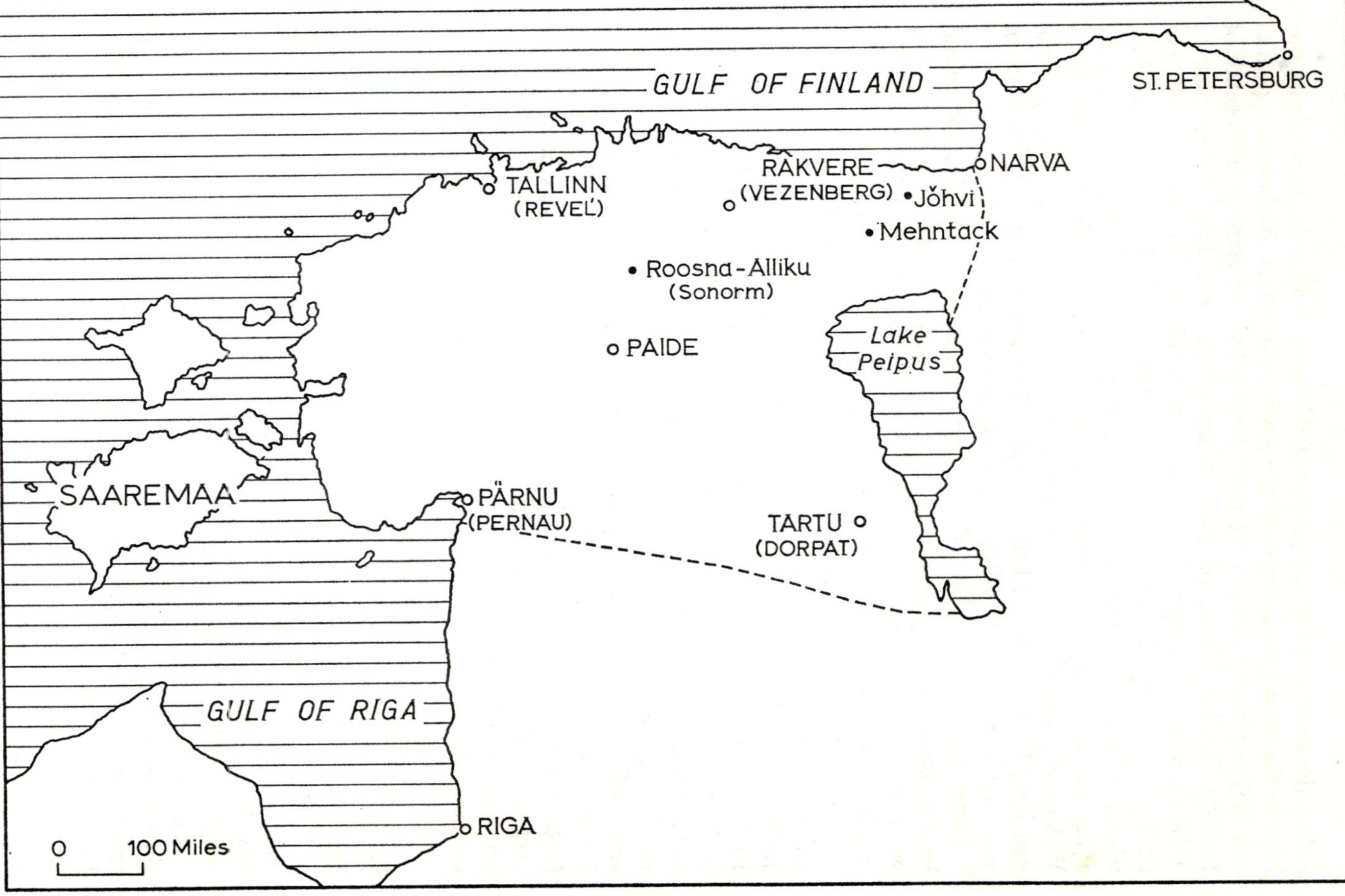

Rozen's Estonia

ceding the birth there of the subject of this book. Rozen the Decembrist was born in the large manor-house of the patrimonial estate, Mehntack, 44 miles east of Vezenberg (Rakvere), 12 miles from Jõhvi and some 6 miles south of Kokhtla (Kokhtla-Yarva, on the modern railway line from Narva west to Tallinn), on the morning of November 3, 1800. He was baptized, according to the Lutheran rite of his forebears, Andreas Hermann Heinrich.[27] His mother, who had barely passed her sixteenth birthday on her wedding day, June 27, 1784, was thirty-two, his father forty-one. He was the third of four sons, Waldemar (Vladimir) having been born twenty-two months after his parents' marriage, Otto nine years later, in 1795. The youngest son, Julius (Yuliy), was born in 1807. Andrey Rozen was robust in infancy.

Baron Eugen Octave, his father, being occupied with the affairs of several local courts of lower instance and, more especially, with his local magistracy, was frequently away from Mehntack. Since 1803 he had been *Kirchspielsrichter* (magistrate) for Kallina, and he took his legal functions seriously. Still, he did his best to supervise the week by week running of his lands, left to him by his father and comprising, in the first years of the century, 1,963 *desyatins* or 14·21 hectares. On his property there were six hamlets: Mehntack itself, Voide, Kollostre, Arroküll, Metskülla, and Kallina.[28] As a result of his industriousness, both on his own estate and, in particular, as a legal official, Eugen Octave seems to have had little time to spare for his young sons. Certainly neither Andrey nor Yuliy, the youngest boys, ever grew close to him. Yet Eugen Octave's absence from his home and growing sons was, in the main, deliberate. The fact is to be borne in mind. After his four-year sojourn at the University of Leipzig (1780–83) where he had studied jurisprudence, Eugen Octave's interests had centred on the courts of law, the nobles and the running of Estonia. The presence in his house of a young family did not, it seems, cause him appreciably to change his views on work, duty or marriage. It fell, therefore, on Barbara, his wife, to take charge of Andrey's moral upbringing and, for his first few years, his schooling. That she did her duty well was to be eloquently proven by her third son's steady bearing under stress during the last days of her life. Barbara Helene Stael von Holstein, the daughter of a landowner of Hannijöggi and herself of ancient Baltic-German lineage, inspired lasting affection in her sons, and the bonds of love and intimacy were broken only by her death on March 18, 1826. So much is evident from the Decembrist's recollections of his youth, as well as from those private letters to her which survive.[29]

The estate, while not large by Uxküll standards, was nonetheless of a considerable size. The atmosphere inside the manor-house, in the wings of which various relatives had settled, was at once active and cool, legal and civilized. Here, all was ordered; all contingencies had been foreseen. Here every man, woman and child had duties to perform and was expected to perform them willingly. Andrey was required to learn to write. He learnt to write. Estate stewards reported to the manor with estate accounts each week. No week passed in their absence. Here, all was regulated, systematic and orderly without being oppressive. Countless youths, no doubt, would have rebelled against such *Ordnung*, such routine, but for the third son of the house it proved congenial. Rozen grew and flourished in the knowledge that specific tasks and duties had been placed on him and him alone, discharge of which would bring him sure rewards and the approval of his father, the judge. To know his place and duty; to perform well, as required of him by those whom he himself loved and respected; to avoid uncertain, awkward situations—such prudent aims are not, perhaps, those to be commonly expected in a boy of ten or twelve. Yet they are distinctly reminiscent of the objects of another youth, barely four years his senior:

> Here is order; strict, unconditional legitimacy, no presumed omniscience, no contradictions. Everything flows, one thing from another . . . everything has its place. This is why it makes me feel so good to stand among these people, and this is why I shall ever hold the military profession in esteem . . .[30]

So Nicholas could tenderly describe the military life—thinking, we sense, of the Prussian corps of Guards no less than the Russian. The parallel should not be forced. For Rozen, we shall see, the military could never, as it did for Nicholas, "represent a kind of secular priesthood . . . submerging personality".[31] He had too much respect for individual dignity for that. Nor did his need of solid forms, unchanging ritual, predictable requirements ever spring, as in the case of Nicholas, from secret and unspoken apprehensions. Rozen was not a nervous man. Still, the comparison of his delight in order and consistency with that of Nicholas is not without its basis. He, too, would come to value that peculiarly tranquil frame of mind granted to officers in well-trained standing armies, and the peace to be discovered in a military way of life "not clamorously aggressive, not warlike, but firmly disciplined and steeped in duty . . . separated from the 'fallen' world of doubt and indecision, and of arguments that have no end".[32] He, too, would find his closest friends and helpers among Guardsmen and their wives. Rozen and his Tsar were to think well of one another as professional officers in 1824–25. The fact is not surprising; their outlooks on the duties and functions of an officer, though possibly on little else, were wholly sympathetic.

From the age of seven to thirteen, the youthful Rozen lived among his relatives, taught by his mother, in a German-speaking, service-conscious, duty-bound milieu. It was a large, well-managed German household. But what, it may be asked, of the Estonian peasantry outside, whose life and work the not yet adolescent Rozen necessarily observed on the estate, week after week? And what of the estate itself (now covered by the large State farm "Maëtaguse", whence came in 1970 nine million eggs, and chickens by the thousand for Soviet consumption)?[33] Let us rapidly survey rural conditions in the north-east of Estonia in the years of Rozen's childhood and throughout his most impressionable years; by doing so, we come to understand his lifelong interests in scientific husbandry and in the economic problems of reform.

Thirty miles south-west of Leningrad, across the River Narova and barely into north-eastern Estonia, the land is squeezed between Lake Peipus (Chudskoye), marsh-fringed and iron-grey in the south, and the chilly Gulf of Finland to the north. The Gulf is chilly because northerly; and a damp wind generally prevails from the north-west, carrying seabirds far inland over the marshes. In this flat, windy and sparsely-wooded neck of land no more than twenty-five miles wide and nowhere more than 200 feet above sea-level, lay the hamlet of Mehntack. It was, in fact, right in the centre of this area known as Alutaguse, and a bare mile from the sluggish source of the small River Pungerja, which wanders south into Lake Peipus. The climate was not mild, or harsh, but damp.[34] Only on hillocks like the one on which the manor-house itself stood was the marshy, boggy soil, which extended northwards from the lake,[35] unable to affect the productivity of an estate. There was always the risk of rotting grain and the likelihood of mildew. When the sun shone in the summer and the wind was southerly, it was a bracing, pleasant land with low horizons. Few villages were to be seen: in Estonia, the population has been concentrated for six millennia in the north, away from both scrub and bogs.[36] But seldom was the sky completely blue over Mehntack, and seldom was it hot. Here, where for years his father had been struggling with indifferent success to grow more rye to supplement his root crops, Rozen was born with the new century. His elder brothers Otto and Vladimir, we have seen, were already five and fourteen years of age. Seven years would separate him from his younger brother, Yuliy. Always, he played alone.

Mehntack seemed a bleak but tranquil place in 1800. Though within easy riding distance of the port and town of Narva, with its ever-growing populace, Mehntack had escaped the main effects of peasant restlessness for many years. It had been unaffected by the massive peasant rising around Tartu in 1784, in the bloody course of which Cossacks and Guardsmen from St Petersburg had slaughtered many hungry serfs, leaving their families to bury them. Tartu was, for those without a horse, far off; what few ripples had been felt in Mehntack and its area had soon been dealt with by Baron Eugen Octave. Surrounded by a modest park, in which little maples and a few unenterprising oaks grew, isolated from the nearest town by woods and empty marshes which few travellers felt any urge to cross, Mehntack was, apparently, a place impervious to change.

Although a cultured, or at least an educated man, Eugen Octave was determined that no literate peasantry should make his life a battle; nor should any peasant dissident so much as threaten to disturb the working of his land. The Estonians on his estate, therefore, received no schooling and no new-fangled foreign implements. The old ways had proved satisfactory for decades, and so could stay unchanged. Yet some things most certainly had been changing in the north-east of Estonia since his youth, and changing, what was more, to his advantage. Like that of all his fellow Baltic German landowners, Eugen Octave's standing in the Province had, in legal terms, been wonderfully strengthened by Catherine II's ukase of May 3, 1783. (In social or political terms, the nobles' strength had already been so great by that year that further buttressing would hardly have resulted in demonstrable change.) By the terms of Catherine's ukase, "all former feudal patrimonies" in Estonia and Livonia with Courland became "inalienable lands" or *votchiny*.[37] Not only were estates hereditary as before, it was also established by Imperial Russian law that only the nobility could ever own, sell or acquire estates. Eugen Octave had no intention of allowing that position to be weakened by seditious, over-educated serfs. Besides, by 1805 his need to make Mehntack as profitable a possession as possible had increased markedly. In itself, a family of five constituted a financial drain of worrying proportions; but his family alone could not account for his precarious position and straitened circumstances which would have seemed inconceivable to the Barons Rosen fifty years before.

The tastes of the Estonian nobility, we see from letters of the period that survive,[38] had changed enormously since Peter's day. More especially, those tastes had been transformed since the middle of the eighteenth century. In the reign of Anna Ivanovna, many Baltic German landowners had lived unostentatious lives. They had had modest means and aims. Content to leave their houses only briefly for occasional excursions to St Petersburg for pleasure or the furthering of their interests, to Riga or to Revel' to maintain useful connections, play their modest part within the *Landrat* and, above all else, to sell their grain, theirs had been lives softened by little luxury. To visit an unheated *myza* (manor-house) by the bleak shores of the Baltic is fully to convince oneself of that.

Not untypical of eighteenth-century Rosens, perhaps, was Baroness Anna von Rosen, whose husband Otto died a Russian prisoner-of-war in 1705, having served the King of Sweden to the end. (He was among the last members of the family to have made that grave mistake.) The Baroness, so far from showing weakness when news came of her husband's death, proceeded to run the ancestral Rosen patrimony of Klein-Roop for thirty years, with never lessening efficiency. Happily, several estate books and ledgers of accounts have been preserved and annotated for the use of Soviet students of agricultural reform.[39] From all of them, we see with painful clarity to what extent the Baroness focused her energies, which were immense, on the problem of extracting sufficient profit from her land, not to buy luxuries and leisure, but merely to meet current debts. Year by year she sold her malt and barley, calculated her expenditure and thought of ways to cut it. Patient, persistent and abreast of current prices, she lived the uneventful life of a majority of eighteenth-century Rosens in Estonia who were not in the State service.

Very different and immeasurably grander were the needs and expectations of her granddaughters and nephews by the close of that century. Once, the peasants of Mehntack had paid their annual dues in goods. With what little resources they had, the Rosens had bought iron, salt, sugar and the other basic needs of life. Now, influenced by French and English tastes and the example of *le beau monde* in St Petersburg, as well as by the rising flood of periodicals in

Riga and in Revel' praising and explicitly describing the accoutrements of life in a polite, polished society, the Estonian German *Herrenvolk* found it ever more necessary to spend large sums on elegant, soft clothing, silks and taffetas, on gold and silver ware, engravings, forte-pianos, paintings and long journeys to the south. This money, moreover, had to be cash: no grain, however fine the quality, could buy statuettes in Weimar or small libraries in Paris. Nor was this all: incumbent on them was the gathering of taxes for the peasantry—in the years 1784–96 70 kopeks per man per annum.[40] And this had also to be paid in cash.

Some measure of the harsh effectiveness of Catherine's taxation policies for the *Pribaltika* may be found in the official State returns for tax and duty revenues. From the Province of Livonia (Liflyandiya), suffice it to observe, the Imperial Treasury collected, in 1782, 919,741 roubles. In 1783, that sum rose to 1,555,947 roubles and it continued to increase throughout the decade.[41] Once more, the peasantry was squeezed; for, so the Baltic Germans as a class reasoned, why should landlords "pay for their vassals" or cover their, or the merchants', share of the burden when the money could be used for better purposes—a trip abroad, for instance, or a little land speculation?

Catherine's sweeping tax reforms of 1784—reforms provoked by imminent rebellion even after the great Tartu rising had been quashed by troops—ought to have brought economic benefits to the whole Baltic region and its motley population. All tariff barriers had been removed between Estonia and Livonia, as between Estonia and the rest of the Empire. The sheer volume of goods leaving Estonia *en route* for growing markets in the east doubled within five years of the pronouncement of the Empress's ukase; and St Petersburg itself provided an insatiable and ever growing market for all surplus crops produced within the Province. Mehntack itself was close to the potential customers of the expanding city; transport was thus no serious problem. How, then, could the Estonians *en masse* fail to reap benefits from this unprecedented upward swing of trade?

Statistics are revealing. St Petersburg did, indeed, provide a splendid market for Estonian goods and produce. The staple crop at Mehntack was, by 1790, no longer flax or rye, but wheat. The volume of wheat sent from Estonian estates to St Petersburg increased accordingly each year from 1784 until 1800. So also did the price, for demand continually exceeded supply in St Petersburg, such was the population growth there. So it was with other crops grown widely in Estonia—barley and rye, for instance. In 1784, a quarter of barley had cost 1 rouble and 85 kopeks in the capital; within three years, that price had risen to 3 roubles 50 kopeks—in fact, it had virtually doubled. In 1784, a quarter of rye had cost 2 roubles. In 1787 it cost 6 roubles or a fraction more.[42] Such circumstances, one might reasonably think, would benefit producers. So, of course, they did. But the producers were not peasants, but their owners. Legally, as we have seen, the Baltic nobles owned their serfs' possessions and skills. Expanding markets for Estonian grain benefited the Estonian peasantry not in the slightest.

Like most Estonian landlords, the Rosens found themselves in ever growing need of funds. There was one simple way in which their income could be raised, and they unscrupulously took it. Since money came from grain, the acreage under intensive cultivation should increase. Nobles annexed the peasants' land. By the hundred, peasant lots were swallowed up by large estates. The effects were quickly felt: nobles staved off their financial problems year by year, while landless peasants grew more desperate, took to vagrancy, and threatened an enormous insurrection. As M. V. Nechkina so baldly writes, "An impoverishment of the Baltic countryside became noticeable at the beginning of the nineteenth century, when landowners were still seizing peasant lands and leaving peasants landless."[43] For the Estonian peasant smallholder especially, matters were becoming simply hopeless by 1800; for as Nechkina further observes, "owners were more inclined to 'spare' a large peasant household but were merciless to smallholders, since a large peasant household guaranteed regular payment of their rents, and regular performance of their labour services". Destitute and homeless peasants were a common sight in north-eastern Estonia, where Mehntack lay. It seems unreasonable to doubt that Rozen saw them as a child.

For a century at least, Estonian peasant households of an average size (seven or eight persons) had provided one fit worker and his cart for the neighbouring landowner three days every week. Now, five days were demanded. So-called "extraordinary services" were extorted, for which traditional liquid payment was occasionally suspended, often drastically reduced. The peasants toiled, and more toil was demanded of them; they were driven to exhaustion, but had no recourse in law should their treatment lead to illness. They murmured, and were silenced. Contemporary records, as Yuriy Samarin remarks, "seem to echo a variety of saturnalia on the nobles' part, in which are fused rejoicing over a triumphant revenge for concessions earlier extorted from them, and a hasty wish to revel to the full in all their temporary advantages . . ."[44]

The peasants had revolted in 1797 and again in 1802. Now, in Rozen's youth, they rose against their lot repeatedly. Year after year there were minor outbursts in the Baltic Provinces. Finally, dispirited and hungry, they resolved to flee. The small trickle of fugitives became a stream. Some peasants slipped into adjacent Russian provinces, St Petersburg or Pskov; others made for Finland. Even in 1797, the port authorities had found it necessary to check all cargo vessels leaving Tallinn and Narva for Finland.[45] Now, in increasing numbers, stowaways eluded them. Fugitives hid in forests by the River Narova and to the east of Chudskoye. They lived in groups of ten, twenty or thirty men. They were hunted down by military parties and, if found, knouted to death or, at the least, beaten into unconsciousness. It was a fragile calm that reigned in north-eastern Estonia in Rozen's early childhood.

By 1805 new economic pressures were beginning to be felt on the estate of Baron Eugen Octave. Always, the family required more money than was readily available. They grew more wheat, but it did not solve their problem.

They started a distillery, and sold vodka to the merchants in the nearby town of Narva. It barely paid their debts. And yet the value of their land itself was rising every year. Fortunately, as Eugen Octave possessed other lands a modest annual income was assured, and Vladimir, Rozen's eldest brother, was financially secure and independent, having reached the rank, by 1812, of Staff Lieutenant-Colonel. But what of Otto, Andrey and the fourth son, Yuliy, the two girls who might need dowries, and the upkeep of the barns and all a landlord's other charges? Eugen Octave thought of selling the estate for a good price, but to do so would be painful. The matter was postponed. At last, during the winter of 1814–15, the problem of the manor-house was solved: the house burnt down. Rozen's parents moved to Revel', where they bought a smaller house and settled down to a more modest life.

Rozen always regretted the loss of Mehntack manor-house and the estate, "better and more splendid for a child than Nice or Naples for an adult".[46] It was the place where, for the last time in his life, he had been oblivious of financial cares, where, after supper and at night he had read Voltaire aloud beside his father; where the governess from Dorpat, Fräulein Charlotte Zaamen, had read to him and taught him both to sing and draw. Later, in December 1823, he would return on leave to find his brother Otto, who had rented the estate from their father, living in a wretched wooden cabin. So punctilious was he in his yearly payment to his parents, still in Revel', that he was unable even to afford to mend his broken windowpanes. Through the open window could be seen the bare, dark walls of the old house. In the carriage-house there stood only a *brichka* and a clumsy two-wheeled cart. Otto, Rozen saw, was the voluntary captive of the family sense of honour. It was a melancholy sight, and one well calculated to impress on him the feeling that the old order was passing, here at least.

In the recent past all things had seemed secure, certain and ordered in Mehntack. Here, the Rozens had their fixed place in the natural arrangement of the universe, and everyone had known it. But the world of Eugen Octave was a world that could not long survive—an anachronism in the nineteenth century. Rozen saw this even in 1812, when he left for school in Narva where the streets were full of rumours of Napoleonic victories and merchants' guilds were flourishing despite the aristocracy. Only in the Baltic Provinces, it seemed, had the nobility contrived to keep considerable vestiges of an ancient feudal power. Only there did a hereditary ruling caste continue to control and guide "its" country, notwithstanding European revolutions that had shattered *anciens régimes* in France, Spain, Portugal, Savoy and other states. Only there, in the whole German-speaking world (and that Estonia had a German-speaking aristocracy is well enough attested by the fact that Baron Yegor' Fyodorovich Rozen, 1800–60, a distant relative of the Decembrist and a prominent *littérateur* during the 1840s, spoke nothing but German until his twentieth year) did the nobility monopolize provincial *Landrat*, courts and administrative organs by explicit legal right, while at the same time retaining their traditional exemption from recruitment and most forms of State taxation. But how long could the opinion of the party represented and directed by the arch-reactionary Baron Ungern-Sternberg prevail in the Napoleonic world? Many years, it would emerge, after the passing of Alexander I's "Livonian Peasant Law" of 1804. Certainly far beyond the publication of such works as J. C. Petri's *Estonia and the Estonians* (1802), a wicked, rabble-rousing tract indeed, and the equally misguided books of G.-I. Jannau which also preached gradual change and slow political reform.

It was against the background of the 1804 reform and its sad aftermath that Rozen's youth was passed. Too young, perhaps, to recollect its passing or the circumstances that had necessitated the enactment of a law prohibiting the arbitrary transfer of a peasant from one district to another, thus breaking up his family and life, he nonetheless witnessed its consequences from close quarters, and for years on end. The conditions of the 1804 reform are not so widely known that they cannot bear stating here.

A peasant, it was stated by Imperial decree, could no longer be removed from his own plot of land and his family at a landowner's caprice—if he had land. Thousands did not, and these, vagrants and labourers alike, could still be arbitrarily transferred from one landlord to another. Peasants also received the right, lost twenty-two years earlier, to own property and to inherit it. But this prerogative was often disregarded by the landowners, to whose disadvantage it could only lead eventually. By the terms of the reform the work of peasants was now fixed in such a way as theoretically to make impossible the imposition of intolerable burdens or unreasonable hours of work. Often, *corvée* went unchecked as previously; few members of the Baltic German ruling class would risk their own financial loss or, worse, the ostracism of their fellow landlords by interpreting the spirit, not the letter, of such laws. For the mass of the Estonian peasantry, little was changed, if anything, by the 1804 reform. In 1805, suspecting that the nobles were withholding their rights, to which the Tsar himself had earlier agreed, peasants rioted in several areas. The riots were suppressed by bayonet. In 1806 there were floods and a general crop failure in the Baltic provinces, together with an order from the Ministry of War in St Petersburg that regional militias be established to withstand expected French attacks. Further rioting again ended in military intervention. Estonia's militia would obviously be formed by peasants, and Rozen serfs became unwilling soldiers. Soon they were ill-clad, half-starving soldiers; for nowhere in the Baltic area were the effects of the blockade known as the Continental System more immediately or painfully apparent than in Tallinn and the north Estonian ports. Here, foreign trade was vital. Tallinn and Narva owed prosperity in large measure to their harbours; within weeks of Tilsit, in July 1807, both harbours were deserted. Few ships ran the English blockade. Warehouses stood empty, the price of salt trebled within a year,[47] even internal trade was radically affected. As always, shortage bore most painfully on the Estonian peasantry.

For the serfs owned by Baron Eugen Octave, the 1804 reform brought no advantages save those of theoretically being able to inherit and own a plot of land. It is generally conceded that the decree, designed to ease the serfs', but more especially the nobles' economic problems, brought harm rather than benefit to the Estonian peasantry.

How the peasants chiefly suffered is a question which has received many different answers. In recent years, Soviet historians have stressed that the growth of harsh, "extraordinary" labour services caused most hardship, together with the fact that, in Livonia, landless peasants constituted almost half the population by the spring of 1805.[48] In the West, greater attention has been paid to the abolition on Estonian estates of the three-field system and to the use of newer agricultural techniques. Here, for example, is the précis of the peasants' miseries in 1805–25 written by E. Nodel in 1963:

> The major change was the change from a three-field system to a many-crop system, where the crops were now changed systematically, in order to limit the exploitation of the soil. This was a result of the economic crisis in the Baltic Provinces due to the tremendous crash in the prices of grain, which, in its turn, was a result of the collapse of world-market prices. The new agricultural policy of the landlords consisted of the introduction of wool-raising and the development of a strong dairy economy. Potatoes and fodder crops, too, became more important. This radical change in agricultural methods became an additional burden to the peasant, whose work increased while his income did not . . . In addition to the maladjustments of these years of experimentation, the Baltic Provinces were plagued with droughts. Altogether the position of the peasant deteriorated steadily. Hunger and starvation became common.[49]

It is possible that Rozen saw these semi-starving serfs in early childhood. One thing is quite certain: like N. V. Basargin, he was witness to grim scenes of cruelty to peasants in his later youth: "I remember how cruelly, in my youth, idle and negligent Estonian serfs were punished: stripped naked, they were tied up to a pillar and whipped from head to feet. In winter, they would be drenched with water outside, in the open, and all kinds of humiliating punishments would be thought up."[50] So prevalent were all the signs of peasant suffering throughout the Baltic Provinces during his adolescence (1813–17), so striking the manifestations of despair, that he would certainly have needed to be blind to have remained unconscious of peasant grievances.

Injustice and despair had led first to revolt, then to attempted flight. Lastly, the Estonians sought some relief from black reality by entering a state of semi-consciousness and following a cult of ecstasy, beginning in 1812. Landowners in Estonia were disturbed by the occasional appearance in their district of peasant "paradise walkers" (*khodoki v ray*).[51] Simple peasants would induce a state of trance by chanting softly to themselves; then they would prophesy. Many of these self-hypnotized seers were girls. They prophesied no imminent disaster, and foresaw no New Jerusalem; instead, they preached the need for continence and absolute humility. But they spoke, not in tongues, but in

Estonian, and the peasants left their villages and walked great distances to hear the *khodoki* speak softly in Khar'yusk, Yarvask, Vil'jandi. Lutheran pastors did their best to ridicule, and so to terminate such unseemly spectacles. The peasants, after all, were in a state of quasi-mystical delight that owed nothing to the Church as recognized by the authorities. Predictably, attempts to quash the movement had the opposite effect to that required and more walkers appeared. Apprehensive landowners represented to the Bishop in Riga that such conduct posed a threat to law and order. If hundreds of Estonians left their villages disaster was imminent—no harvest could be gathered in.

The Church moved quickly to condemn the *khodoki* who were not following the proper and established route to paradise. But matters proved no better when, a decade later, the Estonian peasantry did finally pay some attention to the Lutheran Church. For years a rumour had been spreading through the country that the Russian Government was granting land to all those who applied to have their name placed on a "list". Growing numbers of Estonians walked to Riga, seat of the Russian Governor-General and the Lutheran Bishop. Despite repeated public protestations to the contrary by vexed officials, the rumours spread still wider and the flow of peasants steadily increased. "The police," remarks E. Nodel,

> could not chase them away from Riga. The peasants went to the Russian clergy, there asking for help against the German noblemen, since they knew about the growing rivalry between the Lutheran and the Russian Orthodox Churches. The Russian Church authorities made the mistake of taking the names of the peasants, which increased even more among the latter their conviction of the truthfulness of the rumours of aid . . . Things went too far, however, even for the Russians. Many a bloody fight developed between the Russian army and police on one side, and the angered and desperate Estonian peasantry on the other.[52]

Further reform, it was apparent by the end of the Napoleonic Wars, was necessary if bloodshed was to be avoided in the Baltic region. Even in 1810, members of the *Landratskollegium* of Estonia had started discussion of the practicality of "freeing" their peasants, but not their land, as had been done in 1807 in the Grand Duchy of Warsaw and in Prussia. The Rozens and their class preferred to entertain the thought of "individually freeing" their serfs, to any thought of giving up their right over the land. In the land, it was well understood, lay wealth: and through wealth, power. What more natural, therefore, that even the Baltic Germans who supported the idea of reform (and these were a minority) should seize upon so suitable a precedent as Warsaw? By granting personal "freedom" to their serfs while keeping full control of all their land, they might hope to free themselves of the constraints of the vexatious land reform of 1804 and, simultaneously, to minimize the risk of provoking a rebellion by peasants. Even so genuine a liberal as S. von Himmelstierna, one of the main drafters of the 1819 reform for south and east Estonia, saw no incompatibility between the granting of such "freedom" to his serfs and the continuation of *corvée*; what chance was there, then, that the majority would see it? The ex-serfs, Himmelstierna reasoned, would become "free labourers". Since they would have the choice of whether or not to work a certain noble's land on which they could be short-term tenants, paying their rent with their own toil, they could not justly be viewed as exploited. Once more, ineffectual reform was brought about. Partly because of the concern of the majority of landowners that their economic welfare be protected, partly because the Governor-General of Livonia, Paulucci, urged them to do so, the *Landrat* of Estonia resolved to guarantee the personal liberty of serfs within that Province. The project, approved by Alexander I in May 1816, became effective legally on January 8, 1817.

There is no space here for a full consideration of the effects of the 1816 reform, but the principles on which the "liberation" of the Rozen serfs through-out Estonia was based may be summarized. First, the peasants gained their "freedom" but forfeited all rights to what had been their own allotments. Second, their right to purchase land was recognized in principle. Third, peasants were acknowledged to have full rights to conclude at their own pleasure contracts for renting land from landowners. Fourth, they became members of township communes which, however, were placed under the control of landowners. Fifth, provision was made for the creation of peasant law courts—also under the supervision of the nobles. Lastly, the landowners retained the right to inflict corporal punishment on peasants.

The landowners, as H. Palli and Nechkina so rightly emphasize, made no wider use of free hired labour after the reform of 1816–19 than they had earlier, but merely set the norms for labour services by "free" contracts which they themselves effectively dictated. "The Baltic peasants were impoverished not only by impossibly heavy labour services but also by an extension in the use of short-term rental agreements, through which the landowners were able continually to increase the amount of dues paid by the peasants."[53] In 1830, crop shortage and famine was no less chronic a problem in Estonia than in 1800. By then, however, faulty farming methods had resulted in a partial soil exhaustion in the area where Rozen passed his youth. But at least the suffering from hunger and ignorance of the peasantry among whom he had passed his early life, would benefit another land, another peasantry far to the east. Nor had the spectacle of starving peasant families failed to impress on him the absolute injustice of a system by which some men—his class—brought about the moral degradation and economic backwardness of an entire society. The sufferings of the Estonian peasantry on and around his own father's estate were to yield handsome dividends for others, in the fourth and fifth decades. It is, indeed, not easy to conceive of a more suitable scenario than that provided by Estonia in 1804–12 for the gradual unfolding, in a noble youth whose family were foreigners in their own land six centuries after their coming, of a quiet but deep distaste for legal slavery.

2

YOUTH AND LIBERAL CIRCLES

Rozen the Decembrist, then (to stress what he himself stressed), was of ancient, conservative, and military descent. Having touched upon the Rosens' ancientness and general hostility towards reform, we shall now turn briefly to the militariness of the whole family.

For seven centuries the Rosens had been members of a ruling caste. Their lands and influence they had originally won, we saw, by force of arms. But by 1800 the time was long since past when triumphs of the Knights of the Crusading German Order of the Sword could be spoken of without at least some deprecating nod of powdered heads: the early Rosens, after all, had been so very violent. Now, in the early nineteenth century as for the past two hundred years, the Rozens in the Baltic lived on, by, and sometimes for, their wide estates. They were landlords who, for reasons of prestige, by long tradition, and especially because they needed income, served as Russian officers. "Under Alexander I," as Rozen himself remarks with pride, "one could find a Rozen in almost every Russian regiment and in all the artillery brigades. At the conclusion of the war of 1812–14, moreover, there were in the Russian Army seven Rozens with the rank of General."[1] Army officers by training, they were also country squires on a considerable scale. Theirs, moreover, was no amateur approach to agriculture, but a well-informed, totally practical interest in how to make land pay. Like most Baltic German families in the Province, they were prolific. For three generations, by the time Andrey Yevgen'yevich was born at Mehntack, there had been at least four sons on the estate.

The Rozens liked the military life. Their presence and activity in various Russian army corps throughout that century,[2] as in the Swedish service earlier, gives ample proof of this. All things, in fact, combined to make the Russian army life not only wholly fitting for them, but congenial as well. St Petersburg, the centre of the military and administrative systems for the entire and still growing Empire, was no more than fifty miles away. German officers were held in high regard there. It was a Baltic German, Münnich, who in 1732 had founded the first military school in Russia—the Officers' School;[3] and men of German origin continued to enjoy a reputation for strategic skill and "military learning" of the first degree. In the view of many native Russian officers, indeed, the Germans were the law-givers in military science. In the reign of Anna

Ivanovna (1730–40), herself a princess of Baltic German birth, Russian military textbooks had been written by Germans and in German, then translated into Russian—in the main by other Germans. But it was only recently, in Paul's reign (1796–1801), that the German star had reached its highest point, hovering brilliantly over the Russian General Staff. Certainly, Catherine II had used officers of German origin. Some, notably P. Weismann in Moldavia, had done well and had attained exalted rank. But Paul was a fanatical admirer of the person, style, and attitudes of Frederick the Great, whose capital, Berlin, a Cossack band had actually invaded for a day within the memory of living Russian officers.[4] To the intense disgust of many, "he forced on the Russian Army a tight Prussian uniform, with pigtails, powdered hair, buckles, gaiters and busbies. Even high officials were expected to move with rapid military precision."[5]

All in all, it was a good time for a Baltic-German youth to join the army, and for Andrey the future was marked out even in childhood. Like his brothers, he would go to St Petersburg, attend a military school, and thence embark on the career of the professional army officer. First, however, he would need to reach the statutory age of fourteen, for until then youths were not, in general, admitted to the main, or senior, section of the military Cadet Corps in the capital. Let us here, therefore, glance briefly at his early education, first at Mehntack, then in Narva.

Rozen's father was an educated man—a judge, if not a scholar. His mother was a simple, pious woman of unfailing kindliness. So, at least, we learn from Rozen's memoirs and, though filial duty doubtless plays its part in the long passage of his reminiscences that touches on his childhood,[6] there is no reason to suppose that hers was not, indeed, a warm and beneficial influence. She it was, her husband being ever more preoccupied with bench and service duties, who gave Andrey, and all her other sons, a thorough moral training in the first five years of life. Above all, she attempted to instil in him a sense of right, and showed him by her own life the effective application to the modern world of ancient Christian virtues: faith and charity. (Hope seems to have loomed less large in Rozen's early training; but, of course, the Baltic-German Lutherans were a self-sufficient race.)

> Religious convictions, which so often change during a life, from circumstances or society or reading or from doubts, were deeply stamped on my heart, not by prayers learnt by rote, not from reading and interpreting the Holy Writ, but by the living, hourly example of my parents' piety and practical existence, by their continual submission to God's will and their pleasantness to fellow and servant alike.[7]

So Rozen could declare in middle age, adding, by way of a conclusion, "Since that time I have not ceased to pray; since then I have preserved a religious outlook in spite of all the troubles of my youth, maturity and old age." The question of his faith is considered in more detail in Chapter 6.

In 1812 Rozen was sent to Narva Public School (*Narvskoye narodnoye uchilishche*) twenty miles north-east of Mehntack. He travelled on a cart carrying wine from the estate into the town; the money he received for it from merchants he kept hidden in a special inside pocket sewn into his jacket. On returning to his parents for the holidays, there came the reckoning. He produced the full amount. In Narva he lived with a merchant who was happily called Goethe, his wife and five daughters, who created a hospitable and even faintly cultured atmosphere. There were occasional small parties, and here, for the first time, Rozen saw entertaining of a civilized but also casual variety. He performed well at them. Even better was his day-by-day performance in the public school run by the conscientious Radeker, who taught him Latin, German, history and traces of geography.

School life under Radeker was arduous: the day began at 7 a.m. with the choral singing of a psalm and explanations of the catechism. Six hours of classes followed, Rozen sitting with the sons of local merchants. He worked diligently and, in time, came to admire the careful, uncomplaining Radeker, whom every pupil paid a mere 5 roubles for the year, together with one *sazhen'* of good firewood. What possible reward was there, he wondered, for the pains that Radeker continually took over his charges? Not a financial one—the cost of education did not rise in Narva, it appeared. Nor one of social lustre or prestige, because the *rektor* lived a simple life. It was, Rozen began to understand by his third year, the spectacle of progress of his pupils, and the knowledge that his duty had been done, that rewarded the man. Radeker, like Rozen's own parents, taught him the value of a sense of duty well performed, and of a sense of honour. The lesson was well taken: Rozen, as the Russian saying went, "cared for his clothes while new, his honour while still young".

Finally, in the spring of 1814, Rozen was taken to the capital, there to be entered for the First Cadet Corps. He was accepted, but the Corps, it was at once plain, had been left to drift unchecked into disorder. The Director and Chief Secretary of the Corps were not even in St Petersburg. Russian troops were still in France and under changing war conditions classes had dwindled to the point of disappearing; no fresh cadets could be received for months. Discouraged, Eugen Octave and his son returned to Mehntack. Andrey would have to pass a few more months in Narva. Fortunately the two sons of a relative, Baron I. O. Korf(f) of Salo, outside Narva, were also studying in the town and so he would have company. With the Korfs, one of whose cousins was to be a prominent historian of the Decembrist movement and apologist of Nicholas,[8] he passed cheerful days. As earlier, he slept out on warm summer nights, now staring at the stars (he would recall in sober middle age), now gazing at the fire by which Estonians sang to themselves "or endlessly discussed the main, even exclusive topics of the peasant's conversation—his stomach and his food".[9] Not unpleasantly, the year drew to its close.

With the new year, fresh efforts were made to place him in the Corps. Finally, in the first week of March 1815 word came that he had been enrolled as of that month and should depart immediately for the capital. Eugen Octave and his wife were in Revel' inspecting a prospective home there. Rozen hastened west, gave them the news and, to his pleasure, met his brother Otto and Baron General Fyodor Rozen, recently returned from Paris. Otto was the general's aide-de-camp. The Russian armies, Rozen learned, were even then returning from the West by land and sea, and Otto was travelling to Finland where his unit's winter quarters were; they would escort him to St Petersburg in style.[10]

Understandably, having just seen his brother and heard tales of Russian triumphs in the West, Rozen was impatient to begin at the Cadet Corps. Only by doing so could he advance his career; for even German barons, by the reign of Alexander I, had to serve in a cadet corps if they hoped to reach high rank. Rozen spoke only a slow, imperfect Russian, but any forebodings he may have felt remain unknown, he does not discuss them. The military tradition in the family was very powerful. Never once, if we accept his reminiscences at face value, did even the possibility of any other life present itself to him, though there were several other possible careers open to him. He might have made a good career within the Province of Estonia (Estlyandiya) had he so wished. For the scion of a noble German house, as had been shown innumerable times by his relations, there was always a position as administrator in the *Landrat*, honorary steward of a large estate, head of police, inspector of the forests, district ranger— all suitably *standesgemäss*, lucrative posts.[11] Or he might have flourished in a ministry, like Sievers, Ungern-Sternberg, and so many other barons from the Baltic littoral.

According to the *Gothaische Diplomatisches Jahrbuch* for 1867, of the 1,064 higher dignitaries in Russia, barely a quarter were of purely Russian stock; almost a half were Germans or, at least, had German surnames.[12] Eugen Octave's cousin, General O. F. Rozen (1763–1828), later Civil Governor of Kazan',[13] and several other kinsmen could no doubt have opened doors; and Revel', the administrative centre of the Province, could certainly have offered many promising careers. Notwithstanding the derision of the tired and lovesick Nelson who arrived in Revel' quite against his will in April 1802 ("It is a nasty, horrid place . . ."),[14] Revel' was no longer, by the time that Rozen's parents settled there, a stagnant backwater. On the contrary, it boasted some ten thousand inhabitants, almost one-half of whom were German Balts, and it offered a theatrical and literary life of some distinction. (It was, of course, the adopted town of the dramatist August von Kotzebue. In the private theatre of another distant relative of Rozen's, Baron Friedrich Georg, one at least of Kotzebue's earlier comedies, *Der Eremit Auf Formentera*, was first performed.[15]) Rozen would have had powerful connections in the town.

But the Rozens were soldiers. So, at the age of fourteen, the outline of Andrey Yevgen'yevich's future was settled—to all appearances. He was close-cropped, given a uniform, and found himself a junior cadet. Though his early schooling had not been neglected, his general and professional education was at last, after so tiresome a delay, taken seriously in hand.

Founded in 1800, when the former Artillery and Engineering Cadet Corps had become the Second Cadet Corps, the First Imperial Cadet Corps was, by the time French armies had invaded western European Russia, a school of well over one thousand pupils.[16] Although not as distinguished in its antecedents as the Imperial Land Corps (the *Sukhoputnyy Korpus*), the First Cadet Corps gave a solid general education, with fitting emphasis on military subjects, to boys whose fathers were or had been senior officers. In the main, cadets were in the Corps at least six years, leaving at the age of eighteen, though some stayed rather later; in the junior school, preparatory schooling was given to boys of six or seven. As its statute of foundation tersely put it, the First Cadet Corps was "an institution offering to youths destined for military service in the ranks of officers and, in the main, to sons of senior officers, a general education and a training in keeping with their calling".[17]

Like the many other military schools founded in Russia between 1800 and 1825—and by the middle of the century there would be no less than twenty-four Cadet Corps, most offering a ten-year course[18]—the First Cadet Corps was repeatedly being reorganized. Now because of the Napoleonic Wars, now in consequence of an enormous growth in the entire Army establishment during the fourth decade, specialized classes were added, expanded, split off from the rest and, finally, removed to separate buildings. First an attempt was made to minimize the size of the preparatory class, then, after 1817, a reverse approach was taken. Yet despite the Corps' ever-evolving system of administration and varying class structure, three basic factors did not change over the years. They were observed objectively in the 1850s by Baron A. von Haxthausen, whose comments in his major work, known in English as *The Russian Empire, Its Peoples, Institutions and Resources*, have withstood the test of time. As relevant to the conditions in 1815 in the First Cadet Corps as they are to those of his own day, Haxthausen's summary of military life and education within Russia bears quotation.

First, we see, attendance of the Cadet Corps conferred prestige, since Russia needed Russian officers. Second, it was not considered from an academic standpoint; the military life saturated the whole Corps, which was, indeed, like a military unit in its structure. Third, though the pupils of the Corps were desperately needed by an army which was always short of well-trained officers, they often passed only a few years in the Guards before retiring or accepting profitable places in civil administration:

Whatever may be said against this kind of education in cadet schools, it is the only means in Russia of making the Army independent of the West, from the want of military science in the country. These institutions are the more important to the Army, as the national pride and aversion to foreigners, together with the difficulty of the language, diminish the efficiency of foreign officers . . . According to the Military Encyclopaedia, there are at present in all 28 establishments for the education of officers, one of which is for those of the Navy. The number of pupils amounts to nearly 10,000, of whom 1,000 enter the service every year; about

800 to 900 of these appear to join the Army . . .[19] As the admission of the pupil is generally conditional upon the services of his father, and the education is defrayed by the Government, the children of Generals are consigned to institutions of a more elegant description than those of other officers . . .

The system of instruction in the ordinary institutions is divided into three courses: preparatory, general, and superior. The superior course alone includes a scientific study of military subjects; the two others are more for general education, in which modern languages play an important part. With all are united practical military exercises . . .

Notwithstanding the frequent recruitment of officers from the cadet establishments, these are not at all equal to the demand. Calculating that on average one officer is needed for each forty men, Russia would need, should she call under arms the whole of her regular army, about 25,000 officers . . .

But Army officers, like the nobility who serve the State in general, seem to indulge in luxury beyond all the means of their pay. The promotion, certainly, of educated, brave and well-connected officers is rapid; but this arises not so much from vacancies opened up by death or sickness, as from the custom prevalent among the rich nobility of making their rank in the Army a mere step to the more profitable posts in the administration, or a method of asserting their nobility, and enabling them to retire to their estates. This is one of the causes, too, of the considerable preponderance of Baltic Germans in the higher posts, and is proof that the profession of the soldier has attractions in itself for Germans, whereas Russians will adopt it as a means to other ends . . .[20]

The proliferation of Generals-Major and Generals-Adjutant Rozen in the first part of the nineteenth century has been noted. That Andrey Yevgen'yevich, like the fifty noble youths born in Estonia who had entered the first class of Marshal Münnich's military school in 1732, had every thought of making his a permanent career as a Guards officer would seem plain from the sheer assiduity and pleasure with which, by 1817, he was studying the subjects taught to senior cadets.

Little can be said of Rozen's years in St Petersburg as a cadet (1815–18) save what is to be found in his own memoirs; few letters or allusions by contemporaries cast light upon the period. Some things are clear, however, from his own later reflections on his youth and early manhood, and the many detailed letters of another future criminal and pupil in the Corps, K. F. Ryleyev. His letters, to his parents in particular,[21] shed light not on Rozen (whom he met only when he was soon to leave), but on conditions then prevailing in the Corps. Ryleyev, moving spirit in radical political societies in St Petersburg from 1823, leading protagonist in the rising of December 1825, and martyr in the Soviet calendar, attended the First Cadet Corps from January 1801 to February 1814.[22]

The building that the school occupied was a converted palace—the former mansion of Prince A. Menshikov, built by the Saxon specialist in low baroque, Gottfried Schädel, in 1713–16.[23] High stuccoed ceilings showing scenes from classical mythology, enormous pilasters, great windows overlooking the Nevá (for the mansion was on Vasil'yevskiy Island), such physical exteriors made a strange contrast with the internal working of a military establishment for boys, boots ringing on the parquet floors, orders floating in salons from nearby drill and riding halls. Yet such a clash of ornamental setting and harsh military régime, high boots and vases, walnut cabinets and general parades, had been a salient feature of the Russian gentry's life for many years by 1814. Such palaces as Pavlovsk and Gatchina, Kameno-Ostrov and Oranienbaum (the last also designed and built by Schädel), had rung to raucous orders and the sound of formal floggings in the time of the late Emperor Paul. However, corporal punishment was seldom used on the cadets; the Director of the Corps, though a firm disciplinarian, did not approve of violence towards future officers. He was, in fact, a unique phenomenon among contemporary Russian heads of institutes; but then, he was not Russian.

Heinrich Maximilian Klinger (1752–1831) was a German and a poet. He had also been, since 1803, Curator of the University of Dorpat, and was therefore *in absentia* as Director of the Corps most of the time. He chose to live in Dorpat, where his own language was spoken. Once tutor to the future Emperor Paul and married to a natural child of Catherine the Great,[24] Klinger had long moved in lofty circles. General-Lieutenant and high pedagogue, courtier-cum-dramatist, he had had time, by 1814, to weary of Imperial society. Besides, he was a man of sixty-three when Rozen joined the Corps, and had no wish to gain more stars or orders by performing at the Court. Disinclined to entertain recent ideas on education, or, indeed, to entertain at all, engrossed in his own work and hard of hearing, Klinger had little energy to spare for any adolescent even if, as in the case of A. E. Rozen, he was diligent and spoke perfect German. Through his staff he ran the Corps in a traditional eighteenth-century way: horsemanship and mathematics, modern languages, fortification science, discipline.

"The Director", as A. G. Tseytlin has remarked, "was a staunch supporter of Prussian militarism. Morose in his conduct and sparing of words, he thought the birch a method of educating cadets." (On this point, however, there is controversy, and Tseytlin would seem to overstate the case.) "Besides Klinger, however, there were also serving in the Corps simple-hearted and sincere men, and these managed to establish fairly favourable conditions for the cadets . . ."[25] "Activity of mind and body," Rozen could declare in middle age on the basis of his own experience, "moderation and simplicity in diet and accord among one's comrades—these are key factors in overcoming and enduring the diurnal cares of life; and to this, officers who have been cadets grow accustomed even from childhood."[26] The autobiographical note is unmistakable. Food in the Corps, for which the government was paying, was indeed "simple and moderate", and life, both physical and intellectual, was strenuous.

Rozen adapted well to conditions in the Corps, the guiding force in which, he quickly saw, was not "the white bear", as cadets referred to Klinger (who, when he did enter the building, promptly vanished through six doors into his massive, smoke-filled study), but Colonel Mikhail Stepanovich Persky, Inspector of Classes. Persky was a stern but kindly officer. Once an aide-de-camp to the Tsarevich Constantine, he was a man of culture and, besides, was much attached to the Cadet Corps which, in 1812–18, was becoming something of a poor relation to the newly-formed Lyceum of Tsarskoye Selo and the now reorganized Artillery and Engineering Corps. "The First Cadet Corps", said Count Konovnitsyn, the Director of Imperial Cadet Corps, "is poor, but it is honest." Patient and industrious by nature, Rozen soon won Persky's favourable notice, and reciprocated his regard. Even as a youth, his tastes were catholic. He attended and, more noteworthy, enjoyed classes in subjects as diverse as Russian history and artillery, geometry and poetry. Among the teachers whom he would recall "with the sincerest gratitude" forty years later, were representatives of the precise sciences, the arts, and institutional organization: A. K. Schmidt, teacher of fortifications, M. I. Talyzin, teacher of Russian literature and history, and Persky.

Rozen progressed well in the Corps. By 1817 he was an under-officer (military ranks were given to the senior boys), and was in the highest class. In examinations held that year, he was placed second—behind another Baltic youth, E. I. Korf. That year it even seemed that he would join the Guards: four ensigns were required, and he was chosen. But a subsequent decision to reorganize the Guards Corps made by General N. M. Sipyagin caused him to be passed over. Like the earlier delay in his enrolling in the Corps itself, it was a bitter pill to swallow, but he did not complain. He must needs stay; therefore he would widen his reading. The teachers of the Corps, we see, had managed, by his nineteenth year, to accomplish something infinitely greater than the inculcating of a syllabus: they had brought Rozen to wish to learn more; to view the intellectual life with some respect; even—happily for him in later life—to teach himself. Nothing is more apparent from that section of *Zapiski dekabrista* (*Memoirs of a Decembrist*) which deals with the so-called "Academy" formed by exiles in the prison-fortress of Chita, in 1827–30, than that Rozen, though a man of nearly thirty, was still willing and most able to extend his knowledge in almost any field that might present itself:

> Many of our comrades having received a scientific education, it was resolved that they should enliven our long winter evenings by giving us lectures. Nikita Murav'yov, who possessed splendid military maps and plans, expounded on strategy and tactics; Ferdinand Vol'f gave us lectures on anatomy and chemistry; Pushkin II explained the higher branches of mathematics, while Aleksandr Kornilovich and P. Mukhanov read Russian history, and Prince Aleksandr Odoyevsky, Russian literature. I must add, in gratitude, that this last had for many years the kindness to teach me, a born Estonian, Russian . . . These long years of intimate contact with such highly educated men had a considerable effect upon those of us who had previously had neither time nor any means of improving their mind.[27]

As for himself, Rozen would undertake translations of Heinrich Zschokke and

Sismondi into Russian, experiment with rollers and iron harrows, and, for thirty minutes every day, practise the flageolet.[28]

"Life in the First Cadet Corps", writes Tseytlin, "was not a secluded one: the cadets knew well what was going on in the capital, and beyond its limits, too. They strolled about the city and frequented the theatres of St Petersburg."[29] It was, as the same writer notes, the time of Batyushkov's and of Zhukovsky's triumphs in the field of elegiac poetry, and of the success of *Dmitriy Donskoy*, V. A. Ozerov's most nationalistic tragedy. Certainly it was not chance (as Tseytlin might say), that that play, which dealt with a great conflict between foreign and Russian troops, was such a success in St Petersburg: if 1812 had been a year of national suffering, the following three years brought an unprecedented wave of national pride and a new sense of Russian power and independence. Russia attended the Congress of Vienna as the equal of Austria-Hungary and Great Britain, and as the mighty but magnanimous victor over Napoleon. In the Cadet Corps, too, the prevailing mood had changed dramatically between 1812 and 1815, when Rozen entered it. Three years before, martial enthusiasm and a longing to assist in the great task of bringing down the French had raged in youthful breasts; study had proved all but impossible when there were battles to be fought—and battles had been fought—within the country. Among those youths unfortunate enough to join the First Cadet Corps when others were about to leave their benches for the army in the field was M. I. Pushchin, brother of the Decembrist and a good friend of the poet A. S. Pushkin (who, in the Lyceum of Tsarskoye Selo, twelve miles away, was equally hard put to it to concentrate, French armies having crossed the Niemen). "My entering the Corps in March 1812," recalled Mikhail Pushchin in memoirs published only forty years after his death, in 1908,

> at the time of the most furious preparations to confront the enemy who had approached our frontiers, placed me at once right in the midst of the general animation of cadets who had requested leave to defend their Motherland. And at that very time, some cadets who were not yet fully trained, including Ryleyev, graduated from the Corps.[30]

Pushchin's memory played him false where Ryleyev was concerned: Ryleyev, we have seen, did not graduate until the February of 1814; but in his memory of the prevailing atmosphere of tension and impatience, he was surely not mistaken.

It was, in short, a different St Petersburg that Rozen found, coming after the wars were ended. For him, there was no prospect of immediate action. Nor did war ever seem imminent during his four-year stay as a cadet. Within two months of *his* becoming ensign in the first cavalry company, First Artillery Brigade, Ryleyev had seen half of northern Germany and was advancing into France. When Rozen joined the Finland Lifeguard Regiment, he found himself stationed in St Petersburg. By the end of 1815, Ryleyev had been eighteen months abroad, seen action, and passed several weeks in Paris.[31] Rozen would never fight abroad. "For youth," observed I. D. Yakushkin, Rozen's fellow-prisoner in 1826 but one who, like Ryleyev, had at least witnessed the Russian victories abroad and strolled proudly along the Champs Elysées among Cossack bivouacs,

> life was tiresome in St Petersburg in 1814. During the two previous years, events had passed before our eyes which had determined the destinies of nations, and we, to some extent, had participated in them. Now it was unbearable to gaze upon the empty life of the capital, and listen to the babbling of old men who praised the past and reproached every progressive movement.[32]

Within months of gazing at "the empty life of the capital", however, Yakushkin would have joined with five close friends, all in the Guards and members of the nobility,[33] to found the first organization to lay a basis for the subsequent (Decembrist) Northern Society, the Union of Salvation or Society of True and Faithful Sons of the Fatherland. It was, one need not labour the point, a secret group aiming, somehow and at some future date, to destroy autocracy in Russia. Merely for having known of its existence and not informed the government, many men would spend their middle years in exile as State convicts. Rozen, only sixteen in 1816, was too young to join the Union of Salvation; nor is it certain that he would have wished to do so, even had he had the opportunity. There are no letters to suggest that, like the young A. A. and N. A. Bestuzhev, he was hostile to autocracy even in adolescence or had serious intentions of protesting against serfdom as the basis of the Russian State. Only late in 1825, indeed, did he at length become involved in the activities of the Northern Society. His was no early sense of loyalty to the extreme liberal cause though, as we saw, the seeds were being planted in his youth; rather was it a gradual ripening of an awareness that a change was vital, if the State was not to suffer as the peasantry was suffering. In his memoirs, first published in 1869, Rozen would devote a lengthy chapter to "Masonic, Literary and Secret Societies, 1815 to 1825" (Chapter Three). Because of the controlled and balanced outlook on the liberal movement in its Russian context that that section reflects, but also, and especially, because the chapter is among the most objective of contemporaneous résumés of pre-Decembrist liberal feeling in St Petersburg, certain extracts from the passage bear quotation. They show Rozen at his best, not as a soldier or a farmer or a journalist (though he would prove no less distinguished in all three different trades), but as a political historian:

> Even before the reign of Alexander, in the time of Catherine II, secret political societies existed in Russia, though they seemingly had a religious object. Educated men, not finding sustenance for their intellectual capabilities either in the service of the State or in private life, entered Masonry: for them it had a charm in its mysteriousness and in its outward forms, and because it gave them an occupation, discussions, labour of a literary kind . . . And when Masonry ceased to be merely a pastime or empty formality, and became better known for its

moral and material power, then Catherine acknowledged the Masons to be Jacobins; there began the investigations and constraints from which Novikov suffered most of all. The Emperor Paul protected Masonry, as did Alexander I also; but in 1822, on April 13, a ukase was promulgated ... by which it was ordered that all Masonic Lodges be closed ... But the excited temper of the times, and the considerable effect which a long sojourn abroad, in France especially, had had on many of the officials and Russian officers, had created a strong desire for opportunities for the interchange of ideas and, in consequence, clubs sprang up on every side; the example of the above-mentioned societies was swiftly followed. They were, in fact, the expression of a deeply-felt need. Certain of the Guards officers formed small literary societies among themselves—small côteries which gathered for lectures and for evening entertainment. From conversation about literature, poetry and novels, they involuntarily and imperceptibly glided into discussion of Jacobins and Girondists, *Carbonari* and *Tugendbundgenossen*. The younger officers, especially, were interested in such topics, and tried by all means possible to obtain *entrée* into these literary circles. The political followed the footsteps of the literary societies ...

Unions of this kind might almost be said to have been in the air. Almost at the same moment, another secret côterie was formed. M. Orlov and Nikolay Turgenev wished to establish a separate group, "The Russian Knights", but after some discussion of the question were induced to join the Union of Welfare. M. N. Murav'yov, Burtsev, P. Kokoshkin and Fonvizin joined this Union after the statutes had been revised by Aleksandr Murav'yov, Trubetskoy and Kokoshkin himself, and the paragraphs relating to the taking of oaths, unconditional obedience, coercion, and poisons and daggers, had been struck out ... The members were then divided into four classes ...[34]

Rozen proceeds to summarize the workings of the Union, its organization, and its apparent dissolution in late February 1821, continuing his narrative with an assessment of the growing influence in Tul'chin, Second Army Headquarters in the south, of A. P. Yushnevsky and Pavel Pestel'. He surveys the forming of the Northern Society, to which he had himself adhered in its last weeks, as follows:

Meanwhile, in St Petersburg, the secret society had almost gone to pieces; but at the end of the year 1822, when the Corps of Guards returned from Lithuania, it began to revive again, and starting at this time it assumed the name of "Alliance of the North". It was divided into two parts—the leaders, and those who were merely their followers or imitators—upper and lower circle. The upper circle consisted of the original founders, and these selected the members of the directory; they alone knew the measures to be taken to attain their object, and the time appointed for its execution. Nikita Murav'yov became the head of this revived society, and at the close of 1823 the Princes Trubetskoy and Obolensky joined him in it. When Trubetskoy was placed on the Staff of the army in Kiev, Konrad Ryleyev took his place ...

It now remains only to say a few words as to the cause of the unusual political activity shown by the Russian Army of that time in originating and encouraging all these societies—activity of which not a trace was to be found a few years previously. It must be remarked that the liberal reforms started during the reign of Alexander I for the advancement and development of the educated classes were the more effective for the harsh manner in which everything of the kind had been repressed under Paul. The extraordinary events of 1812 had also brought about a powerful feeling of the people's strength, and a sense of patriotism of which no one had before had a conception. Then came the eventful years of the Franco-German war.

The Russian and Prussian troops of occupation had remained for some time in France after the taking of Paris . . . To the young Russian nobility, more especially the Guards officers, the Franco-German campaign was nothing less than an entry into a world of civilization—a world which was hitherto unknown to almost all their number. Under a milder sky, in fresh surroundings, which bore the stamp of a higher civilization, under the influence of softer manners and a more humane outlook on life, many of the Russian officers acquired some new ideas about the government of their own country. To the young men who had spent the greater part of their lives in the monotony of distant Russian country towns, or in the bacchanalian uproar of St Petersburg feasts, a new and beautiful world opened up on the sunny banks of the Loire and the Garonne, to whose charms they yielded with delight. With profound interest and attention, the young strangers watched the party political strife which then filled every part of France. The most zealous and most active spirits of the Russian Guards enthusiastically imbibed the concepts of liberty, citizenship, and constitutional right, and threw themselves with energy into the life of the people for whose conquest they had come from the distant east.

So far as it goes, the passage is unimpeachable; but one thing grows more obvious as we read on: Rozen himself was never a Mason. Nor had he been a member of the Free Society of Lovers of Russian Letters—the literary-cum-political society of which he speaks so calmly. Nor, for that matter, had he ever joined the Union of Welfare. Clearly, Rozen's own position *vis-à-vis* liberal societies in St Petersburg in the years immediately following his leaving the First Cadet Corps (1818–24) deserves scrutiny. Superficially at least, it might appear that, far from sympathizing with the Liberals in the Guards, he was totally indifferent to their designs. Let us pause and survey the salient features of his army life.

It was in April 1818, after long delays, that Rozen joined the Finland Lifeguards as an ensign (*praporshchik*). The life that he led in St Petersburg was, for the first two years, constrained: his father could not spare him funds enough to allow him to purchase a carriage or to visit the theatres of the capital. He played cards because it was the custom in the regiment, and sometimes lost. He read widely and in private.[35] In 1819, while on furlough with his parents and his brother Otto in Revel' (where he danced at splendid balls given by Baron Eduard von Dellinghausen, Count Buxhoewden and the Civil Governor himself, Baron Gotthard Budberg), he was promoted second lieutenant (*podporuchik*). For his family, the news was bitter-sweet: Otto, his brother and an officer five years his senior, a veteran of the Napoleonic Wars, was as yet only a full lieutenant in the army, that is, not in the Guards. It was an awkward hour, but no acrimony arose between the brothers.

By 1821, Rozen was in contact with literary circles in the capital. Through his service comrade P. I. Grech he met N. I. Grech, and through him Zhukovsky, N. I. Gnedich, and other writers of a younger generation. He held authors in respect, poets even slightly in awe. In the same year, while in Dorpat or Polotsk, he came to know another officer, Captain A. V. Malinovsky, his future brother-in-law. Malinovsky was the son of the first Director of the Lyceum of Tsarskoye Selo, Vasiliy Fyodorovich, and had himself received a first-class education there as the comrade of Ivan Pushchin, future Decembrist, and of "the sacred brotherhood of poets": Del'vig, Pushkin and V. K. Kyukhel'beker. Once again, liberal and literary connections fused.

Supposedly to help to re-establish "true monarchic principles" in Piedmont and the States of Italy then in revolt, the Russian Guards were ordered south, in April 1821, on their abortive "campaign" of "liberation". The campaign, as is well known, was quickly proved unnecessary: matters arranged themselves in Italy and Piedmont without the Russians' aid. Such an event, however, was not to be foreseen by the Imperial General Staff, and in the second week of April, seven days before his regiment *en bloc*, Lieutenant Rozen was dispatched south from the capital in charge of a peculiarly unaggressive band: sixty trained bakers. Such inglorious beginnings to a struggle with the hydra of democracy! Such prosaic duty! Yet the troops must needs be fed at every stage of their long march; Rozen was to supervise a complex, if exceedingly unglamorous, operation.[36] It was a premonition of Siberian events. There, too, he would be made responsible for food, kitchens, and military supplies. Significant, perhaps, that this, his first modest command, should be one involving careful, detailed planning, not decisiveness, and that it should demand, not acts of bravery, but cool administrative skills. Rozen, to summarize three months of cautious effort in a line, discharged his duties well. He won the public thanks of the Colonel of his Regiment, General B. S. Rikhter, while managing his office so adeptly that, on marching out of Narva, he managed to arrange a hasty visit to his parents. From Narva, Rozen's bakers moved to Dorpat (Tartu), Lemzal (where they baked bread for a month), Polotsk, and so to Drissa.

Winter quarters in the neighbourhood of Grodno (where, as officer responsible for purchasing provisions for the First Battalion, he was, so he asserts, "vexed" by the Jewish traders who "proposed to teach him how to steal"— always Rozen was a very *upright* subaltern); evenings in the castle of Ishchelna (as he spelt it), with a Polish noblewoman and her daughter who would play the harp and listen as, in tender tones, Lieutenant Rozen read from Lamartine, Chateaubriand, or Madame Cottin's *Mathilde, ou le retour du croisé*: and, alas, losses at cards. Such were the scenes of Rozen's service life of 1821–22.

In February the regiment moved out, *en route* for St Petersburg, passing through Minsk and Vil'no. There was time enough to form a sound impression of the Lithuanian and Polish peasantry, gentry and clergy. Rozen was shocked by the perpetual spectacle of poverty and drunkenness:

> Having passed a year and a half in Lithuania, I came to know that country and its inhabitants fairly well. Then, the nobles or landowners were distinguished for their insolent haughtiness towards the lower classes and the poor, and for their flattery of their superiors and the rich. With their peasants, they behaved as strictly as with slaves, while their principal and favourite occupation was the hunt—and coupled with it, the inseparable pastimes of cardplay and the drinking-bout . . . Both by their condition and in their appearance the peasants are indeed slaves in the full sense of the word. Everywhere there is poverty . . . In their Roman Catholic churches, the clergy comfort them in Latin, which they do not understand, and terrify and threaten them in Polish only in confession; certainly they do not defend them against landowners or courts or the police authorities, for they themselves are kept and are protected by the gentry—and from peasants there is nothing to be taken . . .[37]

In several respects, it is an interesting passage. First, we see the youthful Rozen's genuine disgust with a nobility able to lie and flatter—a nobility, in fact, that is no longer noble, having lost its sense of honour (or rather, *his* impression of that honour). Second, we catch a glimpse of various antipathies: towards Roman Catholic priests (but not, it must be said, towards Roman Catholics in general terms); towards adventurers; and, in the passage leading on from this, towards ever-busy, money-grubbing Jews.

Until now, Rozen had had little or no contact with Jews. If he had shared, and still shared, the antipathy towards the Jewish race ever so painfully in evidence among his class and caste, that prejudice had been, in him, based solidly on theory, not experience. Now, at the age of twenty-two, he found himself precisely in that region of the Empire where Jews were numerically most significant: the region around Vil'no. Nor, here and in the smaller towns, was it possible to overlook their presence, for they were, both by their choice and by Russian law, distinctive in appearance:

> The Jews had not been integrated into Polish society but, as in other Western lands in an earlier age, had been given a special status under royal protection. They were not subject to the ordinary judicial and administrative authorities; in each major town they were authorized to elect their own officials . . . Thus, Polish-Lithuanian Jewry lived among, but distinct from, the general population. They were set apart not only by their religion and by the special judicial and fiscal regime, but by language, dress and cultural traditions . . . Still more important, perhaps, the Jews performed special economic rôles. Although they constituted about one-eighth of the total population of the country, a Polish census in the late eighteenth century had found only fourteen Jewish families engaged in agriculture. On the other hand, they controlled three-fourths of the export trade.[38]

Bearing in mind this Jewish dominance in trade, let us look again at Rozen's condemnation of the Jewry, clergy, gentry, and nobility of Lithuania. We see that his anger and impatience with the state of serfdom thriving about Grodno rest no more on an awareness of natural rights or moral wrongs than on his realization of *the economic folly* of the system. The Jews and nobles thrive, the clergy wheedle what they can, the peasants groan: such is his sketch of Lithuanian conditions. Yet (he insists in every line) such a deplorable state of affairs need not be tolerated. "Everywhere there is poverty...": *this* is the core of Rozen's irritation. He himself was excellently versed in the effects of economic and political "reforms", having seen peasants in Estonia suffer needlessly in consequence of them. Always it would be the economic, not the moral, aspect of emancipation that would most engage his interest and conscience. But to return to his Battalion, which marched its way with drums and with a choir of several hundred untrained voices through Dinaburg, Pskov, Luga and at last, on June 20, 1822, Petergof, where Alexander and the Court were entertaining for the Empress Dowager: it was her name-day. The gardens and thin woods around the palace needed sentries, it appeared. Rozen unguardedly asked why. Such questions, he was curtly told by the new Chief of Staff of his Division, General P. F. Zheltukhin, were not asked by junior officers who hoped for long careers. The reprimand was turned into a lecture, within hours, by a certain colonel stationed at Petergof, one A. S. Mandershtern.[39] Troubled times were coming for a number of the subalterns serving, with Rozen, in the Finland Lifeguards; for Mandershtern, all quickly found, was a military pedant of the Schwartz brand. Baltic German barons, in particular, must needs proceed with caution.

In the event, Rozen could not avoid a clash with Mandershtern. His execution of routine duties was ceaselessly found fault with; his orders were discussed and criticized; several times, he suffered semi-public reprimands. M. F. Mit'kov, his company commander, did his best to shield him from unfounded accusations of incompetence, but the air of tension stayed, and poisoned all tranquillity that Rozen might have found beside the Gulf of Finland.[40] Finally, there was an open argument. Rozen went at once to the new Colonel of the Regiment, V. N. Shenshin, with a request to be transferred without delay to the Caucasus. Permission was refused.

Not until 1824 did Rozen's military career mend for the better; but then, when he attracted the attention of the recently appointed Head of the First Infantry Division, the Grand Duke Nicholas, it was transformed. His fortunes had begun to change in April 1824 when he was given a training command. The First Battalion passed the summer months in a pleasant village outside St Petersburg called Krasnoye Selo; and here, untroubled by the dictatorial Mandershtern, Rozen discovered that he had a useful talent: he not only looked and felt well while on ceremonial parade (having an eye for detail and for symmetry), but he also made others look as competent as he. As a drillmaster, he gave soft commands; but the troops responded well and did their best to please him.[41] His superiors looked on with new approval.

November brought its famous floods. The First Battalion was stationed by the palace of Kameno-Ostrov, and struggled hopelessly against the waters. So another winter came. Rozen was again promoted. Now he lived in quarters in Rybatskoye: "I lived in complete isolation. Books, a guitar, singing and study shortened our tedious winter posting in the country eight versts from the capital, into which I went but rarely."[42]

There was a great ball in the Winter Palace on December 12. Rozen attended in the hope of seeing officers who had been recently promoted, in particular, General K. I. Bistrom, now Commander of the Guards Infantry, and the officer who had assumed Bistram's former position as Commander, First Division, Infantry—the Grand Duke Nicholas. He was not disappointed. The Grand Duke snatched his tea away as he was standing by a buffet in a crowded ante-room and, in a loud voice, briskly reprimanded the attendant for not serving Rozen "first-class tea". "I understood", wrote Rozen later, "that he wished to show kindness towards one of his new subordinates; until that moment, he had noticed me only when I had mounted guard in the First Division, our Division doing sentry duty in the Winter Palace and in his own Anichkov Palace. The supper was excellent . . ."[43] It was a strange meeting by a buffet between one who was inept at showing kindness and another who was not expecting it—but who was to meet the Grand Duke Nicholas again in the same palace, twelve months later, under tenser circumstances.

So began 1825, in hope and expectation. On February 14, I decided to ask for the hand of Anna Vasil'yevna Malinovskaya. Having received the assent of her uncle and aunt in advance (they were father and mother to her), I addressed myself to my chosen one. It was, I recall, a Saturday evening; we were sitting in her uncle's study; I had earlier learnt a speech by heart, which I forgot in that solemn moment . . .[44]

The marriage took place on April 19. Never did Rozen have occasion to regret it. Anna Malinovskaya, the second of three orphaned sisters (Vasiliy, their father, had died in 1814), was a plain but even-tempered and well-educated girl. She brought only a modest dowry, it was true, and Rozen was not rich; but the ease and charm of manner that she showed made up for such deficiencies. Besides, the Malinovskys were acquainted with his parents, being frequent visitors to Revel'; and their family was all that one could wish. Anna's mother was a daughter of the celebrated cleric Andrey Afanas'yevich Samborsky, formerly priest in residence at the Russian Mission in London, and so herself half-English. (The priest had married an Englishwoman, and brought her back to Russia with his agricultural machines, seeds, poultry and a dozen pigs.) Later, Samborsky had been tutor to the Grand Dukes Alexander and Constantine Pavlovich. Thus Anna had connections with the Court on both sides of her family; for her father had been Director of Alexander I's favourite educational project, the Imperial Lyceum of Tsarskoye Selo. And as though this were not adequate recommendation for a wife-to-be, Samborsky had established a small school of agriculture close by Tsarskoye Selo. Rozen was thoroughly content.

"Meanwhile, my service career could not have gone better: my superiors marked me out, my comrades liked me, and the troops knew that I liked them very well . . . So, in my military service, I experienced what is found in every walk of life: when a careful, industrious man is found, all manner of duties are heaped on him . . ."[45] Twice at Oranienbaum, where Rozen and his bride settled in May and lived in rooms only a short walk through the birches to the Bay of Finland's stony shore, the Grand Duke Nicholas paid him the compliment of commending publicly the bearing of the men in his detachment. Once, indeed, when Rozen was in charge of sentry change, the Grand Duke shouted his approval of the crispness of the sentries' drill and movement. On the domestic front, too, all was smiling. With his bride, Rozen took an excursion out to Kronstadt, where they wandered round the harbour. In his quarters, he read Say's works on political economy, or simply talked to Anna. The summer wore away delightfully. Anna, too, it is apparent from this short note to her uncle Pavel Fyodorovich, was as cheerful as could be. Pavel Fyodorovich, we see, had prudently been leaving the young couple to themselves in the first weeks of their marriage.

May 21

Dearest Uncle,

For a long time I have been deprived of the pleasure of seeing you, so I take this *earliest* opportunity of writing to you, hoping to receive a few lines back. I can imagine how you are toiling and how splendid everything is at your Belozerka: the weather is smiling here, and every day the greenery grows finer. We came here on Monday. I do a lot of walking, and am feeling much better already. The air is excellent and there are really most *delightful* spots around. Our host and hostess [Col. Tulub'yev and his wife] could not be kinder or more attentive. As soon as the Battalion returns to town, and when you say, we shall be able to enjoy visiting you in Belozerka; but from here it is impossible. However, they say the Battalion will not be here long . . .

Farewell, be calm and healthy, and accept this assurance of my feelings of love, respect, and gratitude.

Your niece,
Anna Rozen[46]

Mundane, even trivial the content of the note may be; yet still its tone can tell us much. Every line breathes absolute normality. A womanly preoccupation with her own and other people's health (later in life Anna would enjoy extraordinarily sound health, despite the trials of exile), even the politely gracious interest in an ageing uncle's gardens—all seems to resolve itself into one message: Anna has not missed the Malinovskys too unbearably.

Still, she wrote with almost clockwork regularity to Belozerka and the gardening Pavel Fyodorovich. Not to have done so, after all, might seem to show but moderate gratitude for the care that he had gladly lavished on her for ten years.

Moreover, he had made a handsome wedding-gift to the young couple. Anna wished to make it clear that she appreciated such great generosity as he had always shown her. But even to write letters twice a week was no hardship for Anna, for she loved her father's brother. The stream of notes continued through the summer months.

St Petersburg, June 2

Dear, most honoured Pavel Fyodorovich,
Our Battalion reached the capital yesterday, and that same evening we were gladdened by your kind letter. We thank heaven that you are well, and look forward to meeting you again impatiently. Here, we are continuously taken up with exercises in the presence of the Grand Duke [Nicholas], so I may be unable to visit you on the day that you appoint. Do please tell us on which days you will be at Belozerka—I'll certainly manage to choose *one* when I can express in words the sincere feelings with which

I have the honour to be your grateful
Anna Rozen[47]

Anna did, indeed, visit her uncle at his house in Belozerka, in July, and letters and civilities continued to flow unabated. Sometimes, Pavel Fyodorovich came to the capital on business; twice, Anna's brother Andrey called on her, while passing east or west.

But what, it may be asked, of Rozen's own activities in 1825—in secret côteries? What of his anti-tsarist feelings? Rozen was a future Decembrist, after all; therefore (it seems reasonable to suppose) he was hostile towards serfdom and autocracy. Where do we see it? How is it made evident? Certainly there seems to be a case for arguing that, if not wholly ignorant of the activity of I. D. Yakushkin, Nikita Murav'yov, Prince S. P. Trubetskoy and other Liberals (as a fellow-officer of Mit'kov, Repin and Prince E. P. Obolensky, Liberals all and in his regiment, he could hardly be *entirely* ignorant), he was at least indifferent to their ever-shifting plans. Let us first, the better to disprove such an assertion, amass the "evidence" suggesting such indifference.

It is a simple matter to point up the distance, psychological as well as physical, separating Baron Rozen, in his first years as an ensign, from the leaders of the Union of Welfare and, after 1822, the Northern Society. In three ways he may be shown indeed to have stood apart from most of the main participants in the rebellion of December 14, 1825—the brief, untimely climax of the post-Napoleonic liberal movement among Russians. First, he did not serve abroad, so had no way of "comparing what was seen there with what confronted one at every step at home: slavery of the majority of Russians, cruel treatment of subordinates by superiors, all kinds of government abuses, general tyranny".[48] But had he not experienced serfdom in Estonia and Lithuania? Did he need to visit France to understand the difference between "distant Russian country towns" and "surroundings which bore the stamp of a higher civilization"? No doubt Revel', Dorpat and Narva were not true metropolises like Paris or Berlin or even Frankfurt; but they were ancient, European centres of learning and of trade. There, at least, a literate middle class was much in evidence, and in Radeker's small school Rozen had met it; there, at least (if not in St Petersburg), few beat their servants openly. There, too, foreigners abounded, and their presence was the cause of no excitement.

But Rozen, it might be objected secondly, had at no time been a Mason. At a time when, in the phrase of a contemporary, the Lodges served as "neutral territory or oases in a desert of bureaucracy",[49] how could Rozen not have felt attracted by them—even if not otherwise than by a curiosity, or as a social pastime[50]— if he was not a young reactionary? The answer is self-evident: the Decembrists came to their political convictions by as many routes as they had pasts. Many had been active Masons, it is true—Pestel' and A. N. Murav'yov in the Loge des Trois Vertus, V. K. Kyukhel'beker in the Grande Loge Astrée[51]—but even more had not been Masons, while to some, Freemasonry was actually objectionable. To the atheist I. D. Yakushkin, for example, its mysterious rites seemed laughable; to Baron V. I. Shteyngel', a deeply religious man, Masonry was simply offensive.[52] Nor is it to be doubted that by 1822, when all Masonic Lodges were closed in Russia, all but a tiny handful of the members of the Union of Welfare had already left them. This was very natural, since Masonry had proved even by then a far too narrow field for politically ambitious youths who, in due time, had felt the need to form groups of their own.[53] Rozen, whose own father had participated in Masonry during the 1780s,[54] never saw the need for complicated oaths, symbols and rites. Yet does that fact imply that he was ever hostile to the aims of officers who either joined a Lodge out of a need for "neutral territory" or, like some Liberals in St Petersburg, did so with the intention of establishing within a Lodge a group with consciously political objectives?

Again, the fact of Rozen's apparent unfamiliarity with works and authors mentioned, in the course of their prolonged interrogations in the early part of 1826, by at least fifteen Decembrists, may be given spurious significance. Under questioning, it might be urged, many Decembrists mentioned Adam Smith, Helvétius, Holbach and Destutt-de-Tracy as having influenced their thought. Rozen, no doubt absorbed in Plettenberg and Kelsch and mediaeval Baltic history generally, had no time for such essential liberal reading.[55] In 1822 he was reading Chateaubriand! In 1825 he was playing his guitar but, by his own admission, took no part in the liberal life of St Petersburg a mere twelve miles away. Yet so patent and so many are the signs of Rozen's consciousness of liberalizing trends that to state them is to emphasize the obvious. He was aware of Jean-Baptiste Say's *Traité d'économie politique*, which he discussed with fellow-officers in 1825.[56] He was perfectly familiar with Sismondi, parts of whose *Histoire des Allemands* and *Histoire des républiques italiennes* . . . he would translate while in Siberia.[57] He was certainly conversant with the recent history of North America, and shared the Russian liberals' admiration of George Washington. Why otherwise should "a companion in misfortune" have contrived to send in to his cell in the Peter-and-Paul Fortress, in 1826, "a newspaper of 1776 which contained an article on North America and in which the 'shameful rebel, General Washington' was continually spoken of"?[58] He knew Voltaire; he probably read Tacitus and Plutarch, whose heroes many liberals admired and strove to emulate, with Radeker. But this, one may remark, was thirteen years before the rising. Many Decembrists, to insist on the self-evident, came to support *la bonne cause* (as Ryleyev called the anti-autocratic movement) only in the final months, or weeks, before the insurrection: Shteyngel', N. V. Basargin, Mikhail Kyukhel'beker, to name only three, were hesitant in their support of the Northern Society almost to the last. Rozen, too, was a latecomer to personal, active involvement in *la cause*.

What, then, was his path to half-commitment to the anti-autocratic, anti-slavery cause? (That he never threw himself whole-heartedly into the radicals' embrace will soon be seen.) Though a century and a half have passed, his route may still be traced with accuracy.

Rozen was by instinct and by training a Liberal, in the context of that word's earliest meaning. That is to say, like the shopkeepers and students in Madrid in 1820, to whom the epithet "liberal" was first applied in a pejorative sense by the Right; and like the discontented Neapolitan grandees, French radicals (Barrot and Thiers alike), and English merchant Whigs of later years (to whom alone it was at length to be permitted to create a liberal party), he believed in the essential right and the effectiveness, first, of free institutions, and second, of untrammelled human reason. By working through free reason and such institutions as the *Landrat* in Estonia, he held that men of good will might bring about progress for all nations and classes, and on several planes: the spiritual, material, and moral. To be free, of course, institutions must necessarily be independent of immediate government control: hence the importance of maintaining *useful* rights enjoyed for decades by the Baltic German landowners of his native province. But those rights were to be exercised, not for the sole advantage of the landowners themselves (which is what happened in effect, as we have seen), but to the benefit of men of every race, class and belief throughout Estonia—English traders, German pastors, Russian legal officers, and the vast bulk of the populace, the Estonians themselves. Reason by itself demanded equable, humane, and thoughtful treatment of the peasants. Quite apart from the injunctions of religion, which, we may add, weighed heavily with Rozen in his middle years, if not before the rising, how was the harvest to be gathered with the greatest possible dispatch, if the harvesters believed that they could never benefit by their co-operation and hard labour? Yet the harvest, and the regional economy in general (always Rozen thought initially in Baltic terms in 1822–25—in Russian, or Imperial, only with more effort) was as important to peasant as to landlord; for all men had to eat. Again, what progress could there be on any plane whatever unless men in power were reasonable and proper in their dealings with inferiors, whether peasants on a large estate or privates in a regiment? Treated fairly, all men are co-operative; treated harshly and unreasonably, most men would make life burdensome for all, and most especially for their supposed or real tormentor.

Such, in broad outline, was Rozen's simple attitude towards man, estate and army management—an attitude both rational and religious, commonsensical and, in its further implications, lofty. As an attitude, it served him well: troops under his command respected him because they trusted him; superior officers thought him reliable because they could predict his views. It was, above all, *reasonableness* that Rozen sought in others. In Russia, clearly, there was little scope for the development of any institutions over which the government would not have absolute control, unless those institutions were clandestine. Reasonably, though sadly, the youthful Rozen faced the fact. But such a situation did not make the exercise of man's glorious reason either less important or, in theory, less easy. The military life made grave demands upon one's freedom, it was true; but still one's intellectual independence was not lost. To be a serving officer was not to be a cipher, an automaton. So, judging by his actions in the pre-Decembrist years, and more particularly in the south-west and in 1821–22, Rozen rationalized the limited condition of the subaltern. By 1825, the strain of such a rationalizing process was becoming evident.

So we are brought to the essential ambiguity of Rozen's attitude towards committed Liberals—those few prepared to act to bring ideals into effect— until the last few days of 1825. He was himself, it has been said, a man of liberal sympathies. As Say's theories condemned the exploitation of the land by a self-seeking, agriculturally untutored few, so the example of his parents had impressed on him the pointlessness of arbitrary rule over the peasantry or rank and file. Prudence, self-interest, the welfare of the masses, natural rights, the dictates of the Church, his better feelings—all, in a religious-cum-political-cum-moral choir of private, silent orders—forced him to be kindly to subordinates. One might attempt to disentangle the emotional and intellectual impulses behind such admirable conduct, pointing out the parts of Say's (or for that matter Heinrich Zschokke's) work that demonstrably influenced his actions,[59] emphasizing the importance in his early life of brothers', teachers', friends' acts or opinions; but the result would be unchanged. Suffice it to observe, then, that Say did influence his thinking in maturity, but that this influence was possible only as a result of earlier, essentially unintellectual factors in his youth: the fact of his mother's humaneness, the fact that as a child he had seen savage punishment wrought on recalcitrant Estonian serfs. *Those* memories would always remain clear.[60]

That Rozen's dislike of cruelty in any form was honest, and his scorn for uniformed and salaried oppressors deep, is hardly open to dispute. Yet it is clear also that the idea of threatening the political stability of Russia was anathema to him; and he opposed all violent steps to change the structure of the State—which necessarily condemned most Russians (and almost all Estonians) to remorseless, endless toil. He wished the ends but not the means or, rather, favoured means so slow and legalistic that no liberal who was not from the

5

Baltic Provinces could fully sympathize with them. (As if Baltic German landowners were not experts in the principles and outcomes of reform! Yet their experience, most said, was inapplicable to conditions in Great Russia.) Rozen, in short, was caught between two impulses: to serve the State with honour, and to act in such a way as to improve the peasants' lot both in Estonia and elsewhere in the Empire. He was no flaming revolutionary, no second Riego. His hesitation and ambivalent behaviour on the day of insurrection, December 14, 1825, would well enough reflect his inability to reconcile opposing impulses. To support Ryleyev and the radicals, of course, would be to break his formal oath of loyalty and allegiance, first, to Alexander, then to Constantine; but to do so would be certainly "to work with the best of his time".[61] Always clashing understandings of his duty and of what was right would worry and harass Rozen until, at last, he could find a fitting explanation for the "young enthusiasts, who should be judged not by a strictly political standard". He was a constitutionalist and a believer in well-drafted, gradual reform. So, too, were the majority of members of the Northern Society in its last year, and, like them, he would be caught up in that flood-tide of events which followed the unexpected death of Alexander I.

But in one respect at least he was as strong a liberal as any man in the Society: he not only *held* that all men should be treated with respect and charity, he *treated* all men in that light. The very sympathy that bound him to his soldiers and to common folk in general—a sympathy rather like N. I. Lorer's in its subtle blend of friendliness and consciousness of self-respect, of warmth and of reserve—speaks eloquently of his natural, even instinctive sensitivity towards the dignity and self-regard of others. Few Decembrists could be more at ease with men of every class than he, few better able to command respect from Polish noblemen, Estonian serfs, Buriat tribesmen and Ukrainians, princes and indigents alike. Let us consider, for example, the reaction of his own troops when, in the third week of March 1826, they met their now disgraced former lieutenant for the first time since the rising, in the grounds of Peter-and-Paul Fortress:

> When I stepped over the threshold of the outer door from the dark corridor, the sun's rays so blinded me that I stood still and involuntarily covered my eyes with my hand. I gradually withdrew my hand, and went on: the ground appeared to shake under my feet, and the fresh air took my breath away . . . Not far from the gateway stood a subaltern's guard; I was delighted to recognize my own soldiers: they hastened at once on to the platform and replied as loudly and joyfully to my salute as they used to do formerly.[62]

True, the men had nothing tangible to lose by showing such a friendly attitude; but neither could they gain by it. The incident, though Rozen possibly dwells on it the longer for its being complimentary to himself, rings true.

Again, let us observe his attitude, seven years later, towards peasants exiled to Siberia for their part in a rebellion against Count Arakcheyev's hated "military colonies". These, certainly were rebels:

> On the 3rd May every year, the Poles all assembled to celebrate Kosciuszko's memory. At the same time there appeared also numbers of soldiers and peasants who had been sent here for taking part in the revolt of the military colonies of Old Russia. Soldiers and peasants had not been able to stand the dreadful situation in which they were placed by the unfortunate system of military colonies of Arakcheyev. They rose like one man, and then, as slaves always do, turned against their superiors, whom they stabbed and impaled. To this day the account of the sufferings of these military colonists makes me shudder.[63]

There is no reason to suppose that Rozen's attitude towards Arakcheyev and his colonies had been different in 1820–25.

But, of course, most men of sensitivity had shuddered on learning details of the running of these "military colonies", where pots and pans were issued, army-style, to peasant-women, and annual child-bearing was obligatory.[64] To ponder on the servitude still binding millions of one's fellow countrymen was to experience guilt, if one were capable of guilt. For men of sense and feeling, happiness was tainted almost necessarily in Alexandrine Russia. Given his temperament and milieu, indeed, it would have been remarkable only if Rozen had not felt the liberal influence of the times. Even by 1815, to be sure, Alexander's own liberal days were over. Having originated from the Tsar himself, however, such exalted notions as those of natural rights, egalitarianism and the international brotherhood of man had for some years been seeping down and outwards through the educated gentry, the class most open to untried and new ideas. Alexander's "Intimate Committee" had long since been disbanded. The ideas first inculcated in him by Caesar Frédéric de La Harpe, republican and hater of all despots, were alive and flourishing in St Petersburg two decades afterwards. There were, by 1820, many hundred educated, youthful Russians who placed their hopes, according to La Harpe's gospel of the Enlightenment, in the power of human reason and free institutions. Along that double highway, they believed, lay progress. Nor did young idealists alone form small discussion groups of the variety described for us by Rozen. Others, of by no means revolutionary temperament, also began to meet informally, but with increasing regularity, in private rooms. But in all cases, the burden of their meetings was the same—that something be changed, and government oppression be controlled, before it swamped all private life. By 1818, private letters were no longer private: seals were deftly broken and repaired, "unfortunate" letters "mislaid". In their frustration, even moderates complained, but without effect.

If not impervious to discontent among the gentry and, closer to home, the Guards stationed in St Petersburg itself, the government was not in a conciliatory mood, as increased spying activity and its extraordinary handling of the Schwartz affair showed clearly. In his efforts to ignore brutality which, he no doubt believed, was not his business as a junior officer, as in his gradually increasing receptivity to the concept of reform in Russia, Rozen was neither more nor less conservative or radical than most Guards officers of his circle, class, and age. Liberal in outlook, but not prepared to act to realize a vague ideal, or, for that matter, to implement a concrete, detailed constitutional design such as that drafted three years earlier by Nikita Murav'yov; generous in impulse, but uncertain of the rightness of revolt against established, crowned authority, and hostile to all thought of regicide, Rozen in so many ways seems to have typified the middle-ranking, middle-income members of the Northern Society of 1823–24. But we must briefly turn again to his professional career which, while discontent simmered in some select circles, and while life continued wearisome for the great mass of the people, had progressed well since he had joined the Finland Lifeguards in 1818.

The Finland Lifeguards Regiment did not have a long history. Formed as a militia unit of crown serfs in Strel'na in December 1806, it had, however, promptly met the French—and shown up well. In recognition of its early services, one battalion of the militia unit was added to the Guards Corps; and in 1811 that battalion became a regiment. Though young in regimental terms, the Finland Lifeguards had a fine tradition for belligerence in action, and had won honours both at Borodino and at Leipzig.[65] However, it was not a fashionable regiment. For prestige it was entirely overshadowed by the grand Izmaylovsky, Preobrazhensky and (until October 1820 and the "Schwartz incident") Semyonovsky Guards regiments. But life in it, by the same token, was less exorbitant for ensigns of assured but modest means than in many other sections of the Guard, and this well suited Rozen's circumstances. Of course, expense was unavoidable: ensigns were expected to avoid walking the streets and to hire droshkys; to purchase their own uniform and all accoutrements; to entertain often and generously: even to safeguard regimental honour where wine and gambling were concerned. Rozen lost heavily at cards until, in 1823, he resolved to put an end to such stupidity and never play again.[66] Small wonder that so many officers looked forward to the likelihood of war since they received, in addition to their (often meagre) pay for rank, a more generous allowance for service in the field.[67] Still, the cavalry was far more burdensome on the finances of an ensign than the Finland Lifeguards Regiment could ever be. Here is the list of clothing which, in the opinion of K. F. Ryleyev, then about to join the Horse Artillery, was the minimal basic wardrobe of all officers of that prestigious arm in 1813: "Two greatcoats, one frock-coat, three pairs of trousers, three vests, riding-breeches, one good fur-coat, one braided scarf, one shako with silver pommels, one sword, one hat or spiked helmet, one *konfederatka*, one sheepskin coat ..."[68]—all to be bought for not less than 1,500 roubles. Throughout the century, as Lermontov was to show so well, cavalry officers would struggle with insolvency. At least Rozen was spared the necessity of acquiring riding equipment and hiring an extra stable-hand.

But what of service life itself in the post-Napoleonic Russian infantry? For the private soldier military service was, in the early nineteenth century, nothing less than a calamity. Quite apart from the extreme length of its term (twenty-five years), which generally wrought havoc with a peasant's family life, the military existence was a barely tolerable one.[69] "Corporal punishment for the least misdemeanour, emphasis on triviality, accuracy of step and uniform, such were the matters of stringent importance in the army. Even the most disciplined of units grumbled against unnecessary cruelty."[70] Something should be said here on the subject of the "Schwartz incident" of 1820; for it is in the setting of the Emperor Alexander's favourite regiment of Guards, the Semyonovsky, and of its celebrated gesture of revolt against that officer's inhuman disciplinary measures, that we may best appreciate the circumstances of most junior officers' existence while on guard or barrack duty, and of Rozen's slowly gathering disgust with all the cruelty that he beheld.

"The Preobrazhensky Regiment is a royal regiment, but the Semyonovsky is mine,"[71] said Alexander. Its officers, unlike those of the Finland Lifeguards, were exclusively selected from among the higher echelons of the nobility, and sections of the rank and file were literate. Morale was high. General Potyomkin, until 1820 officer commanding, was well liked and well respected. Relations between officers and privates were so good as to be cordial, and corporal punishment had been abolished in the regiment shortly before it had returned from France where, like the Finland Lifeguards, it had won numerous honours.[72] Notwithstanding these extraordinary leniencies and a unique absence of tension between officers and men, the Semyonovsky had borne the many hardships of a long campaign without a sign of restlessness. Yet to conservatives, who were unable to conceive of military discipline without corporal punishment, the spirit that prevailed in the Semyonovsky on its return to Russia was profoundly suspect. The Grand Duke Nicholas, for instance, then officer commanding, First and Second Infantry Brigades, thought that spirit "loose, corrupt in the extreme". "Subordination", he complained, "has vanished, having been preserved only while troops were at the front; respect for officers has gone completely [in this regiment], and military appearance is on paper only."[73] Nicholas could not appreciate that soldiers who had been in Western Europe for a period of months or even years could no longer be regarded as, and treated like, brute animals.

Dissatisfaction with Potyomkin and his regiment simmered for years among the Guards General Staff. Finally, in 1820, Arakcheyev and the Grand Duke Mikhail arranged for the removal of General Potyomkin from his post, and appointed in his place one Colonel Schwartz, "a man who, although not a great fighter, had the gift of arousing greater hatred among troops than the cruellest of tormentors".[74] Immediately on taking over the command, Schwartz re-established flogging in the regiment and introduced savage new penalties. On October 16, 1820, several veterans decorated with the Order of St George, traditionally exempt from corporal punishment, were flogged on his instructions. The incident proved more than the First Company could stomach: next day, the Company asked to register a formal complaint against "that German".

The Company was placed under arrest in Peter-and-Paul Fortress, whereupon the regiment's other (eleven) companies left barracks and demanded Schwartz's absolute dismissal or permission to join their wronged comrades. The whole regiment was next placed in the fortress, then, after more floggings, dispersed among a dozen other units. Hundreds of officers and men were sent to Finland, then dispatched south to the Caucasus or (in a few cases) to Orenburg and Omsk—where, naturally, they spread their discontent. The government, in other words, effectively assisted them in the enterprise it hoped to scotch. Colonel Schwartz, it may be said by way of epilogue, was indeed dismissed from his command, but was not court-martialled though found guilty of premeditated cruelty by trial; in 1828 he again entered the army. Only in 1849, when at a second court-martial he was found guilty of personally torturing troops, was he dismissed for life and finally disgraced.

It was a *cause célèbre*, a signal for the radicals, a warning. Discontent throughout the army was, however, general, and not confined to any single regiment. In Rozen's unit, it is true, there occurred no open gesture of revolt; but there, too, every private's lot was, if not unendurable, then nearly so—as was Rozen's own in 1823 when he had clashed with Mandershtern. So swiftly had unrest spread through the Guards at large, indeed, after the "Schwartz incident" that in 1821 a special military police was formed. Ten days after the incident, a contemporary involved in the affair and in its aftermath could write about it in these terms: "*Carbonari* appear only when a people are led to a state of despair; *we have the elements for its appearance*, beginning in the guardians of the State themselves. The military men alone are highly valued in our country, yet at the same time they are the most unfortunate of people."[75]

Army life, in short, was steadily producing explosive material, for by 1824 most troops had much to gain by revolution and nothing to forfeit. Not without good cause did the authorities fear that the "Schwartz incident" might provoke others, in other regiments. Among the documents relating to the period first published in this century are records of the skilful propaganda even then, in 1820–22, being disseminated in the army and the Guards by members of the Union of Welfare. "Pray", asked a member of that union hoping to recruit a comrade, "in whom do you have hope?" "My hope," came the reply, "is in God." "But your hope is unsound," was the rejoinder. "We advise you to listen to us ... You do not yet know our intentions ... If we unite, we shall destroy the burdens of the people and the army, who are oppressed by useless and unnecessary misery ... All will be corrected when we work together. Then we shall have a constitution, then the peasants will be freed. *You* will be free ..."[76]

These were aims with which, by 1825, Rozen could entirely sympathize: a constitution, and an end to pointless suffering by peasants and by troops alike. But would he join a secret group in order to compel the Tsar to grant a constitution? (For it was plain even by 1821 that no hope remained of gaining one through the official, legal channels; no recourse remained, therefore, but to resort to secret action.) He waited. His career, after a stormy interval, was going well. One could sympathize, surely, but keep one's distance from the growing storm? Besides, there was his courtship to engross him in 1824. Alas, the storm could not be long ignored, and finally it overtook him. His earlier acquaintance with Ryleyev, his fellow-pupil in the First Cadet Corps; his contact, week by week, with fellow-officers in the Finland Lifeguards who were also liberals and members of Ryleyev's group—Colonel M. F. Mit'kov (1790–1849), a veteran of 1812, four times decorated, who had recently protected him from Mandershtern; Prince E. P. Obolensky (1797–1865), aide to General Bistrom when, in December 1824, the General became Colonel of the Regiment; and Staff-Captain N. P. Repin (1797–1832)—perhaps even the impact of Ryleyev's poetry (certainly Rozen was familiar with parts of it, and held it in respect):[77] all, though he might struggle fitfully, combined in the last month of 1825 to draw him, hesitating still, into the closing liberal ranks. Why in that month? Because it was on Alexander's death, during the interregnum, that the question of divided loyalty would come to an excruciating climax for "the very upright German", as Yakushkin would describe him. For others, oaths might be a mere formality; for Rozen, with his knightly antecedents and a certainty that honour is a man's dearest possession, to swear allegiance was to be committed—honour-bound. And, in November 1825, he swore allegiance to the Grand Duke Constantine. Could he unswear the oath, merely because Nicholas or others might require it? It was, essentially, the question of the double oath of loyalty that finally brought Rozen to the active liberals' camp, and condemned him to Siberian exile. But this is to advance the narrative. Let us return to 1824–25, and consider Rozen's links with secret groups while he pursued a career that still promised well. (Promotion had been steady; his fellow-officer, N. P. Repin, had served seven years as *praporshchik*, from 1812 to 1818, while he had held that rank for only one.[78] Only wartime might have speeded his promotion to staff-captain—M. F. Mit'kov, a second lieutenant in November 1810, was a staff-captain by January 1813, thanks to Bonaparte, and had reached the rank of colonel by the age of twenty-eight.)

In the Finland Lifeguard Regiment there were, by 1825, four members of the Northern Society: Mit'kov, Repin, Obolensky, and Lieutenant N. R. Tsebrikov. Repin and Obolensky alone played active parts in its working. Tsebrikov's membership, in fact, would give rise to controversy within days of the rebellion itself—by March 1826, three independent witnesses would claim that he had never been a member, Prince Sergey Trubetskoy declaring for his part that he had never even heard of Tsebrikov. (But then again, Tsebrikov had earlier denied being acquainted with Prince Obolensky—hardly likely since the latter was his fellow-subaltern, and had seen him every day for several weeks before the rising. The truth of the matter, one suspects, is that Tsebrikov played only the most minimal of rôles in the Society, or came to hear of it extremely late. Others had hopes, therefore, that his complicity might not be proved, were they consistently and firmly to deny his membership.)

Rozen was never on familiar terms with Colonel Mit'kov. The difference in their ages and ranks militated against intimacy—at least until the two should meet as exiles. Repin and Prince Obolensky, on the other hand, were barely three years older than himself, and his equal, or almost his equal, in rank. Here, nothing barred familiarity, and Rozen did indeed grow close to both in the years 1823-25. Sadly, Repin never had fair opportunity to write his memoirs of the period: he died in 1831 in a log-cabin fire. Obolensky, on the other hand, wrote lengthy reminiscences, in which he made it clear that he, at least, did not view Rozen as a dissident until the very end of 1825. But to help throw light on Rozen's part in the political developments of 1825, we also have Prince Obolensky's statements to the 1826 Supreme Committee of Enquiry, instituted to investigate the rising that had heralded the reign of Nicholas. The statements well reflect the Prince's temperament, and, since that temperament will bear immediately on Rozen's trial (see Chapter 3), it may be well to summarize them here.

Obolensky was a man hounded by conscience. It was essentially out of a sense of obligation to his comrades and their cause that, very briefly, he assumed the overall command during the rising of December 14, 1825—and so made confusion worse. Though a staff-officer, his rank was modest; he was Rozen's equal. Far worse for the rebellion, he lacked initiative. Accustomed to deliberate discussions, he was intellectually ill-fitted to make swift, vital decisions. The same feeling of duty that had prompted him to act in Senate Square, moreover, would later bring him to a frank confession of his guilt. Indeed, his repentance would be total and unqualified: there was, as he perceived the situation in January 1826, no room for reservation. He was, of course, consistent with himself—for was this not simply another moral challenge to be met with deep humility? From his cell in Peter-and-Paul Fortress, Obolensky wrote a letter to the Emperor. It bears quotation here, for it shows what Rozen might expect with such a comrade in the witness-stand:

Having been granted the blessing of Holy Communion, Sovereign, and having thus received the Lord's pardon and been enabled to present myself to Him with a serene conscience, I hold it my primary duty, all-merciful Tsar, to cast myself at your feet and to implore, not your temporal pardon, but your pardon as a Christian—your spiritual forgiveness ... I feel guilty now of only one sin: hitherto I have been giving your appointed Committee only those names which I could not conceal; the rest remained hidden in my heart ... But Faith, having reconciled me with my conscience, has also made me aware of a higher responsibility, and your generosity, Sire, has won my heart. Seeing in you not a severe judge but a merciful father, and trusting in your mercy, I now place at your feet the destinies of your erring sons.[79]

No doubt there is a curious kind of logic here (once the parallel between the Emperor and God has been accepted); but many men though not, in the event, including Rozen, would have reason to deplore Prince Obolensky's restless conscience and his willingness to furnish the authorities with a full, detailed list of *former* members of the Unions of Welfare and Salvation.

Obolensky's statements, then, are to be used with caution. Still it is difficult, on reading through his testimony of January 26, 1826, to escape the feeling that, in mid-December 1825, at least, he and Rozen had been very close. The two had met deliberately three times in sixty hours; they confided to each other their opinions on Ryleyev and the rising's chances of success; they shared their deep misgivings and unwillingness to leave their comrades to their fate, whatever that might be; finally, as is apparent from the following short extract from the full, official summary[80] of Obolensky's statement (on his fellow-officers' involvement in the "preparations" for *der Tag*), the two men worked together, in the last, frenetic days before the rising, in an effort to persuade numerous officers, of many regiments, not to swear loyalty to Nicholas:

> On December 11, Prince Obolensky was in Repin's quarters, where he strove to dispose the officers of the Finland Regiment to participation in what the Society planned. Desiring to convince them that many regiments would refuse to take the new oath, he invited to his quarters the next day, at the suggestion of Baron Rozen, deputies from those regiments in which there were members of the Society: the Chevalier Garde, the Izmaylovsky, the Grenadiers, the Moscow, Finland and Mounted Artillery Regiments . . .

More will be said of Rozen's part in the activity of the Northern Society in the last weeks of 1825 (see Chapter 3). Here, we may usefully lay stress upon the main characteristics of his liberalism (for different Decembrists sought the lessening of privilege, the core of all liberal thought, by many different routes). Rozen's, it must first be said, was a cool, practical, *rational* liberalism. Others might entertain fine visions of a new, purified Russia—a land made new by nation-wide reforms; he, like Nikolay Turgenev and half a dozen other pragmatists, gave thought to the reality of practical, peaceful, and prompt improvement of the peasants' lot. To be sure, he had no serfs himself, and no estate on which he could experiment and introduce reforms as had Yakushkin in 1816–18. Nor did he imitate Nikita Murav'yov and compose draft constitutions. A liberal humanitarian unable to shake off a heavy sense of obligation to his fellow-officers *and* to the State, an officer who saw the economic and political, as well as moral, evil of a system based on serfdom, and so was torn by double loyalties, he was by no means firm enough in his convictions to attempt a written project of reform. Besides, he was too busy, and too ignorant of legal niceties.

So we are brought to the second main characteristic of Rozen's liberalism: he did not choose to draft elaborate constitutions or to ponder on the best system of government for Russia. From the tenor of his later articles and certain letters, we perhaps sense a basic sympathy with Murav'yov's (1822) draft constitution. Like Murav'yov, he too felt that "the experience of all nations and all times has proved that autocratic government is equally fatal to rulers and to society; that it accords neither with the rules of our sacred religion nor with the principles of common sense . . ."[81] Like Murav'yov again, he saw the usefulness of the federal principle (after all, he was a Baltic German), and could in middle life, when discussing nationalism in Estonia, closely echo this broad formulation of the principle: "Only a federal system, or an allied form of government, can . . . satisfy all necessary conditions and combine the greatness of a nation with liberty for its citizens."[82] But these views, like his admiration for the British constitution (an unwritten one, we may observe), are implicit, not explicit, in his writings. He does not dwell on them, or state them boldly. Why so? Because his interests lay elsewhere, in the century-old dilemma which his own experience gave him some right to speak about: the deplorable condition of the peasantry, and ways of lightening their burden while not ruining the gentry by doing so. Was Rozen violently opposed to the republican ideal set forth in P. Pestel's *Russkaya Pravda* (*Russian Justice*)?[83] We do not know, because he does not care to mention that "product of a misguided mind", as Nicholas described it in his anger. In itself, the fact is of significance. Was he aware of the main flaw in Murav'yov's plan—that the peasants would be freed with no land, or (as in the third draft, written in a cell in 1826) with a miserable five acres? It seems inconceivable that he was not; for his own part, he considered landless freedom no true freedom. Such was the attitude, of course, of the Estonian peasantry themselves, and he accepted it.

The pragmatism of his liberal sympathies within the context of his attitude towards Estonian serfs should be emphasized. The fate of these serfs gave rise to two of his lifelong concerns: with the improving of their lives, and with the furthering of a reasonable, informed approach to farming. Two illustrations of his attitude may serve. First, it may be compared with that of other liberals familiar with Estonia. V. K. Kyukhel'beker, poet and would-be murderer of the Grand Duke Mikhail Pavlovich, "impotent playwright, one of Schiller's victims, a heroic Decembrist, a pathetic figure but a brave idealist",[84] passed four years of his later childhood (1808–11) in or near the small Estonian town of Vyru (Verro). Most of his first ten years he passed on his father's estate of Avinorm. Kyukhel'beker was well placed to see the harsh reality of life beside the Baltic and, as might have been expected, he took some interest in the Estonians' customs, folklore, and history. But here his empathy was at an end. A people with an ancient, checkered history, splendid dances and gay costumes, an independent spirit never absolutely crushed—such was Kyukhel'beker's concept of Estonians. He saw and understood the ancient struggle for a remnant of autonomy, of course; so much is clear from *Ado* (1824). But that tale does not involve modern serfs; it concerns the efforts of Estonians of the early thirteenth century to contain advancing Germans. Of course, the past could very well be put to the effective service of the present; in suitable historical scenarios, all educated Russians understood, much could be said that might not be expressed in a contemporary setting. (Plainly enough, even if he concurred with P. Pestel' in viewing all the Baltic German nobles as "usurpers and aggressors" (*zakhvatchiki*) with no right to any of their lands,[85] he could not well express the view so bluntly.)

A. A. Bestuzhev (-Marlinsky), too, turned his attention to Estonia in the early 'twenties. What, then, of that liberal-romantic's *Excursion to Revel'* (*Poyezdka v Revel'*, 1821)? Surely such a title promises a factual account of the conditions, population, points of interest of the town? Quite the contrary: once more, contemporary questions are transposed into a distant and exotic past. Again we find ourselves among the warriors and bards, burghers and barons of a colourfully mediaeval town. Rozen, too, could strike a lofty (though less literary) tone when speaking of Estonia's past, comparing the allegedly grand exploits of his own forebears in dealing with the Ests, with those of Cortés and Pizarro against the Indians of South America.[86] But Rozen's interest was in the facts of history, not in its transformation into literature; and in modern history no less than ancient (though he knew far more of both than either Kyukhel'beker or Bestuzhev ever dreamed of). The Rosens and Pizarro: the comparison is certainly arresting, if not wholly just. But such comparisons are never, in his writings, allowed to set the tone of a whole passage. On the contrary, having delivered such a blow to arid style, Rozen immediately turns from the Estonians' ancient struggles to their freedom, economic and political, and to the sufferings of living men—from the literary to the real. Rozen respected poetry and *belles-lettres*; indeed, he treated verse with reverence, preserving fragments by his fellow-exiles P. S. Bobrishchev-Pushkin and Prince Aleksandr Odoyevsky for thirty years, until at last all could be published (see Chapter 12). By transmitting to posterity poems or tales written by his companions in Siberia, and adding terse, characteristically factual comments to them, he performed as it were a duty to those comrades' memory. But he himself had no literary bent, or rather, no imaginative penchant. Not that he was lacking in imaginative power: to read his reconstruction of events on December 14, 1825, or his account of his own childhood in Estonia, is to convince oneself of that. But Rozen was, by temperament, a man who honoured facts. Therein lies the true value of his memoirs.

As a second illustration of Rozen's unromantic attitude towards serfdom in the Baltic region, we may rapidly consider his modest contribution to the working of the so-called "Academy of Chita"—that casual and loose-knit institution in the frame of which, in 1827–30, the Decembrist exiles whiled away long evenings in delivering and listening to talks.[87] The exiles spoke or lectured to their comrades on the subjects they knew best. Several spoke on historical themes: A. Kornilovich on eighteenth-century Russia ("for many years he and Professor Kunitsyn had had free access to the State archives, and had studied the times of the Empresses Anna and Elizabeth particularly deeply"[88]); P. A. Mukhanov on the rise of Muscovy; Prince Odoyevsky on Russian literature before the reign of Alexander. Rozen, too, lectured on history. "He spoke", recalled Odoyevsky, "on the question of serfdom, with special emphasis on serfdom in the Baltic provinces, and on the legal and economic aspects of reform: emancipation without land allotments, without redemption contracts of any kind, but with a universal right to acquire property, in the form of land, by mutual consent."[89] Not a particularly striking or exotic subject, possibly, but one that had already been engrossing him for many years by 1828, and one that would continue to do so until, to his great joy, emancipation came for serfs throughout the Russian Empire, in February 1861. Rozen felt deeply on the subject of emancipation *"with a universal right to acquire property by mutual consent"* (for Estonians had *always* been small-holders, had never worked in communes, and prized their private land no less than any Western European peasantry). He felt personally committed, by his own family history, to the improvement of the Estonians' lot. And with passion he refuted those who, even in the 1840s, argued that Estonians deserved no greater measure of self-government than they already enjoyed by the terms of the reforms of 1816–19. Here, to give some notion of the strength of Rozen's feeling that Estonians, possibly *more* than other peasantries in the vast empire, deserved greater control over their own social and economic destinies, is an extract from *A Brief Sketch of the History of My Fatherland* (*Kratkiy ocherk istorii moyey rodiny*), which he wrote in middle life. Certain individuals, Rozen observes sarcastically, claim that since the "level of civilization" among Estonians has not altered markedly since Tacitus described them, it follows that Estonia itself does not "merit" the attention of reformers:

> Yet surely it is not surprising that a people does not progress in mores or in conduct if that people has not ceased to be treated like slaves, like machines, or like stinking animals. From the time of their conversion to the Christian faith, I say, to the beginning of the last century, the Estonian people knew nothing of the Christian religion except the name of Christ the Saviour. The Knights had not the leisure to preach, and the first bishop, and even monks, preached only by the sword. The Ests knew neither Latin nor German, so how were they to understand their proselyters? They just toiled, they just endured, and when they no longer had the strength to endure it, they rebelled against their masters thirty times . . . At first the German pastors, not knowing the Estonian tongue, troubled themselves but little with the great majority of their parishioners. On Sundays and on Feast Days they amused themselves with target-practice and by riding through church grounds. They ate splendidly, drank plenty, took bribes, and built themselves fine country-seats. And for all this, the Ests received great quantities of blows from their own pastors, birch-rod beatings from their masters, cuts from bailiffs' canes. How, under such conditions, could they make progress in civilization? They were slaves, and slaves they remained . . . And take any educated Englishman, Frenchman or German, and treat him as the Ests were treated till the early nineteenth century, and I guarantee to you that, even if the first generation of these educated people has sufficient strength to combat ignorance, coarseness, obtuseness, the second generation will unfailingly be just as dirty, just as stupid and as careless as were Ests in Tacitus's time . . .[90]

The heat of indignation warms the page. But Rozen had good reason to grow heated when discussing the condition of the peasants in his native land (and what "native land" connoted in political as well as ethnic and linguistic terms, we shall consider in due course): the first draft of the passage cited here was written between 1850 and 1853, that is, after the passing of the 1849 "Fölkersahm edict" by which all Estonian estates were divided into two parts, the demesne and peasants' land. On the latter (theoretically as it was quickly proved), permanent rights of tenants were recognized; rents in labour were to be replaced by rents in kind; nothing but lack of money (theoretically) now stood between Estonians and their ancient dream of owning all the fields they worked. The landlords, as Jackson puts it, hurried very slowly; and in north-eastern Estonia, that is Rozen's Estonia, peasant resentment grew acute—not until 1856 would the *Landrat* pass its draft of the Livonian edict of 1849, with the proviso that its terms should not apply until 1858. "By that year," writes Jackson,

> the peasants were wildly impatient. They had got it into their heads that forced labour had been abolished and that the barons were acting against the law in trying to exact it. In Mahtra the men refused to perform the customary carting service . . . Nine peasants were killed in the free fight that followed . . . Hardly was this incident over than a similar strike took place on an estate in Harju, where the men saw no reason why they should cut the lord's barley. Convinced that the law was on their side, they took a respectful petition to Tallinn. There Baron Rozen, the acting Governor, was waiting for them: he had them arrested, dragged to the market-place and beaten, some of them to death.[91]

Rozen lived to see the full enactment of the 1849 ukase and all its unexpected fruits: more riots, more oppression, but the gradual emergence of a shrewd class of Estonian peasant landholders who in their turn oppressed the ever-wretched landless peasants (*bobyli*). Still, he met new circumstances, on returning to Estonia from exile, in the same pragmatic spirit as before (see Chapter 9). His was no grandiose or pyrotechnic scheme for the transforming of the State and the destruction of its economic evils—or its yet more glaring moral ills. But neither was his character a grandiose, flamboyant one. Always steady and consistent with himself, always practical in outlook, Rozen's was a balanced liberalism, and a calm, reasoned approach to slavery.

3

DECEMBER 1825

> Early on the morning of November 27, I entered the drawing-room of my quarters, in which I had heard a noise. A joiner, who was employed at the Court and to whom I had given the parquet floor to keep in order, was at work there. He asked me, with a mysterious look, "Have you heard of the great misfortune? The Emperor has just died in Taganrog." Everyone to whom I spoke about this that day assured me it was so. The sensation it created everywhere I cannot attempt to describe. Our regiment assembled towards evening in the street opposite our hospital. The Colonel of the Regiment, General Bistrom, informed me, with a trembling voice, of the death of the Emperor Alexander, and congratulated us upon the new Emperor Constantine's accession, waved his hat, and cried "hurrah". Tears were running down his cheeks . . .[1]

So begins Rozen's account of the unprecedented interregnum of November 27 to December 14, 1825, and of the rising that so bloodily marked its conclusion. As always, the controlled and balanced narrative begins at the most reasonable point: the day on which the news of Alexander's death, eight days before, nine hundred miles away, reaches the capital; the day on which the regiments of Guards there swear allegiance to the Emperor Constantine—ignorant, like the populace at large, of the contents of a secret manifesto signed by Alexander I on August 16, 1823, copies of which were kept in the Uspensky Cathedral in Moscow and the Senate and State Council in St Petersburg. All would discover in due time that, treating the Russian State like a huge private property, members of the Imperial family had come to the decision in 1822 that because of his morganatic marriage to a Polish woman not of royal blood, Constantine, though next in line to the throne since Alexander had no children, should forego his birthright to that throne. And he did formally renounce his right; not wholly willingly, however, but when pressure was applied on him by the Empress Dowager.[2] "The whole matter", as Mazour concludes, "had been prearranged by a small circle of the royal family as if such an important act was a purely family matter and of no concern to the State."[3]

Many complementary accounts survive of the confusion that prevailed both at the Court and in society throughout the next two weeks. One Decembrist, Baron V. I. Shteyngel', writes in his memoirs of framed pictures of "Constantine I, Emperor and Autocrat" which were displayed in shop windows on

Nevsky Prospect.[4] Prince Sergey Trubetskoy records the growing irritation on the part of noble houses with the country's "strange predicament", as *The Times* so crisply put it on January 7, 1826 (N.S.), "of having two self-denying Emperors and no active ruler".[5] Other contemporaries speak of the firm, emphatic way in which both Nicholas, in St Petersburg, and Constantine, Russian Viceroy in Poland, repeatedly renounced the throne, while simultaneously declaring perfect loyalty to the other. "When", it was asked sarcastically, "will the sheep finally get sold?"[6] Rozen, for his part viewing the situation from the standpoint of one implicated in the rising which the interregnum had provoked, not unnaturally perhaps, gives much attention to the fact of Alexander's manifesto not being unsealed. For, as he notes, the senators unquestionably knew of its existence, and knew, too, that on each copy were inscribed the words: "To be preserved until I demand it, but, in the event of my death, to be opened before anything is done."[7] It was, indeed, an act of folly. "For had the will been opened on November 27," as Rozen justly says,

> all would unhesitatingly have sworn allegiance to the Grand Duke Nicholas; at all events, the rising would not have had the excuse of the second oath of allegiance—that oath which annulled the one sworn sixteen days before, and at the same time showed that the will of Alexander had by no means been respected as it should have been, according to existing law.[8]

Here is an interesting emphasis: not the shortsightedness of the Imperial family in keeping such an act a family secret, nor the lack of resolution on the part of all the senators but two,[9] nor even Nicholas's strange unwillingness to take the hint, twice given by his brother Alexander,[10] that he might be called upon one day to take responsibility for Russia on himself, but rather the *unlawfulness* of forcing declaration of allegiance from men who had already sworn an oath. But Rozen was his father's son: it was essentially, one realizes on considering his acts over the next few days, the question of the rightness and legality of swearing an allegiance that had two weeks previously been given to another, that most disturbed him from the first. After all, both law *and honour* made it plain: oaths of allegiance, freely given, are not broken. Others too, of course, gave thought to the dilemma of a double oath of loyalty; but Ryleyev, Nikolay and Aleksandr Bestuzhev, Yakushkin and the other leading spirits in the north were less concerned than he with legal niceties and points of private honour. What, these demanded at a meeting of the Northern Society on December 9, if Nicholas attempted to coerce troops and their officers to swear allegiance to himself?[11] Certainly the law itself demanded that the effort be resisted. But more imperative than this, from any radical position, was the fact that mere political expediency demanded that the state of interregnum and bewilderment then reigning in the capital be turned to good account. If a gesture of revolt was to be made, Ryleyev saw, it should be *then*, not, as had earlier been planned in general terms, the following summer. Already, we see, there was no small disparity between the attitudes towards the interregnum, and the possibility of using it, of Ryleyev and his circle on the one hand, and Rozen on the other.

Next day, December 10, it became known in St Petersburg that Constantine had finally refused to be the tsar. The Northern Society was placed in a dilemma even worse than that of eighteen hours before: now a move had to be made: should it consent to accept Nicholas, or revolt? The one course meant an end of the Society; the other course was still more dangerous.

> Sergey Trubetskoy, as a member of the Council in the North, frankly stated that, once Constantine had renounced his right of succession, the Society must act without delay. Ryleyev supported him . . . Realizing they were facing a situation which might decide the future of the nation, the members elected Trubetskoy as "dictator", and gave him full powers to act at his discretion.[12]

And Rozen? Did *he* favour a rebellion? In his statements made before the Special Supreme Committee of Enquiry in January 1826 he swore that he did not; and there is other, more convincing, evidence that he did not: his attitude, revealed by several comments made to others between December 10 and 13, towards the dissidents and their adherents into whose (as yet unplanned) conspiracy he found himself, little by little and not wholly voluntarily, now being drawn:

> On the evening of December 10, I received a note from a comrade, Captain N. P. Repin, begging me to come to him at once. It was late; I found him alone, walking up and down with his watch in his hand. In few words he informed me that the long foreseen rebellion was at hand; a fitting opportunity had come for action, in order to avoid the risk of internal discord or a civil war. Speeches and argument would now be of little avail; material force was needed—a few battalions and cannon they *must* have. He wished for my co-operation in raising our First Battalion. This, as I commanded only one section, I roundly refused; the readiness of the subalterns to join might be depended on, but not so the captains of companies. However, an *attempt* was still possible, which was all the more likely to succeed as it was claimed that Colonel A. F. Müller and his Battalion would assist. That same evening I repaired with Repin to Konrad Ryleyev's; he lived by the Blue Bridge, in the American Company Building. We found him alone and reading: he had wrapped a large kerchief round him because of a sore throat. In his expression could be read all his enthusiasm for the great cause; his speech was clear, convincing; he pointed out that the impending new oath to Nicholas would cause great confusion among the soldiers, which, with little trouble, could advantageously be used to further plans for a change of system . . .

With its shifting tone and various shades of emphasis, the statement is a fascinating one. Rozen was asked to raise the First Battalion; he refused, even indignantly. (It was contrary to military protocol; was Repin unaware that a lieutenant could not order out a military unit larger than his rank could justify, according to the military code?) On second thoughts, however, he saw that a rebellion might possibly succeed—and certainly he would be glad, if such were to be proved. Captains of companies, unquestionably, would oppose any rebellion—but Repin was himself just such a captain! And what of Rozen's attitude towards Ryleyev, the effective leader in the north by December 10? Admiration shines from every phrase: his speech, his look, all augurs well. But if Rozen was confused by his encounters with Ryleyev and now Repin, that confusion grew when he came to Repin's quarters the next afternoon, there to find,

> to my considerable annoyance, *sixteen* young officers of my regiment, discussing the events of the day—they were partially initiated into the secret of the undertaking. I succeeded in calling our host into a side room, where I represented to him how *ill-advised* was this hasty initiation of novices. He replied that, at the moment of action, they could count on every man then present. But youth allows itself to be so easily carried away. It acknowledges no hindrance, no impossibility: the greater the difficulty and the danger, the greater the thirst for action. Among all those present, not one was a member of the secret society except the host and me; yet each man now lent a willing hand to the projected enterprise . . .

He was annoyed, but also nervous; impressed by all the energy of youth (he was now a married man of fully twenty-five), but also necessarily filled with foreboding. He was a member of a secret group; yet, here as elsewhere in the memoirs, a gulf seems to divide the frenzied actions of its members and himself. Indeed, we might suppose from such a passage that the Rozen of December 1825 was a detached, semi-approving, semi-censorious onlooker. But steadily, remorselessly, conspiracy drew Rozen in.

To return to the political state of the capital: it was apparent, by the evening of December 12, that Constantine not only would not take the throne, but that he did not even mean to come to St Petersburg. Warsaw was his city and the centre of his influence; there he would stay. Nicholas was already aware of the existence of clandestine groups, all hostile to him, in St Petersburg itself. He was uncertain of the scope of his own power. Again he was informed of the activity of secret groups; once more he hesitated. But at last, on December 12, he resolved to act.[13] He summoned General Voinov, Commander of the Guards Corps, and informed him that he had at length decided to accede. Voinov humbly knelt. But time was needed for the summoning of the entire State Council. December 14 was set as the date on which the Senate, State Council, and Guards then in the capital would swear allegiance to the Emperor Nicholas I. Meanwhile, impromptu gatherings of members of the Northern Society were growing frequent and more hectic. Day by day, the liberals met and talked; day by day, Lieutenant Rozen saw himself drawn deeper into treason. But there was little to be done about it now. After all, he was a member and was trusted. And Repin had informed him of the plans for an armed rising. Could he betray the confidence of comrades, or in any other way offend his honour? By that very sense of honour which had led him, two weeks earlier, to question the correctness of a new oath to the Grand Duke Nicholas, he was now condemned to lend support, active or passive, to a rising in the

6

capital—a very different matter from a theoretical distaste for tyranny, or loathing for the brutal facts of serfdom in Estonia.

> On December 12, I was present at a meeting at Prince E. P. Obolensky's, at which the chiefs of the conspiracy living in St Petersburg took part; they deliberated on the means at hand and on the impending crisis. It was decided to assemble the revolted troops on Senate Square, there to collect as many men as possible and, under the pretext of defending Constantine's rights, to refuse the oath of fealty and allegiance to Nicholas; and finally, if victory remained on our side, to declare the throne vacant and immediately to appoint a provisional government consisting of five members to be chosen by the Senate and State Council, including, among others, N. S. Mordvinov and Speransky . . . It was not yet known for certain how many battalions or companies, or which regiments, would support us. In the meantime, the tumult which the new oath of allegiance would excite among the privates must, at all hazards, be turned to good account. The Winter Palace and the major seats of Government, the banks, and the Post Office were to be occupied by enough troops to forestall disorder. In case the number of troops should prove too small, and the enterprise should fail, a retreat was next allowed for, to the military colony of Novgorod, where they would find reserves. These measures were not found either decided or severe enough. But to all objections and suggestions the same reply was always made: "You can't have a rehearsal for an enterprise like this, just as if it were a parade!" All those present at *this* meeting were prepared to act. When I heard them confidently reckoning on some of the battalions of my regiment, whose disposition I knew too well for me to place any dependence on them, I held it my duty to represent to them the difficulty— nay, impossibility—of attempting a revolt thus unprepared. "There may be little prospect of success, it's true; but a step must now be taken—a beginning must be made. Strike at once, and the blow will bear fruit;" such was the answer. The words "A beginning must be made" ring in my ears still. The speaker was the enthusiastic Konrad Ryleyev, one of the leaders of the conspiracy.

Always Ryleyev had considered the demise of Alexander as a suitable occasion for the radicals to act. But now, so unexpectedly, the hour had come and nothing was prepared; even Ryleyev, the prime mover and leading spirit in the north, foresaw failure. Nevertheless, he was insistent upon action, "for it would awaken Russia" and the lesson learnt in failure, should failure be inevitable, could be turned to good account by later generations.[14] Fatalism mingled strangely with ardour for the fray, and keenness for the conflict with autocracy, with forebodings of disaster. For Rozen, too, there dawned a frantic two-day period of disorganized and random preparation. December 12, we saw, found him at the quarters of his fellow officer and comrade Obolensky, General Bistrom's aide-de-camp, then in Ryleyev's book-lined rooms on the ground floor of the building of the Russian-American Company. Next day, his fellow officers brought trouble closer to his hearth, by arriving on his own doorstep:

> On December 13, officers of my own regiment came in to see me. To their

question as to how they should conduct themselves if they had to mount guard anywhere on the day of the rebellion, I replied, shortly and concisely, that for the public safety they must steadily defend their posts. However firm might be my *own* resolve to stand by friends, I thought it unadvisable to entangle others in my own uncertain fortunes. That same evening I received intelligence that the next day was appointed for the swearing of the oath. In the night, a regimental messenger brought me the order that all officers were to present themselves, in a body, at the residence of the Colonel, at 7 a.m.

Here, once again, we find a rich field for analysis. Where, one might reasonably ask, did Rozen's loyalties lie now, on the thirteenth? He was, by his admission, a member of the Northern group, in contact with its leaders, and aware of its intention. Yet he could tell his own subordinates "steadily to defend their posts, for the public safety", in other words, effectively to hamper, or at least not to collaborate in, the approaching insurrection. Again, he knew of, and did not now speak against, the basic principle involved in a rebellion—that the law and government were to be challenged; yet, by cautioning his comrades against any optimism, he heightened the electric atmosphere of gay depression, first at Obolensky's, then Ryleyev's, and finally in his own rooms. "However firm might be my *own* resolve . . . I thought it unadvisable to entangle others in my own uncertain fortunes." Unadvisable! The movement desperately needed all the help that it could find. It was *precisely* as a serving officer, a man empowered by that fact to "entangle" many men, specifically, his own troops, that Lieutenant Rozen was of any use whatever to *la bonne cause* in these vital hours! Some officers, he knew, proposed to use their personal influence over their privates, and to count on loyalty to bring them out on Senate Square; others might do their best to order troops to follow them. It hardly mattered. The point was to produce the troops when they were needed. But Rozen? He advised his own subordinates to guard "the public safety", knowing very well, however, that rifles would be taken by the rebels on to Senate Square. No more need be said. Uncertainty was uppermost in Rozen's mind, ambivalence was clear in all his actions. Perhaps it is the phrase "to stand by friends" that best reveals his feelings in those last, chaotic hours before the rising. Here, surely, is the key to his continuing vacillation—a key to which a duplicate is to be found in his "Sketch of the Secret Societies in Russia, 1815–1825", written, apparently, during the 1840s, redrafted ten years later, and first published in the Leipzig (German) text of 1869.[15] The possibility exists, of course, that twenty years wrought changes in Rozen's recollections of his own earlier attitudes and feelings, and that in the "Sketch of the Secret Societies . . ." he interpreted, rather than echoed, his younger self's reaction faced with imminent revolt. On this score, however, his statements made in 1826 before the Special Committee of Enquiry reassure us. Even then he viewed the very prospect of an armed rebellion with diffidence, if not distaste, yet saw no way of not participating in an enterprise begun by friends and comrades. Let us glance at the last paragraphs of Rozen's later essay:

Knowing that the Emperor Alexander himself agreed with their ideas, the liberals in the Guards supposed that in preparing a reorganization of Russian affairs they would be able to obtain his co-operation. But Alexander, frightened by the liberal movement in Germany, now took a different line, and the young nobles in the Army found themselves in direct opposition to the Government in power. Even some of the soldiers were infected by the French poison, and desired such treatment as they had observed, and grown accustomed to, in France. The *enragés* among the conspirators became still more estranged from the Emperor . . .

The revolt broke out in two places and failed in both. The movers of it had in view a political impossibility, and had only themselves to thank if they proved the victims of their own imprudence. But it is not to be denied that the flower of the Guards, and especially the younger intellectuals, had attempted this master-stroke of 1825. With youthful enthusiasm they clung to a number of highly gifted but impractical leaders; many officers held it a point of honour to share danger and want with men whom they knew to be devoted, noble champions of modern thought. The proud consciousness of working with the best of their time was more powerful than the fear of death or exile; for the first time, they had come into contact with the Ideal, and they could not withstand the lustre of an enter-prise which, it appeared, secured for everyone who took a part in it a place among the best and very noblest of their fellows.[16]

It is, needless to say, of himself and his contemporaries that Rozen speaks. He was himself among the "young nobles" who found themselves opposed to Alexander's every policy. And it had been his own acquaintances and friends who, in 1822–25, had "clung to highly gifted but impractical leaders"—Ryleyev and Pestel' foremost amongst them. He himself, finally, had held it "a point of honour" to stand with the "best and very noblest" of his time. Not any concrete, realizable political objective, we perceive (despite his later plans for land reform), but rather the feeling that his comrades did indeed represent what was best in Russian life and thought brought Rozen to the point, on the fourteenth, of throwing in his lot with the conspirators. What painful self-examination he endured during the night of the thirteenth, we cannot know. In his memoirs, he would write of the necessity of warding off "disorder or individual action" in the city: perhaps, like Baron Shteyngel', he had apprehensions that the masses in the capital might turn against and murder members of the gentry.[17] Necessarily, he was affected by the news, broken at Obolensky's on the twelfth, that the Colonels A. Tulub'yev and A. Müller (Moller) had, like Colonel Shipov of the Semyonovsky Regiment, refused to pledge support for a rebellion—both were senior officers of the Finland Lifeguard Regiment.[18] (Colonel Moller, when approached by Nikolay Bestuzhev, had declared bluntly that he, at least, would not "be a tool and toy for others in an enterprise, the head of which was not fixed firmly on the shoulders".[19]) Still, Rozen had decided to adhere to the insurgents. He was sombre. How lacking in all ardour was his mood the very day before the rising that would mark his life for good, is clear enough when we observe how others passed that day and night. Among those present at

Ryleyev's on the eve of the fourteenth was Mikhail Bestuzhev, who recalled the gathering in these terms:

It was a noisy, turbulent meeting in Ryleyev's rooms on the eve of the 14th. Those present—and there were many—were in a feverish, somehow exalted state, and there were heard desperate statements, impracticable instructions and suggestions, words without deeds for which many, although guilty of nothing and before no man, would pay dearly . . . But how fine Ryleyev was that evening! He was not a handsome man, and although he spoke simply he did not speak fluently. But when he touched upon his favourite theme, love of the Motherland, his face would grow animated, his jet-black eyes light up with an unearthly glow, his speech flow as smoothly as molten lava; and *then* one could never tire of gazing at him. So on this fateful evening, too, during the course of which that cloudy question, *to be or not to be*, was decided, Ryleyev's countenance, pale as the moon but lit up by some supernatural light, would vanish, reappear, and vanish once more in the stormy waves of that sea in which simmered various convictions, many passions . . .[20]

Describing the same evening, Mikhail's brother Aleksandr could add, many years later: "Leaving, we were so utterly determined either to succeed or to die that we did not come to the least agreement in the event of failure,"[21] while Prince A. I. Odoyevsky, then a nervous youth of barely twenty-two, exclaimed in ringing tones: "We shall die, oh, how gloriously we shall die!"[22] Rozen, it will have been observed, was absent from the gathering.

So dawned December 14, 1825—the day on which Guards regiments then stationed in the capital should swear solemn allegiance to the Emperor Nicholas I. The events of the next fifteen hours are too familiar to bear detailed restatement here. To summarize them, then:

Nicholas was anxious that the oath be sworn to him promptly and quietly. At first, it seemed that he would have his way; senators, ministers and members of the Council of State took the oath by 9 a.m. In most regiments of the garrison the oath was taken peaceably. In some, however, troops expressed bewilderment at the swift passage of rulers and the multiplicity of swearings. Seizing upon this mood, some officers brought about three thousand men on to the Senate Square, where they formed up ready for action. The officers who led them hoped that such an extraordinary display of discontent and show of military strength would rally all the troops stationed in St Petersburg, and that their ranks would swell enormously. But this was not to be. Quickly and poorly planned, their scheme was frustrated . . .

Nicholas, meanwhile, was in the nearby Winter Palace, preparing counter-moves. He had no plan. Nor could he help proceeding slowly and with caution, since the troops' mood was unknown to him . . . Nicholas gathered loyal men, especially artillerymen, and carefully encircled Senate Square. Hours passed, and still the rebels had not moved. Cannon were brought up and trained on them . . .

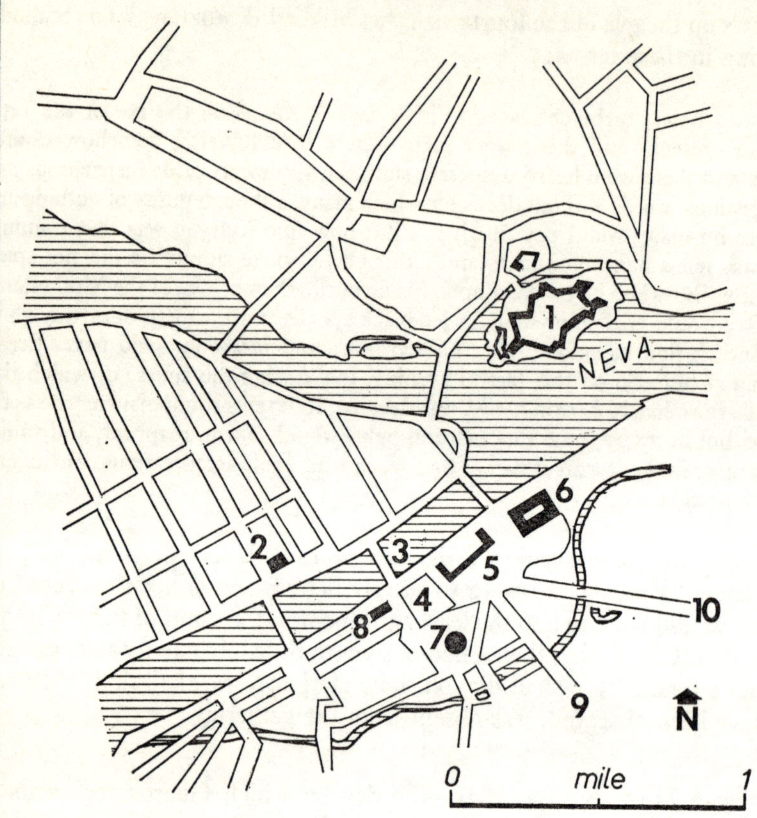

1 Peter and Paul Fortress
2 Academy of Arts
3 St. Isaac's Bridge
4 Senate Square
5 The Admiralty
6 Winter Palace
7 St. Isaac's Cathedral
8 Senate Building
9 Gorokhovaya Street
10 Nevsky Prospect

The centre of St. Petersburg in 1825

The mutineers would not disperse; but neither did they make a move. Finally, between 3 and 4 p.m., Nicholas felt confident of the complete superiority of "his" forces . . . Grapeshot scattered everyone, slaughtering many.[23]

All histories of the growth of liberalism in Russia, indeed, all histories of Russia, spare a paragraph or two for the events of December 14, 1825. That is proper; for on Senate Square, liberal tendencies in Alexandrine Russia came to an unprecedented, brief, premature crisis. It was, in political terms, the high point of the radical movement in St Petersburg itself, the martyrs' day, the *joli commencement de règne* (as Nicholas is said to have remarked to General I. O. Sukhozanet).[24] And yet, one sees on carefully examining accounts of the rebellion itself, all historians have fundamentally relied on the same sources: the eye-witness accounts of Nikolay, Mikhail and Aleksandr Bestuzhev on the one hand, and of Rozen on the other.[25] All historians have thus agreed, implicitly, on the value and reliability of those four versions; and Rozen's memoirs have been taken, in this study, at face value—a great compliment to any memoirist. Before proceeding here with his account of December 14, 1825, let us, therefore, give reasons why it may be trusted and, indeed, why it is irreplaceable for students of the period. (Reminiscences of dissidents, few would dispute, have often proved mixed blessings for historians.)

Rozen's account of the events of December 14, 1825, many of which he saw himself, is, in the main, highly reliable. From the factual viewpoint, it is more accurate than many other eye-witness accounts.[26] Only where precise times and, occasionally, individuals' initials are concerned, may he be faulted. His reminiscences, like those of N. V. Basargin and Baron Shteyngel', reflect an unimpassioned temperament. Where insurrections are involved and where, in consequence, things happen rapidly and details tend to be obscured or lost— whether from the sheer speed of events and sense of chaos, or whether certain writers choose to have them lost—that is itself a fact to give one confidence. Rozen, it has twice been emphasized, was a cool, rational officer. His written style, in Russian and in German alike, reflects his temper splendidly. No less dispassionate or measured than his résumé of reasons why the rising failed (but very nearly did not fail) is his attitude, apparent in all sections of his memoirs, towards the liberal activism that was widespread in the Guards during his early life. Consider, for example, this remark in the introduction to the second (1874) edition of his memoirs: "Well enough do I know that men's characters and actions are very much determined by the spirit of the times and by the circumstances in which they chance to be—a fact that may embitter us towards those who have acted harshly towards ourselves . . ."[27] It is, one may say, an old man's observation. But Rozen's attitude towards his judges hardly changed between 1826 and 1869: this is the point. Within days of the rebellion, he was ready to condemn it, but excuse it; within hours of his arrest, he could regret it, but yet view it steadily, and see it whole. Deliberate and cautious as a youthful officer, he was cautious and deliberate forty years having gone by. He took no foolish risks in later life; nor did he do so on "the day", as we shall see. And here is one more reason why his calm, balanced account of the rebellion itself is of such value: unable to decide to leave the scene of the revolt, but equally unable to advance on Senate Square, hemmed in by government and by his own troops, Rozen saw everything as from a grandstand. For three hours he stood immobile on St Isaac's Bridge with three full companies of the Finland Lifeguards at his back—his own men; for three hours, from that vantage-point, he watched the tide of fortune ebb and flow two hundred yards away, until at last his comrades lost the day and were dispersed by canister. To his left there stood the Admiralty, by the far corner of which appeared the Tsar (or Tsar-to be) and all his suite; on his right hand was the Senate, and, beside it, Galley Street, by which onlookers had gathered by the hundred towards noon, and across which Sukhozanet would be firing. Before him, by Falconet's statue of Peter the Great, stood the insurrectionary companies, stamping and shivering: a cold wind blew all day.

> During the night a light snow had fallen over Senate Square, but when the sun came through the low clouds the snow melted: later the cobblestones gleamed with a coating of ice. As the morning advanced a chill north wind began to blow in gusts across the Neva, while the fog still clung to the islands and the river . . . The air was so raw and cold that many people preferred to stay at home. As usual, fires were burning at street corners, and the few carriages made a leaden sound as they drove through the streets. It was not a good day for starting a revolution . . .[28]

Six hours before, Rozen had made a hasty, futile effort to incite his own men not to swear an oath of loyalty to Nicholas. Then he had driven up to the insurgents in an open sled. Within five minutes, gnawed by dreadful doubts and by the feeling that his own men should be brought on to the Square post-haste, he had driven off again in the same sled. Finally, his company and others had been ordered out of barracks on Vasil'yevsky Island and, having brought at least three hundred men to a complete stop on St Isaac's Bridge, by an earth-shaking cry of "Halt!", he had stood glued to the one spot, neutral to all intents and purposes. He was, to say the least, well placed to view events. What he saw, we see in Chapter 7 of his memoirs. With photographic clarity, disaster unfolds. Yet rarely does the narrative of Rozen's memoirs touch upon his own feelings that day, or on his own conduct, indeed. Since that conduct, between 9 a.m. and 3 p.m., would stamp a permanent impression on his life, though he lived to be a man of eighty-three; since, in short, it was the day that turned his destiny, we may usefully consider his account, not as a picture of the rising in its general perspective (the salient features of the day, as has been said, are familiar enough, and have been well surveyed by Presnyakov and Anatole Mazour),[29] but in so far as it throws light upon his own conduct and changing moods. On neither vital question have we secondary sources.

In his own account, then, we see Rozen first making polite objections to the

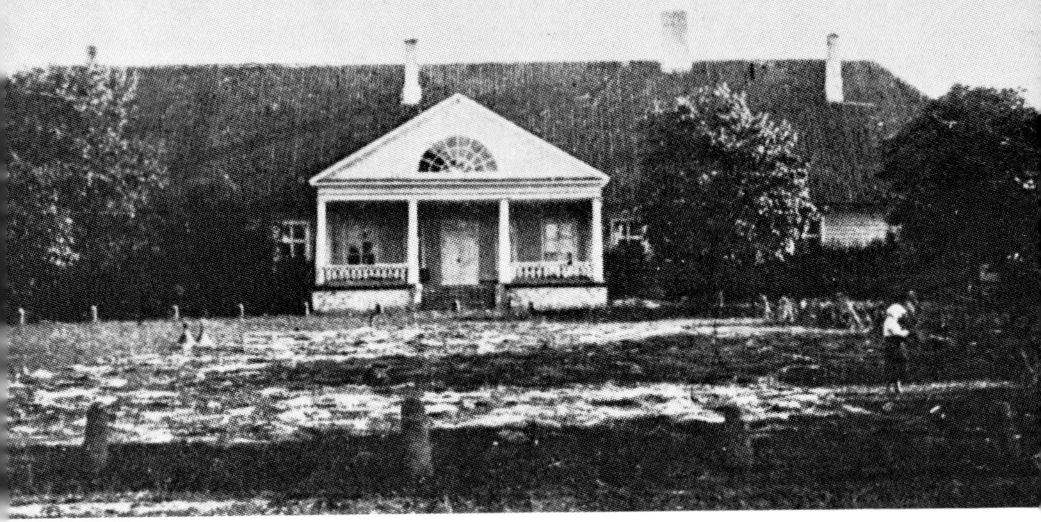

e manor-house at
osna-Alliku early
s century

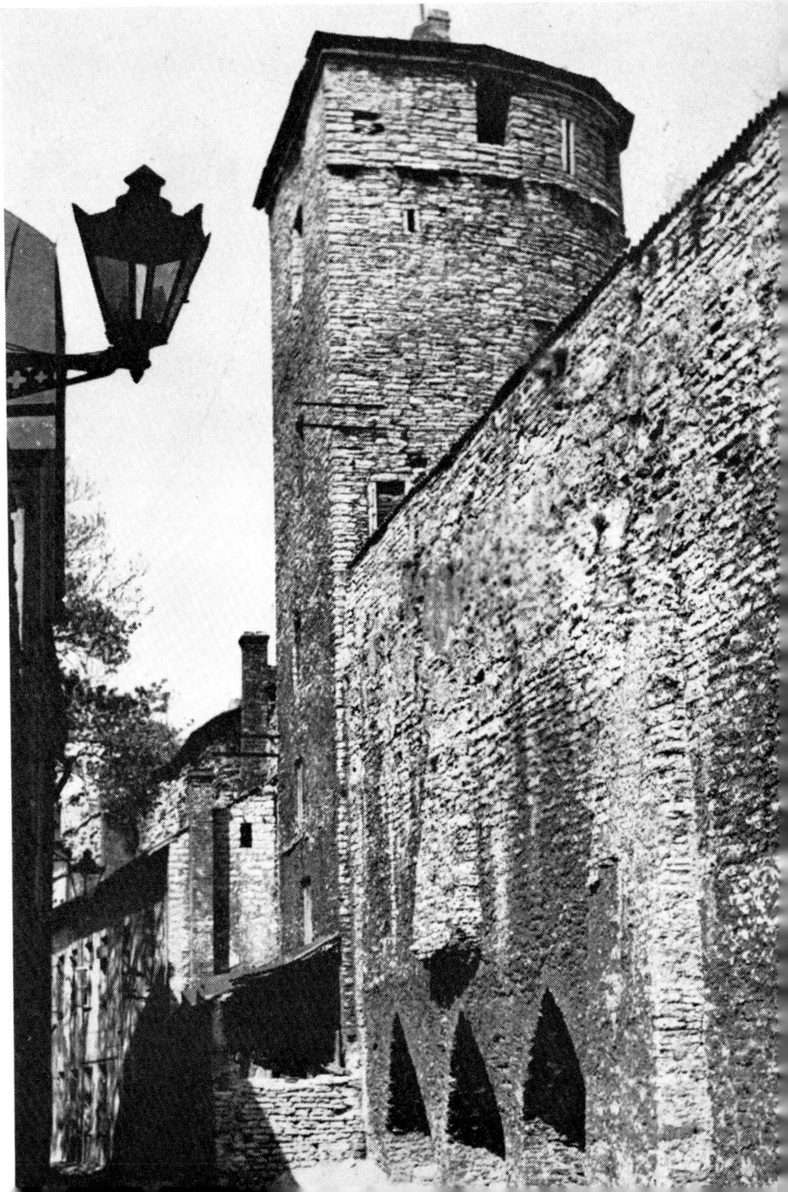

e fifteenth-century
ınkadetagune Tower,
llinn

ERLEAF
e Senate Square,
Petersburg on
ecember 14, 1825;
ter-colour by
I. Kol'man, *c.* 1830

Andrey Yevgen'yevich Rozen, *c.* 1825; water-colour by N. A. Bestuzhev, 1832. *Right:* Anna Rozen, *c.*

St Isaac's Bridge, St Petersburg, where Rozen halted his troops on December 14, 1825; as it appeared in the 1840s (oil painting by Bishbois)

swearing of an oath to Nicholas, and then apparently avoiding the necessity of doing so by not being where the oath was to be sworn. Only he and his section of sharpshooters, in fact, do not swear the oath; the fact, and Rozen's emphasizing of it, are important. Not being bound by the new oath (and so not having infringed his sense of honour), he would certainly not act in a dishonourable way if later that day he opposed the Grand Duke Nicholas—as he would still be, in his sight. Always, Rozen respects the law.

Next we see him free to act with the insurgents in his own sight, approaching Senate Square at 10 a.m. or slightly later. He pushes through a crowd of on-lookers to where a carré formed out of a company of the Moscow Regiment is standing wearily, and he is greeted. He walks up to I. I. Pushchin, who naturally supposes he has come to join the rebels, and asks where he can find Prince Trubetskoy, the "dictator". Pushchin tells him Trubetskoy is absent. Why should Rozen wish to know the whereabouts of "the dictator" and to speak to him? Because, in Rozen's view, only the prince, as the elected chief, could act as a commander and direct him where to go and what to do. It is a matter of procedure. Had Trubetskoy been present, it seems safe to say, *there is no doubt* that Rozen would immediately have done as he was bidden; but Trubetskoy was absent.

Rozen had reached the first of two great turning-points. He went off to do his best, as I. Pushchin put it, "to bring more men". Hastily, he returned to the Finland Lifeguards' barracks on Vasil'yevsky Island. There he ordered all the troops he found to take up arms and leave immediately to "help their comrades". It was 11.15 a.m. Few junior officers fell in, knowing full well that Rozen was proposing to support the insurrection; within his regiment, his membership of a supposedly secret society was an open secret—or had been, since the previous day, when sixteen junior officers had come to him. Adjutants galloped about incessantly, carrying messages. Confusion reigned. If only for that reason, Rozen managed to bring out into the yard the whole battalion—one thousand men. Each officer supposed that someone senior to himself had given orders for a general parade. And now, at the decisive, crucial moment, as the columns are about to march for Senate Square to support the insurrection, the Brigadier arrives. The men set off, accompanied by Generals Komorovsky and Golovin— but not to Senate Square, and not to aid the rebels. On the contrary, they set off to crush them. The situation is, in fact, reversed. Rozen nonetheless goes with his regiment. Events already speed to overtake him. Does he think of aiding the insurgents, of averting the apparently inevitable clash between his comrades and his regiment? Probably he himself could not have said. Certainly the very possibility of helping them seems lost when, by the building of the Naval Cadet Corps, Komorovsky orders the whole regiment to swing left to St Isaac's Bridge. The insurgents will thus be approached both from their flanks and from across the frozen river, and effectively deprived of all escape routes. The Finland Lifeguards march on to the bridge, and halt.[30] Orders are given to load sharp. Many privates, now expecting to be ordered to destroy or maim their equals, cross themselves. Still Rozen watches. He marches to the centre of the bridge, leading his company, then halts again. Komorovsky and Golovin are behind him—perhaps fifty yards, possibly as much as several hundred. The bridge ahead is packed with moving troops, all steadily advancing on the Square. Another spurt of energy, another pang of strained conscience, strikes Rozen. After all, his desperate comrades (and that they *are* desperate is clear from the numbers of troops surrounding them) are still expecting his appearance with more men. He has given I. Pushchin to understand that he will come. He tries to cut a path through the dense mass of soldiery ahead, to reach the Square, and fails. But at that instant, yet again to change the situation utterly, Komorovsky gives the order for a general advance. Rozen reaches his second turning point:

> As I had now convinced myself that the rebellion had no leader, and was totally without cohesion; and as I was determined not to sacrifice my soldiers needlessly (while it was obviously out of the question that I join the opposition), in that instant when Count Komorovsky and the Brigadier gave the order to advance, I decided to halt my men just where they were. By this, I meant not only to prevent my men from being turned against my friends, but at the same time to take from regiments behind me the possibility of their passing the bridge now occupied by my company, and so to stop their acting against the insurgents . . .[31]

The result of this decision, concludes Rozen, was "rather successful": the bridge was blocked. "Rather successful" from the theoretical, tactical viewpoint, possibly: the bridge being an impasse, advance was certainly impossible (although the river ice was thick enough to bear large groups of men, as Mikhail Bestuzhev would show after the rout, and Komorovsky might conceivably have sent units across it). But for the rebels, who were practically in hailing distance now, Rozen's move could bring no comfort. (Many, it would afterwards emerge, remained in ignorance of his presence on the bridge until long after the fourteenth.) He failed to bring them aid in their most desperate hour. But to return to his intentions when he stopped his company: had thoughts of simultaneously preventing the advance of troops loyal to Nicholas and of preventing men under his own command from being turned against his comrades truly, as he claims, decided him to shout the fateful word? Had he, indeed, pondered the matter carefully from various angles? He was, admittedly, a trained, professional army officer. It was as such, on January 8, 1826, that the Grand Duke Mikhail Pavlovich, the youngest of the late Emperor's brothers, would address him:

> The first question was put to me by the Grand Duke Mikhail: "How could you, as commander of a section of riflemen, keep back three whole companies who stood partly in front of your company?"
>
> "When the battalion marched out of barracks," I replied, "it was arranged in columns of companies, so that my section was before the three companies of jägers."

"Pardon me, I was unaware of that," said the Grand Duke in a friendly tone. Dibich thereupon asked me why I had kept my troops in the middle of the long St Isaac's Bridge. I answered that . . . it seemed to me correct to take no action whatsoever. "I understand," replied Dibich, being a tactician, "you had it in mind to form a reliable reserve."[32]

Several Decembrists, too, later regarded his behaviour on the bridge as having been considered and deliberate. I. D. Yakushkin well sums up this attitude: "Lieutenant Baron Rozen, a very upright German, and in everything a very loyal comrade, did not actually come on to the Square. Perhaps he hoped, by staying with his regiment, the more effectively to contribute to the success of the enterprise which his comrades had begun . . ."[33] It would, of course, have been uncharitable to assume anything else; and so it is today. Yet still the feeling lingers, as one ponders on his actions, that perhaps Rozen did not bark out his order having thought the question over; that perhaps, far from assessing the whole situation as he subsequently claimed, and taking an appropriate decision in accordance with the military textbooks, he was *jerked* into the order by the fact of everyone's so suddenly, after a pause of several minutes, moving on towards the Square. Possibly, in brief, he spoke, then thought. The question, it is obvious, can never be resolved once and for all.

Meanwhile, there were already above 2,000 men in the ranks of the insurgents. With so large a force, and surrounded as they were by thousands of the populace ready to co-operate, it would have been easy to bring the rebellion to a happier conclusion, had there been but one efficient leader, especially as the opposing force was wavering and certain regiments assembled round the Emperor seemed inclined to join the rebels. But able generalship was not to be found among the insurgents: the soldiers were kept standing motionless for hours, with only a simple uniform on, in ten degrees of frost and a sharp easterly wind . . .

On Admiralty Boulevard stood the carré of the Preobrazhensky Regiment. The Emperor was prominent on horseback there, with a numerous suite. The Tsarevich, a seven-year-old boy, was in the middle of the Square with his tutor. Before it were positioned cannon of Colonel Nesterovsky's Brigade, covered by a troop of the Chevalier Garde . . . When the men thus arrayed had encompassed the insurgents on all sides with close columns, the crowds of people on the Square around them started to thin. The police grew bolder in dispersing them . . .[34]

Rozen's decision once having been taken to halt on St Isaac's Bridge, it was a relatively easy matter to resist the threats and blandishments of all who, for the next three hours, attempted to make the Finland Lifeguards move away. Most of the troops were disinclined to make a sudden move either forwards or backwards; but in any case, they were hemmed in by other units. So the afternoon wore on. More cannon were dragged hurriedly down Admiralty Boulevard, though ammunition for them was in some cases delayed for several hours.[35] Rozen was now compromised beyond all hope of extrication. He had disobeyed a senior officer; attempted to incite to mutiny; and failed to aid the government (if Nicholas could legally be viewed as such—an arguable point, it must be said) to quash an open insurrection.

But Komorovsky and the other senior officers in the vicinity, extraordinary though it may seem, were unaware of Rozen's effort earlier in the day to lead his men to the assistance of the rebels. Such is the implication of Rozen's being left at liberty throughout the evening following the unsuccessful rising, even having openly declared in the First Cadet Corps' riding-hall that his troops were "in no way to blame for anything". No senior officer, it would appear, was in the regimental barracks in the morning, when Rozen had assembled the First Battalion with a view to bringing it on to the Square; not one, it follows, need have known of his seditious attitude towards the government and Nicholas. Yet is it possible, one wonders still, that *no one* in authority knew of his earlier connections with Ryleyev, Obolensky, Repin, and half a dozen other radicals? It was a curious situation: Rozen, who had openly defied his own superiors within the hearing of a hundred men, found himself free to go to his own quarters when the rising had been quashed. More than this, he was sent out on active duty in the night (having finally sworn loyalty to Nicholas) and, so Golovin later testified, carried out his duties irreproachably![36] But there can be no doubt: for there is ample evidence that even officers loyal to Nicholas and standing by St Isaac's Bridge were unaware, as the day drew to its bloody close, that Rozen had been acting for some hours in a spirit hardly likely to assist the government to scotch the rising. Here, to illustrate that point, is part of the long statement made by General-Adjutant Golovin, of the Finland Lifeguards, in January 1826 concerning officers of his own regiment who were personally implicated in rebellion. The general, we see immediately, was hardly an authority on Rozen's conduct on the fourteenth of December: like several other officers, *he* thought that Rozen had, in fact, sworn loyalty to Nicholas at 7 a.m. that day. What he did not know and had not seen, indeed, considerably outweighed what he had seen:

The company . . . to which he [Rozen] was attached was on watch during the oath-giving. Baron Rozen, with his regiment, loyally swore to serve His Imperial Highness Nicholas Pavlovich. When the First Battalion was approaching Rumyantsev Square, Baron Rozen attempted to persuade the sharpshooters not to go against the rebels, telling them that they had not yet sworn an oath to His Highness the Emperor Nicholas; and on St Isaac's Bridge he halted them, and when certain individuals declined to drop back from the carbineers [who were ahead, and keeping Rozen from the Senate Square end of the bridge], he threatened to strike with his sword the first man who should then advance; to which the whole section of sharpshooters has testified under interrogation. On the return of the regiment from bivouacs to barracks, General-Adjutant Voropanov did his best to ascertain if Baron Rozen had used any other methods in his effort to seduce the troops, but nothing was discovered beyond what was already known . . .

Concerning the action of these officers: although I was with the First Battalion continuously from the very moment that it left barracks until the actual dispersing of the rebels, . . . I was unaware that Lieutenant Baron Rozen had halted his section of sharpshooters, and even earlier had been persuading men not to advance against the rebels . . . All the rest was revealed later. Lieutenant Baron Rozen, however, when the Battalion reached its bivouacs, was employed all night, with other officers, on sentry duty, and carried out his duty with proper exactness, so that it was then impossible to have entertained the least suspicion of him.[37]

So ended the day of the rising; by 3 p.m., dusk was approaching. "The first cannon-shot loaded with blank cartridge roared out, but the second and third sent ball, which hit the wall of the Senate House, or flew over the Neva . . . A moment later, grapeshot fell like hail in the densely crowded Square . . ."[38] By the river, two hours later, many bodies were thrust hurriedly into the gaps made in the thick ice to receive them.[39] On Senate Square itself, blood was scraped off the ground and stained patches were sprinkled with fresh snow. Fires burned at street corners, and beside cannon, near which tapers were still smouldering five hours after the rebels had been scattered, soldiers stamped their frozen feet.[40] But Rozen saw none of these scenes: from 4 p.m. until 7 p.m. he was sitting in his quarters where, considerably to his surprise, he was joined by a distraught and weary Repin: "When the firing began," declared Repin to General-Adjutant Levashev three weeks later, "I set off towards the regiment, which was on St Isaac's Bridge. I went up to Lieutenant Rozen, who told me to withdraw and asked me to call on his wife and calm her on his own account. I went to Rozen's quarters afterwards, and sat there until evening; then I went home to sleep."[41] All night, as we have seen, Rozen was on guard duty. Next day, first in the morning unofficially and by an unknown person, then at 4 p.m. officially, by his company commander, he was arrested.[42] Not having seen his wife again, he was sent off under armed escort to the residence of General-Adjutant A. D. Bashutsky, Commandant of St Petersburg, and then briskly removed to the guardhouse of the Chevalier Garde. On December 22, he was transferred to the main guardroom of the Winter Palace, overlooking both the fortress shortly to receive him and the First Cadet Corps that had once discharged him. The first stage of his expiation started.

We will quickly set the scene for Rozen's coming trial and period of confinement in a dank casemate of Peter-and-Paul Fortress, by saying something of the leading actor in that trial, Nicholas I.

To most Russians, Nicholas was an unknown quantity when he acceded to the throne. Several Decembrists, on the other hand, knew something of his character: Sergey Volkonsky, whose mother was a confidante of the Empress Dowager, had often met him at Court; others, like Rozen, had observed him at close quarters as an army officer and had exchanged occasional words with him, always on service matters. They, it followed, were aware of his narrow and despotic temperament before they met him under such unpleasant circumstances in the Winter Palace for interrogation. "Strict subordination", remarks Masaryk, "and unquestioning obedience—these formed Nicholas's system. In his psychology, men were machines or, at most, animated slaves."[43] As often, Masaryk oversimplifies, yet is essentially correct. Absorbed by the military life and style (he had received most of such education as he had, and all his formal training, in the army—chiefly in the field of engineering), the new Emperor lacked even an average degree of tolerance with men whose views on life, duty, and tsardom differed from his own.[44] His accession, liberals foresaw, would bring a restoration of the days of Colonel Schwartz.[45] As a boy of thirteen, A. I. Herzen, later to become the major architect of the Decembrist myth (by which the tragic but heroic happenings of 1825, and the deaths of the Decembrist martyrs, should prompt all radicals to undertake more revolutionary activities), caught sight of Nicholas for the first time. "He was handsome," he later recalled of his symbolic enemy,

> but there was a coldness about his looks; than his, no face could more mercilessly have betrayed the character of the man. The sharply retreating forehead and lower jaw developed at the expense of the skull were expressive of iron will and weak intelligence, of cruelty rather than sensuality; but the chief point in his face was the eyes, which were entirely without warmth, without a trace of mercy; wintry eyes.[46]

Like Queen Victoria nineteen years later, Rozen would be faced by those cold eyes, and be appalled;[47] but he would meet them soon, at 10.30 p.m. on December 22, 1825. First, however, let us trace his fortunes, and those of the main figures in the rising, in the days immediately following its crushing.

Rozen made no attempt to flee, and was arrested in the capital. His conduct was typical. Each man, of course, went his own way to death or exile; some voluntarily and hurriedly confessed their sins to Nicholas—and, in some cases, crimes that they had not in fact committed;[48] others simply went to bed, like Trubetskoy; others made ill-considered or (in four cases) serious attempts to flee the city. But these were few indeed, and most Northern Decembrists were arrested in St Petersburg, like Rozen, peaceably, and within forty-eight hours of General Sukhozanet's cannonade. An extraordinary feature of the rising, as Rozen would himself remark, was that not a single "ringleader" was scratched, though many bullets flew and, as we saw, whole rows of soldiers fell. All were reserved for other fates.

Nicholas, it is an understatement to observe, took a close personal interest in the capture, questioning, and incarceration of his *amis du quatorze*. Most men arrested in connection with the *joli commencement de règne* were brought before him in the Winter Palace, usually at night. Having put some questions to them, he would scribble orders to the Commandant of Peter-and-Paul Fortress, the wooden-legged General A. Ya. Sukin. More than a hundred of these orders, stating how each prisoner was to be treated, have survived.[49] They show the avid interest that Nicholas took in the whole affair, and his grim determination to squeeze from every prisoner the last possible drop of "evidence", that is, of guilt. "Ryleyev", read the note accompanying him, "to be placed in the Fortress but his hands not tied. Give him writing paper and deliver personally to me whatever he may write each day." "Yakushkin to be treated *severely*, and not otherwise than as a villain." "Rozen to be kept in confinement."

The hatred that Nicholas felt for these officers was personal and deep. The mere thought of them annoyed him. Obolensky in his sight had "a black soul" and "a bestial and mean expression"—an expression strikingly at odds with pictures that we have of that mild-mannered individual. As for Volkonsky, who alone of the Decembrists had a niche in the highest Court society, he was—in Nicholas's view—"a stuffed fool, a liar, and a scoundrel in the full sense of the word ... and a repellent example of an ungrateful villain". The Emperor's artistry in posing for each prisoner in the way best calculated to extract desired information, now as father-figure, now as veteran soldier, now as puzzled ruler, was such as to deceive even La Ferronays, the French Ambassador. Small wonder, then, that he succeeded with the weary prisoners who, with occasional exceptions, took his pretended sympathy at face value.

As in the cases of so many well-born rebels' families (and now the capital seemed to be overflowing with them), the Rozens of the Baltic provinces—a large and numerous clan—promptly disowned their erring son. Not to do so, after all, given the fact of Nicholas's feeling on the score of the Decembrists, one of deep affront and hatred, would have been impolitic; and the Rozens, as a house, were politic. Only Rozen's closest family, his parents and three brothers, even acknowledged his continuing existence in the early weeks of 1826. Here, to give some impression of the swiftness and completeness with which less immediate relatives succeeded within days of the rebellion in blocking Rozen from their mind and memory, are a few lines from a letter headed Wattel (in Estonia), December 20, 1825, from Baron Otto Johann Rozen, later Governor of Kazan', to his daughter Karoline Sophie von Uxküll. News of the rising in St Petersburg, we know, had reached Revel' and Riga by the sixteenth, that is, certainly within forty-eight hours of its suppression. To reach estates outside those towns, admittedly, might well have taken longer. Nonetheless, it must be said that it was *most improbable* that such a man as Otto Johann, with connections in the capital itself, should have remained more than a day or two in ignorance of his own relation's part in a rebellion against the government. His own self-interest was at stake. The participation of a Rozen in the rising, after all, plainly concerned himself—and might conceivably affect his own career. Besides, bad news could be relied upon to travel fast enough. Steps had obviously to be taken to resist the evil influence his nephew might exert upon the futures of other members of the family beside his, Otto's. So, without more hesitation, Otto Johann shut his nephew from his mind. It was as if, in the last days of 1825 as for the rest of his long life, his wretched relative had never been. The note referred to, we may further stress, was to a daughter, not a colleague, or an individual in any way likely to report its contents to authority. Nevertheless, in this as in all his other extant correspondence of the following three

years,[50] the Baron simply wiped Rozen the convict from his personal horizon.
Other members of the family did likewise.

> So haben wir also jetzt unseren Grossfürsten Nicolay zum Kayser da Constantin
> dem Trohn entsagt hat! Das Manifest von Nicolay soll schon geschrieben seyn . . .
> Gott stärke und beschütze unseren geliebten jungen Monarchen damit wir auch
> unter ihm so glücklich wie unter dem allgeliebten Alexander leben können. Das
> Militär hat in Reval dem Kayser Nicolay schon gehuldigt und jetzt auch wol
> das Civil . . .

As a letter from a father to his daughter, it is not expansive. But the Decembrist
rising, others too would find, had cast a chill over the life of the whole Empire.

But to turn again to Rozen's personal fate. Even in the earliest stage of questioning and punishment, his treatment had been proving exceptional. For eight
days he had been held, not in a chancery nor even in the building of the General
Staff, like most of those about to be transferred across the river, but in the
guard-house of the Chevalier Garde, two miles north of the Winter Palace.
When, at last, he had been taken to the Palace for a private interview with
Nicholas and certain members of the newly-instituted Committee of Enquiry,
he had been left there, in a dingy ante-room. Days passed, then weeks. Still
Rozen had been left, with neither books nor company to help alleviate the bore-
dom or distract his mind from terrifying thoughts. He had last seen his wife
the day before the rising, when he told her all he knew of what would happen;
was she well? Would she be suffering as a result of his involvement in a rising?
He was kept in ignorance. Perhaps his special treatment may be explained most
clearly in the context of his first, brief audience with Nicholas, on December 22.
Rozen, it should be added, was interrogated first by General-Adjutant V. V.
Levashev. The General was courteous, Rozen extremely weary.

> Just as my examination started, a side-door of the room opened, and the
> Emperor entered. I went a few steps forward to salute him; he said in a loud voice,
> "Halt!", came up to me, laid his hand on my epaulet, and repeated the words,
> "Stand back; back; back!", following me till I reached the spot where I had been
> standing, in the full glare of the candles which were burning on a table. Then he
> looked me searchingly in the face for a minute, expressed his satisfaction with my
> former service, and said he had repeatedly observed me. He added that heavy
> charges were laid against me, that he expected me to make a full confession, and
> ended by promising to do everything possible to save me. Then he withdrew. The
> examination was resumed as soon as the Emperor had left the room. I found
> myself in a most painful position. There were no grounds for me to deny the facts
> on my own account, yet neither could I tell them the whole truth for fear of
> implicating those who had taken part in, or originated, the rising. After half an
> hour the Emperor came in again, took from the hand of General Levashev the
> paper on which were recorded my answers, and read it. No names were given in
> my statement. He looked at me kindly and encouraged me to be candid. His pallor
> and his bloodshot eyes showed clearly that he worked too much; he heard, read

and investigated everything for himself. On returning to his study, he once again opened the door, and the last words I heard him say were, "I would willingly save you"—*Dich rette ich gern*. When Levashev had ended his report, he handed me the paper to read through, so that I might attest to the truth of my evidence by signing it. I begged him to spare me such a signature, and gave him to understand that I could not reveal the whole truth. Nothing remained for me but to sign the report; but the Emperor was informed of my first hesitation, and must have looked upon it as contempt of his gracious promise. The sentence passed upon me was not only not mitigated, as will be seen, but was made still more severe...[51]

Rozen had at first made an acceptable impression, or succeeded in not damaging an earlier good impression: so much is clear both from the Emperor's final remark (not, however, to be taken at face value) and from the interesting fact that General Martynov, one of the senior officers appointed by Nicholas to inspect the prisoners in the Fortress every six weeks, took it upon himself in early April 1826 to "recommend" Rozen to the Commandant, General Sukin. There is no record of this being done for any other prisoner. Here is Rozen's own account of what occurred: "Martynov, who was my inspector, recommended me to the Commandant, who was accompanying him, reminding him that, on some previous occasions, the Emperor had noticed me."[52] Had Nicholas implied, then, by some casual remark to Martynov, that Rozen should be treated more humanely than some other prisoners? That he hoped that Rozen's part in the revolt might yet be mitigated by a full confession? Martynov, one is sure, would not have taken it upon himself to single out a prisoner for gentle treatment, even had he been a kindly officer, which he was not; and the former supposition is lent weight by Nicholas's last remark, *Dich rette ich gern*. Here, surely, is a comment of significance. Rozen, we are reminded, was a Baltic German, a member of the caste at once so vital and so prominent in Nicholas's Army and, indeed, in every branch of the Imperial Government. V. F. Adlerberg, A. Kh. Benkendorf, I. I. Dibich, and F. G. Tol', such men were his most trusted instruments, the pillars of the new Russian State. On these officer-bureaucrats, not on high-ranking members of the ancient Russian aristocracy which had proved false, he now proposed to place responsibility for the creation of the new, purified Russia. Yet Rozen, though a German, had proved false; he had betrayed his own position and the group on which, more than all others, Nicholas had tended to rely. Highly privileged by birth and situation (Nicholas had been raised to *respect* the Baltic German officer), Lieutenant Rozen must needs undergo a heavy punishment, should he hesitate to make a full confession, or his guilt be demonstrated in some other way. Nicholas waited for the statement that he wished to read from Rozen. Rozen did not write it.

When my first examination was over, I was led back to the ante-room of the Palace guardroom, behind a partition. I received light through the glass doors, warmth through the open top of the partition. This place would have been bearable for a few hours at the most; every moment I expected to be taken to

7

another guardroom or into the Fortress, and therefore I submitted to my fate
with patience. I slept through the night on a chair . . . Christmas came and the
same narrow, dark corner of an ante-room was still my abode. All the passers-by
stared in through the glass door, so I turned my chair in order to show them my
back . . . In this way day after day passed, and every one seemed endless. In the
afternoon of the third day of Christmas, the Grand Duke Mikhail suddenly came
in to me, stood at the doorway, and said, "What? Is he still here?" I made up my
mind not to complain of either cold or hunger. But the most trying part was that
I could not sleep. The chair, the only piece of furniture in the room except for a
table, was so uncomfortable, and the floor was so fearfully cold. I had no choice
but to spend fourteen nights in a sitting position. Often, the men on sentry duty
would take pity on me, wake me up at night, and secretly give me some of their
bread . . . I remained in this miserable corner until January 3, 1826. In the afternoon of that day, the Grand Duke Mikhail again arrived: again he came into the
guardroom and expressed astonishment that I was still confined there. By his
order, I was taken to another room, where a bed and clean linen were given to me.
At last, on the afternoon of the fifth, I was taken by a State courier to the Fortress.
With thumping heart I went through the gate; the carillon of the Fortress clock
saluted me—an artistic piece of mechanism, which tediously and slowly rang out
the tune "God Save the Tsar" . . .

Nowhere in official papers that survive is there any explanation of Rozen's
curious treatment. Certainly there were cells enough in the city to have taken
him—barracks had been converted into jails;[53] nor is it easy to believe that he
was simply, in the constant *va-et-vient* surrounding Nicholas, forgotten. So
we are left supposing that Nicholas expected more from Rozen than the latter,
bound by honour, could provide—and that he subsequently, venting his
annoyance, treated him with more severity than he might otherwise have done.
Such was the interpretation put upon the Rozen situation by the first of French
historians of Decembrism, J.-H. Schnitzler. Even having permitted the Special
Court to read its sentence over Rozen, on July 9, 1826, Schnitzler justly notes,
Nicholas

made certain distinctions, by upholding sentences passed on some men and
reducing them for others, so that he appeared to be establishing a different range
of guilt [from the Court's]. Lieutenant Baron Rozen and one other individual in
the same category were the objects of particular severity: in accordance with the
sentence passed, the Emperor ordered that they be condemned to hard labour
for ten years, then banished in Siberia . . ., while a third man, the naval ensign
Bodisko *junior*, remained sentenced to fortifications work for a period definitely
limited to five years.[54]

Schnitzler is correct to emphasize the special treatment meted out to Rozen and
to M. N. Glebov. Glebov was a Collegiate Secretary, the civilian equivalent to
full army lieutenant, in a ministry department in St Petersburg; Rozen represented something dear in Nicholas's sight, and had proved false. For neither

man did the new Emperor feel any inclination then, at least, to exercise his power of clemency.

Rozen, to continue with his tale, came to the Crownwork (*Kronverk*) Curtain of Peter-and-Paul Fortress on January 5, 1826, exhausted by emotional stress and sheer physical hunger. He found himself placed in a cell compared with which his ante-room had been a veritable scene of luxury. In itself, it has been rightly stressed, incarceration in the Fortress's damp casemates (most covered to a depth of several feet by the tremendous flood-tides of November 7–9, 1824), was frequently enough to break a spirit—or a life.[55] What with the wretched diet, chains, and endless silence, few men could endure the trial and, breaking down, many involved ex-comrades. Even today, their statements are oppressive documents, written by men obviously on the verge of physical and mental collapse.[56] Always there was suspense, always some fear for wives and families, and always ignorance of what others had already said to implicate their friends. Many men collapsed under the strain, or from the noisome air and scanty food. Here is the Decembrist M. A. Fonvizin's recollection of that time:

Methods were used against the prisoners which struck their imagination and destroyed their spirit, inflaming them either by false hopes or by fears of torture, and all this with just one purpose—the extortion of confessions. The door of a cell would suddenly be flung open at night; over the prisoner's head a blanket would be thrown abruptly. Then he would be led through the corridors and passages of the Fortress into a brightly lit courtroom.[57]

But to return to Rozen's narrative:

The town-major [*plats-mayor*] called out: "Artilleryman, open no. 13." Keys jingled, locks rattled, we entered, the doors slammed behind us. The town-major then took the bandage from my eyes . . . My cell was almost pitch-dark; the window was covered by a thick iron grating, through which I could see only a narrow strip of the horizon and part of the glacis. Against the far wall of the triangular cell stood a bed with a blue-grey blanket; against another, a table and bench. My triangle was six feet in the hypotenuse. In the door was a little window with a linen curtain on the outside, which sentries could lift at any moment to watch the prisoners. A little after I had entered this cage and sat down, I heard a guard's footsteps approaching; the keys and locks rattled again; a prison warder entered and gave me a lamp (a wick burning in an ordinary glass filled with oil and water), a bowl of soup, and a good large piece of bread. I asked the man a question, but received no answer. I then, with the utmost speed, devoured the potato soup flavoured with bay-leaves, and two pounds of bread. The warder watched me with amazement; I told him how I came to be so hungry.

The Fortress clock struck eight consecutive hours; then I heard "God Save the Tsar" again. Though I was conscious of the sounds, they did not rouse me from my sleep; and I should certainly have slept on for a full twenty-four hours, if the jailer with his keys had not awoken me. This terrific clatter was no sooner over than the Platz-Adjutant Nikolayev entered: a tall man in a black coat followed him, with the artilleryman acting as warder. I sat down on my bed, expecting another prisoner to come in with them. The Adjutant enquired next how I felt; the man in the black coat, who proved to be a doctor, also enquired after my earlier health. To both I replied, "Thank God, I am well rested." "Excuse our having troubled you, but we must do our duty." And, as silently as they had entered, the trio disappeared; I immediately fell asleep again. When I awoke it was midday, but the casemate was still dark, for the window had been cut in an embrasure and did not admit the full natural light. I never saw the sun or moon, and scarcely did a single star pass by the narrow window-pane. Towards evening, a lamp was brought in. But I had nothing there to read, for in the first months of imprisonment no one brought us any books. Alone, confined in a narrow room, there was no exercise for the body, no distraction for the mind—though the mind alone was free. The future lay before me, uncertain and forlorn; the present offered nothing; the past alone remained to me . . . [58]

Week after week, the newly formed Supreme Committee of Enquiry was engaged in its supposed investigations, unwilling to report to Nicholas in case some detail had been overlooked. "Giving prisoners no time to think, they demanded an immediate, affirmative reply to all their questions. They accepted no self-justifications, invented fictional testimonies by other prisoners, and frequently refused to call those other prisoners in to testify to their own statements."[59] And, of course, they made no effort to appreciate the underlying intellectual force behind the whole liberal movement, or to comprehend its psychological aspects; they had no brief to do so. As Prince Obolensky put it, "They took for truth what had been said or done in moments when the imagination had been guided by some feverish outburst, [60] and used this as solid evidence of evil thoughts and plans.

4

TRIAL AND IMPRISONMENT

Almost immediately after the rising had been quashed, Nicholas had instituted his Committee of Enquiry to investigate, in theory, into all secret societies in Russia. The Grand Duke Nikolay Mikhaylovich, uncle of the last Romanov Tsar, characterized the Committee members thus:

> The chairman was the Minister for War, Tatishchev, an entirely obscure figure, while of the members of the Committee, Chernyshev, Levashev, Golenishchev-Kutuzov and Potapov were known for their servility and heartlessness; Prince A. Golitsyn—for hypocrisy; D. N. Bludov—for his liberalism in theory and cowardliness in practice; only one, Benkendorf, was thought more independent and, in fact, constantly tried to mitigate the Tsar.[1]

The Committee, we have seen, did not hesitate to use all means in the extracting of information or, more accurately, information that its members wished to hear. Physical discomfort, it was found, was but a trifle to most prisoners compared with the more subtle pains to be induced by "loyal" priests, who came into the cells to offer "spiritual consolation". But Rozen, as a Lutheran, at least was spared all this.[2] Moreover, he was treated civilly when, on the night of January 8, he was brought for the first time before the Committee itself:

> The town-major bandaged my eyes so thoroughly that my whole face was covered. I heard talking on the steps of the Commandant's house; through the handkerchief, I could make out the shining lights of a carriage; an ante-room seemed to be full of servants. In the next room, the town-major made me sit down and told me to await his return. I immediately lifted up the bandage, and saw great folding doors in front of me, and a large screen at the far end of the room, behind which were two lights, but no one else in the whole room. I do not quite know why the thought came to me, but it struck me that the doors would open suddenly and that I should be shot. Perhaps this idea was caused by the mysterious manner of the town-major, and by the binding of my eyes. I sat for an hour like this. At last the town-major returned and led me, still blindfolded, through the next room, which seemed full of light. I heard a quantity of pens scratching, without being able to make out the writers. Having finally reached a third room, the town-major said, *sotto voce*, "Stay here." For thirty seconds there was no movement or sound;

then I heard the words, "Take off the handkerchief." It was the Grand Duke Mikhail's voice. I saw a long table before me; at the upper end of it sat the chairman of the Committee, War Minister Tatishchev . . .

Was this Committee of Enquiry intended to be a court martial? Then the whole business might have been decided in twenty-four hours, without the aid of anyone versed in the law. The articles of war would have condemned all the accused to death at once! And this kind of court, in which only officers gave sentence and the plaintiffs served as judges, was the customary method in Russia when an important case was to be heard!

The first question was put to me by the Grand Duke Mikhail: "How could you, as commander of a section of riflemen, keep back three whole companies who stood partly in front of your section?" . . . [Rozen's reply has been considered already—G.B.]

Then Dibich addressed a question to me: "Since when have you belonged to the secret society, and who received you into it?"

"I have never been a member of any secret society."

"Perhaps you mean us to infer that you consider that being a member necessitates peculiar usages and ceremonies, signs and conditions, as in the fraternity of Freemasons; on the contrary, it suffices to know the objects of a society to make one a member of it."

"I have already had the honour of informing Your Excellency that I have never been received into a secret society, and that I can appeal to all those who were really members, without fearing examination before witnesses or a confrontation with them."

I was interrupted by Kutuzov at this point: "Yet you knew Ryleyev?"

"I *know* him—we were trained together in the First Cadet Corps."

"Did you not know Obolensky, too?"

"I know him very well; I served with him; he was senior aide-de-camp in the Guards Infantry Corps. How could I help knowing him?"

"What further proof do we need?" remarked Kutuzov, in his senseless way. I was silent, though it would have been easy for me to retort that, since *he* knew Prince Obolensky, he must himself have been a member of the society.

The chairman, Tatishchev, then informed me that, next day, I should receive written questions from the Committee, and should have to answer each question in writing, according to the headings. Before the end of this interrogation, Colonel Adlerberg said to me: "You are accused of having wished to cut down the second sharpshooter of the right flank, because he tried to persuade some of his comrades to follow the section of Carbineers."

"My men, M. le Colonel, did not chat as they stood in rank and file. One of them, I don't know if he was the second or third from the flank, wished to advance; I held my sword before him, and threatened anyone who tried to move without my orders." Colonel Adlerberg's remark at once showed me that they had been informed of the most trifling circumstance connected with me. The Brigadier and one other man who had reason to fear my depositions had given them this information.

With that, the first examination ended; the chairman rang the bell, the town-major bound my eyes and led me off. My face was covered with a handkerchief, so that the secretary and clerks should not recognize the prisoner. After a few minutes I found myself once more in cell no. 13. Three days later, a sealed packet from the Committee was handed to me.[3]

The packet, Rozen found, included novel accusations. (The Committee found new charges to level against prisoners as other prisoners confessed. It was a brisk snowball effect.) But what, it may be asked, did the Committee know of Rozen's acts on December 14, and with what was he now charged? When the Special Court passed sentence on July 9, 1826, he was found guilty of two crimes: "Lieutenant Baron Rozen: personally participated in the mutiny [*myatezh*], having halted his platoon, which was sent to suppress it."[4] (According to the *Gazette Allemande de Sainte-Pétersbourg*, which printed the Supreme Court's sentences in full for the delectation of its foreign readership, Rozen had been "personally active in the revolt, causing his detachment of cavalry—*kavallerie-kommando*—to halt. So much for accurate press coverage of the trial![5]) But had the Committee been told all this before he had been questioned personally? Let us examine Rozen's "trial" (he himself was never conscious that a trial was even under way). His answers, both written and oral, to questions put to him by the Committee throw much light on his sense of honour. And for Rozen, honour was at stake, not truth or mere political advantage.

The file on Baron Rozen had been opened on December 15, 1825, within hours of his arrest. A report on E. P. Obolensky, N. P. Repin, N. R. Tsebrikov and A. E. Rozen, compromised officers of the Finland Lifeguards, headed no. 5055[6] and addressed to General A. D. Bashutsky, Commandant of St Petersburg, was written by the then acting commander of the Finland Life-guard Regiment, General-Major A. Voropanov. The report gave the reasons for Rozen's arrest:

> Lieutenant Baron Rozen has been arrested for having halted an infantry platoon, trying to persuade the troops that they had already sworn allegiance to the Tsarevich Constantine Pavlovich and threatening to strike with his sword the first man to go after a section of Grenadiers . . . On the first appearance of the company from the Moscow Regiment [on Senate Square—G.B.], Lieutenant Rozen approached it in a sled, threw himself into the carré, where he remained no more than five minutes, then left for his regiment and was not in the carré again; but he was the first to bring news of the insurrection to his regiment, and to state that his battalion should go to it.

At once, official notice had been drawn to Rozen's absolute insistence that an earlier oath be honoured. It was a theme that would recur throughout his trial. But to his trial, it has been seen, the Special Committee took a leisurely approach. For days he sat in idleness while other, more important prisoners were questioned; for three weeks no further papers were inserted in his file save those relating to his interview of January 8. Time passed with painful slowness.[7] A report by a senior officer of his own regiment, that of General-Adjutant Golovin, was cited earlier. Golovin was unaware even that Rozen had been acting in a manner prejudicial to his own command, until he had been told of it next day.[8] From him, the Committee learnt only that the prisoner had behaved well on the night of the 14th–15th—hardly the kind of brick required to build an edifice of solid accusation. For his own part, Rozen signed only two papers in December; one of them bears citing here:

> I did not belong to the secret society. I was educated with Ryleyev, so remained acquainted with him; but for all that, from the time I left the Cadet Corps I saw him only twice: once in his own quarters, and once at Prince Obolensky's. No rumours reached me concerning the 14th.[9]

He could not have made a plainer disavowal. Clearly, if it meant to build a case the Committee needed contrary evidence. And so, in the long interview of January 8 described above, Rozen was asked point-blank if he had been a member of the Northern Society. Here, to complement his brief oral denial, is an extract from his statement written, on January 12, in reply to the Committee's set of questions (the "sealed packet"):

> That same evening (December 10) I went with Staff-Captain Repin to Ryleyev, whom we found unwell and reading a work on world history. We discussed that subject, then the fact that it was still unknown whether or not the Tsarevich had arrived in the capital, observing that it was giving rise to various speculations. While we were talking, there arrived cornet M. of the Chevalier Garde and an officer I did not know, wearing a frock-coat with a red collar; these two left after a few minutes. Having passed a quarter of an hour at most at Ryleyev's, we went with Repin to Colonel Tulub'yev, to whom we reported what we had heard, then went off to our homes. Next day, ensign Bodisko lunched with me; and with him, I went to Prince Obolensky's. There we found Ryleyev and six officers, all unknown to me. The discussion of the previous day was repeated, with the addition that it was agreed to dissuade the men from swearing when coerced to do so, and to lead them on to Senate Square. At this, I said to Ryleyev and Obolensky that only a regimental or battalion commander could effect this. "Then let only the officers who are loyal to their Sovereign appear on the Square," they retorted. To my query, "What will happen there to a flock without a shepherd?" they answered, "Everything'll be there—you'll see, then you'll find out." After this, I at once went to Repin and repeated to him all that I had heard and seen . . .[10]

The statement was in various aspects unsatisfactory to the Committee. That Rozen had attended gatherings in Ryleyev's rooms they knew already from the evidence of Prince A. I. Odoyevsky;[11] that he had hesitated there, and made apparent his misgivings on the score of a rebellion, they had learnt from several prisoners, notably A. A. Bestuzhev.[12] But what of his own membership of the Society, and his participation in the hurried preparations for revolt? The Committee hoped in January to establish, first, that he had indeed been a member of the Northern Society and, second, that he had attempted to seduce others from their "lawful" allegiance to Nicholas, by persuasion and by countermanding orders. Questions calculated to elicit suitable replies on those two points were duly sent, on January 9, 10 and 11, to Rozen's fellow-officers, Repin and Obolensky. The replies proved to be flatly contradictory. Repin's precedes the Prince's: "Members of the Society known to me are: Ryleyev, the Bestuzhev brothers, Pushchin, Obolensky, Arbuzov, and Baron Rozen, who joined from the Finland Regiment at the same time as me..."[13] "Of those *outside* the Society who knew of its intentions regarding December 14 and took part in its events, there were also present, excluding Baron Rozen, Count Ivan Konovnitsyn of the Guards Mounted Artillery, and Malinovsky..."[14]

Contrary evidence was, of course, to be expected in the circumstances: many prisoners were struggling to implicate no other man, blaming themselves for everything conceivable or else, like Ryleyev, repeating stolidly to all questions, "I do not know." This discrepancy, like others, called for an immediate confrontation between Repin and Obolensky, and Repin and the tiresome Baron Rozen. A confrontation was arranged between Repin and Rozen. The Committee gleaned but little information, for now Repin, sensing how the wind blew, merely claimed that he could not be sure that Rozen had, in fact, been present at meetings of the Society. Not, to be sure, that the Committee was in any doubt as to Rozen's guilt; still, "concrete" evidence was wanted—and such evidence eluded them. They persevered. At length, on March 8, sixty days having elapsed since Rozen had denied belonging to the Northern Society to Dibich, Ryleyev was asked the same question. Ryleyev's was a systematic policy of whitewashing associates whenever possible. Not only, therefore, did he casually *suppose* that Rozen was completely ignorant of the aim of the Society (for who had told him?); he denied all knowledge of participation in the rising, or in its preparation, by any officers of the Finland Lifeguard Regiment.

Whether or not Lieutenant Baron Rozen was among the members of the Northern Society I do not know. A few days before the 14th he called on me, and afterwards I saw him at Prince Obolensky's; but in his presence we spoke only of ways of bringing the troops not to swear another oath. The aim of the Society, that is, the utilizing of that opportunity to bring about a change of governmental system, we did not mention. I suppose therefore that he had not been received into the Society.[15]

Never did Rozen formally admit to membership of the Northern Society; never could the Committee of Enquiry obtain a clear acknowledgement of what was certainly as plain to them as to Ryleyev: that Rozen had been deeply implicated in the working of that same Society, though only in the last days of its life, and that he chose to understand and to interpret "membership" in his own, fastidious way.

However, there were other charges to be pressed against him. And Rozen made no effort to deny the truth of the accusations of his having withheld the oath of loyalty from Nicholas and threatening to strike the first man to advance across St Isaac's Bridge. By the third week of January it had grown clear that here, in the matter of the oath of loyalty, lay the core of Rozen's case. By the same token, it was growing plain that Rozen could throw little light, if any, on the topics then of greatest interest to the Committee: plans for regicide, designs to introduce in Russia a republican or constitutional form of government. So Rozen was not troubled after January. Among the prisoners who did cast new and interesting light upon his case, however, was the conscience-stricken Obolensky. The Prince's testimony was summed up by Chernyshev, and included these remarks:

> On December 11, Prince Obolensky was in Repin's quarters, where he attempted to dispose the officers of the Finland Regiment to participation in what the Society planned . . . Next day he invited to his quarters, at the suggestion of Baron Rozen, deputies of those regiments in which there were members of the Society . . .[16]

So Rozen, it emerged, *had* played an active part in trying to convince the officers of several regiments of the correctness of adhering to their first oath of allegiance. To Rozen, the "very upright German", the matter was quite simple: oaths could not be broken. True, political expediency also dictated that the Grand Duke Nicholas be prevented from acceding to the throne. But underlying all considerations of expediency and tactic on the part of Baron Rozen, one perceives, was awareness of the strict demands of honour. In him, training and family tradition both spoke loud.

March gave way to April. As a favour, prisoners were at last allowed some books of "spiritual consolation", and tobacco. Already Rozen's health had been affected by the stale air in his cell. Spring came and, when he left his cell for a few moments, he saw grass and birds. Six more weeks passed. Even in March, his case had resolved itself into two questions: his withholding of allegiance, and his halting a platoon (and thus hundreds of men) on St Isaac's Bridge. Yet still on May 19, on making his summary of Repin's testimonies, Chernyshev was adducing more support for Obolensky's statement that Rozen had discussed the refusal to swear a second oath with many officers: "Though the conversation was indeed about refusing to swear an oath and, in the event of an insurrection, about joining it, still we had not been told the details of how the rising would be carried out."[17] But this was ancient news: the Committee had been told as much four months before. So the Committee rested its case. Yet still no report was submitted to the Tsar, in case some detail had been overlooked. (Were not such scribblers as Pushkin and the playwright Griboyedov, or such foreigners as Count Loebzeltern, the Austro-Hungarian Ambassador, and possibly Lord Canning, or even generals such as Yermolov and Kiselyov, somehow implicated?[18]) Finally, on May 30, a report was presented. Two days later, Nicholas appointed a Special Supreme Court, which held sessions for nine days beginning on June 3. Prince P. P. Lopukhin, whom Nicholas named Chief Justice of the Empire, was conveniently deaf, but there was never any doubt that the Supreme Court would confirm all the Committee of Enquiry's "findings". Prisoners were not called before the court—and therefore remained in ignorance that their own trials were proceeding—but were visited in their cells by members of a special sub-committee, who merely asked each man if statements read to the Committee of Enquiry had been accurate, if the signature beneath them was authentic, and if they had signed under pressure. Throughout their time in the Fortress, prisoners were kept in ignorance of the significance of what they did, wrote, or affirmed. Rozen, like other men, supposed that what he said to the Committee of Enquiry would decisively affect his future lot; in fact, his written statements played a far more vital part in his disgracing than the boldest of his comments.

But to return to his own narrative. We find him now, in May, awaiting news of Anna's first delivery, suffering from scurvy, and expecting to be put to death:

On May 17 there was an unusual stir in the corridor: warders and prisoners were continually passing to and fro and talking loudly; many of the latter, as they passed outside my cell, called out "Bonjour, 13." "Portez-vous bien, treize!" In the afternoon, the warder, Sókolov, told me that some of the prisoners had been taken before the Committee, where they had signed some documents, then had been returned to their own casemates. "What do you think?" I asked; "will their being called in there do them good, or harm?" "God knows," was the reply. "Seems to me that those left here in peace will be best off." I went to sleep at last, still in restless expectation, till the rattle of locks and bolts woke me up suddenly, and the Town Adjutant took me before the Committee. The walk to the Commandant's house showed me how beautiful the spring already was: the air was impregnated with the scent of elder-flowers, and birds fluttered and sang in the Commandant's garden . . .

I was conducted through the clerk's room, not to the place where the Committee had been sitting earlier, but to another room on the right, where Benkendorf and Senator Baranov sat at a writing-table. The answers I had written to the questionnaire of the Committee were handed to me; I was asked "whether the signature beneath it was my own", "whether I had answered under pressure", and "if I had anything to add". I replied in the affirmative in the first two cases, in the negative in the last. I was then made to sign the papers. I read in Benkendorf's face that it would not go well with me . . .

On the morning of July 12, I observed some carpenters at work with heavy beams on the Crownwork ramparts opposite my window, not in the least understanding, however, what they were about. I often went back to the window, and once saw two Generals-Adjutant moving about the place . . .[19]

Rozen was one of five Decembrists to observe the construction of the gallows where, at 4 a.m. next morning, K. F. Ryleyev, S. I. Murav'yov-Apostol, P. G. Kakhovsky, P. I. Pestel' and M. P. Bestuzhev-Ryumin would be hanged— the first three slowly, and with broken legs or bloodied necks, the last two with a merciful dispatch.[20] Happily, as he observes, he did not know what the thick beams were for. That very day, however, on July 12, he was taken before the

Supreme Court. He expected to be sent to meet his Maker, not once having set eyes upon his son, then three weeks old:

The reader may imagine my surprise when I found a room filled with my comrades, and with what joy I embraced them. We were assembled there, I was informed, to hear our sentences. I looked in vain for several of my comrades, who were either not among the accused, or were in a higher category and had already heard their sentence. The condemned were assembled in the two rooms adjoining the session-room, arranged in categories or divisions, so that when the first category went into the session-room, the second took their place, and so forth. There were about twelve categories in all, and I was told off to the fifth; we had a few moments to talk to one another: then the guard came up to our division, which consisted of five men; sentries were standing at each door. We entered, and stood in a line facing the members of the upper criminal tribunal, who were seated at a long table beside the wall. Directly opposite us sat the Metropolitan, with several bishops; to the right, generals, to the left Senators, all in full dress uniform, with orders and ribbons. Among the generals, I observed Bistrom, my own respected chief who was restraining tears with difficulty. Some of the judges had a sympathetic air, others looked hard; many of the Senators showed an unseemly and impertinent curiosity, using not only eye-glasses but even opera-glasses to survey us. In the centre stood the chief State Secretary, Zhuravlev, who then read the sentences out in a clear, loud voice. The verdict had condemned us (in the fifth category) to ten years of hard labour, and after that to perpetual exile in Siberia. This sentence had been mitigated by the Emperor on July 11 for my comrades Repin and M. Kyukhel'beker, who were to serve only eight years' labour, while Bodisko, on account of his extreme youth, had had labour changed to work on the fortifications; Glebov and I expected now that we, too, should be named with those whose sentence had been softened, but Zhuravlev remained silent, and the Commandant made a sign to take us back to our cells. Of the 121 condemned men, there were only three, namely N. Bestuzhev, Glebov and myself, whose sentence was not mitigated . . .[21]

The entire ceremony of the announcing of their sentences to the accused lasted five hours, and took place in the most profound silence. M. S. Lunin, a condemned man in the third category, was alone heard to remark in a loud voice, when the sentence had been read on him and special stress laid by the Secretary on the words *perpetual banishment*, "Perpetual, indeed! I'm already fifty years old!"[22]

Lunin exaggerated: he was thirty-nine, and there were only three men over forty in the whole fraternity of the accused, the oldest being Rozen's fellow Baltic German, Colonel V. K. Tizengauzen (Tiesenhausen), then aged forty-seven.[23] Rozen, aged twenty-six, was in the largest age group (while thirty-seven men were under twenty-six); one generation had passed sentence on another, the judges' average age being approximately sixty. Altogether, 579 persons had been brought to trial in connection with the risings of December 14, 1825 and January 1826, of whom 290 were acquitted. Of the remaining 298 (at least

30 of whom were from the Baltic provinces), 121 were selected as the most responsible conspirators, 61 being ex-members of the Northern Society. The sentence in respect to these "chief criminals", passed on July 9 and made public three days later, was that the five who later hanged should be quartered, thirty-one other men losing their heads.[24] Predictably, the sentences recommended by the Court were modified by Nicholas. He had, after all, to demonstrate his clemency. But the fates of the Decembrists had been settled long before the Special Court had held its final session, in the mind of Nicholas.

Thus dawned July 13. Before sunrise, I was taken to the Fortress courtyard, where stood a large detachment of the Pavlovsky Bodyguards, and another of the garrison artillery. From there, I was taken to the square, where some of my companions in misfortune stood already; the remainder were gradually brought out. I was delighted to see old acquaintances again. We all embraced, and every man sought out his closest friends. I looked in vain for Ryleyev...Prince S.G. Volkonsky walked about, talking cheerfully; Baten'kov had a bit of stick in his mouth, and gnawed it in his anger; Yakubovich went up and down, lost in thought; Prince Obolensky had been thriving in the Fortress, and his cheeks were glowing ... I saw no one in despair; even the sufferings mirrored on the faces of the sick now held their peace. Beyond the square, Generals-Adjutant Benkendorf and Levashev and a few more officers restlessly walked up and down ...

At last, in four groups separated by rows of soldiers, we were led through the Fortress gate on to the glacis of the Crownwork Curtain ... A gallows was now visible above the rampart; I recognized the carpenters' work which I had seen from my own casemate without fathoming its purpose. Our sections were arranged at equal distances. Near each division burned a funeral pyre, an executioner standing by. General-Adjutant Chernyshev was on horseback; on this morning he was not rouged, and his face was pale.

A general was with each division; our former Brigadier, G. A. Golovin, was attached to ours. We were each called out singly, according to the order of the categories. One by one we had to fall upon our knees while an executioner broke our sword over our head, tore off our uniform, and cast the broken sword and the clothes on to the burning funeral pyre. I hastily stripped off my uniform as I knelt down, before the executioner could touch me, the general meanwhile shouting at him, "Tear it off!"; but it was already done. The swords had been filed through beforehand ...

This ceremony lasted over an hour. Then they made us put on striped dressing-gowns, such as are worn in hospitals, and took us back to the Fortress in the order in which we had left it. On the glacis there had been no one to look at us, but at the gate a crowd pressed round. As we were taken back, the gibbet on the Crownwork rampart was awaiting its victims; but no one was to be observed nearby. We turned our eyes towards it, and prayed that God would grant an easy death to our companions. I was taken to the cell in the Crownwork Curtain, no. 14, in which Konrad Ryleyev had passed his last night on this earth.[25]

So ended the initial phase of Rozen's expiation. In his memoirs, he concludes his recollection of it by methodically "touching upon the last hours and remarkable traits" of the five hanged men, "finding it necessary", finally, "to place before the reader two lists: one of those men brought before the Committee on account of the events of the 14th of December; the other, of the punishments inflicted on the individuals implicated."[26] There follows the most detailed and authoritative list of "Those Members of the Secret Societies Who, by Order of the Emperor, Were Brought Before the Supreme Criminal Court on June 1, 1826", to be drafted by any one Decembrist—a list of striking accuracy, showing members of the Northern and Southern Societies *and* of the Society of United Slavs, original *and* modified (July 11) sentences. In the 1874 (Leipzig) edition of the memoirs, the lists cover twelve pages. There is nothing in any other Decembrist memoir to compare with it (just as, in reminiscences published during the 'seventies and 'eighties, there is nothing to compare with his consistent marshalling of facts concerning ageing or already dead Decembrists). But Rozen was the most methodical of all active Decembrists; who better to compile their common record? Let us here, since it will exercise its influence over his own life in captivity and exile, as on those of many comrades, consider in more detail his methodical and steady temperament. Its working was in evidence in April 1826, when he sang each evening "to preserve his health", walking the length and breadth of his small cell for a fixed time every day. It was a temperament that saved him in the Fortress, and would greatly help his comrades in Siberia to face their coming trials.

Rozen's consistency of outlook was apparent to contemporaries. By and large, what had preoccupied him in his youth—the military life, improvement of the peasants' lot, study of history—preoccupied him still in middle age, and as a brisk octogenarian. Not that his opinions were not liable to change; quite the reverse. His attitude towards the "standing revolution" itself changed greatly between 1826 and the time when he was working on the first draft of his memoirs. But opinions are not outlook in totality; and even his conduct on December 14, we have seen, was perfectly consistent with his own beliefs and doubts. Rozen was not merely a consistent individual in the sense that he was little subject to abrupt changes of view. He was, as the nineteenth-century German is popularly supposed to have been, quintessentially methodical by temperament; and underlying method was a sense of self-control.

Rozen had been educated in a hard school. As a child, he saw but little luxury; in adolescence, he had not been overfed. The First Cadet Corps, we have seen, was a place of rigid discipline. Rozen responded well both to its intellectual and to its psychological demands of the cadet: "Activity of mind and body, simplicity in diet, accord with one's comrades—these are the key factors in overcoming and enduring life's everyday cares."[27] Here, surely, is the evidence that Klinger's Corps left a deep mark on him. In Chita, east of Lake Baykal in Siberia, Rozen would in 1828 become general overseer of the Decembrists' prison kitchen. None would complain of the cuisine. But what was his own attitude towards food (always a very useful gauge of character)? Let us hear the satisfaction in the tone of the passage in which he tells us that, while in Chita, even former gourmets were well satisfied with simple, wholesome fare; let us recognize the admiration in his summary of the Buriats' dietary habits: "Often I would wonder at the frugal meals of my companions in misfortune who had all their lives been used to the best French cookery, and to champagne each day; now they were content with cabbage-soup and porage and drank kvass or water ..."[28] "Our Buriat drivers and escort took neither bread nor any other food with them. Twice a day they would leave the camp in groups, and spend half an hour in the forest, satisfying their needs with bilberries ..."[29] As in diet, so also in exercise: Rozen had no patience with the idle or, at the opposite extreme, with those who indulged in excess. "The shamans", he observes with disapproval, "would sometimes reduce themselves to a state of complete unconsciousness by their extravagant bodily exercises."[30] Such folly! For his own part, he preferred to take regular, moderate physical exercise—the course dictated by sheer common sense.

Intermittently for many years, but most acutely in 1837–39, Rozen would be in pain. His discomfiture arose from several causes. First, there was the lack of exercise and of a balanced diet. In the Winter Palace, shortly after his arrest, he had been left for days with little food. As we saw, he soon resolved not to complain. "Certainly, soup from the Palace kitchens would have been enough for those who were to stay only a few hours in the place; but I, and those like me, who were detained for many days yet were allowed no other food, were barely kept from starvation."[31] In 1828, the chains which had been fastened to his ankles two years previously were removed. "Those chains had not permitted us to move much, but we had grown used to them and learned how to tie them up with straps ..."[32] Again he said nothing. Four years later, travelling towards Kurgan in the Province of Tobol'sk, he would suffer from hard frosts, an infant's illness, his wife's absence, the violent jolting of a wagon, a sprained foot and, on Lake Baykal, seasickness and an inflammation of the eyes. He would not complain, but think of ways to meet the situation.[33] It is, above all else, Rozen's silence on the subject of his own sickly condition that impresses on us the determination of his character and the full measure of his self-control. For he was an ill man after twelve months in a casemate, although we would not know it from a reading of his memoirs.[34] And his sickness was continually aggravated by the lack of proper exercise:

Since the beginning of the winter, our walks had altogether ceased; and a miserable lamp scarcely allowed us sufficient light to read from one minute to another; the air in the prison, bad enough before, was rendered even more intolerable by the carelessness of the warders, who now and then let an old glove or greasy rag burn in the iron stove. I felt my strength decreasing day by day.[35]

Even a year before, the situation had been grim. Accustomed from his childhood to the open air, Rozen was less able than many to adapt to the foul air and cramped conditions of a cell. N. V. Basargin, too, suffered great pain in Peter-and-Paul Fortress in 1826–27. Here is his account of his first hours in a casemate:

> Whoever has not experienced confinement in a Russian fortress cannot imagine that dark and hopeless feeling, that failing of the spirit, I will say more, even that desperation, which not gradually but suddenly seizes the man who has crossed the threshold of a casemate. All links with the outside world are broken, all ties snapped. And he remains alone against autocracy . . . Every moment it seems that he has been *buried alive*, with all the attendant horrors of that situation . . .[36]

Rozen, for his part, said nothing but grew weaker: "I myself was suffering from scurvy; my gums were swollen and quite white. The pale and yellow faces of most prisoners testified to the poisonous effect of damp and noisome air."[37] A man of twenty-seven, used to exercise, Rozen needed walks along the ramparts every day; instead, he was allowed out for intervals of twenty minutes, twice a month.[38] Small wonder that he took such pleasure in the sight of birds and grass; small wonder that his practically religious insistence on the need for exercise—a need both physical and psychological, as the authorities would see eventually[39]—would last until his death. Rozen was sick from scurvy in 1825, with a lame foot in 1837, from general exhaustion in 1847; but he overcame all illnesses and did so, in the main, by strength of will, not by the aid of medicine. From the first, he saw the danger of physical collapse and, with the calm, methodical approach natural to him, took steps to ward it off. From the earliest weeks of solitary confinement, he combined his antidote to physical collapse with his private remedy for deeper, inward illnesses: despair, self-castigation, and remorse. Because he knew himself, there was no danger of his losing self-control—of his smashing his head against his wall like the unfortunate Colonel A. M. Bulatov. Clearly his circumstances were beyond his own control, but they could not affect him inwardly. The main, essential battle in himself he had won early in the day. Indeed, that Rozen would survive, given sufficient strength, was never for an hour open to doubt after January 1826. *How* he survived, using methodical, fast pacing in his cell, and poetry, which he declaimed, religious faith and intellectual pursuits, throws useful light on his character. Let us glance at the passage of his reminiscences in which we learn how, in the first days of imprisonment, hemmed in by walls through which few sounds could penetrate, he remained stable:

> I walked backwards and forwards and moved about as much as possible in my constricting cell, in order to preserve my health. Sleep halved the weary hours . . . Often, in the evening especially, I felt constrained to sing; singing strengthened my chest, made amends for want of conversation and, besides, gave some expression to my feelings. I sang prose and poetry of my own, arranged airs, and remembered many old songs.[40]

The prescription for survival crystallizes Rozen's outlook, in early as in later years; and three birds are killed with one shrewd stone. Music and exercise would continue to support Rozen, in exile: four years later, he would walk the Buriat steppe from Chita to another prison-fortress, Petrovsky Zavod, a distance of some 700 versts. ("My wife was in a postchaise, and I walked beside her carriage the whole day, talking to her. I would not get in, having resolved to cover the entire distance on foot.")[41] But this was in the future. For the present, Rozen had no choice but to watch autumn turn to winter, and wonder when, if ever, he would leave Peter-and-Paul Fortress. Meanwhile, other men were going:

The verdict was no sooner given than the deportation of condemned men to Siberia began. I don't know why, but for some reason those sentenced to hard labour were, quite contrary to the usual practice, put in irons for the journey. However, as the men condemned for their part in this rising were continually guarded by a gendarme, and transported to Siberia by post-horses in groups of four accompanied by a State courier *and* a guard of gendarmes, escape was quite out of the question. It was an exceptional measure, our travelling by post, and the reasons for it were much questioned. Some men thought it might be to spare us the long march; others, that it was to protect us from the anger of the populace. Many were of the opinion that it was to avert the possibility of our spreading revolutionary ideas, and that the quickest means of transporting us was chosen for that reason . . .

In August 1826, shortly before the coronation of Nicholas I, the Commandant of the Seversky Regiment of Jägers, Colonel Leparsky, was named Commandant of the Nerchinsk Mines. He was instructed to seek out some place on the far side of Lake Baykal that would be suitable for the building of a temporary jail, to be used until another site should be determined for the building of a strong prison. Leparsky left at once, and chose the Siberian fortress of Chita, between Nizhne Udinsk and Nerchinsk and about 400 versts from the latter town. In expectation of the Commandant's decision and report, the departure of the fifth category (my own) had been delayed . . .

On July 25, my wife obtained permission to let me see her newborn son in the Commandant's house; although in tears, she was composed and firm. My son, aged six weeks, lay on the Commandant's sofa; his blue eyes and the smiles round his mouth seemed to bring us messages of comfort. My wife asked me about the time and place of our reunion. I begged her not to follow me out to Siberia at once, but to wait until our boy could walk unaided and until I could tell her something of our new place of abode.

Every third day, four men and no more were dispatched. We were allowed, when September came, to see our relatives for one hour a week till we should leave. My wife visited me every Wednesday, and my brothers also came at times, one of them from Estonia. My youngest brother, a cadet in the First Cadet Corps, also came; he wept bitterly and regretted deeply, among other things, that by my condemnation I had lost the privilege of ever winning the Cross of St George. I passed seven months in this manner, every day expecting to be taken off to Siberia. A whole year of imprisonment already gone, and still I must needs wait!

8

In the winter, empty cells were filled by Poles who had known of the secret society in Russia.[42]

So began 1827. Rozen read the contents of the Fortress library: Cook's voyages, old newspapers, many of Scott's Waverley novels. Some twenty of his comrades, he was told, had been removed to Finnish fortresses. He wondered why. His gums were white and swollen. His brother-in-law came from Estonia with reindeer skins, which Anna turned into an overcoat. His spirits sank still lower, as another month began. But at last, on February 5, his turn arrived. He had a final meeting with his wife, who gave him "a small wooden cross from Jerusalem", and at night was taken to the Commandant's house, where Repin, Glebov and Mikhail Kyukhel'beker greeted him. All four were overjoyed, and talked until the entry of General Sukin with a sentry:

The artilleryman, who was following him, was holding up the ends of his cloak, which were gathered mysteriously in his hands. The Commandant announced to us that, in accordance with the Sovereign's command, he was to dispatch us to Siberia and, he was grieved to say, in chains. At these last words the artilleryman let fall the ends of his cloak, and the chains meant for us rattled to the floor ... After this, we went out; it was not easy to go down the steps with chains on. I held firmly on to a rail, but one of my comrades stumbled and very nearly fell. The town-major then brought some red cords, which had served to tie up quills; one end of the cord was attached to a ring which joined the bars and links of the iron chains; the other was fastened to our girth, to enable us to move with speed. Gendarmes were waiting at the steps to put us each into a sled; and so began our journey of 6,600 versts. The moon and sparkling stars lighted us on our way. We passed over the River Neva at a slow trot...[43]

5

THE FIRST YEARS IN SIBERIA: 1827–30

Rozen, like all his fellow-prisoners in Peter-and-Paul Fortress, had known profound emotional distress before being released at last from its black cells. Unbeknown to him, however, his life had been saved during his solitary confinement. For several months, Nicholas had been planning, in a general way, that "all the ringleaders" of the rebellions of December 1825 and January 1826 should perish by a bullet or the rope.[1] By April 1826, however, a greater consciousness of the realities involved in sending dozens to their deaths had started to impinge on him. Possible repercussions in some[2] foreign courts, a tarnished image for himself and Russia, practical difficulties, all, he saw, combined to make mass killing on the scale indulged in by the great and admirable Peter highly unadvisable. No less than 579 persons had been or would be tried on charges linked with the conspiracies and risings that had stained the first days of his reign. Of these, 290 would be acquitted; but almost 300 would remain. Such a multitude, the Emperor reluctantly but clearly recognized, could not be executed. So, in the early summer of 1826, thoughts of the inevitable banishment of dozens, if not hundreds, of informed, well-born conspirators and noble villains to Siberia had occupied his mind. From the first, such was the influence and wealth of certain convicts in the making, such as Trubetskoy, Volkonsky, and the Murav'yovs, it had been plain that there would be new, vexing problems. From the first, such was the Emperor's own temperament, details which arose with the necessity of facing those new problems took up a large part of his time. So began, as a result of his attitude towards his "friends of the fourteenth" (one of outrage and revengefulness, not pity or bewilderment), that half-obsessive, personal involvement in their further fates in exile.

New problems to be dealt with in connection with the exiling of Rozen and his comrades to Siberia fell, in Nicholas's view, into two groups: those arising from the exiling itself, such as provisioning, orders to officials in a hundred posting-stations, the selection of routes, dates, parties, and couriers; and those arising from the actual exile of so many highly educated officers—the choosing of a fitting site or sites for jails, the forming of a garrison or special company of guards with officers and, most vital of all, a loyal commander. We, too, must consider the new problems in those two categories, posed by the Decembrists in Siberia in 1826–32. First, however, to provide a proper setting we may summarize the history of Siberian banishment for Russian dissidents and radicals—a history to which, it is so sadly evident from recent Russian literature, at least one sorry chapter has been added in the past ten years.

Even in the time of Peter I, it should be emphasized, exile to Siberia was a rare and therefore noteworthy event. Outstanding heretics and troublemakers, to be sure, had been sent there in the previous century; one thinks of the Archpriest Avvakum. But few serfs, either individually or in families or bands, were exiled to Siberia in the seventeenth or eighteenth centuries. The population of Siberia thus grew slowly, as descendants of the Cossacks who had won the endless plains east of the Urals waxed and prospered, but refrained from intermarriage with the native peoples, Buriats, Tungus, Yakuts, Ostyaks and a dozen more, and were given only small infusions of new Russian blood. Not until the nineteenth century would the population of Siberia as a whole exceed three million.

Yet more recent was the early history of Russian exile in the eastern portion of Siberia, east of Lake Baykal and in the valleys of the Lena and Kolyma. By the "gentry's edict" of 1762 nobles enjoyed the right to banish wilful serfs, and many did so. But almost always serfs were banished to the south-west corner of Siberia (and there, if they were strong and enterprising, they often flourished under much improved conditions). Only under Catherine, indeed, and with the opening of new gold mines in Ekaterinburg and in centres further east, did the government begin to banish to the far east "beggars, tramps, fugitive soldiers"[3] and, for good measure, many serfs whose death sentences had been commuted to perpetual hard labour. Of course, a handful had reached Transbaikalia even in the first years of the eighteenth century. Okhotsk on the Pacific seaboard, we are told by S. Maksimov, first appeared on lists of exile points in 1733.[4] Even during Peter's lifetime, by an edict promulgated on April 10, 1722, it had been arranged that some serf-convicts freed from toil in European Russia should, together with their families (the better to exploit the mineral wealth of regions barely mapped, let alone geologically surveyed), be sent to work the silver mines of Daury. Nevertheless it was, in broad terms, only during Catherine's reign that Russians had begun to be dispatched in large numbers to areas from which, throughout her lifetime and her son's, few men could ever hope to be returned. But Catherine was the most professional of enlightened despots. Hardly could the authoress of the *Instruction* (*Nakaz*) of 1766 ignore so rich a field for the imperial benevolence as settlements and prisons in Siberia. Prison codes were duly written by officials in the spirit of the Empress's own work. In Siberia as elsewhere in the Empire, it was settled (in the first part of her reign) that prisons should be built "in healthy spots" and "outside towns". More than this, they should have hospitals attached.[5] A glorious vision, like Potyomkin's villages in the Crimea! Though John Howard, the deviser of the Georgian penitentiary, was actually sent on Catherine's service to inspect Siberian jails (and died in Kherson in 1790), the codes and the reforms remained dead letters. As to the humanitarian impulse so persistently evinced by would-be institutional reformers under Catherine and, later, Alexander, suffice it to observe that still in 1819 an ukase proclaimed on September 21, 1744 had full effect. By the terms of that ukase, "female and male convicts" were to be kept apart while in Siberian prisons, no matter how long they might stay there. Social and sexual intercourse, in brief, were to be banned—"for to act otherwise is contrary to Christian morals...Such a situation might constitute temptation, and be a cause of sin."[6] Investigating prisons in Siberia and the Russian prison system as a whole in 1819, the reformer M. M. Speransky made appalling revelations. In a number of Siberian jails, he ascertained for instance, individual convicts' records were not kept. Thus, no one could say how long a prisoner had been incarcerated or, at least, kept in one spot, or for what crime he had been exiled in the first place. Many were the tales of injured innocence and cruelty that Speransky heard; many were the incidents of false arrest, confused identity, and sheer vindictiveness. In Tomsk, to cite a relatively unappalling case, there languished in 1819 a Sub-Lieutenant Kozlinsky. Kozlinsky, it emerged, having been wrongly seized in Perm, where many years before he had been recuperating from an injury, had been forbidden to communicate with anyone or to attract attention to his plight. And he, at least, could write; most exiles, being illiterate, could not suffer from the convict ban on correspondence. Kozlinsky's life was ruined. So were those of convict-serfs in hundreds. Speransky recommended great reforms.[7] Like his predecessors in the penal field, he altered nothing in Siberia. For it was a long way to Siberia from St Petersburg. Even if regional authorities east of Baykal were willing to obey orders immediately and implicitly, communication with the capital was slow, irregular, and even unreliable. The Decembrist M. S. Lunin, held in Akatui in 1843–45, would personally witness just such cruelties and practices as had angered Speransky a quarter of a century earlier: men chained to walls, men left in perfect darkness and abandoned to their fates.[8]

Exile to Transbaikalia, then, was a familiar enough phenomenon, though one of relatively recent origin, when Rozen and his comrades were condemned. Many thousands had been sent, specifically, to the large silver and iron works of Nerchinsk—and few returned. But the Decembrists, we must emphasize, posed special difficulties. Not that Nicholas ever considered any other place of banishment for rebels too corrupt even for service in the Caucasus, as private soldiers, against Moslem mountain tribesmen. On the contrary, Siberia was the obvious place for men such as the "stupid Rozen", the "black-souled Obolensky", the "stuffed fool, liar and scoundrel" Volkonsky, and the "murderer and outcast" Artamon Murav'yov.[9] But Siberia was vast; and he himself had never visited it, so could not select from first-hand knowledge a prison site with all the properties that he required for villains of their hue. Chance lent a hand. General A. S. Lavinsky, Governor-General of Eastern Siberia, was on leave of absence from Irkutsk. Lavinsky was summoned for a meeting with the Chief of the Imperial General Staff, General-Adjutant I. I. Dibich. His well-known advice, that "one group of prisoners is more easily guarded than ten",[10] was unquestionably to become the saving factor in the lives of the Decembrists sent, in 1827, to Chita.

Rozen and his friends, the Emperor resolved on hearing the opinion of Lavinsky, last of the non-military Governors-General in Irkutsk, should certainly be held in one remote Siberian fortress. In this way, the possibility of their poisoning the minds of other Russians with liberal heresies would be reduced, if not wholly removed. Besides, it was a tidy plan, and Nicholas liked well-defined arrangements, clear and soldier-like solutions to all problems. Through Dibich, who had told him of Lavinsky's views, the process was begun by which, within a month, S. R. Leparsky would be chosen as the Commandant of the Decembrist settlement-cum-fortress.

First, however, it was necessary that thought be given to the task of sending groups of shrewd, resourceful officers to Transbaikalia. Over a tract of six or seven thousand versts, would men like Rozen not attempt to flee? Rozen, after all, had long been *trained* to be resourceful, self-disciplined, and calm in an emergency. Weeks passed and still the Emperor took no initiative. Two days after the Committee of Enquiry had at last made its report to him, on May 30,[11] he appointed the Supreme Court which, we saw, so zealously "assessed" the "evidence" which seemed to it to lead to the appropriate conclusions. (As E. P. Obolensky put it, the Court "took for the truth what had been said or done in moments when the imagination had been guided by a feverish impulse."[12]) But here, too, problems arose. Was the Minister of Justice named on June 1, Prince D. Lobanov-Rostovsky, capable of grasping the significance of the prolonged, complex procedure over which, as Attorney-General, he had theoretical control? In objective moments, Nicholas had serious doubts.[13] And there remained the invitation to Speransky (to participate in the eventual prosecution of the rebels) to consider. One might trust that, as an ex-thief placed to guard his property, he would appreciate the danger to himself of any leniency shown to the Decembrists, and be harsh; but such conduct was a supposition only. So another three weeks passed.

At last, in the fourth week of June, impelled to action by the imminence of the Supreme Court's passing sentence on the rebels, Nicholas turned seriously to the question of conveying a considerable group of dangerous men to a place 4,000 miles away. Once more, he chose to act through Dibich. In his turn, Dibich issued instructions to the Minister for War, A. I. Tatishchev; and Tatishchev, on June 25, 1826, dispatched a memorandum to the Governor-General of Western Siberia, General P. M. Kaptsevich, through whose territory every exile on his way to Transbaikalia from the capital would necessarily pass. The Emperor, Kaptsevich learnt, desired that Rozen and his friends be sent in carts, in groups of four, accompanied by State couriers (*fel'dyegery*) *and* special gendarmes, and delivered in Siberia to civil governors of districts where they would be held.[14] These governors' responsibility it would become, after delivery, to see that the Decembrists were transported safely onwards from the centre of the province or provincial town (*gubernskiy gorod*) to the place of exile. Later, on August 22, Nicholas would find the time to give some spurious evidence of the expected clemency of kings, by mitigating all but a handful of the sentences passed on Decembrists.[15] That, however, could well wait.

Meanwhile, it remained to organize the transportation of the exiles. Nicholas spared no detail. The carts, wagons, sledges, and horses were prepared. The Corps of State Couriers was briefed. (That Corps, it may be said in passing, was an institution modelled on the Prussian Courier service. It consisted, in 1825, of four officers and seventy-seven men, most aged under twenty-one since peaks of stamina and fitness were required. Many of the couriers were hard, unsympathetic men or youths—though there was only one Zheldybin, notorious for his sadistic tendencies. On the other hand, many Decembrists were well treated by their couriers, who showed themselves both tolerant and reasonable when far from their superiors.[16]) Next came the matter of selecting routes and departure dates. If the former was a question for the Corps of Couriers, under Dibich's control, the latter would remain in Nicholas's hands. Few men indeed, save Sukin, Dibich, and Benkendorf, ever knew details of departures in advance. Even Nicholas's personal suite remained in perfect ignorance where departures were concerned, as we discover from the fact, for instance, that in mid-November 1826 I. D. Yakushkin's mother-in-law, N. N. Sheremeteva, a member of a powerful and wealthy family, approached General Potapov, unsuccessfully, for just such information.[17] Potapov, although a former member of the Special Committee of Enquiry and, in 1826, an officer in Nicholas's confidence, could not help her.

Such arrangements, such a plethora of details, one might think, would have sufficed to over-tax the most industrious of sovereigns. But Nicholas was capable of an enormous quantity of work. Orders relating to the horses, sleds and wagons, provisioning, financing of the indigents among the exiles, the appointment of Siberian guards, even the night hour of the prisoners' departure, all gave rise to further detailed orders and arrangements. Yet Nicholas might simply enough have entrusted most of these semi-routine and minor matters to a special chancery.

Simplicity, however, was distinguished by its absence from the process of removing Baron Rozen and his comrades from St Petersburg. For many of those comrades, it was felt by the authorities even in the late summer of 1826, were the sons, brothers, and nephews of extremely well-placed persons. At first, of course, the Emperor's personal anger had outweighed the joint prestige and influence of the nobility and Guards Corps; so it did still, perhaps, when 1826 came to an end. But steadily, little by little, the influence of the nobility had started to be exercised in various subtle ways long before Rozen left for exile. Some Decembrists, it was true, had been handed over to their enemies by relatives: Trubetskoy records a particularly wretched case of this.[18] But most had been supported, tacitly at least, by some members of their families. Nor were those enemies themselves, the senior officers of the gendarmerie, the members of the Special Supreme Court of 1826, Nicholas's most devoted servants, in isolation from society and so impervious to its influence. Of course, there were *milieux* in which Chernyshev, Adlerberg, Potapov and their colleagues of 1826 were not made welcome. Yet all three attended balls and public gatherings throughout the last part of that year; and Benkendorf, we learn from Pushkin's sister Ol'ga, was an amateur of brilliant balls at which, between mazurkas, "his bitter-sweet smile, like that of a man who has bitten a lemon", was often to be seen.[19] Detested they might be by ardent liberals, but all these officers, like Dibich, Levashev, and the senior officials of the General Staff and, for that matter, the Corps of State Couriers, were in the skein of St Petersburg society. More than this, judges and prisoners were frequently acquainted with each other, as fellow-officers. A few were linked by marriages of sisters. Count Zakhar Chernyshev and General Chernyshev, his accuser, were blood relatives.[20] Like Rozen, then a prisoner in his charge, General Sukin found it wholly natural that, since he was acquainted with an uncle of the prisoner in question, he should permit both handkerchiefs and linen to be slipped into the Baron's cell.[21] After all, mere social courtesy demanded that a favour be repaid.

Here, in short, there was no single, simple policy adhered to rigorously no matter who the prisoner might be—unless that policy was not to incur the Emperor's displeasure through indiscretion. Private orders,[22] secret links and liaisons, "lost" instructions from the capital to high officials in Siberia, all, stemming immediately from the nature of autocracy itself (as Nikolay Bestuzhev understood better than Rozen),[23] added to the inherent complication of a complex situation. Some prisoners were in Siberia by late August 1826; others would remain in Peter-and-Paul Fortress for another eighteen months. Some were well provided for materially, had warm clothes and linen in their cells; others went in need. Thus the unpredictability and prejudice shown to Decembrists in the course of their (fictitious) trials continued unabated. Artamon Murav'yov, who had deserted the Southern Society on the eve of rebellion, thereby inflicting a near-decisive blow to the whole rising in the south, received life exile; Orlov, an officer as morally responsible for the conspiracy as any man, escaped scot-free.[24] Rozen, we saw, had not had his sentence lightened. Others in the fifth category of guilt had fared far better, for no valid legal reason. Alive Rozen might be; but still he was completely at the mercy of the Emperor.

Nicholas proved merciful, when to be otherwise would lend a martyr's lustre to a convict. Thus, no attempt was made to shave off half of Rozen's hair as, by law, he should be shorn. (The relevant ukase, indeed, which was designed to stop escapes, had been signed by Alexander I barely a year earlier, on July 14, 1825.) Thus, no attempts were made—wisely, since they would certainly have failed given the outlook of officials who were, like the exiles' relatives, *dvoryane* —to prevent relations, well-wishers and friends from secretly assisting the Decembrists as they travelled east. Were the officials contravening Nicholas's orders in this matter? Perhaps; yet the result would have remained the same whether or not assistance had been banned. Try as he might, Nicholas could not *command* hostility towards the exiles. And here, in the opinion and sympathy of countless of his subjects, not in the shortcomings of measures he had taken, the Emperor's plans for the Decembrists met a stumbling block. All noble-minded men understood well enough the exiles' aspiration to limit autocratic power. Many landowners of ancient family, indeed, could share their very purpose; for those landowners were utterly excluded from the shaping of state policy— a process in which their forebears had once played their part. Such an attitude was of huge value to the exiles. Outweighing the hostility of certain grandees who, like one countess, donated iron for fetters, it went far to ease their minds, if not their bodies. For did it not confirm their own conviction that their five hanged comrades were, indeed, martyrs, and that they were themselves true servants of the Russian State? As for the common people, whose lot they had wished to improve, they were by nature and tradition sympathetic towards exiles whom, significantly, the Siberian peasantry referred to as "unfortunates". For generations, they had shown new exiles charity, not scorn. Rozen and Basargin, among thirty others, were recipients of gifts of food and drink from kindly peasants on their journey east, and observed a striking custom in Siberia:

> There exists a custom in Eastern Siberia that admirably demonstrates the light in which the rural populace look upon fugitives, who not infrequently leave their place of work or exile because of the oppressive toil . . . In every settlement, under the windows of each house, you will see small shelves on which rye-bread, wheaten rolls, curds, and milk in earthenware pots are left at night. Fugitives passing through by night take all this, as alms . . .[25]

The Decembrists were not fugitives but nobles, though admittedly in fallen circumstances. Still the peasantry of European Russia and, more generously yet, Siberia eased their way. Nor was the peasantry alone in doing so: even merchants and officials felt obliged to make their lack of enmity apparent. Several parties had food and drink pressed on them by humane merchants and kindly governors, postmasters, mayors, and widows. And only once, in Tobol'sk, was a senior official a relation of an exile—D. N. Bantysh-Kamensky was a cousin to M. A. Fonvizin;[26] on all other occasions, neither blood ties nor the likelihood of gain entered into the situation, which was one of simple charity towards unfortunates. Appearances, of course, had to be kept by civic dignitaries. But while shouting at them publicly, the mayor of Kainsk privately let Decembrists use his bath, and loaned them books and linen. Basargin's narrative continues thus:

> We reached Irkutsk three weeks after our leaving Tobol'sk, having passed through Tara, Ishim, Kainsk, Kolyvan, Tomsk, Achinsk, Krasnoyarsk, Kansk and Nizhne-Udinsk. Everywhere along the way we met with real sympathy both from the populace and from officials. In Kainsk, for instance, a policeman called Stepanov—an elderly man of enormous size and girth who had once been a courier—came up to us with two other men. The three of them were dragging a huge basket of wines and every kind of foodstuff. Stepanov made us eat all this or

take it with us, even offering us money which he had with him, with these amazing words: "This money" (said he) "I scraped together somehow or other *not altogether cleanly*, in bribes. In our line, gentlemen, you find yourself doing a lot of things that go against the conscience . . ."

In Krasnoyarsk the Governor, also named Stepanov, entertained us cordially. Indeed, in almost all the towns in which we stopped the officials visited us. At first, they would not dare to start a conversation; but they always ended by offering their services and showing sympathy. And at posting stations, the officials from nearby halts would usually appear with comparable offers, while the common folk crowded around the sleds.[27]

Not all the exiles, one need hardly add, met with such kindness and enjoyed such relatively tolerable journeys out. And even those whose luck held in the main, such as Svistunov, Rozen, Mikhail Bestuzhev and Basargin, knew unpleasant moments. (The last three were in accidents in carriages rolling down hills, and Mikhail Bestuzhev, as he himself later remarked, was dragged "like Hector from the chariot of Achilles", his chains caught in a wheel.[28]) However, the discomfiture of the Decembrists was rarely brought about by the inhabitants of towns through which they passed, or by officials with whom they had brief contact. God, as the Russian saying went, was high, and the Tsar far off. A month's journey from European Russia even Nicholas's power was limited, if a government official was determined.

Rozen was by no means ignorant about Siberia on leaving for it. Conveniently for him, at least two of the best-known descriptions of that country had been written in his native language, German, and he had read them: the *Reise durch verschiedene Provinzen des russischen Reichs* (1774–76) of the great naturalist Peter Simon Pallas (1741–1811), who had spent six years in Siberia, and the same author's *Tagebuch zwoer Reisen von Kjachta und Zuruchaitu nach Pekin . . .* (1781). He had also, it would seem, glanced through the paintings and the text of *A Picturesque Journey from Moscow to the Chinese Frontier*, by A. Martynov, which appeared in St Petersburg in 1819, and was at least acquainted with the name of A. I. Martos (1790–1842), whose *Letters From Eastern Siberia* were to appear three months after his own departure for that region, in 1827.[29] He was, in fact, as properly befitted a historian, familiar with the basic literature on recent eastern trade and history. Had he not been he could not have learnt, several months later in Siberia itself, that "most of these accounts were incomplete and full of errors . . ."[30] Familiar though he might be theoretically with Transbaikalia, however, the fact remained that, realistically, Siberia seemed a threatening land of wilderness and cold. He thought of the approaching journey apprehensively. Still, he did not brood over the prospect of spending the remainder of his life "at the frontier of an unpeopled realm, where ice and frost, like Pillars of Hercules, draw the line for man, saying *ne plus ultra*",[31] as S. I. Krivtsov put it dramatically. Nor, having left the capital, did he imitate

Artamon Murav'yov and loudly curse Yermak for ever conquering Siberia, "the source of anguish and of graves for exiles".[32] What could such conduct have achieved?

Even the first weeks of his journey east, itself so great an improvement on his earlier existence in a cell, made clear to him that sanguine expectations would be justified. There were black moments, certainly, with pusillanimous and petty officials, and lengthy periods of discomfort; but such unpleasantnesses were well compensated for by the impromptu hospitality of ordinary people and occasional officials. Rozen's courier, unlike the infamous Zheldybin, proved civil, even friendly. And within two days it had grown clear that Rozen and his comrades were by no means to be treated, as the sentence of the Special Supreme Court required, as common criminals. Sorry would have been their plight if they had been so treated: common convicts were not dealt with civilly during their journey to the east, and not all who passed through Tyumen', not even all who dragged themselves into Tobol'sk, chains scarring flesh, survived to see the beauties of Nerchinsk. As he was treated better than an ordinary State convict on his journey to Chita, so Rozen would continue to be tolerably courteously treated in Siberia. Not from him would be required the unremitting labour exacted, in the iron and silver mines of the Nerchinsk district, from ordinary convicts and Crown workers. Not for him would be the fate, so heatedly described by M. A. Bestuzhev and Basargin, of "the outcast tribe of peasants and of factory labourers, doomed from their cradle to complete, final exhaustion of the body". For the Decembrists, with few and rare exceptions, would always be regarded either consciously or otherwise, by guards and couriers, peasants and governors alike, as gently-born—and so as deserving of civilities denied to simple convicts. Such attitudes, it soon grew plain to Rozen, could not be changed at will by any edict from a tsar.

The striking landscape, too, as they approached the shores of Lake Baykal, did much to soothe the exiles' jangled nerves. Like Prince Sergey Volkonsky, Rozen had left a wife and infant child behind, so had an extra burden to support; but as he came into close contact with Siberia and its populace, having crossed the Urals and parted company with his first gendarmes and drivers, early fears melted away. Even while still in Tobol'sk, he found himself viewing the future with more optimism than had seemed conceivable three weeks before. As Basargin put it: "The further one moved into the country, the more it gained in one's sight. The common folk seemed freer, cleverer, even more educated than our Russian peasants . . . Here, they appreciate human dignity."[33] Rozen, too, would shortly make comparisons between Siberia and North America.[34]

Released after his long imprisonment, Rozen was bolstered physically and psychologically by the benefits of knowing his destination and of being on his way. At last he was moving, if not active. The change is reflected in the sections of his memoirs that concern the journey east. For the previous six months Rozen, like other prisoners, had been principally preoccupied by thoughts of his survival and that of his close family, his health and theirs; therefore he was inclined to dwell on private attitudes and hopes, though always tempering such tendencies with solid, factual information. Now, he looked out. The journey, one might even say, brought out the best in Rozen's written style. Clear descriptions of the countryside through which he passed, vignettes set in the various towns, pen sketches of the buildings, hills and rivers that he saw (but seldom, we note, of individuals), such are the major elements of Chapters 8 to 10 of his memoirs. Suddenly, natural description looms large in the narrative, as in Rozen's life; we, too, see Buriat tribesmen, wide plains, ranges of mountains, and a wonderfully revived group of Decembrists. It is as if a gust of air were passing through his memory. Never short of objectivity where concrete objects are concerned, Rozen seems to draw on faculties that have been dormant in his cell, growing sensitive to moods in other men, and so to changing atmospheres. Seeing different things, he also sees them differently. Here, first, to give a notion of the clarity of Rozen's swiftly drawn scenaria, is his account of the first week out:

We sped on incessantly like couriers, day and night: sleeping in the sled was practically impossible; passing the night encumbered with clothing and with fetters was not comfortable either: we could only snatch a few minutes' sleep while the horses were being put to; and the rapidity of the journey became hourly more intolerable. Kostroma, Makeyev, Kotoluich, Glazov, Perin, Kungur, Ekaterinburg and Tyumen' passed before our eyes like apparitions. We spent a night in Glazov, and here our fetters were removed for the first time while we changed our linen. But having reached *this* distance from the capital of European Russia, we began to learn the special practices of the State courier who was accompanying us, and to perceive how skilfully he lined his pocket. From Tikhvin, he allowed only four sleds to be harnessed; he invited me to sit in his sled with him, placed my gendarmes in the sleds behind us, and thus the money that should properly have hired horses to draw a fifth sled for a full 3,000 versts—went straight into his pocket . . . Always he was striking the postilion with his sword, shouting, "On, on!"; and by his oaths and threats he urged the man to such a crazy speed that I was obliged to cover up my mouth and nose with the sleeve of my fur-coat, for the rapid passage through the cold and bitter air robbed me of breath. By these tricks, the greedy rascal brought things to such a pass that merely on our way out to Tobol'sk, seven horses fell dead to the ground. In vain I remonstrated; and often I could scarcely contain myself when I saw the postilion thus losing his best and most spirited horses, and sobbing as he had to cut the traces . . . However, when we came to posting-stations kept by Tartars, which became more numerous on the eastern side of Tyumen', the power of the State courier was at an end; *they* demanded the money in full, and drove so fast that he could not say anything to the postilions . . .

Now we were travelling along the great highway that traverses Siberia diagonally. Everything was arranged here with a view to the transporting of State criminals; every posting-station was a military station too. The district south of this great road is the most thickly peopled in the whole country, though the population is so small that towns are from a hundred to four hundred versts apart.

At Tara, we could not avail ourselves of the hospitality of the chief of police, Stepanov, a Caucasian warrior of Yermolov's time, since we did not pass a night in the town; but some of our companions, whom we later joined, could not praise the generosity of this good man enough . . . We passed our nights in the clean huts of Russian peasants, who received us cordially and refused all payment . . . I will give just one illustration of the charitable disposition of Siberians: on certain days, and at fixed points on our way, we saw crowds of peasants standing by the roadside, under an open sky. It was the custom for the villagers living near the great road to assemble and await the passing of "unfortunates" (as they called men exiled to Siberia), in order to sell food, warm stockings, and the like. To the poorer ones among us, they would always give things free. This happened twice a week . . ., and I was told this Christian custom had existed there since ancient times. They received us kindly everywhere, from Tobol'sk to Chita; warm wraps were fastened round our open sleds, our feet were carefully packed with hay, and blessings would be showered on our heads.

Our route lay through the towns of Tara, Kainsk, Tomsk, Achinsk, Krasnoyarsk, Kansk, Nizhne-Udinsk and Irkutsk—nine towns in all, over a stretch of 3,000 versts. From Krasnoyarsk we were put on wheels, and drove for several stations. The undulating hills of yellowish red chalk had here thrown off the snow, and the road already tended to be dusty. The main street of Krasnoyarsk consisted of well-built stone houses, many of them of two stories. We stopped at the police station in the market place, where several of the town's inhabitants disputed the honour of accommodating us. At last, an old man begged the chief of police to let him take us to his house; this was a merchant named Stargov. And this Stargov gave us his best room, lodged us luxuriously and, according to the Russian custom, had a hot, refreshing bath prepared for us.[35]

Hectic though the journey was, Rozen was able to form several clear impressions of the western regions of Siberia. The soil, he noticed, was extremely rich; the populace was generous and healthy; the hilly panoramas and, at length, the mountain ranges were more grandiose than anything he had seen beside the Baltic. And, of course, there was a distinctly and increasingly exotic tinge to all that met his gaze. By March 22, his little group had reached Irkutsk, parting company with the second guard and taking in another, a Cossack; only two stations to the east lay Lake Baykal, "The Holy Sea", then frozen over. Here, one might meet Tungus, and Buriats, and Old Believers, and exiled Little Russians, Poles and even German colonists, but no one who had ever seen Estonia. Climatically, ethnically, geologically, it was another, larger world:

We drove across Baykal: the horses went sixty versts without a halt. The drivers had taken some boards in their sleds, to make bridges over ice-fissures if necessary, but the horses jumped the cracks, which were often many feet wide, with such dexterity that the long sleds barely touched the water. Siberian horses are amazingly strong and hardy, although small and ill-proportioned; they can go eighty versts at a stretch without exertion. On the far side of Baykal was the monastery of Posol'sky. The beautiful environs of this monastery, which I would afterwards come to know well, now lay under a thick covering of snow, the uniformity of which was only broken here and there by villages, mountains, and trees. As we drew near to Chita, we saw yurts for the first time [the felt tents of the nomad Buriats]. At Klyuchi, the station before Chita, our sleds were replaced by stage-coaches, because here the snow does not lie all year round. This place stands very high, and so enjoys a clear, unclouded sky; if snow does fall occasionally, the wind soon carries it down to the valleys. In a certain sense, indeed, it may be said that Chita is too cold for snow: the thermometer sometimes stands at 40 degrees of frost (Réaumur), so that mercury freezes and only spirit thermometers can be used . . .[36]

Now the driver was a Buriat—and a very careless one at that: because he tied the harness up with string, not with stout rope, the harness broke. Rozen was dragged down a steep hillside and so nearly killed. But Chita came into sight on the evening of March 29, 1827. Before Rozen arrives, let us rapidly survey the prison-fortress that would house him for the next three years.

Even before the five supposed leaders of the Decembrist conspiracies had died, Nicholas had understood the need for new arrangements in Siberia. In mid-July Colonel S. R. Leparsky, a russified Pole and veteran officer of seventy-two, was formally invited to become Commandant of the Nerchinsk mines—and thus of the Decembrist prison-fortress—in terms so flattering that he could not refuse that offer. Leparsky's was, as it could only be, an Imperial appointment. Recently retired, he had been personally acquainted with the Emperor some twenty years when Nicholas, now seeking a man both loyal and tactful, recalled their earlier relationship. On Nicholas's orders, Dibich offered him a salary of 8,000 roubles per annum, "with messing allowances to 12,000 roubles per annum", if he would undertake "the special, strict, but reasonable surveillance" of State convicts in Nerchinsk.[37] Even had the salary not been alluded to, Leparsky would, in every probability, have felt obliged to take up such an offer: his senses of loyalty and of honour were something Rozen could well understand, and always the two men would like each other. But sentiments of loyalty apart, Leparsky's own financial difficulties made his re-employment desirable. Twelve years before, thanks to the inefficiency of the Second Army's Commissariat in Kiev, he had been obliged to borrow the alarming sum of 21,000 roubles to buy forage for the horses of his regiment. For twelve years, his (just) claim had remained unsatisfied by the authorities concerned.[38] Now, unexpectedly, he was offered a position with a salary as high as that of General S. B. Bronevsky, the Governor-General of Eastern Siberia. In a terse but grateful letter of July 24, he accepted that position.

Nicholas received him in Moscow, and issued his instructions while dressing for a ball.[39] Leparsky was to name his own assistants, and to do so hurriedly. He had authority to name one town-major, two town-adjutants, and a military surgeon. All would receive four times the standard rate of pay for their rank. Without delay, the ageing but still energetic officer wrote to his only nephew,

Osip Adamovich, to offer him the post of town-major if he wished it. Captain Osip, also of the Seversky Jägers, accepted. Within days, two junior cavalry officers, Staff-Captains Rozenberg and Kulomzin, had agreed to serve as adjutants. A surgeon was next found—one Dmitriy Il'insky, the son of a Siberian priest and a recent, undistinguished, student of anatomy at Moscow University. Finally Mikhail, Archbishop of Irkutsk, named Father Pyotr Gromov "to service with State convicts condemned for the revolt of December 1825".[40] All was ready. Accompanied by Osip Adamovich, Leparsky crossed the Urals to settle on a site for his new prison-fort.

For him, as for his future exiled charges, the journey to Siberia marked the beginning of another stage in life. Yet how much more of life he had observed, by 1826, than any of his charges or subordinates! Leparsky had been forty-five even before the nineteenth century began its work of turning countless minds against the concept of divine right; before Nicholas or Rozen had been born, he had campaigned first in a regiment of infantry (the Kargopol' Carbineers), then with chasseurs. Among his many virtues were the virtues of the age of Chesterfield: decorum and a sense of etiquette. Again, all augured well for the relationship so shortly to begin between Leparsky and the Baltic officer barely one-third his age, Lieutenant Baron Rozen.

As a subaltern himself, in 1795, Leparsky had become familiar with the region of Nerchinsk: in that year, he had been called upon—he, whose father was a Pole!—to escort into Siberian banishment a company of the defeated Polish patriots, Kosciuszko's fellow-rebels. He had carried out the mission without mishap, and so moved one rank closer to the colonelcy that would be his in 1800. (Always, Leparsky had been recognized as a most *tactful* officer; to his regiment, we read,[41] were often sent those guardsmen who, for faults or indiscretions, had been demoted to an army unit. For he, better than other men, was able to assuage their wounded feelings and so obviate unnecessary unpleasantness. Here, surely, in his courtly interviews with wealthy guardsmen sent into the army in the field, we see pleasantly foreshadowed his later, longer meetings with the wives of the Decembrists in Chita. Here, too, we see the fruits of early training in the Jesuit Institute of Polotsk, where he had received a solid liberal education, as of a cautious, steady temperament.[42])

Had Leparsky seen the valley of the Ingoda in which, surrounded by a gently undulating meadow steppe, lay the strongpoint (*ostrog*) of Chita? Had he seen the site of Rozen's future exile, five years before Rozen had so much as managed to be born? It is highly probable since, whether he approached the fortress of Nerchinsk across the frozen surface of Baykal or by the southern track around the lake, and so through Kyakhta, he would need to pass the valley of the Ingoda, then as now cloaked by great woods of larch and pine. Certainly he would recall that valley's bracing climate, so superior to that of many areas on the same latitude in Western Siberia: Pavlodar and Semipalatinsk on the Irtysh, Tselinograd on the Ishim. And, of course, he would have recollected the sparseness of the population in the region of Chita itself.

Even if Leparsky was familiar with Chita before 1826, however, few other men from European Russia were. Only three of the Decembrists, indeed, had any real acquaintance with, or knowledge of, Siberia; and though G. S. Baten'kov's first years had been passed in Tobol'sk and Baron Shteyngel' had received his schooling in Irkutsk and—even more romantically—Kamchatka, neither had had opportunity or reason to inspect that tiny, unimportant outpost.[43] One Decembrist only was familiar with the name of Chita—D. I. Zavalishin. True, he had not *been* there, though he had crossed Siberia.[44] Still, he alone of the Decembrists (so he tells us with his customary sense of self-importance) had known of the existence of Chita since early childhood:

> The word "Chita" had a strange ring to my ear, and it recalled two incidents to memory. One of these was among the earliest recollections of my childhood, the other, from the very recent past. As a child, I had been most inquisitive. I never played, so I was never given toys as presents, but always things related to study, such as books, pictures, instruments and so forth. On my seventh birthday, my father gave me a wall-map of Russia on which European Russia and Siberia were represented on the same scale. This map, which was of enormous dimensions and glued on canvas, I hung on my wall. And, naturally, Siberia occupied almost the whole map, and European Russia only a small area to the left. Each time I stood facing the middle of this map, I noticed that the map's meridian passed through Transbaikalia and through some place called *Chitinsky ostrog*. I became curious to find out what kind of place this was, and discovered from some geographical gazetteer of the time (Shchekotov's) that it was a *plotbishche* [log-built strong-point—G.B.] on the River Ingoda. Even then I became occupied by the idea that there must be communication between Chita and the Eastern Ocean by way of the Ingoda, Shilka and Amur Rivers. Later, I questioned Treskin and Kornilov, former Governors of Irkutsk, about Transbaikalia. They told me much of interest; but about Chita they could tell me nothing in particular.[45]

Zavalishin's precocious interest in the development of Transbaikalia and the Amur, it may be said in passing, was to grow obsessive, as in N. N. Murav'yov-Amursky, Governor-General of Eastern Siberia and his great antagonist during the 1850s.[46] Finally, in February 1863, a new Governor-General, M. S. Korsakov, would find an opportunity of sending such a wearisome "authority on Eastern Siberia" (as Zavalishin was, having lived thirty-six years in Chita) to "a milder climate".[47] But in 1826 even Zavalishin knew but little of Chita in concrete terms. And, in fairness to Treskin and Kornilov, one must add that there was little "in particular" to say about the place. Once a major fur depot, look-out and Cossack strongpoint of importance to the Muscovite advance into the recently-subdued Siberian khanate of the Tartars, it had long before lost all strategic value. As to the trade on which it had prospered in the early eighteenth century, that had moved to towns nearer to sources of rich furs and pelts. There were many kinds of fur, of course; forest pelts were bought and sold in various centres in Siberia. But this had not staved off the decline of

Chita. Other places in the *oblast'* of Nerchinsk, moreover, had seen a new prosperity from mining in the last part of the eighteenth century. Nerchinsk itself, we learn from V. Shunkov,[48] was producing silver by the ton even in the reign of Anna Ivanovna; but Chita sat on no silver veins. A static settlement within a modestly expanding district; a place that *had* enjoyed commercial and strategic importance—such, then, was Leparsky's choice.

It was, by any standards, a remarkably unbusy spot in 1826. There was no fair to draw outsiders even once or twice a year. There was no posting-station even, although this would now be remedied. Its two dirt streets were quiet. As to reminders of its busier past at least a century before, there was a single group of buildings: the dilapidated shells, more than once rebuilt or strengthened but again falling apart thanks to extremes of cold and heat, moisture and dryness in the area, of what had been the settlement's first structure of importance and, indeed, its *raison d'être* in its first years—the Ingoda wintering place (*Ingodinskoye zimov'ye*), erected by the Cossack Beketov in 1653.[49] Here on a grassy incline, and around the small stockaded point, had once flourished a little Cossack *sloboda* or village. In the eighteenth century, a modest trade had developed between colonists of Russian peasant stock and native peoples of the area, notably Buriats.[50] Some Russian artifacts thus found their way south to the River Argun', into China, while Chinese goods—and games and superstitions—were imported by nomadic Buriats to the district of Nerchinsk. But no building in Chita suggested Chinese influence; architecturally, if that is not too grandiose a word for huts, Chita was wholly Cossack still.

For decade after decade, Beketov's fort had been ignored by the authorities, first in St Petersburg, then in Tobol'sk, then in Irkutsk. Before St Petersburg was founded, indeed, the wintering place had been allowed to grow or fail entirely as it pleased. By 1649, the Cossacks had established outposts on the Pacific (the Sea of Okhotsk) and the Arctic Oceans (Nizhne-Kolymsk, 1644). There were *portages* to explore—by 1700 it was possible to go by river from Tobol'sk to Okhotsk via Irkutsk and Lake Baykal with only five of them.[51] There was land and independence to be had from oppressive Muscovite control; the exodus of Cossacks and of peasants to Siberia which had followed the revolt of Sten'ka Razin and his bands in 1670 was only one of several that would push the total number of Russian settlers east of the Urals to 200,000 by the start of Peter I's reign. Who could trouble with a spot called Chitinsky Ostrog (as Beketov's *zimov'ye* or wintering place was known by then), when it had neither strategic significance nor promised an immediate return? It was left to its devices. In 1821 it was officially named a settlement (*seleniye*). There were new arrivals—Russian peasant colonists. But the arrival of a dozen peasant families and fifty bachelors could hardly change the fortunes of the place; and by 1827, when Rozen reached Chita, not five hundred peasant labourers could have done so. The River Chita was too shallow in the summer months to benefit from Eastern Siberia's increasing water-borne commerce. Not until the twentieth century, indeed, would hydro-electric power resuscitate Chita,

9

enabling it to grow into the modern city of 300,000 people.[52] Many times the regional authorities of Rozen's day might try to turn the settlement's position at the confluence of two rivers, the Chita and the Ingoda, to good account, and so to foster economic growth. Always they would fail—and none more memorably than that most ambitious of Governors-General in Irkutsk, N. N. Murav'yov-Amursky.

A small and undynamic ex-frontier settlement, then (for the frontiers of effective Russian power had advanced 500 miles towards Mongolia since Beketov had died), Chita was a commercial backwater. In 1826 it had an idle[53] population of 300, and consisted of one wretched wooden church, some twenty peasant cabins, one barn, one storehouse and three stone houses, lived in by officials. The place belonged almost in its entirety to the Department of Imperial Mines and Factories, on whose behalf a mining engineer, S. I. Smol'yaninov, managed most aspects of the lives of those inhabiting the "few tumbledown huts", as Mikhail Bestuzhev characterized Chita.

By what, it may be asked, was the settlement, if not distinguished, at least distinguishable from a hundred others like it in the region of Nerchinsk? Not, to judge by most Decembrists' reminiscences of 1827–28, by its residents. "As is general among old Siberian settlers," records M. Bestuzhev tartly,

> these were poor and idle, and . . . sold both their poor produce and their meagre services at a high price . . . Accustomed to make money easily, the inhabitants of Chita soon fell into penury after our departure in 1830, and their poverty was greater than it had been previously. Idleness went hand in hand with drinking now, and so, progressively degenerating, they lived until their poor village was named the district town. They themselves were then called Cossacks, and resettled at Atamanovka, twelve versts away.[54]

Idleness, apathy, and drunkenness: not an inspiring picture. Nor were most inhabitants of Chita attractive to the eye—charcoal burning turned the very skin dark, and charcoal burning went on year by year.[55] Smol'yaninov, for his part, was at least an honest man. But, alas, he was a poorly-educated officer whose greatest single claim to our attention lies, perhaps, in the coincidence that, as Basargin puts it: "Annenkov's maternal grandfather, General Yakobi, had once been Governor-General in Siberia and of service to the father of Smol'yaninova. She could not forget this, and held it a sacred duty to repay the grandson for the grandfather's good deed."[56] Here, at least, the Decembrists in Chita would find one person of worth; and if Annenkov would taste much of Smol'yaninova's cooking, Zavalishin would become her son-in-law. Never could the man allow himself to be outdone.

It remains only to mention the most colourful of those subsisting in Chita in 1826–28, Monsieur Pereis. Chita, like many settlements throughout Siberia, boasted its ageing exiled foreigner. Unlike his fellow-countryman Champagne de Normandie, whom Lorer would encounter five years later in another village,[57] Pereis had contrived to keep his self-respect, and to remain sober. Once in the Prince de Condé's army, he had emigrated to St Petersburg, duelled and been arrested, fled and been recaptured, killed a guard and, as his punishment, had his nostrils torn, his back flayed, and been exiled to Siberia. When had all this occurred? Pereis, like Count Kakhovsky whom Lorer also met while in Siberia and "who had once played cards with our mother Catherine",[58] and like the cautious Karl, sometime church caretaker in Riga who entered Rozen's service as a "yardman" in 1832,[59] had kept careful track of time. Like the indigent Kakhovsky, Pereis had spent thirty years in exile. Since his banishing, indeed, criminal law itself had changed in Russia. "Since the decree of December 25, 1817," records the expatriate and liberal I. Golovin, "the practice of tearing out the nostrils of criminals had ceased. Now, those who have undergone chastisement by the knout . . . are branded on the forehead and cheeks with the Russian letters BOP, that is, thief."[60]

So much, then, for the inhabitants of Chita, whose fortunes were so shortly and so radically, though only temporarily, to be improved. Let us turn briefly to the physical surroundings of the place. All at once, the Decembrists' situation of 1827–30 assumes a rather different and a far more smiling aspect; for on one thing all Decembrists who left memoirs are agreed: Chita, its valley and environs, was beautiful during the summer months and bearable enough in winter.

Thanks to the sketching skill of P. I. Borisov and V. L. Davydov,[61] among other exiles, but above all to the talents of Nikolay Bestuzhev, who had briefly trained at the Imperial Academy of Arts and was a painter of some stature, we have many aquarelles of Chita as it appeared in 1827–30;[62] of the valley ringed by scrub-grown hills, the ten-foot-high stockades of sharpened stakes, and the River Ingoda in which Decembrists bathed in summertime.[63]

Perhaps there is no stronger preconception about "Russia", among Europeans and Americans, than that Siberia, time-honoured place of banishment for Russian dissidents, is a land of endless snows and icy wastes. Soviet historians, too, though for their own reasons and not from ignorance, have sometimes tended to insist unjustifiably on the rigours of the climate of Siberia; after all, the Decembrist myths deserve a proper setting.[64] In reality, of course, the climate is far harsher in some parts of Canada, Sweden and Finland than in most parts of Siberia. Again, excessive generalization is the pitfall of the dogmatist. (The Decembrists suffered in Siberia; *therefore* the climate was indubitably terrible.) Terrible it was for Europeans in many *northern* settlements, such as Sredne-Kolymsk and Verkhoyansk, to which Decembrists of the eighth degree of guilt were banished in 1826, and of the seventh in 1828. But Chita was not in the far north. Nor can the climate in most regions of the former Province of Tobol'sk, where vast forests of silver fir, cedar and pine grow now, as they were growing in the 1830s, be called unpleasant. Continental, yes; but most Russians are accustomed to a continental climate, with extremes of cold and summer heat. Chita, in short, enjoyed a tolerable climate. Other places to which exiles would be sent in 1826–28 were, compared with it, exceedingly unpleasant.

But, of course, dark preconceptions of Siberia were prevalent in Russian circles, just as in the West, during the early nineteenth century. Too few were the officials who had first-hand knowledge of that land, and had returned to St Petersburg to share it; too many were the grim or lurid references to Siberia in Russian, as in Western European, literature, to allow a just impression of the country to permeate the minds even of educated men. Siberia, in fact, belonged to fiction—and to the Archpriest Avvakum's autobiography. Three Decembrists only, it was seen, had real knowledge of Siberian conditions. Many more left for their exile with a feeling that their last years were about to drain away in a vast wilderness.

Yet life in Siberia proved bearable, for Rozen as for others. The climate proved acceptable. Summers in Chita would prove delightful. The facts must be insisted on, if only to do justice to those exiles who survived in northern settlements, and kept their sense of balance. And as reality contrasted in Chita with the Decembrists' earlier fears, so the morale of many exiles in Siberia—a morale lifted so swiftly from the nadir of long, solitary confinement by the very act of moving east—contrasted greatly with those exiles' previous moods. Here, for example, is N. V. Basargin on the region of Nerchinsk:

> So magnificent, so astoundingly beautiful is the countryside of Eastern Siberia, and that of Transbaikalia in particular, that one cannot—and could not—help standing in wonder and in rapture, and simply gazing at the scenery and objects all about one; so rich is that region in flora and in landscapes pleasant to the eye. The air, too, was so beneficent and steeped in the aromas of fragrant flowers and herbs that one felt a special delight when breathing it.[65]

Fragrant flowers and herbs . . . So much for endless wilderness and never-ceasing winds! Other Decembrists too, notably Rozen and Volkonsky, would feel a sense of simple joy on seeing the extraordinary greenness of the valley of Chita in spring. In their cells, in 1825–26, they had had no single blade of grass to look at; now, in Siberia, they had irises and lilies:

> Towards the end of May [Rozen records], a greenish tinge began to show on the fields and mountains around Chita. This little settlement lies on the great road between Baykal and Nerchinsk, on an elevation surrounded by high mountains on two sides. The little River Chita falls near the settlement into the navigable Ingoda, and forms a delightful valley. To the north lies Lake Onon, on the shores of which Genghiz Khan held his court of justice. (He used to drown criminals in the seething waters.) The descendants of his Mongols, the Buriats, still wander through this country with their felt tents—a country abounding in rivers and lakes . . . The climate here is healthy, and the speed with which things grow amazing: both corn and vegetables ripen within five weeks of the frosts' ending, that is, between mid-June and late July . . . As to the valley of Chita itself, it is

renowned for its flora, for which reason it is called the Garden of Siberia. Never have I seen finer specimens of lily, iris and other bulbs than are to be met with here.[66]

Rozen admittedly was by training and by temperament a horticulturist—the sight of grass and trees alone made him feel cheerful. Again, one senses his awareness of, and curiosity about, the picturesque aspects of Transbaikalia: the Buriats with their yurts, the "seething waters" of Onon. Such an awareness could, and did, blunt many exiles' consciousness of the more humdrum disadvantages of their position for a few weeks. Again, the very dates or times of year presented in so warm a tone do not, on cold reflection, strike one as fitting sources of delight. The frosts continue until June; the grip of winter does not loosen until May. Such facts, one might have thought, would sober a native of Estonia, not soothe him. Yet Rozen spoke for the majority of the Decembrists in Chita, for whom life could have been so much worse in 1827. In the perspective of earlier apprehensions, and compared with solitary confinement, who among the exiles in Chita (in contrast with the exiles in remote hamlets) could complain about the summer? It lasted for a good third of the year, if one included torrential floods in spring: "In fact, the situation and the climate of Chita were excellent. The luxuriance of the plant growth there was extraordinary; everything that grew reached amazing proportions. The air, moreover, was so good . . . In general, we all grew healthier in Chita."[67]

All in all, in fact, it was a healthy spot. Winters might be long and hard, but the summer months were blazing. In June, Rozen records, there was a veritable explosion of every kind of grass and flower. Very different would have been his lot had he been kept, as was proposed briefly in 1826, in Akatui. There, in the silver-mining centre on the arid plains that stretched towards Mongolia, M. S. Lunin was to die, in pain, in 1845.[68] There, indeed, foundations for a new jail had been laid before Leparsky could convince the Imperial Staff that so noxious was the air in Akatui—no bird was to be found within a radius of a hundred miles, because of silver poisoning—that to send the exiles there would be tantamount to sentencing them to a lingering death.[69]

For a temporary jail, Leparsky settled on the shell of Beketov's old fort, which he ordered to be strengthened and rebuilt to his own specifications. Next, and using all the labour available from exiles who had reached Chita by early summer 1827, he set about erecting another, larger prison. It was well that he did not waste time in doing so, for Rozen arrived to find that sixty prisoners had preceded him; by the end of 1827, eighty-two Decembrists were packed into three cramped, dark, noisy buildings.

Most aspects of the Decembrists' lives while in Chita are clear enough from Rozen's recollections of that time: none-too-demanding work in the so-called "Devil's Grave", a co-operative or *artel'*, much horticultural enterprise, some correspondence with relations 7,000 versts away through wives who had arrived in Transbaikalia by 1828. To continue with his narrative:

We were received in Chita by the captain of a line regiment, a town-adjutant, a clerk, and some sentries. The captain asked if we had any cash or valuables on us, as this was strictly forbidden. I took from my neck the silken cord on which hung a portrait of my wife, a locket with my parents' hair in it, and a little packet of earth from my native land. When I had handed these things to the captain, he noticed the gold ring on my finger, and shouted in a stentorian voice, "What's that on your finger?" "My wedding ring." "Off with it!" I replied civilly that I had been allowed to wear it in the Winter Palace and in [Peter-and-Paul] Fortress, and that the wearing of such things was not forbidden us. "Off with it this instant, I tell you," he shouted yet more roughly. "Take the ring and the finger with it," I replied calmly, folding my arms and leaning quietly against a stove . . .

The next day, we were visited by our Commandant, S. R. Leparsky, an old cavalry officer who for many years had commanded the Seversky Jägers, of which the Emperor Nicholas had been Colonel before he had mounted the throne. Whenever any officers were obliged to transfer into another regiment, on account of some unpleasantness in theirs, these so-called unruly characters were invariably transferred to Leparsky's; for he well knew how to handle them, and never made an enemy of them. Though his entire life had been passed in the garrisons of remote towns, it was plain to see that he had had a solid education in his youth. He had been a pupil in the Jesuit school at Polotsk, spoke Latin, and could also express himself fluently in German and in French; he was, in addition to all this, a man of noble character . . .[70]

Leparsky lived up to Rozen's expectations of him. The physical conditions in the camp in the first months, however, were appalling: men slept packed together and the air, heavy with rank tobacco fumes, greatly oppressed Rozen and other men who, like him, did not smoke. Still, there was congenial company, and most exiles were youthful and by no means in despair; indeed, the Government's passing of such savage sentences—sentences quite disproportionate, in most cases, to the offence—gave many prisoners a sense of righteousness, almost of justification, that lesser sentences would not have given them. By punishing the exiles less, in short, Nicholas might well, by leaving their consciences to work, have punished them the more effectively. It is remarkable, in fact, that Nicholas should have committed so immense an error as to grant them all the solace of each other's company; for to have left them isolated would most certainly have broken their morale and crushed their spirits. (Fearing a general insurrection in Siberia, we saw, Nicholas had accepted the unintentionally humane advice of A. S. Lavinsky.[71]) Drawing strength from one another, the Decembrists in Chita and, later, Petrovsky Zavod were mercifully enabled, as Nikolay Bestuzhev put it, "to exist politically beyond political death".[72]

At last, in April, the weather grew a little warmer, and at the end of May the earth began to thaw and we could start our work. One morning we were taken out to an open area, where we met our comrades from the other prison building. Our meeting was a very happy one, and was repeated twice a day, from eight to twelve in the morning, and from two to five in the afternoon. Our regular employment now began. A quantity of spades, mattocks, shovels, carts and wheelbarrows had been collected; our first task was to dig foundations for our own new prison and the ditch around it. This work reminded me of the fortress of Zwing Uri, which the Swiss were once obliged to build for themselves ... Every day, except on Sundays and on feast days, the under-officer on duty would enter early in the morning with the call of "Gentlemen, to work!" In general, we left with songs upon our lips, energy in our hearts; no force was used on us ...

The Buriats still wander through this country with their tents of felt; now they are here, now there, always on horseback and often armed with matchlocks, though in general only with bows and arrows so as to save powder, with the use of which they are perfectly familiar, for special need. Part of this tribe has given up nomadic ways and settled down; these Buriats practise agriculture, and their fields and meadows are as soundly irrigated as those belonging to the Milanese ...

The population of the settlement in which we lived had reached three hundred. Like all miners, they are poor. They lived in little huts, on which a miserable church looked down, supporting themselves by agriculture and by fishing, which pays well along the Ingoda and in Lake Onon. The land belongs to the Crown, by whom it is allotted to the peasants; these were therefore greatly taken up with burning charcoal, which had to be conveyed by water to the Nerchinsk mines ... In the three years and six months that we passed in Chita, the place took on a totally new aspect, as much from the many new buildings as from the new guests, in whose suite came military authorities and guards. On our arrival, Chita boasted only three real houses, lived in by the Commandant, the mining superintendent, Smol'yaninov, and the town-major, but twenty-six small cabins ...

We were ordered to fill in a large hollow near the road, with earth and sand. This hollow, down which foaming mountain torrents rushed, was threatening to undermine the road. In a few days, the waters washed away the work of an entire summer, so we found ourselves obliged, the following year, to build a dam of logs in order to create a base for our dyke of earth and sand. We called this hollow the Devil's Grave.

Life passed in cheerless monotony. At first, we had very few books, writing was strictly prohibited, and neither paper nor ink was to be had ... Our rooms were so tiny that we could not keep them clean as we wished. We had beds made out of boards, covered with felt rugs or furs; under the boards were our boots and portmanteaus. At night, when the doors and windows were shut, the air became intolerably oppressive, for the doors were closed at sunset.[73]

1828 began. The wives of more Decembrists came to join the first arrivals, Murav'yova and Naryshkina, Ental'tseva, the Princesses Volkonskaya and Trubetskaya. In St Petersburg, encouraged by the (theoretical) success of I. Yakushkin's eighteen-year-old wife in gaining permission to join her husband with her child, Anna Rozen, too, sought permission from Benkendorf. She was refused, the General remarking that Dibich had acted "rashly" in assisting Yakushkina.[74] Perforce, Anna found herself respecting her husband's earlier request that she remain, at least until her son could walk. In Chita, meanwhile, Rozen's own life acquired a rigid pattern. Physical conditions had improved somewhat when, in the late September of the previous year, the exiles' new prison had received them; Rozen shared a large room, furnished with iron beds and several benches, with seventeen companions. The room was known as Pskov, after the sister-city of Novgorod (the next room). Colonel I. S. Póvalo-Shveykovsky was elected prison senior, to speak for all the exiles to Leparsky, to organize a small co-operative, and to purchase stores. At Rozen's suggestion, a kitchen-garden was established and tended near the prison.

Rozen fixed a strict timetable for himself, and adhered to it. Translation into Russian from German or from French (Mondays and Thursdays); discussions with his fellow-exile, K. P. Torson, who had sailed with Bellingshausen south to the Antarctic in 1820–21 (Wednesday evening); physical exercise each morning at the same hour; lunch at midday sharp; and in the evenings— music. Spartan and peculiar to himself, the pattern never varied, week by week. Hardly surprisingly, some of his comrades found such regularity faintly amusing —though there were men in the vicinity leading far stranger lives, like the semi-recluse and Roman Catholic Lunin. Several, in their memoirs, would allude to Rozen's clockwork habits. None, however, gives more useful information than does another sailor, A. P. Belyayev (1803–87). Belyayev, it is evident from the whole passage touching on "the baron", was neither very intimate with Rozen while in exile, nor in the least like him. The two, indeed, could not have been less similar. Belyayev, a good-humoured former warrant-officer later to serve, to his own surprise, in the Kabardinsky Hussars, was indifferent to religion; Rozen was religious, and a Lutheran. Belyayev was gregarious, Rozen was not. Belyayev, like his brother and fellow-exile Pyotr, was given to enthusiastic outbursts and periods of depression. Rozen was controlled by temperament. Yet, it is no less obvious, the two exiles respected one another. Moreover, they had common interests: both sang well and both, moved by concern for Russia's literacy, would open private schools, Belyayev in the settle-ment of Minusinsk, Rozen in Khar'kov (see Chapter 10). Here, now, are A. P. Belyayev's recollections of Rozen as he was in 1830:

Rozen, I recall, would also work on the hand-mills, but for reasons of hygiene— to be active, to maintain his health . . . Many of us had resolved to take exercise without fail, specifically, to walk for several hours and to keep our health by doing so. But the most punctilious of all, in this regard, was Andrey Yevgen'yevich Rozen, whom we nicknamed Kuno von Kyburg. Rozen was a man of chivalrous nature, truthful, upright, always self-possessed, serious, and unswervingly precise in the fulfilling of all tasks that he had set himself for every hour. He was liable to inflammation of the eye then, and at this time had begun to take French snuff which, by drawing the congestion away from the eyes, soon dealt with *that* ailment. But he afterwards refused to let himself take snuff, regarding the habit as a caprice. In the evenings, he would usually play the flageolet with Falenberg, but only for the fixed time, ending the music at the appointed hour. Wits even used to say he had a rule as to which hand was to be used to cleanse the various different portions of his body in the bath . . . Healthy, energetic, with a clear memory and intellect, he now [1880—G.B.] passes his time in continual labour, composing and translating.[75]

Others, too, found it amusing that Rozen, with no obvious need to do so, should pass his every day with such unbending regularity. Few knew of his intense sufferings during interrogation when, penned up, deprived of exercise, and in a wretched cell, he had been sick indeed. He did not speak of it. One thing, however, was apparent to his comrades as a group: his was a temperament well suited to lend stability to life in any gathering, and to help others in their trouble. Like Shteyngel', a man seventeen years his senior, Rozen became a sure support for men less able than himself to cope with long-delayed emotional disturbances—the stresses of disgrace. He was, in short, an asset to his comrades. That they thought him absolutely trustworthy is plain from the mere fact of his election, first, in April 1828, as prison senior in Chita, then, two years later, as the head of one of the two parties marching west to the new prison of Petrovsky Zavod. Rozen justified their faith in him.

How can one measure the success of an administrator whose accounts have gone, whose work could by its nature leave no mark, whose reminiscences touch only indirectly on his earlier responsibilities? Only, perhaps, by the opinions of the men whom he administered. Rozen, suffice it to say, earned no hostility during his term as senior, but great respect from the majority of those in contact with him. (Colonel Póvalo-Shveykovsky had been charged by some with skimping at the table, in his efforts to be economical.[76]) Even to have improved the kitchen standards in Chita to the extent spelt out in memoirs was a considerable achievement; for Rozen enjoyed few facilities—only common sense, an ample source of labour, and a useful skill at growing vegetables. ("When, after Shveykovsky's return, I was elected prison senior, I salted down in brandy-casks 60,000 cucumbers from our own garden."[77]) Always he was courteous, always the same; and so he won the confidence (though not, it seems, the love) of men of every kind of character, from the dyspeptic Zavalishin to the volatile but gentle Poggio, the moody Gorbachevsky to the amiable Nikolay Bestuzhev. But Rozen's was a larger and more lasting achievement than the organizing of a kitchen-garden, or the winning of the trust of many men. His achievement it was, as spokesman for the exiles in 1828, to establish on a footing of civility and mutual respect, reason and decorum, relations between prisoners and Commandant that would subsist until, during the 1830s, the Decembrists were released from Petrovsky Zavod and sent to settlements throughout Siberia. Punctiliously courteous but also cool, Rozen's quasi-official personality, in speaking to Leparsky, was not unlike Leparsky's own in dealing with his charges. The two promptly established an *entente* that had been missing in relations between the ageing Commandant and the less equable Póvalo-Shveykovsky. Both Rozen and Leparsky were professional and tactful men; each understood the other's true position. Here is Rozen's summary of their relationship:

On occasions, I had to transact business with Leparsky in connection with affairs of my companions in misfortune. He always received me with marked courtesy. Often he said, "What will be written about me everywhere in Europe? They will call me a hard-hearted jailor, executioner, oppressor, while the truth is, gentlemen, that I only retain my present post in order to protect you from the persecutions and injustice of unscrupulous officials."[78]

As a group, the exiled Decembrists trusted Rozen, though they might not love him. It was his property, it seems, to inspire respect, not love. His regular, unchanging way of life, even his self-possession prompted confidence. So much is plain from his election as prison senior, in which position he bore full responsibility for literally thousands of roubles—all the funds, in fact, which all the prisoners who chose to contribute to it gave to the Chita *artel'*, or co-operative. Cook, soldier and historian, gardener and prisoners' diplomat, Rozen's was a many-sided talent.

Another of his skills, it became clear in 1828 and 1829, was to live economically. The right to receive money from relations was strictly regulated by the government. The law permitted exiles to receive (on leaving for *seleniya*) not more than 2,000 roubles for "settlement purposes" and not more than 1,000 annually.[79] Sums were paid out in instalments by Leparsky's nephew, Osip Adamovich. But there was little danger of Rozen's being sent excessive sums: Anna had sufficient funds in 1828–30, but not a lot to spare. Not that he was ever among those—thirty-four exiles in 1828–30, and most from the Society of United Slavs—who received no aid at all, so were dependent on the government's paltry subsidy of 114 roubles $23\frac{1}{2}$ kopeks a year.[80] Still, he was well able to benefit by the efficient working of the camp *artel'*. Many of the Decembrists in Chita had been, and in practice were still, men of property; he himself, through Anna, controlled lands in the Ukraine. Four or five, however, were grandees and in receipt of massive sums through wives already in Chita; and these, most notably the Murav'yovs and Trubetskoy, could contribute generously to the *artel'*, so guaranteeing that no man should lack essentials. Trubetskoy and Nikita Murav'yov both received between 2,000 and 3,000 roubles annually from family estates, government regulations notwithstanding, while Volkonsky received up to 2,000, and Ivashev, Naryshkin, and Fonvizin often up to 1,000.[81] In Chita, where goods and services were cheap even allowing for inflation caused by the presence of so many wealthy prisoners, these were considerable sums indeed. And in ten years that they spent as State convicts, that is, until 1836, Decembrists would receive from home almost 355,000 roubles in cash, and the wives, including Anna Rozen, another 778,000 roubles.[82] And this was through official channels only. Yet Rozen remained relatively poor in 1828–32. Though the fact did not alarm him, it perhaps led to his throwing all his energies into the agricultural enterprise, four years later in Kurgan, that could bring him a considerable income—and did so, thanks entirely to his knowledge of the land.

I have already mentioned that about half of my comrades were not well off at all, and that many were neglected absolutely by their relatives while some were very rich indeed. So, every time a senior was chosen, at the end of a three-month spell, a paper would be sent round on which every man wrote down his contribution in proportion to our common expenses. The sum collected would be spent by the senior on tea, sugar, and viands, besides household necessities. Clothes and linen we had all to obtain for ourselves. The wealthy bought necessities and shared them with the poorer brethren; everything was divided in a truly brotherly way, money as well as suffering. So as not to spend funds lavishly, our clothes were cut and made by some of our own comrades. The best tailors were Pavel Pushkin, Prince Yevgeniy Obolensky, Pavel Mozgan, and Anton Arbuzov. The best hats and shoes were made by Nikolay and Mikhail Bestuzhev and Pyotr Falenberg . . .

From September until May we were taken twice a day into a special building outside the prison courtyard, where hand-mills had been set up. We were each obliged to grind eighty pounds of rye a day, and at first we found the work hard, until our hands and arms grew used to it; the strongest and the healthiest among us helped the weaker ones to finish off their share.[83]

But what of the intellectual life? Most of the Decembrists in the capital were, after all, well-educated officers. It was improbable that specialists in several fields of science and the liberal arts, doctors, writers, travellers and craftsmen, would do nothing to distract themselves. And so there came about what has been called "The Academy of Chita". Within one year, that settlement had been transformed into the intellectual centre of all Russian territories east of the Urals. Never before, indeed, had so many intellectually distinguished individuals been confined in one small outpost in Siberia. Irkutsk itself was quite eclipsed. Nor, we may note, was the effect a transient one: when, in 1885, the American George Kennan visited Chita, he found there many amiable, shrewd, and highly educated political exiles, though the two Governors-General of Siberia and their staffs continued to maintain themselves elsewhere. Then, and until the present century, exiles sometimes gathered in the evening in a building that had once been the Decembrists' carpentry and joinery shop.[84]

Predictably, given their antecedents, the willingness of most Decembrists to acquire new knowledge only grew while in Siberia—indeed, it had been sharpened by two years of intellectual starvation. Informal lectures were arranged. Each "academician" took it upon himself to study subjects of which he knew little or nothing, while speaking on his speciality. Through their wives, books, periodicals and newspapers in several languages were starting to arrive. The library built up between 1828 and 1830, and then transported to Petrovsky Zavod, was accessible not only to all exiles, but also to the local populace.[85]

Nikita Murav'yov, who possessed beautiful military maps and plans, expounded strategy and tactics to us; Ferdinand Vol'f [Wolff, formerly a Staff-Surgeon in the Second Army Corps—G.B.] gave lectures on anatomy and chemistry; Bobrishchev-Pushkin *junior* explained the higher branches of mathematics; Aleksandr Kornilovich and Pyotr Mukhanov read Russian history; Prince

Aleksandr Odoyevsky, Russian literature. (I must add with gratitude that he had the kindness to teach me, a born Estonian, Russian, which I knew poorly.) At 9 o'clock in the evening, our doors were shut and every light had then to be extinguished. As we could not fall asleep so early, we would usually talk for quite some time, or listen to tales told by M. Kyukhel'beker, who had made a voyage around the globe . . .

These long years of intimate contact with such highly educated men had a considerable effect on those among us who had previously had neither time nor the means of improving their minds. Some now began to study foreign languages. Zavalishin was our greatest linguist; he learnt not only Latin and Greek but eight modern languages as well. And he found a teacher for each one of all these languages among his comrades . . .[86]

Torson lectured on political economy and state finance, Nikolay Bestuzhev on the arts of seamanship, and several Decembrists on historical themes, including, we have seen, Rozen, who spoke on serfdom in the Baltic provinces. Through periodicals, the exiles kept in touch—at a distance of three months and several thousand miles—with political events in Western Europe. On hearing news of the July Revolution in Paris, they formed a choir and sang the Marseillaise.[87]

But the influence of the "Academy" was not confined to Chita itself. Outside in the surrounding countryside its presence could be felt in various ways. The Decembrists' work, for instance, in the fields of medicine, education and agriculture has been adequately covered by Soviet scholarship.[88] Dr Vol'f's renown was widespread; he saved many lives, possibly including Leparsky's; but Vol'f was not the only prisoner with a knowledge of medicine. Zavalishin, Naryshkin, Mikhail Kyukhel'beker and Princess Trubetskaya also understood its elements. Nikolay and Mikhail Bestuzhev, for their part, sought permission to teach local peasant children to read and write, and were refused. They thereupon requested leave to instruct the local populace in liturgy and church music, for which a fair degree of literacy was obviously desirable. Permission was eventually granted. Later, after the main body of exiles had left Chita, Zavalishin would found a primary school there.[89] As for agriculture, in which Rozen took a lasting and informed interest, the exiles were immediately made conscious of the main problem: the almost total absence of a wide variety of vegetables and fruits. The horticulturally inclined, headed by Rozen, Poggio and Volkonsky, tackled the issue, introducing barley, melons and cauliflowers to Transbaikalia.

It would be wrong to think, however, that the exiles were concerned only with local problems; on the contrary, questions of regional, national, and even international significance also engaged them. While Basargin undertook a general survey of Siberia's economic, social, legal, and administrative problems,[90] the Borisov brothers formed a huge insect collection, classifying as they went along.[91] It is not only in the scholarly activities of Nikolay Bestuzhev, compiler of a Buriat-Russian dictionary, or of Shteyngel' and Murav'yov-Apostol in the 1840s, that we see the influence of the "Academy of Chita"; it is discernible in schools to which came hundreds of Siberian peasant children;

n a new attitude towards farming adopted by progressive-minded settlers in
he area; in a glimmering of enlightenment where earlier there was none.

Leparsky's rule, it rapidly emerges from Rozen's and from other men's
accounts, was by no means an oppressive one. With wives hovering by it could
not be, for some of them had Court connections still. The majority of the
Decembrists in Siberia, moreover, were still relatively young, and did not feel
that all was ruined in their lives. (As long as they remained in Chita, one perceives, where the native population as a whole was well disposed towards them,
most kept their hopes of general amnesty on the occasion of, perhaps, a royal
birth, or of a military victory. Physical deprivations blended, in these years,
with a certain youthfulness of spirit.)

Rozen took an active part in the work of the "academy" and in the tending of
the kitchen-garden, in the musical activities and in the no less regular religious
life of the Decembrist exiles. Of his interest in these last three fields—horticulture, music, and the spiritual life—more will be said. Here, we shall consider
his greatest single intellectual interest while in Chita, indeed, throughout his
later years: the study of history. For, perhaps alone of the Decembrists, Rozen
is of threefold interest to the contemporary historian. He was himself a
connoisseur of Baltic German and of Russian history; he was a prominent
participant in great historical events, which would have permanent significance
for Russia and, by obvious extension, for the Baltic states; and, after the event,
he was the self-appointed analyst of happenings that had transformed his own
life and the lives of all his comrades. Of his part in the confused events of 1825,
something has been seen; his work as the recorder of Decembrism, and as a
living link between the 1820s and the readership of the historical-cum-literary
periodicals of the 1870s, *Russkiy arkhiv* and *Russkaya starina*, will be treated in
due course (see Chapter 10). Here, something will be said of Rozen's interest
in history *outside* the context of Decembrism—of his taste in books and chosen
fields apart from the disaster of his early life. For to regard him as no more than
a participant in the Decembrist rising, ironical although "no more" may be in
such a context, is to belittle him.

Many Decembrists, one must say at once, took an interest in Russian history.
Certainly it would have been remarkable had some at least of Rozens' fellow-
exiles, their lives utterly dislocated by the tragedy of 1825, not been curious
enough to make some study of more recent Russian annals. After all, their very
presence in Siberia prompted questions of a patently historical variety: how
had autocracy developed among Russians? When had the first secret societies
been formed there, and when had the first move been made to combat tyranny?
Like Rozen, Yakushkin, Zavalishin and Lunin all wrote "sketches" of the
history of secret political societies in Russia in the nineteenth century, less to
inform the public, one suspects, than to clarify the matter in their own minds
and to see their own conspiracy in true perspective.

But some of the Decembrists were more than merely curious about such
questions. Jolted into their fields of interest by the events of their own lives and,

frequently enough, disposed to study history by temperament, some were highly knowledgeable in various areas of ancient, Russian and, less often Western European history. Nikita Murav'yov, for instance, had in 1818 written *Thoughts on N. M. Karamzin's History of the Russian State*, which, though banned by the St Petersburg censorship committee, had circulated widely as a manuscript and showed a no less solid understanding of the underlying sociopolitical issues of eighteenth-century Russian polity than had the several articles on Petrine Russian trade by the outstanding archivist among the exiles in Chita, A. O. Kornilovich. Kornilovich's *History of Journeys Within Russia* (1822) and *Historical–Statistical Atlas of Russia* (1824), the former largely given over to the wanderings of Peter Bruce, had been acclaimed in learned circles in the capital. Again (and very naturally, the great majority of the Decembrists being army officers), there were among them military historians: I. G. Burtsev had published in at least three periodicals before the rising. Naval history, too, was represented: Nikolay Bestuzhev's *Essay at a History of the Russian Fleet* had enjoyed a great success among, admittedly, a narrow readership. And there were those who, like A. Von der Briggen and Spiridov, specialized in, and translated, ancient authors—Caesar of the *Belli Gallici*, and Titus Livy, enemy of modern centralism, and Tacitus, the hater of autocracy. One might also mention the historical essays of P. A. Mukhanov, of V. D. Sukhorukov, and of P. I. Pestel'; but the point is clear. Rozen, the author of a family history, a history of Estonia, and half a dozen articles on former comrades, was in fitting company.

His own family and country: such were the themes on which he could speak most authoritatively. Rozen's interest in history, however, was by no means limited to these two areas. On the contrary, we have ample evidence of a sustained interest in economic, military and mediaeval social history. He read voraciously, and read for two main reasons: the better to escape the walls and wastes surrounding him, and to consolidate his knowledge of subjects that had seized his interest early in life—serfdom and its origins and remedy, the history of warfare, agriculture, husbandry. But here we see a curious point: he read works of economic history, but read them as a respite from contemporary economic quandaries (this in Estonia during the early 'fifties); he read Walter Scott in prison, but viewed him as a chronicler, not as a spinner of fine tales. Hard economic history and colourful romance, accounts of recent battles and the panoply of mediaeval war—Rozen needed distractions of both kinds. Nor could his need for factual information on the one hand, and the pleasures of escape through chivalry on the other, be satisfied by books alone. In his choice of reading matter we see, crystallized and ranged before our eyes, his larger needs. Rozen had but little Keatsian negative capability, and liked to know the truth on all questions. He discussed America with Torson[92] and with M. K. Kyukhel'beker, agricultural techniques with Poggio, music with Falenberg, translation with Odoyevsky. Occasional escape from the reality of Chita, as earlier from his cell, was indispensable. Was Captain Cook's *Voyages Around the World . . .*, as abridged by G. W. Anderson, a work of history? Unquestionably so; but it spoke not only to the intellect, but also to the fancy of a prisoner far from any sea.

Rozen acutely felt the shortage of books in Peter-and-Paul Fortress. In comparison with his more pressing physical ailments, to be sure, the lack was a small matter. But that lack grew more oppressive after many silent weeks, and few Decembrists, judging by their memoirs of that period, suffered more than Rozen from the ban prohibiting the reading of all books in their first four months of solitary confinement. So greatly did he feel the need that he broke his own rule and complained—in vain. He asked Anna to provide him with some books; he was informed that she could not now send him books direct. He approached General Sukin for permission to receive them; permission was refused, but he was given one small copy of the *Psalms of David*. Finally, tormented by the crisp sound of a prisoner in a nearby cell turning the pages of a book at night (it was Mikhail Bestuzhev-Ryumin, shortly to be hanged, making his testimony with the aid of a large French–Russian dictionary, so poor was his command of Russian), he asked Sokolov, the sentry, how to get books.[93] Sokolov advised him to stay clear of trouble by avoiding them. At last, in March, the Emperor deigned to allow all prisoners in the Fortress to read religious works:

> In Passion Week, the Emperor permitted prisoners to have works of spiritual counsel, pipes and tobacco. This was true luxury after so long a deprivation. My wife had sent me Zschokke's *Stunden der Andacht* (*The Hours of Devotion*), and three volumes on the wars of 1812–14, but these were kept back by the censor of the Committee of Enquiry.[94]

Stunden der Andacht (1809–16), by the parson Heinrich Zschokke (1771–1848), author of long, edifying tales of spiritual reform *à la* Pestalozzi, and even longer tales of the romantic past of Switzerland; and a large work on the Napoleonic Wars: a striking combination. Yet plainly Anna Rozen either felt her husband would enjoy such books or, far more probably, had been requested to provide them. Equally obviously, however that may be, Rozen was familiar with Zschokke by 1825. Yet Zschokke's novels had been popular in Russia only very recently; best known, perhaps, were his exotic tales with Swiss scenaria, *Der Freihof von Aarau* (1823) and *Addrich im Moos* (1824). (One indication that Rozen was familiar with one of these at least was his familiarity with the Zwing Uri incident, which, we have seen, the exiles' work in Chita brought to mind.) As to the history of the recent wars, that, surely, was a wholly natural choice. Only if he had *not* maintained some interest in military affairs would it have been remarkable. The wars had, only twelve years earlier, convulsed the whole of Europe. From them had flowed such consequences as had led, albeit indirectly, to his being in a cell himself. Acquaintances and regimental colleagues had participated in them personally; and Rozen was himself, though now disgraced, an army officer. Naturally he took an interest in the recent history of warfare: as Basargin would remark, of the Decembrists' interest in recent happenings along the Turkish and the Persian fronts in 1827–29,

> The progress of these wars could not fail to engross us; we had not yet forgotten our military service or grown indifferent to the successes of our arms—practically all the officers most active on our side, after all, from the C.-in-C. to the last general, were known to us. Many of those who distinguished themselves in these campaigns, indeed, were our comrades, and some even our friends.[95]

It was in August 1826 that the library of Peter-and-Paul Fortress, such as it was, had been opened to the Decembrists, or rather, that a few books had been carried out to them. Rozen describes his happiness when that occurred:

> I read all Walter Scott's novels with the greatest pleasure—the hours would pass so fast then that I often failed to notice the ringing of the Fortress clock. Through Sokolov, I shared my books with a fellow-prisoner. Sometimes I would devour four volumes in a day, and I spent those hours not in the Fortress but in Kenilworth Castle, in a cloister, in a Scottish inn, or in the palaces of Louis XI, Edward, and Elizabeth. When evening came, I would rejoice in the thought that next morning I should start another book . . . Those prisoners who had no relatives in St Petersburg received books from the Fortress library: Cook's *Voyages*, the *History of the Abbé Laporte*, and old Russian newspapers; to me, a comrade once sent in a newspaper of 1776 which contained an article on North America . . .[96]

Escape into the towers and naves of mediaeval England, and the ramblings of Joseph de la Porte; Captain Cook's dry narrative of life aboard H.M.S. *Resolution* in Pacific waters, and records of a Russian group in China: the mixture of romance and fact is now familiar. The Fortress library contained a curious blend of old and new, facile and ponderous. Few self-respecting libraries of the 1820s, certainly, did not boast George Anderson's "abridgement" of Cook's *Voyages Around the World . . .*, reprinted from the 1784 edition three times by 1820. Rozen was probably confronted with Loggin Golenishchev-Kutuzov's valiant (1796) misrepresentation of that work, "translated" from a poor French paraphrase. Again, most Russian libraries, private or public, would contain at least a few of Scott's Waverley novels; Rozen apparently started with *The Abbot* (1820), *The Monastery* (1820), and *Kenilworth* (1821). But *L'Histoire Littéraire des femmes françaises*, by Joseph de la Porte (1713–69), with the voluminous assistance of another arch-compiler and contemporary of Fréron, Lacroix de Compiègne, could hardly be considered fresh in 1826. It had been published fifty-seven years before.

As in St Petersburg, so also in Siberia: Rozen pursued a double interest in Russian (and Estonian) history and foreign travel, the exotic and the factual. He himself gave lectures on the history of serfdom in the Baltic. Here is part of his account of the delights of hearing experts speak in their own fields:

Aleksandr Kornilovich and Pyotr Mukhanov spoke on Russian history. And A. Kornilovich would occasionally relate episodes to us from the history of his fatherland, with which he had much occupied himself as editor of the periodical *Russkaya starina*. For many years Professor Kunitsyn and he had had free access to the State archives, and had made a special study of the times of the Empresses Elizabeth and Anna. But after six months we lost this most accomplished comrade...[97]

Admiration shines from every line; and Kornilovich, it has been seen, was indeed no mean historian. Greatly would both Rozen and Kornilovich have wondered had they known that, forty years having elapsed, the former would be intimately linked with the revival of *Russkaya starina*, refounded by the journalist Mikhail Semevsky in 1870. Rozen's interest in history did not falter, however, after Kornilovich's unforeseen departure for the Caucasus (where he shortly afterwards died of a fever). By the end of 1830 there was sustenance enough for those with academic leanings. Mikhail Bestuzhev summarizes the improvement in Petrovsky Zavod over earlier conditions in Chita, where the exiles' library had been formed:

Our store of books, and sensible books too, grew very large. This store was built up, and given over to the general use, from all that was sent to each one of us, or was received by our ladies to their husbands' orders. Of one accord, we subscribed to the most noteworthy political and literary works of the time, through our ladies, as also to the finest periodicals, Russian and foreign alike. Everything at all remarkable then being written and published in Russia, everything printed abroad and worth reading whether in periodicals or monographs, we received without exception.[98]

Among the papers and journals received, we may note, were no less than three German-language ones: *Journal de Hambourg*, *Allgemeine Zeitung*, and *Preussische Zeitung*. Here, Rozen's hand may be discerned.[99]

Year by year Anna, who had finally been reunited with her husband on the trip from Chita to Petrovsky Zavod in August 1830, bringing many letters with her,[100] subscribed to works published in Moscow, St Petersburg, and Revel'. And Rozen found another reason for continuing his studies: he himself would have to educate his sons. Another boy, Konrad (Kondratiy), named after Ryleyev, was born in 1831. He took his work a stage further, embarking on sustained translation projects. One of these, we know, was from Jean-Charles de Sismondi's *Histoire des républiques italiennes du moyen âge*, another from the same dynamic author's *Histoire des Allemands*. Sadly, not a paragraph of Rozen's text survives. Which of the sixteen volumes of the former history did he broach? We cannot say. The fact of his attraction to Sismondi, however, remains, with its two major implications.

Sismondi was a prolific author. His most famous work perhaps, during his life as now, was the twenty-nine volume *Histoire des Français* (1819–42). Yet

10

Rozen chose in preference to this his smaller history of the German people. Second, Sismondi was essentially a socio-economic historian, and it was in this area that Rozen's own interests lay. In 1819 had appeared the French historian's last work of socio-economic theory, *Nouveaux principes d'économie politique*. The main idea expounded in that work, that economic science had too long been principally concerned with how best to augment wealth, and ought to pay attention to the problem of promoting happiness *through* wealth, would be echoed unmistakably in two of Rozen's longest articles, "An Opinion on the Affairs of Estonia" and "A Sketch of the Activities of an Arbitrator of the Peace in Khar'kov Province, 1869" (see Chapter 10). It was no coincidence. Rozen mentions by name only one work by Heinrich Zschokke, yet was demonstrably quite familiar with three; why, then, should we suppose that he was not acquainted with Sismondi's greater, economic texts?

By training, as by temperament, Rozen was a respecter of historical research. From casual allusions in his writings to George Washington and North America (with which he twice compared Siberia, such were the latter's "natural endowments and advantages"), to Scottish, French, and Polish struggles for autonomy in other times, above all, to the Russian and Estonian past, it is apparent that he was himself familiar with the histories of many lands. Of course, his memoirs are themselves a basic text for every student of the Russian liberal movement. Yet it is not so much Rozen's acquaintance with events and individuals lost from the sight of his contemporaries that strikes one, as his attitude towards the past. He was, if Lewis Namier's ghost permits the phrase, an historian by instinct. He recorded accurately: his survey of Estonian history, balanced and terse, is of considerable value still. He stored materials with care, often for decades, thus preserving several articles and poems by his fellow-exiles in Siberia. He assembled facts not merely systematically (his, we have seen, was the one Decembrist memoir to contain a full list of the prisoners of 1826 by categories), but in a way designed to give due weight to their importance, and to place the isolated incident in overall perspective. Here, to illustrate that skill of organizing, but of simultaneously *animating*, factual records—a skill he made his own in middle life—is Rozen on a pair of fellow German-Balts, the Decembrist A. von Briggen and the favourite of the Empress Anna, Münnich:

Our comrade A. F. von Briggen was settled [in 1832—G.B.] in the town of Pelym, rather to the north of us, but still in the same province. He had lived a year with us at Chita, whence he was transferred to the settlement. For six years we had not met when, to our common joy, he was sent to Kurgan. Briggen had served in the Izmaylovsky Guards, and had then retired. In 1825 he had wished to travel abroad and was already provided with a passport when he was detained for the whole winter by his wife's illness; during that time he was arrested. He had taken no part in the conspiracy itself but, like so many of my comrades, had been punished for his "way of thinking" and "expressions". I have kept some highly interesting letters from him, written in Pelym. In one of them he describes the life which the celebrated Marshal Münnich led during the twenty-one years that *he* passed in that town (throughout the reign of Elizabeth). Briggen had been given details of the life of this famous general and statesman by the children of eye-witnesses, and even now they are of interest. Münnich lived in the very house which he had earlier had built to his design for his enemy Biron, when he had overthrown the latter and had sent him into exile. Biron was subsequently sent to Yaroslavl', and Münnich took his place. After the dethronement of Anna, whose honours and favours were declared forfeited, he was sent as an exile to Pelym, where he was never allowed to leave the house and could exercise only by walking on its roof. He occupied himself by drawing plans of battles and sketches of fortresses, by completing a pamphlet on the reorganization of the administration of Siberia (afterwards submitted to the Empress), and in reading newspapers; in the evening he would play at Boston with the officer on guard duty or his own *valet-de-chambre*. He never missed the moment when the cattle returned from the fields. Then, he would go up on to the roof and gaze with delight at the herds returning to the town, listening to the sound of cow-bells, large and small, around their throats . . . His strength of body was no less remarkable than was his strength of mind. After his return from Siberia he lived for four more years, partly in St Petersburg and partly on his property in Courland.[101]

Controlled and clear, it is a passage, like many in the memoirs and in Rozen's articles, no less informative than it is entertaining. But for Rozen, many years had yet to pass before, like Marshal Münnich, he could go home to the Baltic. By summer 1830 the new, permanent prison at Petrovsky Zavod, 430 miles west of Chita, was ready. And on August 7 and 9, in two parties, the Decembrists left, with wives in carriages, for the unknown. The six-week promenade proved to be more delightful than any man had dared to hope.[102]

Preparations were made quickly; portmanteaus were packed; our vegetables and everything belonging to the garden, including our wooden tools, were given to the local residents. We were to march in two divisions on the way, the first going under the charge of the town-major, Lt.-Col. Leparsky, a nephew of the Commandant; the old colonel himself headed the second. Each party was guarded by a sufficient escort of soldiers and Cossacks. Carriages were hired to transport our belongings . . . Our nights we were obliged to pass in yurts—cone-shaped felt tents capable of holding four men. These tents, when spread out in a line, had the look of a small military encampment, especially when surrounded by sentry-posts and pickets. Our cooking was done in the open air; in rainy weather we would make a temporary shelter out of sticks and brambles, to protect the kettle. The autumn air which, although warm enough by day, went down to eight degrees of frost by night, together with the journey through a mountainous terrain, invigorated and refreshed us all. For several days, our road led over hills and dales; mountains rose up on every side of us.[103]

Once more, Rozen found himself in a position of responsibility: his task it was to ride ahead at dawn each day, buy stores if necessary, and have supper ready when the main party reached night-camp. So, until Anna Vasil'yevna came while the Decembrists were by Óninsky on August 27 (galloping straight into her husband's arms, so we are told by Baron Shteyngel'[104]) he had ample opportunity to watch the Buriats accompanying him and to observe the scenery and various groups of colonists—Old Believers, Little Russians, even Germans —that they met along the way. The Buriats, in close contact now, produced a mixed impression on him: on the one hand, they were hardy, strong and cheerful; on the other, they were generally dirty, smoked incessantly, and were idolaters. He was fascinated, but repelled: they had no sense of order, no idea of cleanliness. They were semi-savage and lacked self-control:

The uncleanliness of the Buriats reaches the highest possible degree—they have no linen, and wear furs next to their bare skin, with boots made of chamois-skins and little fur caps both in summer and in winter. Their heads are shaved, except for one tuft which crowns the top. Little eyes, low and flat foreheads, square faces with broad, prominent cheekbones and pale yellow complexions, such are the distinctive features of their race. Among themselves they are called Mendu . . . Families of Buriats would sit around the fire on felt rugs in the middle of their yurts, naked children tumbling about amongst their elders, who spend their time tearing and cutting the skins of animals with their bare teeth, or shaping arrows, casting bullets, milling felt . . . And the people have a passion for tobacco, which they smoke in little copper pipes. When they light them, they inhale all the smoke.[105]

Exotic scenes indeed, and placed in suitably romantic frames: the River Selenga, with its glistening banks of black, yellow and red granite and lime; Tarbagatay, the village of the diligent *Semeyskiye*—sectarians from Dorogobush —where wheat and corn grew in abundance, and where Rozen ate fresh sturgeon; Desyatinkovo, where Rozen met a man sent to Siberia in 1733, now aged 110. Here, there were mountains. A little to the south lay the Mongolian wastes. It was 6,000 miles to Revel'.

6

PETROVSKY ZAVOD

Petrovsky Zavod, Rozen at once saw, was no makeshift prison but a specially designed and solid jail. With its twelve identical sections, long, dark, draughty corridors, and all-pervading sense of discipline, it was a sombre edifice. In itself, such architecture (if the word can be applied to what was, as the exiles rightly claimed, essentially a huge and furnished stable with a hundred stalls) militated against casualness of any kind. Each prisoner had his own cell now. Neither cells nor prison sections were interconnecting; indeed, each cell had its own door on to a corridor, and each section its distinct, separate yard.[1] Here, all turned inwards, and the tendency must necessarily be for humans, too, to turn in on themselves. It was as if the Emperor deliberately proposed to encourage the Decembrists to live separate existences—to break all sense of kinship and community. No longer could the exiles, as for three years in Chita, casually foregather in one place for meals.[2] Gone—and soon lamented by some men— were the constricted days and nights which had, however, bred tolerance and not contempt or pettiness. Now, individuality was to prevail, and the pursuit of private interests. No rattling chains or other din would stop a man from passing an entire day as he chose, within the limits of an ill-lit room and a routine requiring three or four hours' work. The new situation suited many well enough. Indeed, for every man who was unhappy in Petrovsky Zavod in 1830–32 there seem, to judge by the surviving evidence, to have been at least three happy ones. But here, of course, is the essential point: some individuals, like Rozen, adapted easily to a changed situation. Others did so with the greatest difficulty. Some Decembrists were to feel less personal distress in the new prison, where privacy was to be had, than they had earlier in Chita. On others, solitude or semi-solitude, combined with perfect liberty to idle for a large part of each day, was soon to have a sadly deleterious effect.

Now, in 1830, those individuals with special interests could follow them with greater ease than since before the risings, and they did so. Others pursued interests acquired while in Siberia—the flora and economy, administration, peoples, game, geology and native superstitions, *inter alia*, of Siberia itself.[3] Other men played cards. Considerably blurred during the first chaotic months of banishment in 1827, the lines dividing individuals one from another, but not, it must be emphasized, one group from other groups, grew sharper in the fourth decade. Personality acquired a new significance; and, of course, there were less prisoners packed into cells, so personalities had room in which to grow. Eighty Decembrists had lived in cramped conditions in Chita; sixty-five came to Petrovsky Zavod, and two more would leave for settlements (Repin and M. K. Kyukhel'beker) within nine months of their arrival.[4] Moreover, individuals could use their rooms precisely as they chose, provided that some neatness was retained for occasional inspection purposes. Some rooms were speedily transformed into dark studies (Rozen's, Obolensky's, Zavalishin's, Pushchin's), others into workshops with machinery and lathes (N. Bestuzhev's, Artamon Murav'yov's), others into sitting-rooms (Volkonsky's, Trubetskoy's). Now, there were less constraints on individualistic habits. Smokers could smoke each day, since tobacco was obtainable at reasonable prices; readers were at liberty to read, and worriers to worry. In his room, Lunin could arrange a little chapel, pray, recite his prayers aloud, declaim the breviary, burn books—no one disturbed him.[5] In his, Mikhail Bestuzhev could try his eyes by reading to excess. Many men now found or fostered earlier interests, interests that would sustain them in the lonelier years of banishment to come: I. I. Gorbachevsky in shamanism, for example, and Yakushkin in meteorology. Andrey Borisov and Ya. M. Andreyevich grew sicker, not in body (Vol'f was always near), but in spirit. In short, the exiles' coming to Petrovsky Zavod marked the beginning of a time of flowering individualism. With forces and resources now acquired, some men, including Rozen, would be well enough equipped to face the unforeseen demands of life as a Siberian settler when released. Other men would be so ill-prepared that hunger and collapse would threaten them.[6] All but a few would survive the first half of the fifth decade; but the fittest would fare best.[7] Now, in 1830–32, characteristics that would virtually guarantee the continuing stability of some exiles grew plain: a willingness to work and learn beyond what seemed to be the minimum or necessary limits; cheerfulness under duress; a sense of simple balance.

What, then, of Petrovsky Zavod itself in 1830? It was, we can immediately say, a place of far greater industrial importance than Chita had ever been. The very speed with which its population had reached 2,000 was evidence of that: for the settlement had not even existed in 1786. Its importance was, indeed, an essentially industrial importance. It had no administrative significance: since the establishment by Catherine II of the three immense Siberian "vice-regencies" (*namestnichestva*) in 1782–83, even Kyakhta, two days' journey to the south of the new ironworks, had lost what small importance it had formerly enjoyed. Naturally, the affairs of the ironworks themselves were controlled by representatives of the Department of Factories and Mines—unscrupulous and grasping engineers, if we believe N. V. Basargin, until the appointment of A. I. Arsen'yev, "a good, just man".[8] But as far as regional administrative policy, and even economic planning, was concerned, Petrovsky Zavod was entirely under the control of the centre both of its "vice-regency" and of its *oblast'*, Irkutsk. Speransky might make sweeping changes in his time as Governor-

General, decreasing the importance of Yakutsk, Okhotsk and Nerchinsk as centres of the other *oblasti* in the (by 1823) defunct *namestnichestvo* of Irkutsk.[9] But nothing he could do or did affected the commercial and administrative rôle of Irkutsk within Siberia (it was, after all, the stronghold of the merchant class,[10] and commanded the great valley of the River Angara below Baykal), or the industrial importance of Petrovsky Zavod in its own region. Administrators came and went; the ironworks of Petrovsky continued to expand beside the confluence of two small rivers, the Myrkyta and Balégi. Soon, it was planned to dam the Balégi, which sank too low in summer to be otherwise of use for industrial purposes. A dam was built, and a large saw-mill from Irkutsk installed. The mine-shaft was extended, and new seams of ore discovered. Convict-workers were transported to the mine from other regions. But the government had little need to introduce fresh colonists or workers, settlers or traders by coercion. Prosperity drew many to the spot. This was no Chitinsky *ostrog*, with twenty-five or thirty wretched huts. The earth was full of minerals, and the Siberian peasantry, as foreign visitors observed, were not as idle as the peasants of Great Russia.[11] If they did not relish actually mining in the earth, they were not slow to take the economic opportunities afforded by the presence of less fortunate Siberians than they—the convict-workers who, as we shall see, were horribly exploited by the mining chiefs.[12] The convict-workers and their guards and overseers, after all, had to be fed. Traders set up shop. "Indeed, the Siberians throughout are more industrious and independent than any Russian peasant, and live more comfortably . . ."[13] More men arrived, more ore was mined. New branches of the iron industry were tried: iron wire was drawn, then hoop iron was forged. Finally, in the first years of the nineteenth century, iron artifacts were cast. So was established the local industry which, notwithstanding all the various measures applied throughout the century to ensure that the industrial hegemony of Moscow and St Petersburg should not be undermined by the Far East, was to develop into the contemporary Soviet city of Petrovsk, a major engineering, iron, steel and machine-tool centre.

Yet there were adverse factors, too, in the new settlement's location on such shallow streams as the Myrkyta and the Balégi: neither river was navigable by craft larger than skiffs. Thus, ore could not be readily transported by water to Irkutsk or other centres; and other metals in the region, such as silver, had also to be carried overland at least to the east bank of the River Selenga. The distance, admittedly, was not great; but even an expanse of fifty miles of hilly terrain from navigable water militated powerfully against commercial growth in the new century.

Another discouraging factor was the dampness of the climate in Petrovsky. To be sure, the climate was extreme; yet it was certainly not as extreme as that of Chita—the relative proximity of Lake Baykal guaranteed that. Nor was Petrovsky built at such an altitude as many of the factories to the east; on the contrary, it stood in an extensive flat depression, surrounded by low hills which, to the south and west, grew larger by degrees and so resulted in a great deal of precipitation on Petrovsky and its prison. Of course, crops could be grown. But the climatic conditions and the soil left much to be desired, from the small-holder's viewpoint: even root-crops often failed in and around the settlement as a result of boggy soil, or frost, or both. Influenced by the French physiocrats, an educated handful of officials in Irkutsk might view the giant forests on the east bank of the River Selenga as an area of wonderful potential.[14] But for workers in Petrovsky Zavod, who knew the district, such notions seemed at best chimerical. They knew, as the Decembrists would soon learn, that though wheat grew well only a day to the south-east,[15] in Petrovsky it was hard enough to cultivate potatoes, beetroot, cabbage, and a little low-grade rye. So agriculture was, in general, abandoned once sufficient quantities of root-crops had been grown and picked and stored to answer the immediate local need. No soft fruit grew near the place.

But if the climate of the area was moister in the summer months and rawer in the winter than had been that of Chita, the micro-climate by the prison building, to judge by several memoirs, was even more dispiriting to would-be horticulturists. There, we are assured, cold dampness crept out of the boggy ground at sunset, and the moisture of the soil, which lacked a clay base, caused whole wooden structures to subside. Even the design of their new prison made it difficult, climatic and soil factors apart, for Rozen and his comrades to grow vegetables or fruit successfully. Considerably higher than the palisades at Chita, the log stockade surrounding the whole prison and the fences dividing up the separate yards within it cast long shadows. By 3 p.m., more than half the area of the courtyards was in shade—and this was in September, when the sun's arc was still relatively high. Matters did not promise well for late autumn or early spring. Why had Leparsky fixed upon a boggy site, far from all trees, houses, indeed far from the centre of Petrovsky settlement? Conceivably because, as Zavalishin claims,[16] he feared the risk of fire in a large wooden building. The prospect of a fire there would, indeed, have been an awful one; and, as would grow clear, stoves placed directly against wooden walls, with no protective iron sheet at all, were sources of real danger. No river flowed in the immediate vicinity. Therefore Leparsky ordered that fire-buckets filled with water be kept in readiness on every roof. At least, thanks to the prison's siting, guards could easily find standing water near at hand with which to fill those buckets. But let us turn from buckets to the furnishing and layout of Rozen's new, "permanent" home.

The prison in which Rozen and his colleagues were about to pass two years, if not considerably more (for men in the first and second categories of guilt), was shaped like a great U. At the centre of the front façade (the bottom of the U) was the main guardroom; other watch-houses were placed along the wings. In the walls of every guard-house were loop-holes, through which, in case of need, Leparsky's troops could shoot at rioters or would-be escapers. (Those embrasures were never to be used.) By the main guardroom, in the front façade, was the only entrance into the prison. The top of the U was closed off by a palisade. The whole area, enclosed by buildings on three sides and by this palisade on the fourth, was divided up into eight courtyards, to serve as exercise areas for the Decembrists. The prisoners were spread over twelve sections, in sixty-four rooms; each section contained five or, in the case of corner sections, six men. A separate building held a kitchen, storerooms, and a mess. Four sections, 1, 2, 11 and 12, had their own courtyard; 3, 4 and 5 shared one large yard, as did 8, 9 and 10.[17]

> The whole building was divided into twelve sections. On each side there were three, and on the front façade, on either side of a guardroom, six. Each of these sections had its own door into a courtyard and was separate from the others. Each section consisted of a corridor and five separate rooms, the exits from which were on to that corridor, which was kept warm . . . We were quartered in our casemates immediately on our arrival. Because there were not enough of them, some of us were obliged to share one room. As to the rooms themselves, they were fairly high and spacious, but windowless. The light came in through the door, which was immediately opposite a window in the corridor. As a result, we had to place our tables by the doors and do our reading and other work sitting beside them. So the doors remained open all day. At night, we were locked in, but not each man in his room—the whole section was locked up. Each section had a sentry, a retired soldier.[18]

The corridors were warm, of course, only if the stoves, which served two rooms so that each section contained two or three of them, were perpetually being stoked. Again, the risk of fire brought itself to the attention of the exiles. "Fairly high and spacious", says Basargin; other witnesses suggest that each room measured six paces by seven, and corner rooms seven by eight. This advantage enjoyed by men in corner rooms, however, was soon revealed to be a doubtful one. For when the whole structure warped and bulged, as a result of careless building aggravated by the damp conditions and intense heat generated by the stoves, openings appeared in the corners of those corner rooms. Someone had provided timber in short measure, and so lined his pocket. Predictably, it was Zavalishin—who occupied a centre room—whose indignation at this villainy attained the highest pitch:

> Petrovsky Zavod, lying in a deep depression surrounded by high hills, presented a most unattractive aspect, with its decayed and blackened mine buildings; not a single decent house was to be seen. Only in the distance could be seen the prison, with a red roof, no windows, and boxes of some kind on the inside—so the inner courtyards looked, encircled as they were by their immense stockades. On the inside, the impression made was not a happier one. Dark rooms, dirty and boggy yards, bare and unsquared walls—everything suggested storerooms or barns rather than habitable dwellings . . .
> As a consequence of thieving by the engineers, the prison had been wretchedly built. Many short logs had been placed in the walls, and others had been set in place so poorly that one could draw them out by hand. The stoves, too, had been

very poorly built, were repeatedly cracking and—to the great horror of the Commandant—constantly giving rise to fires . . .[19]

The worst problem, however, was presented by the absence of windows in all rooms except the guard-house. Through the wives, whose contacts in the capital protested noisily, and even by the Commandant himself, pressure was brought to bear on Nicholas to order that windows be made in outer walls. But Nicholas, the exiles should have known, was not amenable to pressure of that kind. The winter passed and still they crouched over a candle or beside an open door, wearing two coats. Some men, most notably Nikolay Bestuzhev, placed planks on one side of their room at a height of three or four feet from the floor. In this way, and sitting on their improvised platform, they could utilize the extra light that came in through a *fortochka* or little window over their door. The winter of 1830–31 was a sombre one for Rozen and his comrades. When stoves became too dangerous, the inmates of whole sections would be moved to other rooms while bricks were placed around the danger spots; when chinks appeared in outer walls, as a result of earth subsidence or shoddy workmanship, prisoners shivered. For six months Rozen was disturbed by moves, small fires, alarms, false moves and false alarms, and workmen coming in to plaster walls:

As to our cells here, they had been put up in haste and so wretchedly that they were continually being repaired. More than once, fires broke out in walls . . ., while the *corridor* walls bulged out and had to be supported by stanchions and by bolts! Even in the cells it was not very warm, but in the corridors it was sometimes positively cold, so that it was not always possible to open one's door and let a little light in. So we sat over a candle during the day . . . And in the daytime we were allowed to wander freely from our section to any other that we chose; but at 10 p.m., all rooms were locked, as was the section as a whole. Next, the gates of each separate courtyard were locked, and so, finally, was the outside main gate. Each of us thus slept behind four locks.[20]

Finally, in April 1831, permission was received from St Petersburg to make small windows in the cells. Windows were duly made—approximately one foot square and so near the ceiling that even A. I. Yakubovich, one of the tallest exiles in Petrovsky, could see nothing through his postage-stamp but sky. Still, it was an improvement to have any extra light at all, particularly for the prisoners who in 1831 were doubled up in cells (the Borisov, Kryukov, and Belyayev brothers), or who were sharing cells during the daylight hours with wives.

For her part, Anna Vasil'yevna had had much to tell her husband of happenings on her journey to Siberia. She had known tribulations on the way sufficient to prepare her well for all the tribulations to be borne in 1831. Her eldest son, Yevgeniy, whom she had brought to Moscow from Estonia, she had left there in the keeping of her youngest sister. Parting had been tearful. On leaving Moscow on June 17, 1830, she had travelled ceaselessly, stopping only for one night to sleep before arriving in Tobol'sk. In Irkutsk, on July 31, a signed renunciation of her "rights of gentle birth" had been demanded of her; she had willingly complied with the demand. She had crossed Baykal in haste in stormy weather, only to be told that, as the River Selenga had burst its banks, she must wait another week or more. For ten days she had existed in a barn, spending as little money as she could. At last, exhausted, she had reached the exiles as they had been "promenading" from Chita to their new prison—and had gratefully swallowed the "excellent soup" which A. I. Yakubovich had prepared expressly for her.[21] As to Enny, her son, she now found far less time to worry; she had done all that she could for him and trusted that, as she herself had evidently caught the eye of God when, "only a hundred paces from Moscow, a wheel had broken, spokes sprung out, and my carriage had turned over" leaving her unharmed, so Yevgeniy too would be "sheltered and protected" by the Lord. ("*Not a word* about my separation from my child and from all those dear to me: I have entrusted them to Divine Providence, this is all that I can say."[22]) Certainly she had needed faith on catching sight of her new home. Rozen spoke for her, in expressing his dismay at that bleak spectacle:

As we drew nearer, we could see an enormous building with a number of brick chimneys, and stone foundations reaching high up into the walls. It was window-less, except for one small projecting part which held the entrance and a guard-room . . . Each cell was seven paces long and six in breadth. These cells were practically pitch-black—the only light came from the corridor, filtering through a grated window made over the doors! It was so dark that even on a clear day it was quite impossible to read or to make out the hands of a watch! By day, we were allowed to leave the doors open and to work in corridors in warm weather; but how short a time does the Siberian sunshine last! Even in September we had to make our choice of burning candles or of sitting in the gloom. Our first impres-sion was a very painful one, all the more so for its being unexpected. How could we have imagined, having passed four years in the small but tolerable prison of Chita, that we should now be punished—for no reason—by removal to a far worse place, and even be deprived of natural light?[23]

However, Rozen and his wife settled into their section of the building, which was given over to married couples, with the Trubetskoys, Naryshkins, and Fonvizins. A kitchen was established; in the winter, ice hills were constructed down which prisoners could slide, an area was flooded for the skaters, and life went on in the dark building which, Leparsky told the exiles, had been per-sonally designed by Nicholas. Rozen's eyes grew weak from reading by a candle. Anna suffered from the cold (and by November it was very cold outside the cells, especially along the draughty corridors). But spring arrived at last, and with it tiny windows. Once more, Rozen established for himself a strict, un-varying routine. Again the emphasis was on regularity and self-control:

My wife and I lived rather apart from the others, having our own, regular occupations: every hour of the day had its appointed task now, excepting those in which we had to walk about the court for exercise. Every day at 10 o'clock my wife went to the rooms that she had rented [in the settlement—G.B.] to attend to her house-keeping. At midday, all the food to be consumed was taken by the cook into the guardroom, whence a sentry brought our separate meals into the corridor.

So our work went on in common, as in Chita: in summer we were occupied laying a road and labouring in the kitchen-garden; in winter, we worked hand-mills. We each employed our leisure hours according to our taste, and fortunately had no lack of books. Prince Odoyevsky visited me twice a week and corrected my writings and translations. An old sailor, K. P. Torson, spent every Wednesday with me relating his voyages around the world, his past work, and his future plans.[24]

On November 5, 1831, three months after she had moved out of the jail into a house which had been Princess Trubetskaya's, Anna gave birth to her second son, Kondratiy. Repin and Mikhail Kyukhel'beker left Petrovsky Zavod. The "academy" reopened and functioned yet more vigorously than before; and Rozen, while maintaining a slight distance from his friends and living "rather apart" still (though not in isolation like the enigmatic Lunin), played his part in the life of the fortress. In two areas in particular he contributed to the general activity: music and religion.

Even in St Petersburg, Rozen had sung in his cell to make amends for missing conversation, to strengthen his chest, and "to give expression to his feelings". By doing so, he had succeeded in establishing a vital human link with his own sentry, Sokolov, then in July 1826 with a fellow-prisoner, Colonel Worzel:

Once, late in the evening, I was singing the universal Russian song, "In the Level Vale Grew the Shady Oak". At the second verse, I heard another voice accompanying me behind the plank partition. I recognized my warder's voice. "A good sign," I thought; "if he sings with me, he'll talk to me, too." I repeated the song from the beginning; he knew the words better than I. When he brought me my food, I thanked him for the accompaniment of the song ... Then a Colonel Worzel took the place of Bobrishchev-Pushkin opposite my cell. He did not know of the fate of the rest of the condemned men, as he had spent many months in another fortress; he asked me about his neighbours—those incarcerated opposite me—and about his old acquaintances, his questions being disguised by being sung in French. I replied by singing, "Pendu, pendu, exilé à Nerchinsk."[25]

Singing, in short, was a timely source of solace. But it was a solitary exercise, as had been his guitar playing in 1823. Very different was the situation in Siberia, where music was essentially a shared, communal pastime. And it was in Chita and Petrovsky Zavod that Rozen's singing talent came most happily into its own, giving pleasure to himself and to those others of the exiles who, in the winter of 1827–28, formed the first Decembrist choir:

Chess was our sole amusement in the time between work and sleep. Playing-cards might have been had through the warders, but we had passed the word to each other not to allow card-playing, in order to avert any cause of unpleasantness or of dissension. When we were all together, however, we formed a company of singers from among ourselves, which shortened many a sad hour.[26]

From the very first, music was linked with solace and religion for the exiles; and it was natural enough that those who sang should form a choir to sing church music, seldom though they were escorted to the local church. Always the Decembrists who were musically inclined, headed by Rozen, M. N. Naryshkin, P. N. Svistunov and Prince Odoyevsky, *used* music, to alleviate their lot and to cheer themselves: "Our work, which consisted of turning millstones, was frequently accompanied by melodious singing: one musical comrade [Svistunov—G.B.] was appointed conductor; the church music of Bortnyansky was, I think, especially well rendered."[27] When, on August 30, 1828, Rozen's fetters had been permanently removed, he had "almost regretted them", "so often had they accompanied my songs as I beat time with my feet".[28]

More light is cast on Rozen's musical activities in exile by the memoirs of A. P. Belyayev. Here, Belyayev describes the choir which met, in 1830, in Chita, in the prison dining-room, where, fairly regularly in the early years, an Orthodox priest from Irkutsk would celebrate matins: "To the right of the 'choir' sang our choristers, with Svistunov as precentor, and very well they sang. Especially good was the setting of 'The Flesh Once Stilled' for three voices . . ."[29] Rozen was in the choir. Also in Chita, inspired by the examples of his comrades, he took up the flageolet, and practised diligently every day for thirty minutes.[30] Why the flageolet? Because he was "too conscientious to torment" his friends with the violin. There are references to musical activities in exile in the reminiscences of several Decembrists. Belyayev, for his part, continues thus: "We had guitars and a flute, I recall, which Igel'strom played, while Rozen and Falenberg both played the flageolet. Music in general and quartet music in particular, in which the works of the finest composers were performed, afforded us real pleasure and considerably brightened up our prison life." Talent was plentiful among the exiles: Vadkovsky and N. A. Kryukov played the violin proficiently, while P. N. Svistunov played the 'cello well. A. P. Yushnevsky, whose wife arrived at the same time as Anna Rozen, was a fine pianist. Naryshkin, I. F. Shimkov and Lunin all played the guitar, as well as Rozen himself.[31] Sometimes whole evenings would be given over to performances of chamber music. "There were even," writes Basargin, "concerts, or musical soirées. Odoyevsky's fine, sonorous verses, which reflected our condition and were consonant with our opinions and our love for the Fatherland, were often sung by a choir and to the notes of one of our musical comrades."[32] One consequence of Rozen's attempt to learn the flageolet—a successful attempt, it should be added—was a growing friendship with Lieutenant-Colonel P. I. Falenberg. The two men would correspond regularly until Falenberg's death in 1873, when he would be buried in Khar'kov Province not far from the Rozen–Malinovsky lands. Ten years later, in 1883, Rozen would publish a manuscript that Falenberg had given him some thirty years before, "A Tale

From the Time of 1826", concerning Falenberg's relations with Prince A. I. Baryatinsky in Tul'chin, and his joining the Southern Society.[33]

For Rozen, then, music in exile was essentially connected with relief, and with the spiritual life. Let us briefly consider his religious views—views which remained unchanged throughout his life, and which reflect his mother's training in his first five years.

> My parents, and especially my unforgettable, tender, and wise mother, who had more leisure than my father who was occupied with elective service and the running of his properties, instilled the holy faith and strict morality in me from early childhood. Religious ideas, which so often change during a lifetime from one's circumstances, from society, from reading and from doubts, were deeply impressed in my heart, not by prayers learnt by rote, not by reading and interpretation of the Holy Writ, but by the hourly, living example of piety in my parents' practical lives.
>
> Since then, I have not ceased to pray; since then, I have preserved my religious feeling despite all the agitations of my youth, maturity, and old age; since then, I have not parted with that treasure without which one cannot be always calm, always contented. For where is one to turn when, in sickness, consultation with the most experienced of surgeons makes it clear that there is no hope of a return to health? And what is to be done when a man is separated from his family and from society and locked up close and dark? To whom can one turn when a just man suffers exile and is ruined as a consequence of the suspicion or malice of an influential, avaricious man? Always and in every case, directly to the Saviour. Unfailingly He saves, and until the last Salvation, He will strengthen and console you.[34]

Rozen was, of course, a Lutheran. As a young adult, he attended church with regularity. But it required the crisis of his solitary confinement and his wife's first pregnancy, in 1826, to give urgency to his belief—to make him pious. So it was with many other prisoners in Peter-and-Paul Fortress; few indeed were those who, like Yakushkin and Prince Baryatinsky, were atheists in 1825 and died as atheists. Encased by walls so thick that practically no sound passed through them from the outside world, many had time enough to ponder on their future life, on death, and on their Maker. Was Rozen truly so impressed in childhood by his parents' piety? Perhaps; but the passage cited has a filial ring. Yet however he may earlier have viewed the Lutheran Church—as a powerful, living force in his own life, or as a grand inheritance from distant German forebears and a social obligation—his religion had unquestionably become a vital factor in his life by April 1826. His only child, it seemed, would never know him; he himself might shortly die:

> The time of my wife's confinement was approaching, and she wished us once again to receive each other's blessing. I tried to cheer her up in every way on the score of my coming fate. The hour soon passed and the Commandant dared not prolong it. We separated, commending ourselves to the Almighty Father; and I returned to cell no. 13 with a heart full of thankfulness to God.[35]

April passed, then May, and still no word arrived of a successful birth. Rozen lived from day to day in a state of constant tension. In his dreams, he saw his wife crying for help; he became sicker. Finally, on June 19, his first son was born, and he heard the news three days later. Rozen blessed his child in his thoughts, "and in prayer asked that the Everlasting Father replace the earthly father to him".[36] Can one doubt that such experiences might well turn any sane man's thoughts towards his death? Is it not sure that most men, faced by such a likelihood of death, might well recall their Maker? For Rozen, 1826 brought crisis after crisis: on March 18 his mother died; in June his wife gave birth; he thought himself about to die. Instead, five comrades hanged and he survived, though not, we saw, without having observed the building of the gallows on which Ryleyev perished. The day after the hanging, he was taken to the cell, no. 14 in the Crownwork Curtain, in which Ryleyev had just passed his last night with the Lutheran priest Reinboth—for he, too, was a Lutheran: "I entered the casemate, feeling as though it were a sanctuary, fell on my knees, and prayed for him, his wife and daughter; it was here that he had just written his final note to them. In the tin mug there remained still what was left of his last draught. I put it to my lips, to give my soul fresh courage."

Rozen survived to see his son, then aged six weeks, become a Captain of Uhlans and a landowner in Khar'kov Province.[37] But the religious frame of mind, first laid in childhood, then developed under stress in prison, did not leave him. Perhaps it was, as he records, "with pleasure" that he took a picture of the Virgin Mary from his wife to give him comfort in Siberia; but it was with simple piety, on leaving, that he grasped "a little wooden cross from Jerusalem, which had rested on her breast and on that of my new son".[38]

Those exiles with the strongest and most active Christian faith formed a small prayer and study circle in the prison-camps of Chita and Petrovsky Zavod. They were known, by those outside, as "the Congregation", and were watched with tolerant amusement and affection by Yakushkin:

> Every man's personality showed itself very plainly in several ways at Chita. The views of some differed from those of others so that gradually there were formed little groups of individuals closer to one another in their inclinations and conceits than to the rest. One of these groups, laughingly called "the Congregation", consisted of those men whose circumstances, during their confinement, had led them to piety. Among their various other occupations, these would often meet to read didactic works and to discuss the subject closest to their heart. [Bobrishchev-] Pushkin stood at the head of this group—formerly an officer in some dignitary's suite and a man of outstanding intellectual ability. The members of "the Congregation" were mild, quiet individuals who bullied nobody, and who were therefore on the best of terms with the rest of our comrades.[39]

But these "mild individuals", most of whom came from the south and had known far more modest circumstances than had Rozen, were Orthodox believers. For this reason possibly, he did not take a full part in the regular and semi-public meetings of the group, although he much respected Pavel Bobrish-chev-Pushkin and was sometimes present at their weekly gatherings. Here and there in Rozen's memoirs, one must say, there is evident reserve towards both Orthodox believers and, more markedly, towards Roman Catholics. True, he was sympathetic towards Polish exiles, whose songs delighted him and whose cheerfulness and energy impressed him favourably: but do we not detect a trace of mild distaste, or faint amusement possibly, in this thumbnail sketch of Lunin's practices?

> M. S. Lunin lived in a *most* peculiar way. He lived in cell no. 1, a totally dark casemate in which no window could be pierced as a guardroom had been built outside it. He did not share our common table, and kept his fasts according to the Roman Church, which he had joined some years before after he had been the pupil and disciple of some well-known *Meister* while in Warsaw. One third of his cell was shut off by a curtain, behind which, elevated on some steps, was a large Crucifix blessed by the Pope, which his sister had sent him from Rome. All day long, loud Latin prayers could be heard in his cell.[40]

Essential to Lutheran practice was a lack of ornament, simplicity of ritual and setting; and Rozen, it is obvious from his descriptions of the mummery that he beheld in 1837 in a large church in Voronezh, had no patience with an ornamental faith, whether Orthodox or Roman. Here, surely, we observe the ancient and traditional misgiving of the Protestant when faced, in Rozen's phrase, "with the accoutrements of high observance":

> Voronezh, the inhabitants told me, had grown greatly in the past few years and most particularly since the relics of St Mitrofan had drawn so many pilgrims to his shrine. The next day, according to my promise to my escort, we went to hear a Mass said at the coffin of the new saint. The church dedicated to him is adorned with a richly gilt altar, blue and white marble columns, gilt cornice and capitals; on the right, near a window, stands the coffin, draped with a crimson velvet covering trimmed with a gold fringe and with tassels . . . When Mass was over, a priest-monk came with a key, raised the velvet covering and revealed to our sight a golden coffin, in which we saw the "uncorrupted" body of the saint—surrounded on all sides by miraculous caps, gloves, jackets, little bottles, and the like . . . The priests naturally made a good thing of it all, as gifts of money poured in freely.[41]

By way of contrast, here is his reaction to the fundamentalist and diligent tractarians of Tarbagatay, near Verkhne-Udinsk, whom he had met ten years before *en route* to Chita:

> Here they live, the so-called *Semeyskiye*. When these exiles crossed Lake Baykal and arrived in Verkhne-Udinsk, they received orders from the local authorities to establish themselves in an empty spot and far from other settlements. The government commissary led them to an ancient forest by the little River Tarbagatay, and allowed them to select what site they liked: they were exempted

from payment of Crown taxes. How huge was the surprise of these officials when, returning one year later, they discovered a well-built and handsome village, kitchen-gardens, even fields, in a spot where twelve months earlier there had been only a dense forest . . . Like all the Old Believers, these people have no use for tea, tobacco, wine, medicine, or inoculations, as they consider all these things sinful. However, *I* have never seen a man among them marked with smallpox. They are a God-fearing people, read the Holy Scriptures diligently, and observe the rules of their sect with the greatest strictness.[42]

Simple living, strict adherence to a set of rules, and diligence: such were features of a small community well calculated to please Rozen. However, in the fortresses there was no spartan Christian life for him to watch—only the "Congregation". So, mindful of even those men's piety and charity, and of his situation, he attended the local Orthodox church on the rare occasions when the prisoners were taken there—at Christmas, at Easter, and on great feast-days. In the camp itself, he occupied a delicate position on the fringes of the "Congregation", as Belyayev's memoirs show:

When we were still in the large prison, a special archpriest was appointed to us from Irkutsk, who celebrated matins with the greatest solemnity . . . On Sundays, religious readings were arranged amongst ourselves; and a little religious society, of those who loved the Lord and were believers, would gather in some corner. Readings began with an apostle, then from a prophet and a Gospel, and to conclude a chapter would be read from the *Hours of Devotion* in the translation of Andrey Yevgen'yevich Rozen, who always read it himself.[43]

Rozen was at ease with, but not of, "the Congregation". Their practice, after all, was unpretentious; only for pomp and gaudy coverlets, "miraculous caps, gloves and jackets", had he no time. Here, to give some impression of the evergrowing value of religion in his life in exile, is an extract from that section of his memoirs dealing generally with 1828–30:

Only once a year, in Lent, were we led to church to take communion; on the eves of great feasts, a priest would come to the prison to hold divine service. Never shall I forget how impressively and solemnly this service had been celebrated on the eve of Easter 1828 when, before the tattoo, at about 9 o'clock, there resounded from all sides the shout of "Christ is risen!", and the chains of prisoners clanked as they threw themselves into each other's arms in fraternal affection. In thought, we embraced at the same moment all our distant relatives and friends who were, we knew, united with us in prayer.[44]

Rozen was no theologian. His was a simple creed. To be a "heathen Buriat" was a misfortune; to be a Roman Catholic was suspect—and also a misfortune, since one was subject to the wiles of the Catholic clergy; but if one loved one's neighbour and adored one's God, even in ways quite different from the Baltic Germans, it was well, and one was saved. Not that Rozen took it on himself to imagine the celestial life. Still, he could sympathize with those who, like Bobrishchev-Pushkin, strove to do so. In 1871, six years after the latter's death, he would send a modest article entitled "A Poem By Pavel Bobrishchev-Pushkin" to Mikhail Semevsky, the editor of *Russkaya starina*. The poem in question, "An Imitation of the Thirteenth Chapter of the First Epistle of St Paul to the Corinthians", had been in his keeping for four decades.[45] Of a length in keeping with its title (one hundred iambic pentameters), the poem had been written by Bobrishchev-Pushkin at Chita in 1829. Surely Rozen would not have copied out the piece by hand himself, or another by the same author which would appear in the same periodical in 1873, "The Exile to His Parents" (a title inspired by Odoyevsky's epistle to his father, perhaps), had he not found the ideas expressed in both congenial? (For that either poem is of great literary merit, few would argue.) The former piece begins as follows: "Let the evil plait the crown;/ We shall leave them to themselves,/ Our souls take wing/ Towards the heavenly and holy truth!/ Pour, celestial fire, into our hearts . . ." In the same vein, though more opaque in several passages, is "The Exile to His Parents", which ends thus: "Friends! God and our happiness exist/ Not on this earth, but in heaven./ God lives in the souls of sufferers./ A momentary unhappiness will pass/ To show an even brighter day./ And so, dear friends, let us now/ Cease our futile murmuring."[46] The crown is, obviously, the crown of thorns, the "murmuring" (*ropot*), that of some dispirited Decembrists in Siberia.

Not unlike Bobrishchev-Pushkin's, very different though were their attitudes towards the Church and Christian life (Pushkin would obey all men, doing as he was bid no matter who commanded; but no one ordered Rozen to do this or that), Rozen's was a practical and serviceable Christianity. He did not preach love of his neighbour, but demonstrated it by helping as he could, by learning rudiments of medicine, by acting as a bulwark for less stable men. He did not *claim* to speak the truth—he spoke it. His was, indeed, as Belyayev puts it, "a chivalrous nature". Whether or not Alexander II ever said, as Rozen claimed, "I know that Rozen will never write or publish anything harmful", cannot be proved convincingly; the mere fact that Rozen *does* claim it, however, is a reason for supposing that he did.

To illustrate the practicality of Rozen's Lutheran creed, let us, in conclusion here, take three examples of his unsolicited and open charity. First we may recall his attitude towards his jailors and supposed judges of 1826. Here, surely, there were grounds for secret enmity, memories to rankle with the years; yet there is no invective and no hatred in those chapters of the memoirs that concern interrogation in the Fortress and the pseudo-trial. Rather is Rozen's effort to diminish the enormity of Nicholas's crimes against legality. Where allowances can possibly be made, they are invariably made; where facts alone are eloquent, no hostile commentary is added for its own sake. Rozen did not have a vindictive temperament, and harboured no known grudges as he aged.

A no less striking illustration, secondly, of his readiness to see the best in all men and not only friends, is his sorrowful objection to that passage in the memoirs of Belyayev in which the author castigates "certain ex-Decembrists", that is, traitors to the exiles' cause. "Even men with fine feelings and lofty aspirations," wrote Belyayev bitterly, "quite consciously accepted and embraced the perfidious, jesuitical rule that the end may justify the means . . ."[47] Rozen held no brief for Count D. N. Bludov, once a member of the liberal Society of Arzamas but later a judge of liberals and tool in Nicholas's hands; but he defended him, seeing clearly that he was Belyayev's major target. He had no personal knowledge of the circumstances to which Belyayev savagely referred, it was true; yet he felt obliged, Bludov being unable to reply (he had died in 1869), to enter the debate. It was a generous, though probably misguided, impulse.

Most of all it is Rozen's never-failing decency towards men of every class that strikes us—the ease with which, throughout his life, he won the ready sympathy of peasants, drivers, labourers and soldiers, as well as his superiors in the service. In him, charity had reasonableness as a shadow; and common sense tempered a sense of his own dignity. He was a nobleman; therefore he must act nobly and discharge all proper duties towards others, and thereby towards himself. His cordial relations with his warder in Peter-and-Paul Fortress, Sokolov, and with his own men in the Finland Lifeguard Regiment, were touched on earlier. Suffice it to recall here that relations no less generous (though more mercenary) were immediately forged between him and his peasant hosts in Kurgan; with the peasants on his own estate in Izyum, Province of Khar'kov, for whom he built a private school; with simple soldiers everywhere—in St Petersburg and Georgia, Transbaikalia and Estonia. Rozen, peasants appreciated, was a man to be relied upon. He was consistent. As his obituary would put it, in the forty-second volume of *Russkaya starina*: "His was a clear mind and a healthy outlook. Under all conditions, everywhere, he strictly followed the pattern of a high, moral, laborious life which he had established for himself. Everywhere he preserved his cheerfulness, his inner strength and faith."[48]

One way in which he kept his cheerfulness while in Petrovsky and Chita was through religious observance, another was through music, and a third through the pursuit of history and conversation with his academically inclined companions. But there was a fourth way—a way which, like his daily walk, kept him in condition; which, like his musical activities, gave him a sense of contact and community with others; and which, like the pursuit of history, reminded him of other, happier days. It is time to consider Rozen the horticulturist and market-gardener.

Many Decembrists, as the sons of landowners or landowners themselves, took an informed interest in farming and in all aspects of husbandry. Some, like Prince Volkonsky and A. V. Poggio (who would die on the former's huge Russian estate), proved highly competent farmers and market-gardeners in Siberia when, as "free settlers" after 1835, they were granted small allotments by the government. But no Decembrist took a deeper interest in agriculture or, in Chita and Petrovsky, horticulture, or at the same time showed a deeper feeling for the soil, than did Rozen. It was a strange chain of events that had brought him from the poor soil of Estonia, a small packet of which, we saw, he carried into exile, to the "rich, enormous plains, ... the golden territory of Siberia".[49] But here, in the east, he would first realize plans made long before to overcome soil poverty and general mismanagement of land. Small were the risks of meeting here, where summers were so torrid and the air so crisp, the difficulties that had prompted his first interest in farming in Mehntack: despairing of prevailing against standing water and incessant damp, his father had considered giving up the planting of all grains but rye, which at least produced a high-priced vodka, and had concentrated now on his potato fields (which also gave a *kind* of vodka), now on introducing good beef cattle to the marshlands.[50] Disgraced, exiled, no longer young, Rozen found himself on richer soil and with a far more favourable summer than his own father had ever known. It was ironical. True, the winter was severe and long; but Europeans, like the Buriats whose fields recalled those of the Milanese, must needs learn to adapt, and sow such seeds as flourished in the area.

Like Poggio and Volkonsky, Rozen had a deep feeling for all that grew. His pleasure in the sight of grass and flowers communicates itself to us. Here is an extract from his long description of his walk, on May 17, 1826, from the Crownwork Curtain of Peter-and-Paul Fortress to the Commandant's house— a walk of just 300 yards:

> The walk to the Commandant's house showed me how beautiful the spring already was: the air was impregnated with the scent of elder-flowers, the birds fluttered and sang in the Commandant's garden ... On my way back to the cells, I avidly drank in the May air. I picked some blades of grass as I passed by the garden hedge. Then I quickened my step, lest my heart grow too tender; but feeling hearts will readily believe that I kissed and caressed those blades of grass. When they had withered, I examined each blade and compared their varieties of beauty. These were the only links with the natural world that had gladdened my eyes for months.[51]

Paradise is traditionally represented as a garden. Certainly Rozen thought of green and waving fields as paradisical after five months of solitary confinement, and of places where no crops would grow as hellish. In 1832, Colonel Tizengauzen, doyen of the Decembrists and Rozen's fellow Baltic German, would settle by the small town of Yalutorovsk; and here, in late August, Rozen would visit him and learn that he had had enormous difficulties with his wooden house, which he had built himself and which had three times been burnt down. But the old man had not despaired, though arson might have been suspected: "From the *débris* that remained, he had contrived to build himself a little cottage, had worked diligently in his garden, and had cultivated many fruits and vegetables which had never before ripened in this clime."[52] How warm is the tone of approval! The fate of some of Tizengauzen's and Rozen's friends had proved very different. Sent, at the end of terms of labour at Petrovsky, to settlements throughout the barren north, some went mad. "Theirs", remarks Rozen mildly, "was an especially hard lot, for *they* were settled one by one ... in a country where the earth will not even bring forth grain."[53] This at least he was spared; and it was well that he was spared it, so obvious was his pain at the mere sight of a spoiled harvest. Rotting fields produced in Rozen an almost physical reaction, a jarring of the nerves. The smell of abandoned rye seemed to him to "poison the atmosphere".[54]

But what of Rozen's horticultural activities in Chita, with its freezing winters and intense, short summers? Rozen himself best sets the scene, in a descriptive passage which, with its delighted emphasis on greenness and luxuriance, stands in sharp contrast both to N. Bestuzhev's aquarelles of a depression ringed by scrubby hills and other memoirists' balder accounts of their first day in Chita. Basargin, for example, also noted the luxuriance of the area in summer; yet, as comparison of his with Rozen's opening description of the valley shows, for him, the military administrator, the spectacle answered no such fundamental need as Rozen was experiencing even as he jolted on his sled into Siberia. Here, first, is Basargin on the place where he would pass three years and more:

> Both the situation and the climate of Chita were excellent. The luxuriance of the plant growth was extraordinary; everything that grew there reached amazing proportions. The air, moreover, was so beneficent for me in particular that nowhere else and never before had I enjoyed such splendid health ...[55]

Tall grasses, an invigorating air—all is observed with an objective, unexcited eye. Here, like a colour photograph beside one in black and white, is Rozen's more intense and personal introduction to the valley. For him, it is immediately apparent, green fields meant more than health; they were an invitation:

> The high altitude of the settlement of Chita no doubt considerably increases the cold in winter; but still it has a fresh and bracing climate and is healthy. The sky is almost always clear except in August, when thunder is continual for days on end. Then follows a shower, beginning with enormous single drops, which in a few hours floods the whole road—for water rushes down the slopes gouging deep trenches as it runs. The great electricity of the air too is remarkable: the slightest movement of cloth or wool produces sparks or crackling. And as to the rapidity of growth of vegetation, it is quite extraordinary ... Many species of vegetable were then wholly unknown throughout the country [of Siberia—G.B.]; one of my comrades [Poggio—G.B.] first introduced the growing of cucumbers in the open air, and of melons in hot-beds. As to the vale of Chita itself, it is famous for its flora. Never have I seen finer specimens of certain species of lily, iris, and other bulbs, than one sees there.[56]

Enthusiastic but informed (Rozen did not, like Nikolay Bestuzhev, compare the local views with those from mountainsides in Switzerland[57]), the first reaction did not change with the onset of the autumn. Already he gave thought to what might grow around the prison. Irises were very well, but they could not be consumed; and the prison diet, it was soon only too clear, was painfully monotonous: beef, cabbage soup, black bread and pickles, milk and eggs. Rozen had comrades skilled in carpentry make gardening tools, in preparation for the spring. The very pattern of Great Russian expansion eastwards from the Urals since the 1650s, the Decembrists knew, had been influenced by the absence of fresh vegetables in northern and eastern Siberia, a problem which had borne considerable political results.[58] Could that problem not be solved? As Rozen tells us, it both could and was. During the 1820s, M. Murav'yov successfully grew millet in the district of Vilyuisk.[59] Poggio, in Chita, introduced the cultivation under frames of melons, asparagus, cucumbers, and cauliflowers.[60] Rozen, through the wives who had arrived in 1827–28, ordered seeds from European Russia. Meanwhile he discussed with Poggio where and how, in 1828, to create a kitchen-garden.

Spring came; with Rozen's manual assistance, a kitchen-garden was laid out, and the Decembrists sowed. Elected prison senior in place of I. S. Póvalo-Shveykovsky, Rozen participated personally in the running of the garden, and organized the salting down of 60,000 cucumbers. Thanks in large measure to his zeal the garden was in fine condition when, in 1829, Bobrishchev-Pushkin was elected senior, and Mikhail Kyukhel'beker market-gardener (one of the three main posts in the co-operative newly established).[61]

Encouraged by the visible success of 1828, several Decembrists ordered seed from European Russia, and exchanged among themselves whatever crops they grew. It was a chain reaction that Volkonsky's, Poggio's and Rozen's early interest and energy had caused. The consequences shortly benefited the Siberians themselves. For exiles showed that, by persistence and experiment, success *was* possible. Rozen himself taught local peasants to grow rye. Others taught the peasants in the regions where they found themselves on their release from Petrovsky to grow buckwheat, barley, millet and tobacco, and how most economically to produce hemp oil.[62] By 1830, when the exiles left Chita, horticulture was an established factor in their lives; to continue and expand earlier efforts seemed only natural in later years, notwithstanding the less favourable climate of Petrovsky Zavod. To the Siberians, Rozen gave the fruits of all that he had learnt, first on his family estate, then in Chita. He was happy to assist them, for he both admired and liked them and could sanguinely compare their children's future with Americans'. ("There are three strong pledges for Siberia's well-being in times to come: there are no privileged classes, very few officials, and the people are quite capable of governing themselves."[63]) Moreover, they had treated him with kindness.[64] All the exiles took some pleasure from the knowledge that their presence had brought benefits to the Siberians and native tribes. But Rozen could with justice claim to be the moving force behind the *general* Decembrist entry into the field of horticulture in Siberia. No doubt many of his comrades would have learnt the lessons that they learnt even had he not been there, but their success would have been slower, and more limited. Inspired by the apparent ease with which Rozen raised his crops, other prisoners, during their sojourn in Petrovsky Zavod, started allotments. As Yakushkin put it: "Many of us then had beds of flowers, melons and cucumber in our separate courtyards. In the summer, we engrossed ourselves in cultivating fruit—an exercise entailing major difficulties because of the unfavourable climate in Petrovsky."[65] Discouraging the climate was indeed: only a day's trip to the south, wheat grew in plenty. In the prison, morning frosts quite often killed potatoes.[66] Still, Rozen and his comrades struggled on, and from the extra lessons learnt now, in 1830–33, some at least would reap great benefits as settlers in later years, while others, ignorant of the land, would know great hardship and go hungry. Petrovsky Zavod, it could not be denied, was an unhappy place for agricultural or horticultural experiments. Rozen, however, had already seen enough of the Siberians and of Siberia on his journey east to sense that, one day, farming would be carried on over vast areas, with satisfactory results, in what was in the 1830s still an empty, open jail. Never was his enthusiasm for Siberia dampened; never did he change his view that corn, not gold, would form the true wealth of "the golden territory":

Wherever the climate allows of it, agriculture and cattle breeding are carried on with very great success [in Western Siberia—G.B.]. The trade is down the great highway from Tyumen' to Nerchinsk, which is the channel through which the products of these rich, enormous plains will be made available by future generations. Even in the reign of Catherine II, Siberia was called the golden territory because of the abundance there of precious metals; but though the river-beds and mountains of Siberia do, indeed, contain rich goldfields, the chief wealth of the land lies in the fruitfulness of the soil. Many places in the Provinces of Tomsk, Irkutsk, and Yeniseysk have most abundant harvests, and the land there needs as little dressing as the plains of the Ukraine.[67]

And now, in 1832, the time was approaching when he would himself depart for a Siberian settlement; though unaltered by the terms of the ukase of July 11, 1826, Rozen's ten-year sentence had been shortened on August 22 of that year, to six. His term of hard labour in Petrovsky Zavod ended officially on July 11, 1832. One after another, the Decembrists were released and sent to settlements and hamlets in Siberia, both west and east of Lake Baykal, where they would stay, according to their sentences, until the day they died. The first small group (men in the seventh category) had been released from Chita in the spring of 1828; in 1832, "major offenders" saw their terms reduced from twenty years to fifteen, and from fifteen years, on the occasion of the birth of Nicholas's fourth son, to a mere thirteen. Most left Petrovsky Zavod between 1834 and 1837. But though freedom was now closer—or, at least, a crypto-freedom— middle age was closer still for many. Their lives, most realized at this stage, were damaged quite beyond repair. Some Decembrists were prematurely aged, others optimistic or naïve, but almost all were inexperienced in dealing with the traders and officials of their new country. Some, indeed, like Prince Volkonsky, were unhappy at the very thought of leaving Petrovsky; they had infants, or financial problems to resolve, or both. They gave pretexts for remaining in the prison for a few more weeks.

The Rozens did not know where they would go until the month of their departure. Anna's aunt, Aleksandra Samborskaya, they knew, had petitioned Benkendorf to see that they were not sent to an area where the climate would be harmful to Rozen's health. In fact, Samborskaya had been attempting since May 24 to have them settled in the southern portion of Tobol'sk Province. On that date, A. S. Lavinsky, Governor-General of Eastern Siberia, wrote to his counterpart in Western Siberia, General Vel'yaminov, to inform him that Samborskaya had petitioned Nicholas through Benkendorf, and that the Emperor had ordered that Lavinsky personally make the choice of settlement.[68] Where precisely, asked Lavinsky, did Vel'yaminov have in mind for the Baron and Baroness Rozen, assuming that Western Siberia would be "suitable"? General Vel'yaminov, it emerged, was thinking of Kurgan, a settlement 2,000 miles closer to Revel' than Chita. So it was settled, slowly, and in triplicate. Of the fifteen prisoners who left Petrovsky Zavod in 1832, only three, Rozen himself, N. I. Lorer, and M. N. Naryshkin, left for Western Siberia. Anna, expecting another child in mid-September, went on ahead to Irkutsk with her second son, the one-year-old Kondratiy. Alexandrine Murav'yova made her a folding travelling chair, Torson, a cloth hammock, Obolensky, a blue cloak for the baby. Rozen was to join her in Irkutsk as soon as possible; but that was not to be until August 1:

My delay had two causes. The Governor-General, Lavinsky, forgot to inform the Commandant at the right moment of my destination. Leparsky did not receive the letter until July 20, but dispatched me that same day; I had waited in prison nine days beyond my term. The second cause of my arrival being postponed was a storm on Lake Baykal. I bade adieu to my comrades and to prison on July 20, 1832, then ... Now, I drove as fast as possible, not halting for a moment. The charms of the River Selenga passed unheeded before my eyes, their beauty lit up now by brilliant daylight, now by the pale moon. My thoughts were far away with my wife and child in Irkutsk, or in the prison I had left so recently, and I hardly saw what passed before me. Instead of going to the Posol'sky Monastery, where boats generally lie in harbour, I drove—on the advice of my companion— along the shore of the Selenga to the little river port of Chertovkino, whence large fishing smacks go to Irkutsk when they descend the river to Baykal. But I had scarcely reached this village when I saw, a verst away, a boat that had just put out; there was no other vessel in the port, so there was only one course open to me—to drive along the bank till I drew level with the boat ...

We drove on and on along the shore, flying over field and lea to catch the vessel up. In half an hour we had reached the next stage, where sailing vessels called. I shouted with all my strength to the helmsman: "Stop! Take me aboard!"

"Will you give me twenty-five roubles?"

"Willingly."

"Give me thirty?"
"All right."
"Thirty-five roubles?"
"Done."
"Forty roubles, then?"
"Anything for a boat at once!"
Two fishermen jumped into a small boat and put off to the shore. My companions and I stepped in. With me I had only a portmanteau, a basket containing some bread, and a bottle of wine which Princess Trubetskaya had given me for the journey. I had had no time to supply myself with any more provisions; but the wind was favourable, and we hoped to cross Baykal within five hours . . .[69]

But the sailors were lethargic and unhurried, and the wind soon dropped away. The day went by. Rozen himself struggled to pull the boat along the bank and out into the open lake, persuading those escorting him to jump out, too, and tug. But he sprained his foot in jumping out. It was a wretched augury:

When I woke up the next morning, I perceived that the river bank was far away. We were on the lake now, with the sail hoisted, but the wind was failing fast; and finally the sails flapped idly and the gaff creaked on the mast, slowly swaying from side to side, coming at last to a complete rest. There we lay . . .
Though I bathed it continually in water, the pain in my foot became intolerable; I had to ask the skipper to demand his payment from my travelling companions. Thus we lay for two days, motionless, in the middle of the lake. On the third day out a storm blew up. The vessel, though secured by an anchor, rocked like a candle moved by an impatient hand. Still the winds were contrary. Every hour my situation was becoming more unbearable. Night and day we tossed upon the waves, while the reflection of the sun over the water and the high winds caused such inflammation of my eyes that I could barely read a few lines at a time from Goethe's *Genius*, which happened to be in my pocket. And to add to all this, I was sea-sick.[70]

At last, as July turned into August, he reached Irkutsk—only to find that his second son was ill. The milk Anna had taken from Petrovsky had turned sour while she had still been travelling, and the child had refused to drink it. She herself now had no milk to give him; and Kondratiy had declined to take rice-water. For Rozen, as for Anna, August was to prove a testing month. His son was sick, his wife nearly exhausted. Time was pressing—if they meant to reach Kurgan and settle there by winter, they must leave at once. However, to depart at once was quite impossible: he must needs wait, and master his emotions. And master his emotions Rozen did, in various extraordinary letters to relations and old friends. Now, when troubles seemed about to rise and swallow him again, he actually struggled to console his friends. Now, when all seemed bleak, he wrote a heartfelt letter to his father, assuring him that all was well with him. If ever coolness had existed between Rozen and his father (and that the two were far from close in Rozen's adolescence there can be no doubt), that coolness had quite vanished when these lines were written in Irkutsk on August 2, 1832:

> Since my reunion with Annette, my dear father, a new existence has begun for me. But you know Annette, and must well appreciate the happiness that she spreads about her as a good wife and a splendid mother. My dear Enny, my patrician son,[71] consoles me greatly with his excellent development in body and in mind; I receive news of him regularly, every eight days. My Atty [Kondratiy— G.B.] is an exceedingly gentle and good child. I do not know what more God will be sending me in the near future, but I do know that the education of my children will be my major occupation and will require a good deal of attention and much preparation. I aspire to no path of glory now: I am dead to society, and my ultimate happiness can only be based on the real happiness of my family. However, do not think, dear father, that I have grown misanthropic towards my neighbours. On the contrary, throughout my time of confinement in the fortress and of wearing irons, in short, throughout my exile, I have—with the aid of Divine Grace—kept a kind and loving heart, which takes a lively interest in all that happens in this world and which rejoices greatly over the prosperity and great deeds of others. Society has lost nothing in me. But if each individual must perform some good for his country, have I not enough fine fellow-countrymen in our blessed Estonia who, in doing their own duty well, may also pay my debt? I stop my pen here, lest I give way to the ardour of my feelings.
>
> To calm you yet more on my account, I must tell you, father, that in the whole time of my separation from you I have lacked nothing whatever; and I may be thankful for having been treated in a humane, civil, and proper manner. For this, I shall always preserve a deeply-felt sense of gratitude. Of all the money sent to me, of all the letters and belongings, not a sou, not a thread or line has been mislaid.
>
> I beg you, my dear father, to write to me from time to time, when your service duties and your feeble eyes permit it. Your letters will be fine gifts for me and for Annette, who esteems you so deeply and who joins with me in assuring you of filial love and respect . . . Covering your hands with tender kisses, I entreat you to believe that a sincere gratitude for all your kindnesses to me, and to my family, will never leave the heart of
>
> your devoted son,
André.[72]

It is to be hoped that Baron Eugen, whose sympathetic interest in his grandson, Yevgeniy, is alluded to ("your kindnesses"), was soothed as Rozen meant by this kind letter. Certainly the writer was himself promptly rewarded for such "filial respect"—by the recovery of his own small son. In Irkutsk, fresh milk was readily available. Anna could travel when he wished. So, gratefully, State convict Rozen sought an interview with General I. B. Tseydler, the Governor of Irkutsk; he was given papers for travel onwards, and a Cossack under-officer, Nechayev, was appointed to accompany him westward.[73] The little party hurried on:

Almost joyfully, despite the new form of imprisonment to which we were now hastening, my wife and child and I continued on our journey to Kurgan. We drove very fast, hurrying in order to reach Kurgan early—it was no less than 4,200 versts from Petrovsky to our new destination, and the unforeseen delay in my departure and the hindrance on Baykal had robbed us of three weeks of the best time of the year. It was August already, and the night frosts had set in. But at least we were now spared the little flies which so torment both man and beast during the short Siberian summer that it is impossible for either to work during the day. I have already described the extraordinary speed of the Siberian horse. We drove on night and day without a stop . . .

The River Yenisey divides Siberia into two parts, east and west. The former part is mountainous, cut up by torrents; all the rivers there are bright and clear. Western Siberia has more plains, and its rivers are muddy; but the soil of both regions is equally productive, except of course in northern, icy regions. The farm produce of Eastern Siberia is disposed of in the mining towns, and China, too, while that of Western Siberia is consumed at home, save for great quantities of tallow, butter, skins, and soap, which are bought by the great merchant houses in Russia . . . There are three and a half million persons in Siberia, not counting the inconsiderable number of Ostyaks, Samoyeds, Tungus, Yakuts, and Buriats . . .[74]

Notwithstanding the speed of the journey, Rozen had attention enough for the farming that he saw around him now. They reached Tobol'sk in early September, but did not linger there. Anna was past her time. In the hamlet of Firstovo, between Tara and Tobol'sk itself, labour pains began. Vasiliy was born in a peasant hut on the morning of September 29. The family drove slowly to Tobol'sk, where Rozen found good lodgings with the regional police chief, Alekseyev. Six days later, they set off once more, passing through Yalutorovsk where two ex-Chita men lived, A. V. Ental'tsev and Baron Tizengauzen. Both men complained of boredom, though the latter had his garden to occupy him. At last, Kurgan came into view:

We had to drive some versts, before reaching the last station on our journey, over deep sands, through a wood, and then across a sweeping plain. At last, the church tower of Kurgan came into sight. The town lies on the left bank of the river and has three long streets, which five others diagonally cross; these are lined on either side with wooden buildings. Kotzebue makes special mention, in his book *The Most Remarkable Year of My Life*, of the one stone building in the place—the court of justice. Having now reached the end of my long journey, I found that the thought of ending my days here as an exile, and of my wife and children passing their entire lives here, made my heart sink within me.[75]

7

KURGAN

August von Kotzebue, the German dramatist, was in his thirties when, as a new citizen of Revel', he met, was patronized by, and became the friend of Baron Fridrikh Rozen. He formed a curious link between Estonia, Kurgan, and A. E. Rozen. The circumstances of his presence in Kurgan, from June to mid-September 1800, were yet stranger. Travelling to Russia with his family, he was seized by the police at the frontier and dispatched immediately to Tobol'sk, and thence on to Kurgan. One of his works had much displeased the Emperor Paul. Four months later, another play having delighted Paul, he was recalled to St Petersburg, showered with honours and appointed, at a handsome salary, Director of the German Theatre in the Russian capital. Shortly after the murder of the Emperor, Kotzebue wrote and published his account of *The Most Remarkable Year of My Life*—a work with which Rozen was perfectly familiar. Kurgan, it is apparent from the playwright's recollections, had changed but little over thirty years. Here is Kotzebue's first impression of it as it was in 1800:

It was 4 p.m. in the afternoon of June 15 when we first caught sight of Kurgan. A single, mean-looking tower projected from a scattered, meaner-looking group of dwellings. The little town lay on the opposite, slightly higher bank of the River Tobol', and was surrounded by bare steppe which everywhere stretched on for several versts to wooded elevations, and which was cut up by a quantity of little reedy lakes. The wet weather contributed nothing towards making the whole aspect smiling. The name Kurgan, which actually signifies "a barrow", had long seemed to me a prophecy of my fate. With troubled breast and sad gaze, I saw lying before me a prospect of sufferings endured and of sufferings to come. Since we were obliged by the inundation of the steppe to approach the small town slowly and by way of ceaseless windings, I had time enough to examine my open grave from all sides.

Below a group of wooden huts, which were all of just one storey, there rose a single stone house, fairly elegantly built—a palace, in this place. I enquired as to the owner, and was told it was a certain Rosen or Rosin, formerly a Vice-Governor of Perm, who held estates in this district. The strange whim of acquiring estates in this desolate neck of the woods did not exactly make me pant to make the man's acquaintance. However, his name sounded so German. At least I could suppose he was of German origin. Besides, that name had been dear to my heart for many years: it reminded me of my good friend Baron Friedrich Rosen and his excellent spouse, my second mother—a noble couple, who had cheered so many of the sad hours of my life, and who called out comfort to me from afar . . .[1]

Here, now, is Rozen's own account. Kotzebue's memory, we see, was still fresh in the district:

We arrived in Kurgan on September 19, 1832. I presented myself to the inspector of police, Lieutenant-Colonel F. I. Burenkevich, and then moved into the house of my comrade, M. A. Nazimov, where I met an old acquaintance, I. F. Fokht. They found me a house on the same day . . .

Our new place of abode presented no remarkable features. The town takes its name from an old castle which stands on a high mound about five versts distant, on which there stood, 140 years ago, a watch-tower surrounded by a deep ditch as a protection against the Kirghiz. Kurgan had 2,000 inhabitants, and one church. I was shown the house where Kotzebue had lived as an exile in the reign of the Emperor Paul, and met many people who recalled him still and who are mentioned in his celebrated works . . .

The best society in Kurgan, I found, had kept entirely to their former habits and way of life till my arrival. The merchants are not rich there—they chiefly trade in foreign money, and as commissioners of wealthy houses. Some of them had built tanyards, soap and tallow boiling houses, on the other side of the Tobol'.[2]

It was, all in all, a dull spot, although not so dull and wretched as Vilyuisk, where M. I. Murav'yov-Apostol' had suffered for some years by 1832, "a place neither a city nor a town, nor yet a village, and where in winter-time the days became so short that it was necessary to sit the whole day through beside a candle".[3] In Kurgan at least the climate was acceptable to Europeans. The Rozens looked around. They found pleasure-loving labourers, "horses in swarms", boring officials (thirteen of them, including the tax-collector and postmaster), several exiles, Tartars, Jews, and gypsies. Moreover, the land was rich in places. There was less tedious company, as well: not only were M. A. Nazimov and Fokht both settled in Kurgan—in March 1833, their terms of labour shortened by two years in honour of the birth of the Grand Duke Mikhail Nikolayevich, N. I. Lorer and M. M. Naryshkin arrived.[4] And V. N. Likharyov was in the area. (After Rozen's time, A. F. von Briggen and I. S. Póvalo-Shveykovsky, too, would settle in Kurgan.) The situation might have been far worse. On December 4, Rozen and Anna and their six-year-old and three-month-old sons moved into another house, which they had purchased for 800 roubles from a district judge newly promoted to Tobol'sk. It was a large, old-fashioned wooden house, with massive Russian stoves, a verandah, and a garden of two acres with a long acacia avenue and birches. They settled down and faced another winter.

What was Rozen like, on arriving in Kurgan? Temperamentally, we know, he was unchanged, still calm and steady and approaching every problem with the method that amused his fellow exiles in Petrovsky Zavod. An indication of his physical appearance is given by a "Record of State Convict Andrey Rozen, Sent to a Settlement on July 20, 1832", drafted by Leparsky and dispatched to Vel'yaminov. "Andrey Yevgen'yevich Rozen, of gentle birth, aged 33," the General read,

> is 2 *arshins*, 9½ *vershki* in height [5′ 10½″—G.B.], pale in the face, with light-brown hair and eyebrows, a nose oblong in outline [!], with blue eyes and a slender waist . . . He is a Lutheran, and knows no crafts; married to Anna Vasil'yevna *née* Malinovskaya, daughter of State Councillor Malinovsky, and with two sons, Yevgeniy and Kondratiy, the latter born in Siberia.[5]

Inevitably, there were minor problems in their new establishment and life: the infant Vasiliy was unwell briefly; Anna's two young maidservants, Yevdokima Krasenkova and Natal'ya Yatsenkova, proved more troublesome than helpful. Both women, serfs from Anna's own Ukrainian estate, had served her cheerfully while in Petrovsky; but now the Rozens would be needing more constructive help with children, house, and land, and neither woman seemingly was able to give physical assistance of the kind that Rozen now judged necessary. Nor did Anna even want their help in dealing with her infant son. She petitioned A. N. Murav'yov, the Governor of Tobol'sk, for permission to return them to her lands in the Ukraine. There were trifling complications. Because the women had departed *from* Eastern Siberia (though they had previously entered it from Russia), the permission of the Governor of Irkutsk, General Tseydler, was required. After a month, permission was received.[6] Murav'yov (who had himself so narrowly escaped the consequences of complicity with the insurgents of 1825–26; condemned by the Supreme Court, he was sent by Nicholas to Irkutsk, without losing nobility or rank, however) informed Vel'yaminov. Vel'yaminov wrote to Benkendorf. Benkendorf warned the Kurgan chief of police to see that neither woman, on departing for the Ukraine, concealed letters on her person. The police chief spoke to Anna on the subject. And, at last, Yevdokima and Natal'ya left for Russia. It was a foretaste of the bureaucratic jungle that the Rozens, and all other recent settlers, would have to cross to accomplish any project in Kurgan. As Mazour remarks so mildly, "Living under the constant watchfulness and petty restrictions of the police, compelled to struggle with poverty, far removed from civilization and the pulse of national life, the Decembrists found political activity very difficult, if not impossible."[7] Rozen, at least, spared not a moment for political activity in 1832–37; there was the problem of survival to be dealt with on a family basis.

Happily, neither he nor Anna missed the social life of a large town. Nonetheless, they found the social round of Kurgan wearisome. Arguments among officials were continual. Great distances, however, made speedy reconciliations necessary; even the loss of one large family was a blow to social life in such a

settlement. And reconciliations, it transpired, took place on major feast-days.
Visiting was then obligatory:

> Everyone in Kurgan celebrates his own name-day and that of every member of his
> family. Two days in advance, the host sends out his invitations: "M.N. greets
> you, and trusts that you will come to breakfast, dinner and tea with your spouse
> on such and such a day." These social reunions are heavy to a degree that can
> hardly be conceived. In the morning, the guests assemble for breakfast; at
> 2 o'clock they return to a well-served dinner; after dinner they drive home to have
> a sleep and in the evening they meet yet again at eight, for tea, dancing, and
> supper, and finally disperse at two in the morning. During the dance, lemonade
> and dried and preserved fruits are handed round. The ladies are very well dressed,
> and possess the most beautiful jewellery—the Urals being so near it is easy to get
> precious stones . . .
>
> Besides their name-days, the officials of Kurgan kept an annual common festival
> on the last Sunday of Carnival Week. On this occasion, an enormous sled appeared
> made of six ordinary peasants' sleds; supports were placed at the four corners,
> made secure on top by laths laid crosswise. In the middle of the cross was a
> horizontal wheel, on which a grimacing harlequin performed antics and made
> faces, while a flag floated over the whole. The officials and musicians sat on
> benches on the platform. Six horses drew this *équipage*, an outrider preceding
> them. At every door, the mistress of the house met them with pancakes and
> with wine . . .[8]

At the height of winter, there were sledge races over the ice of the Tobol',
and in spring the river would be blessed and men plunge through a hole hewn
in the ice; and every Thursday mail arrived, outgoing letters being sent to the
local chief of police, thence to Vel'yaminov, and so eventually to the Third
Department of His Majesty's Own Chancery—and Benkendorf's secret police.

1833 wore on, and a more insidious problem grew apparent for the Rozens
and for other exiles, too: enforced idleness. The Decembrists were forbidden
to find regular employment in anybody's pay. Time hung heavily. Rozen and
Anna studied the elements of medicine, learning that there was one doctor for
each district of 40,000 people in their region of Siberia. They worked their
garden and, "in order to be able to instruct the children", Rozen translated
further passages on economic history by Sismondi. It was fortunate indeed that
their financial situation was now sound: throughout her sojourn in Siberia,
Anna received regular remittances from her conscientious brother, Ivan, who
was managing her lands in the Ukraine, while after his arrival in Kurgan, Rozen
too was sent sufficient funds, now by his ailing father, now by his brother Otto.

Several formal letters from Anna to her brother—letters written not to show
affection or to send home news, but merely to express her approval, as proprietress, of acts performed by him on her behalf in the Ukraine—have happily
survived from the Kurgan period (1832–37). One such letter, dated November 15, 1835, may be given here as representative of the whole group. It was,

as is apparent from the phrasing and whole tone, designed for lawyers' and officials' eyes:

> My dear brother, Ivan Vasil'yevich,
> Having examined the accounts of receipts and expenditure for 1833–34 on my estate in the Province of Slobodsko-Ukraine, hamlet of Stratilatovka, I find them to be quite correct. I am also satisfied that all due to me on this same estate has been performed for the current year, 1835, to which I now bear witness on this inventory. I take this opportunity to thank my dear brother sincerely for his constant solicitude over the management of my estate, which I fully appreciate.
> Anna, Baroness Rozen, *née* Malinovskaya.

The Rozens were, in fact, with the Naryshkins, the wealthiest exiles in Kurgan. By law, a State convict who was a bachelor could receive, from friends or relatives, 300 silver roubles per annum whilst on a settlement, and a married man 600; and these sums were sufficient in Kurgan, where meat cost a kopek a pound and a cart-load of hay 30 kopeks.[9] But the Rozens both received up to 1,000 roubles annually from relatives, as well as handsome extra sums for the restoring of their wooden house, occasional "fine gifts" (as Vel'yaminov's chancery obscurely termed them), and packages of tea, sugar, cloth, candles, and furs.[10] Vel'yaminov, through whose offices all gifts and sums of money sent to exiles in Kurgan must needs pass, might, had he so wished, have made complications monthly for the Rozens. But, as Lorer says, that high official was at heart

> a decent old man. He occupied himself with *la littérature* a good deal, read widely enough, and was in correspondence with the learned Humboldt. But he governed the enormous tract of territory entrusted to him poorly. He informed us that we should be living in Kurgan, that this spot was the Italy of Siberia, grapes ripening and cherries blossoming there, and so forth![11]

The General did not interfere, and the Rozens' capital grew quickly. Finally, in November 1833, Anna was able to complete the purchase of a handsome house from a Collegiate Councillor Ivanov, one of the thirteen local officials. She paid him 2,900 roubles, then spent another 1,500 roubles on repairing and improving her new property (Rozen could not have bought it in his own name). It was, by local standards, a considerable sum. The Rozens lived like gentry in Kurgan, although deprived of titles and political and civil privileges. Other Decembrists, less well shielded by their relatives from need, might find themselves amalgamating necessarily with the peasantry around them. (Some, like Frolov, Falenberg, Mikhail Bestuzhev and Prince Obolensky, would eventually marry peasant girls and establish families in small Siberian settlements.[12]) For the Rozens no necessity arose of mingling with the local peasantry and merchants, or even with the small official class, more than courtesy dictated. Yet, we shall see, they chose to have close dealings with the peasants, as employers and associates—not equals.

Three times in 1834 their house looked out on to great crowds: life in Kurgan was periodically enlivened by enormous fairs, on March 18, October 27, and December 20 each year, to which came traders from afar—Surgut, Tyumen', even Kazan'. The scenes were unlike anything Rozen had witnessed hitherto:

> From early morning until late at night everything was astir, almost every customer being a merchant at the same time, and throughout the ceaseless holiday to which the fair gave rise the streets, so empty usually, would be filled with a gay bustle which often lasted late into the night. Samovars were set up in the streets, around which many buyers clustered; nearby, other groups gathered around wandering musicians who played songs and dances on the accordion. Many men carried their own handiwork about for sale—boots, gloves, wooden vessels, woven baskets, and so forth. One prominent figure was the seller of chamois and reindeer-leather breeches, of which he carried many pairs over his shoulders. Riders and horses swarmed, meantime, on the banks of the Tobol', where Russians, Kirghiz, and Gypsies bargained over little, mettlesome Siberian horses. The answer to a query about the price of a horse was always, "Oh, it'll be two or three sacks." So little gold and silver coinage is there in Siberia that all the currency is in the form either of paper or of copper. The latter is counted out ready in bags of twenty-five roubles . . . After sunset, booths are closed, and the peasants all retire into the neighbouring villages for the night, returning to town at sunrise. Some of them, however, prefer to pass the whole night in the open, lying round a watchfire.[13]

The garden round their house bloomed. The vegetables did well. Translation work was pleasant. But always, Rozen was combating boredom; more physical and mental occupations were required. At last, early in 1835, the opportunity arose to make a formal application to acquire land and to work it seriously: sent to investigate accusations (unfounded) that a Polish officer, Count Moczinsky, was involved in fresh sedition in Siberia, General Musin-Pushkin, of the Emperor's own suite, came to Kurgan and asked that exiles there make known their needs in written form. Rozen at once informed the General that, as far as his own and his wife's needs went, they were amply satisfied by sums of money sent from Russia; but that he had young sons, whose needs were growing greater every year. Might he be given leave to receive a lump sum of 10,000 roubles from relatives with which, in the immediate future, to purchase land in or around Kurgan, either from a landowner or from the Crown—and to build a house on it, and try his hand at stock farming?

Musin-Pushkin carried the request to Benkendorf. Benkendorf enquired of General Sulima, the new replacement for the elderly Vel'yaminov, what his reaction was to the suggestion that the exile Rozen be allowed to purchase land. Sulima saw no problem. But now those trying to help Rozen unwittingly damaged his cause: the 10,000 roubles, it had been arranged by Anna (who would give up her rights to land in the Ukraine), would be sent to her by General-Major V. D. Vol'khovsky, her younger sister's husband and aide-de-camp to the Commander of the Separate (*Otdel'nyy*) Caucasian Corps.[14] Vol'khovsky

12

spoke to the Commander on the subject. The Commander was a very distant relative of Rozen's—General-Adjutant Grigoriy Vladimirovich Rozen. How would it look, the latter asked himself, if he seemed anxious to assist a former prisoner and radical merely because he was a relative and bore the family name? He wrote coolly to the Minister for War, Count A. I. Chernyshev. How did Chernyshev view the matter? Chernyshev, close to Nicholas since his participation in the work of the Committee of Enquiry of 1826, approached the Emperor himself. Nicholas came to an immediate decision. "His Imperial Highness", wrote Chernyshev to Sulima on March 18, 1835,

> has deigned to find it inappropriate that Madame Rozen be allowed to purchase land to the value of 10,000 roubles; for, reckoning by present land costs in Siberia, she would be able for that sum to acquire a vast area, for the working of which she would have to hire outsiders, or to rent out land; and this, giving her the appearance of a landowner of sorts and placing her in the necessity of entering into relations of a kind unfitting to her situation, would be incompatible with the object of the present rules governing State convicts and their wives who follow them into Siberia.

Legally, the decision was a sound one; pragmatically, it was unsatisfactory for, as Nicholas knew well, many exiles were in desperate financial straits. Some lived in areas where prices were far higher than in Kurgan, and had only their 300 roubles per annum—or what was left of it when they had drunk, gambled, or aided peasant families—on which to keep themselves alive. Several depended almost wholly on the generosity of wealthy exiles like the Murav'yovs, Volkonskys, and Trubetskoys; and, as Mikhail Zetlin writes, "the Murav'yovs' mother seems to have spent the greater part of her vast yearly income in helping her sons and their friends".[15] The Trubetskoys and the Volkonskys might live in massive houses, and employ twenty-five servants each during the later 'forties and 'fifties; but others were struggling. Some measure of the hardships undergone by many in the years 1832–35 is the frequency of the appeals addressed by proud men to the government.[16] So, within three months of Rozen's being told that Anna could not purchase an estate, Nicholas ordered that each settler be granted, free, fifteen *desyatins* of land (some forty-two acres) to gain a livelihood. Happily, not all the exiles in Kurgan needed or wished to work their plots. Fokht and Likharyov at once and willingly gave Rozen leave to work their land as if it were his own; so in effect he had more than a hundred acres. Here is Rozen's recollection of that amicable settlement:

> After some months, we each received permission to have fifteen *desyatins* of arable land in the vicinity of the town. A Crown surveyor then came to Kurgan and made the divisions. My field abutted on to Nazimov's plot, as well as on to Lorer's and Fokht's. Naryshkin's and Likharyov's plots were further from the town and contained both pasture and meadowland, which was most fortunate as Naryshkin had ordered some handsome horses and some valuable brood-mares from

Moscow as the basis of a stud. My comrades left me the parcels of land which touched my own to do with as I liked.[17]

The Decembrist farmers fared quite differently one from another. Some men were given land so poor that a ten-year investment of labour brought almost no results.[18] Others were unfamiliar with the tilling of the soil, or lacked the capital and implements with which they might have succeeded. Igel'strom, one of the least successful farmers (and least willing), remarked bitterly: "So I am requested to plough the land! I spent ten years in a military school, ten on military service, and seven in various prisons; the question is, where could I possibly have studied agriculture?"[19]

None, to state the matter briefly, succeeded more completely than did Rozen. Latterly he had experimented with the growing of vegetables, buckwheat, barley, and rye. He had capital. Now, after a decade of imprisonment, he had land, and not a pocket-handkerchief of soil, like the prison kitchen-garden in Chita, but enough from which to make a livelihood. At once, before the summer waned, he put himself to work. Lorer watched him toiling: "Rozen, who was a great agronomist, was highly delighted with his acquisition and, knowing that I did not mean to occupy myself with agriculture, asked me to sell him my parcel of land too. But I let him have it for two pounds of tea!"[20]

Happily indeed, as a result of shrewdness and experience, did matters soon resolve themselves for Rozen. Others, too, had fine ideas: Naryshkin with his stud, Briggen, five years later, with his wheat-fields. But Rozen had both energy and expertise, and all the lessons of the past were turned to good account. The tale of his earlier success is best told by himself:

I began my work on the land in the late spring of 1835. Sixty *desyatins* of arable land gave me a large field for activity. On the town side, my plot was bounded by Boshnyakovskoye Lake; the shore was sandy and saltish and not even grass grew on it. I manured this barren place with a huge quantity of ashes, thrown out over the past several decades by a soap-boiling plant. This operation paid me dividends within two years. It proved necessary to fence off the field lest the town cattle trample it down. (The field was so near our house that one could get to it on foot in fifteen minutes.) My arable land was naturally first-rate: the soil was black, and in the greater part of the district of Kurgan, indeed, not a single stone was to be seen. Such a soil will not bear dressing, but I manured several acres nonetheless, and peas did marvellously well on them. For agricultural implements, I used the so-called two-horse Siberian plough, similar to the Belgian plough in form, and which is very light and most convenient. Following the advice of Teyer, I introduced the extirpator, a roller made of larch-wood, and iron harrows of a special kind. I turned my three-field husbandry into a four-field alternate husbandry. Several experiments answered well; only Himalayan barley and potatoes did so poorly that I barely recovered the seed. It was hard to get people for money in the busy season, as Siberians call the harvest-time; the population is so sparse, and every man is busy on his own field. But one had only to announce in the neighbouring villages that I *invited* a hundred men to help me on a previously fixed day to be sure that all that number, and even too many, would come. Why will these people not agree to come for wages when, in harvest-time, a rouble or more per man is readily given? Because Siberians, once they have seen to their own most pressing needs, love to make merry, and help is for the man who gives a dance. After supper, they would dance to music all night long. Yes, the required number of men, women, and maidens would soon enough assemble, each one bringing holiday clothes and implements as well. From early morning till late in the evening, they would diligently work while my wife was having pies baked, and cabbage-soup and porage made, and preparing a table in the middle of the court-yard. Work stopped at seven in the evening, and the people gathered to the sound of the fiddle and two flutes to wash and dress. Then they would greet the lady of the house, sit down to table, and eat with an appetite ensured by fourteen hours of work. After the meal, dancing would start which lasted almost uninterruptedly until sunrise. To me, it was incomprehensible how they could find the strength for it, for even while the musicians were taking a break there was no halt. The men and women then took it in turn to sing. Brandy and beer were freely handed round; and the girls refreshed themselves with gingerbread and nuts.[21]

The peas and grain-crops flourished in the summer of 1835, and again the next year. But by then, Rozen was not content merely to keep the local cattle from trampling down his crops; he meant to breed his own cattle. The price of corn being too low to make possible any considerable return, cattle would be more profitable and, besides, would keep his family provisioned with fresh meat. Profitable: the word starts to appear with frequency in Rozen's correspondence. No longer, by 1836, was it enough to eat well; the future of his sons depended on a measure of stability, on wealth even, and he must needs increase his capital. The house in which he lived had sadly weakened Anna's own security, for 4,400 roubles could not quickly be recouped. Property prices were rising, to be sure, but only slowly. To grow grains was not the way to become richer. Although there were industrious agricultural workers in the settlements around Kurgan, none were wealthy, for prices were so modest that a peasant always failed to amass capital. Rozen planned his actions carefully. Pea-straw could be used as cattle-fodder.

Cattle-breeding, which is anyway inseparable from farming, would be tolerably profitable. I cultivated peas on a considerable scale, as they were greatly in demand during the fast and pea-straw was also good fodder for horses and cattle. My herds grew rapidly, and with them my income, while my interest in farming was, in addition to all this, a means of restoring me to health. We hired servants and they served us well and faithfully though they were convicts sent from European Russia. My coachman, a very estimable man, was branded. Wages were not high: a man-servant received $1\frac{1}{2}$ silver roubles, a maidservant 80 kopeks per month; but these small sums were sufficient to enable them to dress well . . .[22]

Rozen the capitalist has not drawn the attention of Soviet historians. Yet it was with the bolstering of his family's position in hard currency terms that the

Decembrist was preoccupied during the 'thirties. He succeeded quite beyond his expectations. Other exiles, too, proved highly competent as farmers, stockbreeders, agronomists: one thinks of Matvey Murav'yov-Apostol, of Volkonsky, even of Lunin. But Lunin's undeniable success in Urik, near Irkutsk, in 1837–42 —a success based less on science than endurance and extraordinary will-power— itself provides a fascinating contrast with, and throws into relief, Rozen's more spacious triumphs. In Urik, it is true, the soil was poor and the struggle necessarily more wearisome than in Kurgan, far to the west. But still Lunin's approach, so well reflected in a letter to his sister of May 19, 1838, points up Rozen's greater knowledge of the art and industry of agriculture. Here are the opening lines of Lunin's letter:

> Dearest sister! Here are the results of my farming activities in 1837: calculating what is ordered and sold, and deducting all my expenditures, I have a clear income of 141 roubles 75 kopeks, besides winter wheat, which is promising well. God be praised, there is enough to eat, though last year was in general a poor one for harvests and my first in a settlement. There were many obstacles: the holding back of money, a ban on trips away, and the timidity of the authorities. However, I was spared taxes and *natural weaknesses*; the gains were worth the losses. The truth is, however, that my main obstacles were my studies: Plato and Herodotus do not get on with the harrow and the wooden plough. But what is to be done? The mind demands thought as the body demands sustenance. Still, much has been accomplished in eight months: the soil, boggy, unworked and thorn-choked, has been drained, fenced, and turned into pasture and arable land. In the middle is an English garden with sanded walks, a summer-house, a quantity of flowers, and a kitchen-garden . . .[23]

Lunin's was an unprofessional interest in land. He prided himself on doing all things well, and in fact did many well; but he had little expertise, and learnt (with exemplary speed) from his mistakes, year after year. He lived in moderate comfort with an ageing servant and six borzoi hounds; Herodotus and Plato kept him company while he wrote letters to his sister which were, in effect, disguised political tracts; why should he strain to build up capital? Rozen's was an opposite approach. And Rozen's great success soon proved of benefit to many in Siberia: first, he employed local peasants, and taught them the elements of grain farming; next, he spent his new wealth in the area of Kurgan; finally, on leaving, he gave much of the money he gained from the sale of Anna's house to his needy companions doomed to linger in Siberia.[24] Meanwhile his family expanded and engrossed more of his energy each year. By November 1836 he had four sons, Yevgeniy aged ten, Kondratiy aged five, Vasiliy aged four, and Vladimir aged two, and a two-week-old daughter, Anna, as well. The responsibility was great: he had no choice but to educate his sons himself—sons who would perforce depend on their intelligence and wit, for their nobility and other rights had gone before they had been born. Only the brief annual visit of Governor-General Sulima, and of occasional Lutheran preachers, broke the rhythm of the Rozens' life.

Then, on December 22, 1836—Anna's birthday—occurred the accident that was to cast a shadow over Rozen's life for the next four years: he slipped on ice, and fractured his right leg. The day was freezing cold. He was carrying a dozen little tapers and hurrying to get out of the wind and reach the house, where he planned to decorate a Christmas-tree. He fell on planks coated with ice, only a minute's walk from home:

I collected all my strength and tried to get up. But I had hardly put my right foot to the ground before the leg gave way and I again fell and again lost consciousness. The servants carried me in, and placed me on a sofa; when I came round, I could not move the right leg; the pain in it was so violent that I screamed aloud at every movement while my clothes were being taken off. The district doctor was sent for, but he was away on duty. And when finally he *did* come he said he was no surgeon and could not say what the injury was. The hip was greatly swollen and inflamed: first they put on many leeches, then warm poultices of herbs and linseed, but all was in vain—the pain did not give me a moment's respite. The anxiety of my poor wife and my children may readily be imagined. I was bled for the first time on Christmas Day, and then, in order that I might be strengthened by a little sleep, they gave me opium. But this merely induced a kind of stupor from which I could not be aroused until my strength had considerably decreased. Friendly neighbours came to and fro, advising and suggesting, offering all kinds of herb concoctions; some asserted that the bone itself was broken, others that the bone was drying up. No one had the faintest knowledge of either anatomy or surgery. I lay in bed until April; my whole nervous system was shattered . . .[25]

Week after week he lay in bed, or hobbled around the house on crutches with the aid of servants. The cattle were abandoned. Fields were not overseen. Anna grew sick with agitation, so affecting all the children. But to sit or lie all day proved no less painful, after several months, than to place the leg upon the ground inviting shooting pains. The situation was becoming desperate: Rozen could not leave Kurgan. There was no surgeon in Kurgan. The leg, if broken, was not healing. Weeks passed, and there was no reply from the new Governor of Tobol'sk, Kh. Póvalo-Shveykovsky, to Anna's urgent plea that Rozen be allowed to travel to Tobol'sk for treatment. For some time, she wrote, her husband had been quite unable to control his leg muscles at all; he was in pain both day and night. Póvalo-Shveykovsky punctiliously addressed himself to the Governor-General, forwarding the testimony of the Kurgan district doctor, Malinin, that *he* at least had failed to improve anything. The Governor-General was extremely busy; no reply came for some days. Finally chance brought relief to Rozen in the person of the Grand Duke Alexander, the Tsarevich, who was about to start on an unprecedented tour of Siberia. The father had condemned, the son relieved.

At about four in the morning of June 6, I drove to the house of the district judge, where the Tsarevich was lodging, brought my droshky to a stop in the middle of a dense crowd of people, and hopped on my crutches to the door. The inspector of police came up from a little distance to meet me, and begged me not to put him to the pain of refusing me admittance, as the Governor-General's aide had given strict instructions that none of the State convicts were to be let in . . . I was obliged at length to yield to the good officer's request, and sought the lodging of the staff-officer of gendarmes who was accompanying the Tsarevich; he was a Lieutenant-Colonel Hoffmann. I met him in the street and entreated him to obtain an audience for me. This request he was obliged to refuse, but he expressed himself willing to deliver a petition if I had one drawn up ready. When he heard that I had nothing prepared, he asked me to wait a moment—he would enquire if there was any possibility of my request being granted. [Rozen hoped to ask the Tsarevich to care for his children and wife, should he die—G.B.] While I was waiting for Colonel Hoffmann to return, a stately figure wrapped up in a military cloak came straight to me and said: "You must be Baron Rozen! My friend Krutov made me promise solemnly that, if I came to Kurgan, I would see you and do all I could to help you; would you care to step inside to see me?" The speaker was I. V. Yenokhin, physician to the Tsarevich.[26]

It was an extraordinary piece of fortune: Ivan Yenokhin (1791–1863), who in 1827 had accompanied the Emperor on a tour of European Russia and was now to travel with his son, the future Alexander II, into Siberia, was not merely a skilled practitioner; he had, twelve months before his meeting with Rozen in this small, distant, surgeonless township, published a treatise on the treatment of spinal disorder—*Tractatus de Medulla Spinali*—for which Moscow University had awarded him a doctorate of medicine *cum laude*.[27] Here in Kurgan, where there was no hope of skilled treatment, where centuries had passed without a surgeon's coming on the scene, Rozen happened on an osteopath in the Imperial service, than whom no man in Russia was more eminently qualified to treat him! Yenokhin had army surgeons in the Grand Duke's suite undress the happy exile and place him on a sofa. He himself examined him, and diagnosed part-dislocation of the limb. The ignorance of Malinin had allowed a hurt, of small significance at first, to develop into a real evil, of which the cure would necessarily be long and tedious; so Rozen was politely told, as he dressed again and heard Colonel Hoffmann approaching. Good luck, it seemed, was with him for an hour: Hoffmann conducted him into the house where the Tsarevich was asleep and introduced him to a General-Adjutant Kavelin, aide-de-camp to His Imperial Highness. But here the streak seemed to have ended. An audience, Kavelin told him was impossible. Rozen had no written petition. What was the request? Rozen repeated it. Kavelin advised him to write down his request and hand it to himself before the Mass soon to be celebrated in the town. After the service, the Imperial party would move on. How could Rozen organize his thoughts in thirty minutes? He had no paper. The party would be gone within an hour for, so he heard in the hallway, the object was to reach Zlatoust', more than two hundred versts away, that very day. He stood in indecision, and the minutes passed. But even as he moved he was approached by another courtier who asked him to convey a message from the Counts Grigoriy and Aleksey Konovnitsyn to their sister, Madame Naryshkina, his fellow-exile in Kurgan. Again he made to leave, and this time was delayed one moment by the sight of the Tsarevich himself, who was standing by a window. His expression, Rozen thought, was sympathetic. His thoughts now in confusion, he rushed home, to discover an elaborate gilt carriage by the door. It was V. A. Zhukovsky, tutor to the future Tsar, poet, and a former slight acquaintance of Rozen from the days before his trouble. He was playing with the children.

I told him of my vain attempts to speak to the Tsarevich, and of how General Kavelin had advised me to prepare a petition. "You've no time now," said Zhukovsky; "we're just starting; but rest easy, I shall represent everything to His Imperial Highness. I have been with him daily now for thirteen years, and have long been sure that his heart is in the right place; when he can do a good deed, he does it *de bon coeur*."[28]

Even as Zhukovsky spoke, church bells began to ring; and Rozen learnt that it was the desire of the Tsarevich that "those gentlemen" of whom he had heard much since early childhood, his father's "friends of the fourteenth", should be in church. Only there could he appropriately see them. And so it came about: Rozen was hurried to the church by messengers sent out to him by the local chief of police.

The Tsarevich and his whole suite stood before the high altar; to the right, and by the wall, stood my comrades; to the left, Madame Naryshkina . . . During the service the eyes of the Tsarevich often turned to my unfortunate companions, and tears were glistening in them. I myself failed to arrive at the church in time; but as I was leaving the house with my children, a hurrah, which rent the air, announced the departure of the Grand-Duke—the only guest whose appearance in this place of banishment could have excited either hope or joy. The people exulted in having seen their future Sovereign, and a few trembling old women crossed themselves, saying aloud: "Well, God be thanked that we are still alive!"[29]

Zhukovsky kept his word. On August 8, the exiles in Kurgan learnt that the Grand Duke had dispatched a courier to his father from Zlatoust', twenty-four hours after seeing the Decembrists, requesting that they all be given civil liberty. Returning to the capital himself, the Tsarevich later spent one day in Saratov, where he was introduced to Rozen's youngest brother, Yuliy (Julius), then a major of artillery. Had he a brother in Siberia, the Grand Duke asked? "Then I am happy to tell you," he continued, on hearing the affirmative reply, "that I have seen him. Although he is on crutches, his health may yet be quite restored—and I have already asked the Emperor to mitigate his fate." This was said within the hearing of a dozen officers. Alexander Nikolayevich took a deep interest in the Decembrists, the arch-foes of his father and the enemies of order in the State; and, curiosity apart, it was natural that he should do so. Nicholas had not repeated with his son the mistake which had been earlier committed in his own case: he initiated Alexander early into public life, and obtained a firm, loyal supporter of the autocratic system. Though kind by temperament, as Zhukovsky emphasized to Rozen, Alexander was a true Conservative; and the poet had himself strengthened the Grand Duke's cautious instinct where politics were even half involved. It was impossible that Alexander should, in early manhood, *not* take a great interest in the past, present, and future of the rebels of his childhood—the human fiends cursed by his mother and condemned in Court society for years; now, in 1837, he was mature, and clearer-sighted than his tutor, Zhukovsky. The Decembrists, he saw, had suffered and were suffering considerably; were not dangerous; but could be dangerous politically if they were left to become martyrs. By taking their part, he would himself be acting regally and would in no event embarrass his father, whom he steadily supported. So the courier departed for the capital.

Anna Vasil'yevna, meanwhile, had not been slow to take advantage of Yenokhin's diagnosis to convince the regional authorities that her husband must unfailingly be taken to Tobol'sk for special treatment. On June 6, 1837, Yenokhin made a note of Rozen's condition. It ran as follows:

> Rozen, it is to be presumed from the variety of blow and the attacks which pained him at the start, is suffering from partial dislocation of the leg, forward. The patient's stoop, which began after the fall, and the deviation outwards of the damaged limb from the healthy one (although the extremities of the dislocated bone cannot be felt beneath the femur curve), sufficiently indicate such a dislocation.
>
> Since the dislocation has been neglected, setting should not be undertaken before the patient is prepared for it by means of all manner of warm baths and emollient embrocations on the upper leg, and then by polyspast. An appropriate extraction of the limb's extremity must be occasioned by drawing it out gently until it is level with the healthy limb.[30]

There was no possibility whatever of applying polyspast in Kurgan; nor were there embrocations there, or even fitting saunas. Rozen would *have* to consult a second doctor, in Tobol'sk. But Vel'yaminov and Sulima had departed from Tobol'sk and with them every likelihood of Anna's new request being considered speedily, or even sympathetically. The new Governor-General of Western Siberia, Prince P. D. Gorchakov, though not a hard man, was unwilling to make prompt decisions favouring a woman whom he did not know, and did not wish to know. Another factor, too, entered into the matter: Gorchakov had, in the first days of August, received further instructions from the capital concerning the Decembrists. The way to European Russia for those gentlemen, Nicholas announced on receiving the Tsarevich's appeal that they be freed, could lie only through the Caucasus. Rozen and his family were to depart at once for Georgia. The Caucasus, as Zetlin says,

> was thus to serve the Decembrists as a sort of purgatory. Although to be permitted to fight ferocious Turks or rugged Moslem mountain clans as an ordinary

foot soldier, amidst constant danger and hardship, without much hope of ever regaining their lost commissions, many of them welcomed it, even the aged and infirm, for whom this was in most cases merely an additional hardship. For it offered them some hope, and sometimes even a means—however hazardous—of regaining their cherished freedom . . .[31]

With chilly courtesy, Gorchakov informed Anna that it was impossible for her or Rozen to travel to Tobol'sk. The Imperial order that they leave at once had to be executed; and *immediately* they must leave.[32] Not that Gorchakov did not act properly. He wrote promptly to the Governor of Tobol'sk, to the effect that Rozen could be let into the town only "if Rozen gives evidence of being in such a condition that, without doctoring, he *is unable* to set out on his appointed journey". Yenokhin's work was bearing some results. Now, in August, Rozen could walk well enough over short distances, using his crutches. He informed the Governor of Tobol'sk that he was able to travel to the Caucasus. The reply was swift: he would depart for Tiflis (Tbilisi), via Orenburg, having made arrangements in Kurgan for the sale of his property and distribution of his goods. For little could be taken to the south. Within a week, the sale of the house was well in hand. The heavy carriage in which Anna had arrived from Moscow was inspected and prepared for a second enormous journey; fortunately it had been well made by a German craftsman in Moscow—and now it seemed conceivable that his prediction that she would return in it, as well as leave in it, might be fulfilled.[33] The house was sold, and money distributed to the Rozens' comrades still in Transbaikalia and to local families in straitened circumstances.[34] Horses and stock were sold, too, for a profit. Money was offered to the one Decembrist exile in Kurgan to whom Nicholas's latest mitigating order did not apply—A. F. von Briggen; but Briggen would not take it.[35] At last, on September 6 and with their special escort, a retired lieutenant named Timashev who had risen from the ranks and fought at Austerlitz, the Rozens left Kurgan for ever. All were sombre; many friends were left behind, and the future was uncertain. Now, it seemed, Rozen would have to fight embittered mountain tribesmen on his crutches; and, to make the situation yet more painful, a relation was commanding the Caucasian Corps, the reactionary Baron Grigoriy Vladimirovich Rozen. From him, no warm reception could be expected. As a private soldier, Rozen the Decembrist would be liable to knouting, should his officers or under-officers see fit. Unwilling to meet trouble prematurely, Rozen gave his attention to the countryside around, and to his escort:

He had been made a prisoner at Friedland and carried off to France, whence he went as a volunteer to Spain, besieged Saragossa with the French, and defended himself bravely with his bayonet against Palafox's sword. But in these wanderings he had completely lost his memory, and his recollection now extended only to where the most sparkling beer, the strongest brandy, the finest ham, and sweetest grapes were to be had. A wag, like every Russian veteran, he chatted and argued on every possible occasion. If my little daughter of a few months started to cry, and he heard it from the box, he would ask permission to soothe her with a Spanish ditty; and then, instead of a Bolero, he would howl a Tyrolean song.[36]

The journey was a hard one, notwithstanding such distractions. Rozen could not be comfortable in the carriage. The weather became bleak. As they travelled through the shipping town of Samara, on the Volga, with its "innumerable masts and waters covered with large and small craft",[37] Kondratiy and Vasiliy were both sick. But they hurried on. Rozen's one-year-old daughter Anna cut a tooth. His wife developed migraine. They came into Saratov:

And here, after a separation of twelve years, I again saw my youngest brother. I had heard in an inn that he was quartered with his regiment of artillery in the town, and that he had recently married. I sent at once to let him know that a relation from Revel' had arrived and wished to see him. In thirty minutes I was in the arms of a man whom I should scarcely have recognized as the brother I had left when a boy in the Cadet Corps. But our meeting could only be a hurried one; the advanced season made me hasten on as quickly as was possible.[38]

Julius's military career already promised well. He had fought with distinction in 1828 against the Turks, and would reach the rank of General-Major before retiring, like both Otto and Vladimir, to become a landowner. Regrettably, however, his enemies in actions of 1849 and 1863 would be Hungarian and Polish liberals, not infidels.

From Saratov, the road to Georgia lay through Astrakhan. Anna wished to see her brother in Khar'kov. So, in order to persuade Timashev to agree to such a detour, it was proposed that they inspect the latest Orthodox saint, Mitrofan, in Voronezh. Timashev agreed, and they hurried on to Kamenka, the Malinovsky estate 130 versts from Khar'kov. Their path almost crossed that of Nicholas, travelling south to Tiflis, but the Emperor reached the River Don one day before them, and was gone when they arrived among the Cossacks. Next, as if fated to meet royalty when they had no desire to do so, they came across the massive carriage of the Grand Duchess Yelena Pavlovna, its axles vanishing in mud despite the frantic efforts of "sixteen steaming horses".[39] Two days were spent in Kamenka, later to be Rozen's home, and then on again. But now, on the stretch between Ekaterinograd and Vladikavkaz, the realities of intermittent warfare with the Moslem tribes impinged for the first time on the Estonians from Siberia. Only twice a week did travellers, the mail and army transports leave, with heavy escorts; always there was the possibility of sudden raids. The Rozens' carriage, part of an unwieldy cavalcade, rolled slowly south over the plain of Kabarda—so slowly, after several days, that Rozen could keep up with it on crutches, and preferred to do so since it gave him opportunity to overhear the soldiers and use his leg.

Early in the morning, a train of provision wagons drawn by oxen had been dragged through the town of Ekaterinograd and halted on a plain outside. This was followed by our *équipages*, the carriage of an apothecary, a postilion with letter-bags, a loaded cannon with a burning match, a detachment of infantry, and ten Cossacks galloping up last of all and dividing on either side of the transport. The infantry had sent a vanguard on ahead, and a rear-guard followed; trumpeters gave the signal to move out, and step by step the lengthy train of men and carriages advanced. Half an hour having gone by, the mists which had until then veiled the land started to lift, and a glorious view of the Caucasian mountains burst upon our sight. From the Caspian to the Black Sea, mountains were piled up on the horizon like masses of white cloud and, illuminated by the sun, were glistening like polished crystal, snowy summits alternating with the silvery glaciers, and their colour changing to a dazzling gold and purple. The whole wall of these mountains was broken only by the giant heights of Elbrus and of Kazbek. It was a sight of indescribable grandeur . . .[40]

October gave way to November, and still the exiles travelled south. In Chita or Petrovsky Zavod, or even in Estonia, to journey so late in the year would have been far from pleasant. But here, on the fringes of Georgia, no frosts or snowdrifts gave discomfort; on the contrary, the weather was delectable, the sky invariably blue, and the evenings cool but mellow.[41]

8

ROZEN IN THE CAUCASUS

Caucasia was, in 1837, a troubled area. For decades, Cossacks had been pressing south from the Kuban River, erecting forts and, under the direction of A. P. Yermolov, great military roads. For decades, the Circassians of the plains and the Ossetes and other mountain tribes of the south-east had been resisting Russian arms. Nor had Georgia welcomed Russia open-armed, although the weak Erekle II had placed his country under Russian suzerainty in Catherine's day: in 1803, Queen Mariam had murdered the Russian General Lazarev with a short dagger. As for the Ossetes, "they were forced to toil without payment on the roads and were mercilessly flogged, some dying from their injuries. Others perished from cold in clearing away snow drifts . . ."[1] The tribesmen of the mountains, for their part, knew all about Imperial Russian policy and military rule. "I desire", Yermolov had declared, "that the terror of my name should guard our frontiers more potently than chains of fortresses, and that my word should be for the natives a law more inevitable than death."[2] So there began, in the last part of Alexander's reign, a species of imperialist *jihad* on the Muslim tribesmen of north-eastern Caucasia and, especially, of Daghestan.

Little by little, the Russians overcame the independent Muslim khanates east of Tiflis: Ganja, Shekki, Baku. Steadily, the Lezghians were tamed. In Georgia itself, the national Church was ignominiously suppressed. One Theophilact Rusanov, the officially appointed Exarch, patently "regarded his flock as ignorant barbarians, and did his utmost to replace the Georgian liturgy with Slavonic forms of worship".[3] Opposition was suppressed by force. And in 1820 a Cossack killed the popular Archbishop of Kutaisi. Yet still the Chechens, Ossetes, and other tribes continued to harass the Russian lines. And in the final hours of 1825, assisted by a Persian army, the tribesmen overran whole areas and recaptured Ganja (Elizavetpol').

Yermolov was relieved of his command by the new Emperor, Nicholas. His successor, I. F. Paskevich, defeated the Persian army under Abbas Mirza, taking Yerevan, Nakhichevan, Tabriz.[4] By the Treaty of Turkmanchai (February 1828), Persia was eliminated as a factor in Caucasian politics. But this did not subdue the Muslim mountain tribesmen north of Georgia; on the contrary, it gave them the courage of despair. Cut off now from direct contact with Muslims outside the new frontiers of the Russian Empire, the more warlike tribes viewed the remorseless advance of Russian unbelievers with rage. To the south, perhaps, all had been virtually mastered by Paskevich's successor, G. V. Rozen, by 1835. Very different was the situation in the mountainous terrain of Daghestan. There, travellers continued to go in danger of their lives, as Muslim tribesmen swept down from their fastnesses, attacking baggage-trains, patrols, small garrisons, Christian civilians. Worse still, from General Rozen's viewpoint, was the advent of a leader of stature for those Muslims: Shamyl. This was the Caucasus that Lermontov would know:

> North along the banks of the Valerik—the River of Death—Cossack outposts stretched . . . Here the Cossacks lived and died, raided and were raided. Stretching across the narrow span of the Caucasus, from the Caspian to the Black Sea, was a handful of dusty little garrison towns . . . where water-buffalo snorted in dried-up streams, where bad champagne, tattered packs of cards and easy women were the only distractions for the young Russian officers quartered there . . . Farther to the north, cradled among gigantic peaks, were the newly-built mineral spas where St Petersburg society found all that it interpreted as exoticism and danger.[5]

Exotic life might be for visitors to Pyatigorsk (Besh-tau), Zheleznovodsk, and the other northern spas. For ordinary Russian troops, in 1835–40, the Caucasus meant only heat and thirst, *ennui*, danger and death. And Rozen the Decembrist was to be a common soldier. As such, he might expect to meet, if not Shamyl in person, then his followers.

> Shamyl began his rule by strangling the boy prince of Avaria and throwing his body over a cliff. Early in 1837, his followers inflicted a severe reverse near Gimri on a detachment under General Kluge von Klugenau. In the summer, Baron (Grigoriy Vladimirovich) Rozen decided to send an expedition against Shamyl's headquarters at Ashilta, which the Russians took in the face of the Murids' desperate resistance. A truce was then concluded . . . The Russian governor of Western Georgia, with some 12,000 troops, had joined forces in 1835 with General Vel'yaminov, the commander in northern Caucasia, in an expedition to subdue the Abkhazians and Circassians, and to prevent the Turks from landing arms . . . But in 1836, the Russians proved unable to protect Kislovodsk in North Caucasia from a raid by some eight hundred Circassians, who also attacked the town of Pyatigorsk.[6]

It was, in short, a beautiful but far from tranquil territory through which the Rozens rumbled in their carriage. Not for nothing were provisions for the occupying troops both in Tiflis and in areas to the south and east conveyed to them with caution by armed escorts. But days passed, and no attack by the Circassians or other tribes ever seemed probable to Anna and her family:

> So, on the third day, we reached Ordón, a fortress considerably larger than the previous two. We then went on through Dradaz to Vladikavkaz. About ten versts

from this town we left the escort and wagons behind, and proceeded at a trot. To the left of the road we saw the houses of the so-called "peaceful Circassians", that is, those who had become Russian subjects. I ordered the driver to stop, and went into one of these roadside houses, in which a Circassian farmer was living; his clothes, his boots, his gait, all were essentially Circassian; but his house and his surroundings were, like his furniture, an exact but poor imitation of a Russian farm. The distrust of the Russians for these new subjects of the Emperor was then so great that my companion warned me against entering the house; to calm him down I was obliged to say that I relied upon the courage of the hero of Saragossa.

We left Vladikavkaz on November 6, and journeyed on along the left bank of the broad and peaceful stream of the Terek, penetrating further into the country. The road wound up and down hills all the way, and as we neared the mountains in the evening, a singular spectacle was presented to our eyes: fires without number blazed on every side, now slowly and now briskly, as the wind caught at the flames and drove them down the mountain sides; peasants had set fire to their fields and pastures to cleanse and improve them for the following spring. On the right was this sea of fire, on the left, the foaming Terek, which seethed faster every minute.

But in order to reach the high mountains we were obliged to follow the course of the Terek. Along the left bank of this river, an excellent road takes the traveller into the interior between rocks of giddy height. Beneath us foamed the raging mountain torrent, while above us the rocks seemed so close together that only a streak of sky was visible in the pass of Daryal, where we now found ourselves. Here and there the way was barred by fallen boulders or stopped by sudden twists in the river. After the long sojourn in Siberia, the charm of being thus transported into splendid mountain scenery of a thoroughly southern type was indescribable. In spite of the burning sun, the air we breathed in the defile was cool, aromatic, and invigorating . . .[7]

In Siberia, too, around Baykal, Rozen had passed through mountains; but these were of a size that he had never seen before. Here there were streams and water-falls in every cleft, and the remains of Tartar villages, and every likelihood of minor avalanches beside Kobi, where the road became so dangerous that thirty-six more soldiers were attached to the procession of *calèches*, wagons, carriages, cannon, and carts. In Siberia, the drivers had been certain of the route, having travelled it so many times before; here, south of Kobi and above the Guttagora pass, the whole caravan was lost for several hours in darkness and an unexpected snowfall, while soldiers actually supported the Rozens' carriage by its wheels above a chasm that dropped vertically three feet away from Anna.[8] There was even an adventure (if this was not adventure enough): a chain which soldiers had attached around their waists and to the rear wheels of the Rozen carriage snapped, and it was only with a massive, hour-long effort that they managed to secure the heavy vehicle with ropes. The party reached the River Aragvi, with its "luxuriantly green banks and well-grown trees, around which vines were clinging". It was November 8. So, at last, they came to Tiflis. For the first time, Rozen found himself in an oriental town. Using one crutch, he made his way along the streets, through a bazaar, and, wearily but in good form, presented himself, according to instructions from Prince Gorchakov, to the Commander of the Separate Caucasian Corps, General G. V. Rozen. He went with deep misgivings.

Grigoriy Vladimirovich Rozen (1781–1841), his new superior, enjoyed a double reputation in the Caucasus: of being stern with troops, but a congenial *bon viveur* among his senior officers and aides. A veteran of the Napoleonic Wars, he had commanded a detachment of artillery (seconded to the Special Guards Corps[9] in 1817), when his namesake from Estonia was a schoolboy still —or a cadet, at least. When Andrey Yevgen'yevich had joined the Finland Lifeguards as an ensign, G. V. Rozen was already a General-Adjutant. Attached to the *Litovsky Korpus* (Lithuanian Corps) and the Grand Duke Constantine in Warsaw, in 1827, he had distinguished himself during the troubles four years later and been moved, by way of a reward, to Georgia as Commander of the Separate Caucasian Corps. For five years he had been struggling with indolence, deceit and peculation in the south when Rozen came to Tiflis; for five years he had been watching the movements of the Persians and the Turks in Transcaucasia. He was a shrewd, unsentimental officer of fifty-six, who believed in corporal punishment, regular drill, and target practice.[10] And here was a liberal and rebel whom the Emperor had banished to Siberia—an officer who had been deeply implicated in a flagrant revolt! Well might Rozen the Decembrist have faced the coming interview with apprehension. But the General was not disposed to launch a swift attack on the new private, and the meeting ended civilly. A. E. Rozen had known for some days that he would be attached to a Jäger Regiment, having been told so by his brother-in-law, V. D. Vol'khovsky; the General requested that he leave at once for the head-quarters of that regiment, the Mingrel'sky, then stationed in a village three days' journey to the south, Belyy Klyuch. Again preparations were made. Now, however, there were helping hands: Rozen's sister- and brother-in-law and his eldest son, Yevgeniy, who had travelled to the south and to whom he had to introduce his other sons—a strange and moving ceremony. As General G. V. Rozen's aide, Vol'khovsky was a person of some influence in the town; preparations for the journey to Belyy Klyuch proceeded none too quickly. Three days were given over to family celebrations and to relaxation. The General did not intervene, as well he might have done in view of the instructions received from General-Adjutant A. I. Chernyshev, Minister for War, five months before on June 21:

> State convicts Naryshkin, Lorer, Likharyov, Nazimov, Fokht, and Rozen, all presently in settlements, are to be made privates in the Caucasian Corps, having been appointed to various battalions, under strict surveillance, and in such a way that they discharge normal infantry service, *with no mitigations whatsoever.*[11]

The orders were explicit, and Rozen had no choice but to depart. Four days, however, were enough to form a good impression of Tiflis:

Next day, as soon as I woke up, I walked over to my window and perceived that in Tiflis every face and object has a quite un-European stamp: the houses with flat roofs, Armenians with loaded camels, Georgians with their bullock-carts, the women veiled, the asses with bundles of firewood, the horses with rawhide water-skins on their backs—skins filled with water or Kakhetian wine. Persians led splendid Persian stallions by my windows, gifts from the Shah to the Emperor. The drawn-out sounds of Georgian and Armenian words in which the gutturals, pronounced nasally, were particularly audible, mingled with the lively and abrupt speech of the Russian soldier. There were so few women on the streets that one barely met with one among forty men.

But most of my readers know what a thoroughly oriental town Tiflis is. Until thirty years ago, the Asiatic element predominated. The bazaar and the renowned baths were still on a completely Asiatic plan, and were served only by orientals.[12]

Neither disapproving nor approving, the tone is strictly neutral. Only the interest in novel sights is plain. Rozen was an objective observer of the Georgian scene as it was in 1837–39. He himself, after all, was from a province of the Empire which, like Georgia, spoke a language of its own and held a people of its own. Linguistically and ethnically distinct from Great and Little Russians, as from inhabitants of all the other regions of the Empire, Estonians shared this at least with Georgians, that the Russians were a foreign, conquering nation in their midst. Of course, Rozen saw the absolute political inevitability that Estonia, with its German-speaking aristocracy, remain incorporated in the Russian Empire. Of course Estonian Lutheranism, or, rather, Lutheranism in Estonia, was not to be compared with the beliefs of the non-Christian peoples of the Caucasus. Yet still there were connections between southern and Estonian positions *vis-à-vis* the Russians and their military might. The longer Rozen lived among the Georgians and Circassians, the more he came to sympathize with their claims to separate identity and a fair measure of regional autonomy in cultural, linguistic, and commercial matters. We shall return to this still living issue.

The Rozens visited the oriental baths, sampled *churyak* or Georgian bread and kid roasted on a spit; there was socializing with the Princess Nadezhda Dolgorukaya, *née* Chernysheva and sister to Alexandrine Murav'yova, who lay buried in Petrovsky Zavod; and there was opportunity for Rozen to converse with his first son, Yevgeniy, still in 1837 half a stranger to him. The Mingrel'sky Jägers, however, were not to be ignored. In a thunderstorm, the family departed as a group for the wild regions where Decembrists, including Aleksandr Bestuzhev and A. O. Kornilovich, had already died, some, like the former, at the hands of Muslim tribesmen, others, like Kornilovich, from fever. By leaving when they did, they missed events of great significance in Tiflis: Nicholas arrived, discovered that Prince Alexander Dadiani, General G. V. Rozen's son-in-law, was using troops as smiths, carpenters, and shoemakers, and hiring out his soldiers for non-military purposes, and, at a general parade, he stripped off the Prince's epaulets and ordered his arrest. General Rozen himself shared

13

the disgrace; he was appointed a Senator, and banished to the capital. Vol'khovsky was named chief of a brigade—an effective demotion from his earlier post. Yet many officers had long been hiring troops. Indeed in the opinion of most Russians in the Caucasus the employment of troops by their superiors for services other than military was not merely justifiable, but necessary. The Georgians would not work, and if the customary amenities of life, soft chairs for instance, and prompt service, were not to be forgone by every officer, who else but Russian privates could provide them, for a reasonable payment? The controversy raged, some claiming that the Emperor had no knowledge of conditions in the Caucasus, so was unfit to judge Dadiani (and countless other officers no less to blame than he), others regarding such remarks as jacobinical and dangerous. But in this the Rozens took no part, being in their garrison. Another visitor to Tiflis whom they missed, in October, was the poet M. Yu. Lermontov. Three weeks after their departure, Lermontov met the Decembrists Nazimov, Odoyevsky and Naryshkin in Stavropol'. Traces of the encounter would be visible in "Princess Mary", in *A Hero Of Our Time* (1841), as in the poem "Memories of O[doyevsky]".[13] But in Belyy Klyuch, where two battalions of the Mingrel'sky Jägers were continually quartered while the other four were out on expeditions against hostile mountain tribesmen, Rozen had but little time to spare for either literature or scandal. He had sons to educate.

It was, he quickly saw, a wretched village. Exiles abounded. The regiment itself, in fact, was almost totally made up of men of dubious political beliefs. There were many Poles, participants in the unhappy struggle of 1831, and at night Polish national airs could be heard along the dusty streets. The houses, to be sure, were neat enough: made of split, thin tree-trunks, plastered carefully with mud and later whitewashed, they stood trimly in a row along the main street. But when winds blew they were filled with draughts, for proper glazing and efficient stoves were altogether absent. Among the garrison officers was a former Finland Lifeguards man, Captain Dobrinsky, sent to the area ten years before because of a suspected sympathy with the Decembrists. He was married to a Georgian girl, and cheerfully introduced Rozen to her and to the other officers. Conversation ran on military lines: expeditions, purchases of horses, likely death. Now, having seemed a curse for seven months, Rozen's crutches saved him from all normal service duties, Chernyshev's order notwithstanding, but a fresh embarrassment arose: only on wearing a private soldier's greatcoat was he permitted to take walks outside his house. He was a common trooper with no privileges; yet he was also treated as a gentleman, even by the Divisional Commander, General Frolov, when he came for a review in Belyy Klyuch. Officers in the regiment regarded him with open sympathy; yet it was necessary to keep a weather-eye open for any under-officer in the vicinity, for Rozen must perforce salute. It was a wearisome and awkward business. After a month he ceased to walk abroad, giving his energies to the task of teaching five-year-old Vasiliy to read and six-year-old Kondratiy to write. The local officers talked on. Still he used crutches. But Vol'khovsky and his wife, all unbeknown to him, had been petitioning again. Clearly he would remain a cripple unless given proper treatment, as prescribed by Yenokhin; and in Belyy Klyuch there was no treatment—only illness, and monotony, and claustrophobia induced by a ridiculously heavy greatcoat. The Vol'khovskys wrote to Lieutenant-Colonel Grinfel'd, acting chief of police in the Caucasus (for Rozen, as a suspect under regular surveillance, was the responsibility of the police and, ultimately, of the Third Department). Grinfel'd contacted his immediate chief, who wrote to Benkendorf. Benkendorf, through Chernyshev, sought advice from Nicholas. Still every thread, from the remotest hamlet in Siberia or the Caucasus, led web-like to the bureaucratic centre of the Empire, the army and police, the Emperor himself. Rozen, Nicholas read, was crippled and unable for that reason to perform military duties. Medical attention was required. The Tsar issued instructions to Benkendorf who, on December 16, 1837, sent the following note to Chernyshev:

> Hearing from the acting military chief of police in the Caucasus region, Lieutenant-Colonel of Gendarmes Grinfel'd, of the sickly condition of State convict Rozen, who has been assigned to service duty with the Caucasian Corps and walks only with the aid of crutches, His Imperial Highness deigns to command: Rozen to be quartered in Pyatigorsk, where he will find every facility for treatment.[14]

In Belyy Klyuch, meanwhile, life for the Rozens had been animated by the unexpected arrival of an aunt, Anna Andreyevna. But yet again a family reunion was curtailed. On January 22, 1838, Vol'khovsky sent a courier with the news that the Rozens were to leave for Pyatigorsk. Rozen was seconded to the Third Caucasian Line Battalion. Two days after Benkendorf had written to Chernyshev, informing him that Rozen was to go to Pyatigorsk for treatment, Chernyshev had enquired of General G. V. Rozen, so soon to leave the Caucasus disgraced, precisely to which unit he proposed that Rozen should be sent. "In accordance with the Sovereign's will," replied the General on January 25, "I have appointed Rozen, private of the Mingrel'sky Jägers and former State prisoner, to serve in ... Kislovodsk."[15] There it was, among the sulphur springs, that the Third Line Battalion was quartered. Again the Rozens travelled: through the village of Greek colonists, Tsynskary, through the cultivated lands of German settlers from Württemberg and Baden, back to Tiflis, and so on to Pyatigorsk, centre of the Caucasian mineral water spas:

> Pyatigorsk is the most invigorating and best known of the Caucasian mineral waters. Lying on the left bank of the River Podkumok, the baths every year bring together a number of officers, officials, and soldiers, who come seeking a cure for wounds or the restoration of health broken by overwork. A little way outside the town innumerable sulphur springs of various temperatures (from 21 to 37 degrees Réaumur) issue from a mountain. So full of sulphur are these springs that the air is impregnated with the smell and almost every piece of metal carried round by

people becomes tarnished; the silver epaulets and ornaments of officers who come here annually turn quite yellow after a time, and almost all coins do the same. The regular course is for bathers, who arrive in April, to leave Pyatigorsk in late June and then go to the iron springs of Zheleznovodsk nearby, or to the chalybeate springs of Kislovodsk, or the alkali and soda springs of Sentuki. In this way it is possible to go through a whole course of several different baths in a summer, and thus to complete a cure with no fatigue of travel and at very little cost.

The life that one leads at these Asiatic spas, especially at the romantic heights of Pyatigorsk, is most peculiar. Bathing society is made up of European and Asiatic Caucasian elements; and from the fact that officers of the Caucasian Corps frequently have Circassian features, the Asiatic type seems to a stranger to predominate. Down the broad lime avenues which form the chief promenade of the visitors, conversation can be heard in every kind of language: French, Russian, Polish, Circassian, and occasionally German; here a couple of ladies in the latest Parisian fashions are walking up and down, while a few paces away from them a richly-decorated oriental servant exercises his master's horse. A regimental band acquaints the public with the latest dance music and operatic airs of Western Europe, and once a week the more healthy and robust portion of the community gathers in the great salon of the *Kurhaus* for a fashionable ball . . .[16]

Here, at last, there were splendid medical facilities, and every likelihood that Rozen would be cured. The family consulted several doctors—the town was full of them, in the military hospital, attached to local units, and in private practice. One recommended the Aleksandrovsky spring, set in a cliff-face and with water at 37 degrees. Rozen went, immersed his leg for periods of ten minutes, then lay sweating on a wooden board. After twenty dips, he could just touch the ground with the toes of his right foot. The doctor recommended that he take another twenty dips. He did so, and was afterwards so weak that he could scarcely stand. Anna sought out another doctor, and discovered one Karl Roscher, a native of Stuttgart who had studied medicine at Dorpat, then, lacking all patronage, removed himself to Tara in the Province of Tobol'sk. Roscher was an excellent physician. With him, moreover, Rozen could speak German, and discuss Vel'yaminov, in whose service in Tobol'sk Roscher had been four years before. Roscher called on the Rozens every week.

Spring came, and with it an appreciable increase in the small town's population. Soon there were sights to be observed each morning: officers cavorting on Circassian steeds down narrow boulevards, walkers departing for the slopes of Mount Mashuk. Rozen himself, avoiding other walkers and the likelihood of having to salute—an awkward operation, with a crutch—strolled slowly up the hillsides and visited the so-called Scottish colony, then mostly peopled by industrious Württembergers, with its Lutheran mission. Here, after so many days among the pleasure-loving, talkative, and indolent, he met men whose spartan lives called out to him. Always, Rozen responded to the sight of simple living:

Pastor Lange, a member of the Basle Missionary Society, was a great favourite of mine; he distinguished himself by the successful way in which he combated the excessive brandy drinking which was the main vice in the Scottish colony, and which was much encouraged by the fact that the colonists have the privilege of a distillery. This most excellent man lived in penury, almost in want: despite the high prices prevalent in Caucasia, he received a mere 250 roubles in all as a stipend. Another very interesting person was the missionary Zaremba, a Polish count who had studied at Dorpat and had subsequently given up his property and his position in order to devote himself entirely to missionary work ... The grave faces of these worthy men, who seemed dead to the pleasures of the world and the attractions of ambition, were remarkable.[17]

We hear familiar echoes: Rozen always respected dignified demeanours, whether worn by Buriats or Christians; he viewed unnecessary ornament or luxury with puritan distaste; but here there is another note. These men, he saw admiringly, had cast off all ambition. Their aims were not like most men's; their rewards were not society's. And had not he, too, to grow used to the reality of his position? Certainly there was no chance of *his* ever achieving the ambitions of his childhood. His life was blighted by an unredeemable mistake. How sensible, this being so, to emulate the Lutheran missionary Lange and be dead to worldly vanity. Already, we may note, Rozen had ceased to drink; twelve years had passed since he had touched a playing-card; his needs were small, his appetites controlled. But it was now that the *ideal* of simple living, of devoting mind and body to the welfare of one's family and friends, most forcibly appealed to him. Earlier, in Petrovsky Zavod and in Kurgan, just such an attitude had seemed to him desirable; but then he had had other occupations—farming on a small scale, organizing prison life, translating. Now, this attitude was necessary. He rationalized his situation. He could not be a general, nor even run without some pain. What more fitting to him, then, than to devote his energies to his five children, in the home, avoiding company and all temptations to spend money that he needed or would shortly need? (Yevgeniy was thirteen in 1839; provisions for his further education could not be delayed.) Crippled, with a growing family, far from his native land and with small possibility of ever going back, Rozen had grounds enough to be downcast and withdrawn. But he did not lose heart, although eleven years had passed since he was banished. His was a steady temperament. As it had been an asset to his comrades in Siberia, so now, in 1838–39, it supported and encouraged Anna. As in St Petersburg, Chita, and Petrovsky, he took daily exercise indoors or in a yard. Now, as earlier, he faced each problem logically. Yevgeniy needed to be taught; he taught him all he could. He was required to bring himself before the Commandant, Simborovsky, with regularity; he therefore did so. Rozen was a self-controlled and rational, but not a chilly, father. Let us consider his behaviour on the death of his second daughter, Sof'ya, born on April 3, 1839, and buried on the 13th. It is not the conduct of a man of little feeling:

Towards the end of March, whooping-cough appeared in our town and the environs. The sickness grew so powerful that all my children had a choking cough, and blood flowed from their noses, so that tears were mixed with blood. On April 3, my second daughter, Sof'ya, was born—and on the 10th she was no more; the whooping-cough had reached her, too. Meanwhile my second son, Kondratiy, had such an inflammation on his side that all the efforts of Roscher, who spent hours at a time by his bed, watching him, listening to his breathing, were to no avail. On the 11th, I ordered a grave dug for my daughter; by midnight I had sent to tell the gravediggers to dig another by it for my son. Even a day before the doctor had given him musk, and at 10 o'clock the boy's breathing was barely perceptible. Roscher went off and said not a word. I stood by the bed, leaning on its railing . . . On the 13th, I buried my daughter on the southern slope of Mount Mashuk; from the little grave there could be seen two roads, one leading to Kislovodsk and one to Zheleznovodsk. A few days later I erected a wooden cross above it with an inscription, and four years later I instructed Roscher to replace it with a stone one. We would often go and visit the grave with the children. My son Kondratiy, who had once been dying, grew more lively every day. Pastor Lange had visited us before the crisis of his illness, and I had asked him to pray for our children. "I have already done so," he replied . . .[18]

There were other tribulations to endure before, in January 1839, Rozen heard that, through the agency of General P. Kh. Grabbe whom he had met the previous spring, Benkendorf had been induced to ask the Emperor if State convict Rozen might not be released from "active" service. Then, in the few days before he left the Caucasus, he had to bear the hostile attitude of a new Commander of the Separate Caucasian Corps, General E. A. Golovin. Rozen, Golovin had told Simborovsky the previous July, ought certainly to have been hanged. Knowing that Golovin was to arrive as their Commander in the nearest future, Simborovsky had several times, to Rozen's mild perplexity, urged him to petition Nicholas for a release. Now Golovin had come. Rozen's name was cursed at Staff headquarters in Tiflis. Fourteen years, it seemed, were not enough for a Decembrist to redeem himself; the stain of 1825 was to be borne throughout a lifetime.

Family joys and tribulations can, however, be of only secondary interest to students of Rozen the Estonian in the Caucasus—the German-speaking Balt among Circassian-speaking tribesmen. And perhaps there is no more arresting aspect of Rozen's narrative touching upon his twenty-one-month sojourn in the south than the reflected attitude towards subjected peoples in the Russian Empire. Rozen, it was noted, saw Armenians and Georgians as distinct and national entities, deserving of good treatment by the government, that is, of respect as unities outside the Russian ethnic pale. It is time to consider in more detail his approach to the inherent, age-old problem of the conqueror proposing absolutely to control a conquered people, the problem of ingrained identity or, conversely, of a stalled assimilation. (For that the Georgians or Armenians or Circassians were about to adopt Russian ways, save in externals, or to think or act or even walk like Russians, no one with the least experience of the region could have claimed in 1840; yet the Russians had been present in the Caucasus, in growing force and with a firm, though yet unstated, policy of russification, for a century or more. Would the Caucasus ever become a safe, integral part of the whole Empire, as Estonia seemed to be?)

Rozen, it must be said immediately, failed to find either Georgians or Circassians (with Armenians he had only occasional and fleeting contact) a sympathetic people. They were idle and slovenly, despite their pride; he respected order, they saw no virtue in it; he was abstemious, they either ate the simplest fare or indulged themselves like Buriats. He prided himself on his word, they would deceive each other and, where honour was involved, murder each other. The dagger was the code in Belyy Klyuch, though Russian officers carried a sword. But in practice, Russians killed using a musket—in the bullet, mountaineers and Russians found a common friend. Above all, it was the Georgians' scorn of work that irritated him:

> The children of the soil here looked on any work which they were not obliged to do for their own wants as a disgrace, and gave themselves over to idleness the moment they had procured the necessities of life—which were in general quite easy to obtain; and from this idleness it was impossible to rouse them. The laziness and incapacity of the [Georgian] peasants reaches such a pitch that there are none to be found for ordinary work, even if they are offered splendid wages. Once you are off the great post-roads, for instance, it is impossible to find anyone able to drive! The Georgians journey on horseback and have all their baggage transported by oxen . . .[19]

Here, in the valleys of Caucasia, where there was food enough for everyone without such reckless labour as the German colonists from Württemberg chose to indulge in, work had no intrinsic virtue. Only a foolish man or slave toiled for the sake of toil, or to produce a surplus; between Rozen and the Georgian peasantry, mutual incomprehension reigned. But Rozen had no choice but to be occupied: temperamentally he could not be both idle and content. The very sight of families lying beside a roadside aggravated him; and at the age of thirty-nine he was too old to grow accustomed to a different *Weltanschauung*, a different set of values. *He* at least, one senses in the memoirs that deal briefly with the southern episode, would never let himself rot slowly in the sun. An outsider and a visitor, he looked on and recorded what he saw with an unfailing *akkuratnost'*. In Pyatigorsk, he took a bath in water at 37 degrees; he arrived in Kobi at 12.30 p.m. on November 7, 1837; Belyy Klyuch was 50 versts from Tiflis. Such detail, page after page, is perhaps idiosyncratic; but it is also, in its fashion, reassuring.

The Georgians and Circassians, then, were very different in outlook, dress, and speech, both from himself and from the Russians who controlled them. But the difference, for Rozen, did not automatically involve hostility. The Russians, he observed, were in 1837 highly nervous of the Emperor's new subjects, the so-called peaceful Circassians, and expected insurrection or, at least, outbreaks of arson every day. He himself, despite the protests of his escort, walked unarmed into the house of such a subject and observed what he discovered there; imitation Russian chairs, rich oriental clothing. And Rozen saw no reason to admire the imitation furniture, or the military authorities' attempts to russify the local populace without delay and in all details. So we come to the crux of his attitude towards Caucasian peoples: that their identities, both cultural and linguistic (but neither ethnic nor, of course, political) should be respected. Neither in the short nor in the long term would it *benefit* the Russian Government to do otherwise; for arbitrarily to impose systems of law, administrations, alien codes, on native peoples with no common history with Muscovy and, in the case of the Circassians, with no mutual strategic interests, would almost certainly foment resentment and eventual open conflict with that government. By respecting the identities of Georgians, Circassians, and Armenians (and the first and last were not un-civilized by any stretch of the imagination; indeed, their histories extended far beyond the history of Muscovy), the Russian Government would stimulate good-will, thus rapidly reducing the necessity for ever-watchful garrisons and, by discouraging fraternization between Georgians and Armenians and the Persians or the Turks, actively strengthening its own position in Caucasia. It was the policy of common sense; or so, rather, it seemed to one whose own country, Estonia, had been struggling for many generations—and with some success so far—against the menace to the *Landrat*: Imperial centralization. There can be little doubt that Rozen's personal heritage, as a German-speaking Balt, deeply affected both his attitude towards cultural, linguistic, and ethnic problems in Caucasia and, still more significantly, his attitude towards the Russian Government's (unstated but persistent) policy of swift russification in *all* regions of the Empire, especially those newly won by arms.[20] Because he was a German Balt, in brief, he saw Georgia in a different light from his fellow ex-Siberians, Nazimov, Lorer, Odoyevsky; because he was an exile from Estonia, he inclined to view what later generations would refer to as "the nationalities question" in a light that they could never share, no matter how sincere their federalism, no matter how intense their liberalism. Some Decembrists, to be sure, had from the first seen the necessity of an equitable, logical, and sound federal system that would grant a major measure of autonomy to certain regions of the Empire. To compare their various proposals with the views expressed by Rozen on the subject is to feel the sheer intensity of the latter's anti-centralism.

The best-known expression of a constitutional project in the Northern Society was, in Rozen's early manhood as today, Nikita Murav'yov's plan—a plan inspired directly by the Constitution of the United States of America. The first lines of its introduction, in the first draft, were familiar to Rozen as to all the active members in the north: "The experience of all nations and all ages has demonstrated that autocratic power is ruinous alike for the ruler and the

Cells in the Crownwork Curtain of Peter-and-Paul Fortress

Exterior of the Curtain

DECEMBRISTS IN CHITA
Above: Annenkov (*extreme left*), Lorer (*left*), Baryatinsky (*right*); water-colour by N. P. Repin
Below: Repin, Rozen, Yakushkin, Fonvizin, Obolensky; sketch in Historical Museum, Moscow

The siege of an aoul by Russian troops

The manor-house of
Edise (Ets), as it
appeared in 1972

Rozen as an Arbitrator
of the Peace, *c.* 1862

nation: it corresponds neither to the teachings of the holy faith, nor to the principles of common reason."[21] The arbitrary will of one man could not serve as the foundation of a modern, rationally-ordered State. But, Murav'yov wondered aloud, "What kind of government is appropriate to the Russian people? For small nations are generally prey to neighbours and do not enjoy independence. Populous nations suffer from domestic oppression . . ." Appropriate to the *Russian* people, we observe—not to the peoples of the Empire. The note, once struck, runs through the text of Murav'yov's whole first and second drafts: "the people are the source of sovereign power". Which people? The Russian people, necessarily. It was a striking lapse by one who was, in other ways, extremely sensitive to the essential problems of constructing a new State. Murav'yov always envisaged a federal system, yet failed to pay attention to the fact that Russia's was a multi-national empire.

Very different was the approach to national groups within the Empire of the virtual creator of the Southern Society, Pavel Pestel', whose *Russian Justice*, constantly emended and improved over four years, remained unfinished in 1825. *His* Russia was to be a centralized, unitary State, like revolutionary France. Perhaps because he was himself of German ancestry, had been educated in Germany, and had spent so many years in the Ukraine, Pestel' was, unlike Murav'yov, acutely conscious of the non-Russian nationalities. But his solution was to abolish all distinctive nationalities by merging all inhabitants of "Russia", that is to say, the Empire, into a single culture. Here is an extract from the first chapter of *Russian Justice* in the second draft, a chapter headed, ominously for Estonians and Caucasians alike, "The Right to Nationhood and the Rights of Convenience":

The definition of the borders of a State as large and great as Russia is an important matter. The number of different races who, from east to west and north to south, are subject to the Great Russian nation and annexed to its State, is very great . . . Now, if every State were composed of one nation or race only, its borders would be automatically defined by the area on which its people were settled; but since all great States, and Russia especially, encompass within their borders many different races, it becomes extremely difficult to define the boundaries. This difficulty stems from two contrary desires. Peoples subjected to a great State and of different origins from those of its dominant nation . . . want independence and a separate political existence for themselves: they base themselves on the right to form separate States and call this the *right to nationhood*. On the other hand, every large State strives to secure boundaries which are strong because of their location and natural defences: basing this striving on its right to security, the large State terms it the *right of convenience*. Whether to favour the former or latter right must be decided on the basis of a third consideration: the right to nationhood exists in truth only for those nations which not merely enjoy it, *but can preserve it* . . .

Finland, Estonia, Livonia, White Russia, the Ukraine, the Crimea, Georgia, the entire Caucasus, the lands of the Kirghiz, all the Siberian peoples . . . have never enjoyed and never can enjoy their independence; always they have belonged to Russia itself or, at some time, to Sweden, Denmark, Prussia, Poland, Turkey, Persia, or in general to some great State. And in the future too, such is their weakness, they will never be able to constitute separate States; for this reason, they must . . . for ever relinquish their right to be separate nations.[22]

There follows an elaboration of ideas raised in this passage: Russia's "right" to security should lead her to annex Moldavia and part of Mongolia at once, and permit her to determine the final boundaries between herself and Poland. There is no space here to consider the extraordinary vagueness of Pestel''s concept of Georgian and Crimean history, or the doubtfulness, from both the moral and the legalistic standpoints, of his view that "the right to nationhood exists in truth only for those nations which . . . can preserve it". Suffice it to observe that, far from totally neglecting the whole issue, Pestel' gave detailed though occasionally muddled thought to the problem, inescapable in his opinion, of the wish for independence of whole peoples in the Empire. Not unnaturally, as a disciple of eighteenth-century radical French theorists, he had little patience with the feudal system surviving in the Baltic States:

> The inhabitants of the Provinces of Estonia, Livonia and Courland are divided into two types: the native peoples and the newcomers. The newcomers are Germans, who invaded these lands and divided among themselves the property and persons of the conquered people. The Provisional Supreme Administration pledges, (1) to pay great attention to the condition of the Letts and to the feudal system that has raged so long in Western Europe and has pushed its rotten roots down even here; and (2), to take all measures for the full, definitive eradication of the remainders of feudalism. The present political organization of these Provinces, therefore, must be replaced by the new order which will be established throughout the entire State.[23]

Rozen's class, in other words, was to be stripped of privileges incompatible with (Pestel''s idea of) the rational and equitable Russian State, while the Ests and Letts were to become Russian by adoption. And the language problem, one might ask? Were the Estonians and German Balts alike to be required to speak another, foreign tongue? Pestel' had been dead thirteen years when Rozen left Caucasia for Estonia; had he lived, perhaps he would have given thought to problems inherent in the practical realization of his theory that the Rozens of the world be, if not dispossessed precisely, then treated like the Ests and Letts. Never had Pestel' supported anything, in economic matters, but moderate liberalism; no doubt there would have been a further draft of Section Six, "Concerning the Lettish Race", of *Russian Justice*, had a hangman not deprived him of his own right to independent life on July 13, 1826.

What, then, of Rozen's attitude towards Caucasian autonomy or cultural identity, semi-freedom or oppression? (His attitude towards Estonian national problems will be treated separately.) Here, first, to set the scene for his annoyance both with actual Russian practice and with outlooks of the kind evinced by Murav'yov and Pestel', very different though they were, is his crisp account of the removal, in the winter of 1837, of the Commander-in-Chief of the Separate Caucasian Corps, Baron G. V. Rozen:

In December, a copy of *The Russian Veteran* sent to me by the regimental commander brought me some most unpleasant news: the Commander of the Corps, Baron G. V. Rozen, had been appointed a Senator; neither the place nor the duty were in keeping with his rank, since younger generals than he were members of the State Council. V. D. Vol'khovsky was appointed a brigade commander—also an unsuitable appointment. Both appointments indicated dissatisfaction, or a punishment, and were the consequences of the Emperor's own inspection of the district . . .

Why such sudden disgrace after the greatest trust had been placed in General Rozen? One wonders. However, the system of centralization, the desire to impose the same civil administration and the same judicial system on the various different regions and on subjects of various races, the desire, in short, to introduce a general division of the land into provinces and districts, resulted in the sending of a Senator von Hahn to Tiflis, there to gather all the necessary data on the spot and to draw up a new plan for the area. As usual, the Senator was given private secretaries and special functionaries—people all unfamiliar with the new land— and off they went to write! What they wrote I do not know; I only know that the country was divided into provinces and districts, new officials cropped up everywhere, and judges and district police officers began to pass sentences on the various mountain tribesmen who understood neither the courtroom procedures nor the language. The Senator and his officials could have drawn up such a project in St Petersburg, or in Kostroma, or in their own homes. Involuntarily, such guests in a country remote from the centre of government, and distant from the sovereign power, became the special centre of intrigue.[24]

Here, surely, speaks the citizen of Revel'. Was Rozen in agreement with the officers who thought General Rozen's removal, and Prince Dadiani's worse disgrace, a blot on the Emperor's own record? It seems not: while he saw and appreciated the necessity for soldiers to perform non-military tasks, since local labour was unsatisfactory, he also understood that abuses were too frequent, especially in distant garrisons where there was extra opportunity for peculation and great temptation for the poorer officers to hire out men at very useful wages. Dadiani's fate might serve as a reminder of military regulations to others, and might thus prevent abuses in the future. That Rozen's own interest was less aroused by the General's sorry fate than by the narrow-mindedness of Hahn, however, is apparent. Indeed, the very mention of attempts to foist unified laws and courts, customs and languages, on to non-Russian subjects of the Emperor, here and elsewhere in his writings, brings into Rozen's generally measured, steady prose a quite unusual touch of heat. The folly of treating dogs like cats, Russians like Georgians! Exclamation marks, rare visitors to Rozen's prose, grow prominent during the Dadiani passage, as also in the summing-up to Chapter 15 of the memoirs, "The Caucasian Mineral Waters". In several respects, the sections of his memoirs dealing with the southern sojourn adumbrate the major themes and emphases of Rozen's later writings; here, for the first time, we find obituaries—long, polished accounts of lives of men known personally to Rozen and admired by him. His brother-in-law, V. D. Vol'khovsky, checked in his military career by the rebuke of 1837, died four years later, an embittered man. Midway through his reminiscences of life in Pyatigorsk, Rozen pauses, and provides a balanced, generous, above all, calm assessment of Vol'khovsky's life; it runs to 1,600 words. Two years earlier, in 1839, Prince Aleksandr Odoyevsky had also died. Prompted to do so by his own account of Vol'khovsky's life, Rozen performs the same comradely service for his former friend in exile. And here we come upon a second trait that is later to grow most significant in Rozen's work: the urge, having discussed a fellow-exile, to publish an unknown fragment of poetry or prose by him. A. I. Odoyevsky was essentially, in Rozen's sight, a poet. How more appropriately, then, to honour him in death than to make known one of his poems? So, after a verse fragment by Lermontov and another by the prince himself, we find in Rozen's memoirs all eight verses of Odoyevsky's "Epistle to My Father"—the poem which, perused by Nicholas, had resulted in its author's being sent far earlier than was "required by law" from Siberia to the Caucasus. A third trait later to grow prominent is Rozen's willingness to dwell on the temperaments and interests of other former comrades: in the Caucasus, we read, he met Odoyevsky, M. A. Nazimov, S. I. Krivtsov and N. R. Tsebrikov, Prince V. M. Golitsyn, and the Naryshkins. It was, inevitably, a time of reminiscing. Never would Rozen lose personal contact with Nazimov or, until they died, with N. I. Lorer, D. I. Zavalishin, and Prince E. P. Obolensky (see Chapter 12). Never would he cease to wish to write about his exile and, by doing so, to give a faithful record for posterity of such eventful times; the recorder of Decembrism is much in evidence in Rozen the returning prisoner of 1840.

But it is in his attitude towards the conquered peoples of the Caucasus that Rozen most transparently foretells his own coming preoccupation in Estonia: the problem of identity and national consciousness in a non-Russian people. Let us consider the conclusion of the section of memoirs dealing, first, with the continuing sporadic warfare in the south and, second, with the Russian Government's most fitting attitude towards the conquered peoples:

Farewell, Caucasia! For more than 140 years already, Russian arms have rung in your ravines finally to subject your multi-national dwellers—insignificant in numbers, and wild, but strong in battle and invincible behind the strongholds of inaccessible mountains; otherwise, the Russian bayonet would long ago have completed your conquest. At first, it is true, warfare was not continuous—there were merely forays to the Kuban and the Terek rivers; occasionally the Russians crossed the Caucasus for the defence of Georgians against Persians and the mountain tribes; but for the past fifty years neither men nor funds have been spared, and the Russians had the great advantage that in 1801, by a manifesto from the Emperor Paul, all Georgia was annexed to Russia without conflict, thanks to the will and impotence of the last ruler of Georgia. For many years now Russia has controlled the plains on this side of the Caucasus, and on the far side of the mountains our possessions now extend in Transcaucasia beyond the former boundaries of Persia. But still Caucasia is not ours! Neither the traveller, nor merchants, nor manufacturers yet dare go beyond the lines without a military escort, without danger to both life and property . . .

Who can count all the sacrifices borne by the Government each year, in men and money! These significant sacrifices no longer permit us to draw back from what has been begun; besides, Caucasia will be necessary to us in the future for trade links. Much has been done, but much remains to be done, and not only by force of arms. Many mountain tribesmen have already become naturalized Russians, and are now familiar by the name "peaceful Circassians". These people should be given all possible advantages and privileges, and left their own system of justice and of punishment, not bound by our courts and police officers. The well-being of these conquered mountain tribesmen, and of those who have already become naturalized of their own will, would in a few years bring us more reliable and solid gains than could be guaranteed to us by a hundred thousand troops and by a hundred million roubles.[25]

Such comments have the ring of common sense. To contemporary authority, alas, their justness was by no means obvious. Russia did, indeed, have more than 100,000 troops in Caucasia in 1840, compared with Yermolov's 40,000 thirty years before; obviously, the government believed their presence to be necessary. And had not every Russian commander in the area, from Prince P. D. Tsitsianov to Paskevich, from Zubov to Kotlyarevsky, and Lazarev to G. V. Rozen, found the native populace restless and unreliable? Had not treachery been added to disease and ever-stretched lines of supply to make life for all these generals oppressive? For Rozen, arguments along these lines were retrogressive, backward-looking, wrong; but he was not in a position of authority, and could not hope to influence Golovin. Besides, he had more personal involvements to engage him: on January 10, 1839, he was released from service and granted the Imperial permission to reside as a civilian in his own home, in Estonia if he wished, but under surveillance: Decembrists were Decembrists still in 1839. Where should he live? How should he live? Arrangements had of course to be completed on such matters before, with his large family, he could again set out on a long journey. At last, in early May, all was prepared.

The Rozens travelled via Rostov, on the Don, to Kamenka, there to stay briefly with Vol'khovsky. It was the third time Rozen had seen life in the Ukraine, where the Malinovsky lands were situated; as before, it made a favourable impression. As by the mountains of the Caucasus after Kurgan, so now he was refreshed by the change in scenery. Southern paysages were certainly exotic; but here, in the district of Izyum, there was plenty, and a wonderfully fertile land. Merchants were growing wealthy from the sale of wool in Khar'kov, and of wheat in ports along the Azov shore; for six weeks the sun shone pleasantly and Rozen, with his wife's brother Andrey, went to a large fair in

Izyum. They discussed farming and rebellion: Andrey, suspected of involvement in the insurrection on the Senate Square, had been placed under arrest, then freed, then seized again; now, having fought with honour in the Turkish War of 1828–29 and been a steady landowner for years, he was still under surveillance. Over his life, too, the rebellion of 1825 had cast a lengthy shadow. From him, Rozen learnt how it felt to be under perpetual observation.

The family moved on, through Chuguyev and the military colony founded by Arakcheyev; through Khar'kov, fifth town in the Empire by volume of trade; through the tobacco fields of Chernigov Province; into Pskov, beside Lake Chudskoye, and so to Narva—and Estonia. It was in Kamenka that Rozen had decided to return to Estonia; now, as he approached his "native land", he felt justified in that decision. True, Anna still had rights to a Ukrainian estate with dark, rich soil compared with which that of Mehntack and the surrounding area was poor indeed. But there he felt a visitor, a guest:

Splendid though it had been in Kamenka, still it was necessary to part with our good relatives and from that blessed country. The choice of where to live depended on me; my wife owned a third portion of Kamenka, so why should I prefer to the Ukraine a tiny spot in the north, a flat region, an unfertile, marshy soil, in short, the Province of Estonia? Because that was my own land! There, by the shores of the Varangian Sea, the progeny of sword-bearing knights had long before forgotten the perennial wars and despotism of an earlier age, but had kept their courage, and their word, and their continual striving for true culture. Piety and uprightness are the distinctive traits in their character. And not only love for my fatherland, but also the social system of a free people, lured me back there from afar . . .

Just as soon as we had crossed the Chornaya stream [the eastern boundary of Estonia in 1839—G.B.], we stopped and alighted from our carriages. And the rain ceased, and the clouds dispersed, and the sun began to shine. With tears of joy my wife and children embraced me, and we thanked God; and my youngest son, Vladimir, urged on by his mother, seriously and importantly declaimed Zhukovsky's verses, "O Sacred Fatherland!"[26]

Rapidly they pressed on to Mehntack, where Rozen's brother Otto farmed, arriving on the morning of August 15, 1839. After fourteen years, little had changed there—or so at first it seemed.

9

THE RETURN TO ESTONIA

Otto Rozen had retired from active military service in 1820, having twice been decorated for outstanding bravery at Leipzig. He had married and become the leaseholder of Mehntack, working it in his ageing father's absence; Baron Eugen Octave had lived in Revel' till his death in 1834. In 1839, Otto was a busy man of forty-four, active as a factor for the *Landrat* and, more especially, as a successful grain-farmer. When Rozen had last seen him, he was struggling; now he was tolerably wealthy. He received his brother and his family with warmth and generosity. The ground floor of the manor-house of Mehntack he gave over to their use, while he himself lived overhead or made long journeys in the Province. For some days Rozen absorbed the scenes around him, noting continuity but, often, change in the conditions of the area:

What happiness, what joy to return to my blessed fatherland after my exile! Everything, on both sides of the road, was familiar to me; only in a few places did I observe new manor-houses. After the Siberian and Caucasian mountains, the Vayvar hills no longer struck me as enormous, to be sure, but still they were delightful. And I was happy to meet the Estonian workers: their faces were the same still, but in their dress and gear I found a great change—all was neater and finer. As for my brother Otto, he looked older in the face and was now greying, but in his heart and enterprising nature he remained as I had known him. After many and long wanderings, I was again within those walls where once my cradle stood; the huge stone house had been rebuilt after the fire and internally arranged quite differently by my brother, and offered all the conveniences of modern life. In fifteen years my brother had made himself a wealthy man . . .[1]

The two families lived together in the large stone house, and filled it. Rozen's younger sons made the acquaintance of their cousins, Herman and Konstantin. Also at the table sat a governess, a tutor, a "supervisor", and a secretary; day and night, there was continual movement and unceasing conversation. Outside, the summer blazed. So heavy was the grain harvest and the potato crop, from which Otto made cheap spirits for the capital, that threshing had not finished by the first week of October; the peasants toiled—and drank—unceasingly. Six days after his arrival in Estonia, Rozen, with his wife's sister, had travelled to Revel' to present himself to the Governor, Pavel Benkendorf. On the way, however, they called in at Rozen's married sisters, Varvara and Elizaveta: having seen the Governor, they knew, he would be forbidden to leave his place of residence, wherever that should be, without good cause and special papers. So it proved. Rozen at once returned to Mehntack. But here he soon found it oppressive to be idle while his brother worked. Life was unexceptionable, certainly; but he wanted a place of his own. Otto, who was now rich enough to do so, obliged. Rozen and Anna were installed in a house beside the ruins of Ets Castle, on another small estate owned by his brother. Stove-makers came from Dorpat, house-painters from Revel'; the move was made by January 29, 1840. And here it was a simple matter to go bathing—the Rozens rented a small cottage beside Sakgof, where a cliff dropped sheer down to the Baltic Sea.

Neither pleasure nor activity, however, caused Rozen to neglect Yevgeniy's future. Since the previous October, indeed, he had been settling with the Director of the School of Jurisprudence in St Petersburg that "Enny" (as Anna called her first child) should sit the entrance examination when he was fourteen. Both family and friends approved his plan. "Rozen", wrote I. I. Pushchin to Obolensky on February 28, 1840, "has probably written to you by now; all is going well with him in Estonia. He's shortly sending his eldest son off to the School of Jurisprudence—and doing well in doing so." Rozen had, indeed, written to Obolensky, and wrote to him each month. In May he wrote again to Pushchin in Turinsk. Pushchin passed on the most recent news to Obolensky on June 27: "Rozen has sent me an Easter letter. He's performing on his crutch as a good and solicitous father must, and sending Enny off for an examination at the School of Jurisprudence." Off Yevgeniy went, accompanied by Otto, in July. He brilliantly passed the general examination, was accepted by the School, and seemed destined to become an advocate or Secretary in the Ministry of Justice. (Founded as recently as 1835, the School offered a six-year course "to train noble youth for service in the law". On completing their course, all pupils were required to serve at least six years in a department of the Ministry of Justice.[2]) Enny, however, did not mean to be a lawyer, as his father would discover in due time.

But meanwhile, on the Baltic coast, life wore on pleasantly enough for the whole family. Anna visited relations and was visited in turn; and Rozen's leg continued to improve. The crutch was replaced by a stick. Spring came, and warming breezes:

In Ets, I lived with my family in a large house, and my brother called on us as often as his own affairs permitted. Every evening, the overseers of work and the storehouse keepers would assemble at my place for half an hour, and I would note down all the workers who had toiled that day, marking them off carefully in lists; and I myself controlled all the expenditure and all the income. In this way I taught myself agricultural book-keeping, which afterwards proved very useful to me. I liked it in Ets. When the innkeeper from Mehntack whom I had known from childhood, Lev Belyayev, first visited me there, he said: "You live as if you were in church!" Probably he had in mind the high stone vaults in every room, instead of level ceilings—or perhaps the Christian works and the devout life of my wife, about which there was always talk. Visible from the windows on one side of the house were the church and cemetery where lay my parents' dust, and I would often go there; from another side could be seen the coach-road out to Revel', and from another, the estate and house of my neighbour, Colonel Toll. From the fourth side, beyond a fine fruit garden, could be seen the ruins and the walls with two embrasures of the ancient Castle of Ets, mentioned in all the chronicles of knightly times . . . After a while, I received permission from the Civil Governor, P. Benkendorf, to move to Bol'sháya Sóldina under the pretext of the closeness of the town of Narva, where my wife and children might have their own Orthodox church near at hand. On April 3, 1841 we went there for a house-warming. The postmaster from the Jŏhvi post-office stopped me on the way, and handed me some money for our house in Kurgan, which one of the Poles exiled there had bought.[3]

The decision had been made: pleasant though it was to live beside the ruins of a mediaeval castle (it was his sojourn in Ets that led Rozen to embark on a "sketch" of Estonian history), a move had now to be made in order to find employment, and some gainful occupation. Otto was rich, it was true, and Anna had a modest income; but still Rozen found his indolence intolerable. He would farm. The house at Bol'sháya Sóldina, which Otto had inspected, was in poor repair: the roof leaked and the cattle-yard, stables, and barn were threatening to collapse from negligence. But so much the better: problems could be tackled one by one and would serve to occupy the newcomer. Besides, the soil around the house was fertile, although there was some boggy land as well. A mere five miles from Narva, the estate of Suure Soldina (now covered by a small electric power plant in the suburbs of the modern town) was rather less than half the size of Mehntack, covering 902 *desyatins*. Still, it was large enough for Rozen's most immediate needs. Yet again the family moved.

But no sooner had they done so than Rozen found another, more disturbing problem to be coped with: the peasants on and all round the estate were ruined. For years, the small estate had been controlled by tenants who had totally ignored the needs of the Estonian ex-serfs; in consequence, some families were starving or had struggled with their poverty for years, while others, with more energy or youth, had simply gone—some to Siberia, to form Estonian settlements.[4] Aggravated by the prevalence of old and ageing men in the vicinity, one tenant, with the agreement of a former owner of Bol'sháya Sóldina, had had several families transported to another district and imported "stronger" workers; but these had proved incompetent as traders and had failed to prosper notwithstanding the increasing wealth of Narva. It was as if the last reform, of 1816, had resulted in the gradual destruction of Estonian society in the district. The sound state of affairs at Mehntack, Rozen saw, had blinded him to the reality of peasant life among Estonians at large. In Bol'sháya Sóldina, a bare thirty of 160 inhabitants had a sufficiency, ate well, and worked consistently. The remainder were all landless peasants, or *bobyli*, whose condition was

14

deteriorating yearly. Happily, the area had enjoyed a better harvest than had most parts of Estonia in 1840; no one was actually starving. Still, Rozen saw that nothing had been done to prepare for a harsh winter. He bought horses for two peasant households, and lent money to two others. In vain did he enquire of the local Lutheran clergy if they could not help him in his efforts to alleviate the other peasants' lot: there too, it transpired, the peasants had their problem, for the pastor, though an educated man, was wholly ignorant of Estonian and full of prejudice against the native people. In return, Rozen observed, he met with hatred or aloofness concealed behind false reverence. German pastor and Estonian peasantry lived in two separate worlds. Only in the collecting of his dues (for the man received no salary) did the "church-lord" (*kirikuhärra*) or pastor come into emotional contact with his flock—and then it was a matter of persuading the Estonians, sometimes with the assistance of a senior court official, to part with a proportion of their poultry, firewood, wool, and meat. For Rozen's new Estonian neighbours, church dues were a form of private tax. *Kirikuorjus*, they termed them, or church-slavery. Even a native *köster* or sexton failed to improve the situation in Bol'sháya Sóldina. Rozen was shocked and, though preoccupied with the repair of his own house, which went ahead with an amazing speed thanks to his novel practice of paying off the workers every Saturday, turned his attention to the peasants' plight.

The problem, he perceived, was many-sided; but so by now was his experience of farming, handling men, and of bureaucracy. Hardly could he have had a more perfect opportunity for the enactment of (non-social or political) reforms, and for the introduction of procedures in husbandry and management that had once filled his thoughts in Chita and Kurgan. Liberals had discussed the exploitation of the peasantry at length, in 1821–25. They had developed splendid theories and even plans of action; but here, in Estonia, a Decembrist had the chance to *act*, not merely talk. Few others had that opportunity. In Siberia, Decembrists who proposed to farm, like Volkonsky, certainly found a peasantry with problems; but *their* problems, stemming for the most part from imported, dull, and ignorant officials, were eminently soluble compared with those of the Estonian landless peasant. Again, those who would settle in the south and west of European Russia, a dozen Decembrists at least, would have ample opportunity to assist the local peasantry; but there, the soil would generally prove good—not boggy, or flint-filled, or sandy, as in north-eastern Estonia—and the peasants, grave and complex though their problems would remain even during the 'seventies, would at least not face a cool, rapacious clergy of the kind reviled (in vain) by such Estonian Liberals as Himmelstierna and Hamilkar von Fölkersahm in the late 'thirties and 'forties.[5] And here was the crux of the matter: general amnesty *would be* announced for the Decembrists in 1856; those Decembrists with the energy to do so, who were not too tired or sick to leave the circle of their families, *would be* old men with few years left to undertake new projects for reform. Several, admittedly, would do so—N. V. Basargin in Vladimir Province, I. V. Kireyev in Tula, Obolensky in Kaluga;

a handful would be active still, like Rozen, Matvey Murav'yov-Apostol and Nazimov, in the 1880s.[6] But by 1856 emancipation would be near, and the problems of the peasantries of Russia and the Baltic lands alike entirely different from those of 1840. For Rozen, opportunity was knocking to exemplify his notions in his actions; the Estonian peasantry needed his help and he could give it, always granted his constrained political and social situation, now. Within his limits, in his own domain, he could influence the gentry of the neighbourhood, his relatives and children, and clergy who depended on his brother, to be reasonable and honest in their dealings with the native population. He resolved to do so. Tempered by his experience, altered by years of exile, his liberal, humane, above all common-sensical approach towards the problem that had troubled him in early manhood, twenty years before, was about to bear results. The problem was, of course, serfdom and its removal. The results would soon be felt where he was born.

What, then, had caused the peasants' present state of wretchedness? Rozen asked himself the question; we must follow his example. The problem, it was clear, was not of recent origin, but had been festering unchecked since he himself had last been in Estonia. Here, to introduce the major themes (incomprehension of the leasehold-based agrarian economy and the collapse of the age-old manorial system), is Professor Nodel's summary of the rural situation in Estonia in 1840, when Rozen came to Ets:

The disappointing outcome of the agrarian laws of 1816–19 was due to the manorial labour which followed. During the 1830s and 1840s, this manorial labour system greatly hampered the development of a stronger peasant economy which had been the original intention of the liberal nobles. Though the Estonian peasant could now leave his community, the rigid guild laws in the cities stopped him from entering the crafts. In order to stimulate the peasant to work harder and improve his land, liberal-minded landlords proposed abolishing the manorial system and substituting for it monetary rents. But this idea did not find immediate support among the landlords, who feared losing their grip on the peasants. Nor did it find immediate support among the peasants, since the latter, used to century-old manorial labour, saw in every new order another trick by the landlords to keep them in bondage. However, after Baron Theodor Hahn-Postenden first introduced monetary rent on his Courland estate in 1839, squires in all the Baltic Provinces followed, slowly but steadily.

It took more than twenty years to change from the manorial to the rental system in Estonia and northern Livonia. During this time conditions in the Estonian area changed very much. The great majority of the peasants did not own their land, but rented it. Those of them who paid in money obtained it by cultivating flax, which impoverished their soil. Since they did not own the soil, they cared nothing about its preservation; and though they cultivated sixteen times more land than the German landlords, they produced only twice the amount of major products— a fact which indicates the low standard of their life and tools. How did the Baltic nobles look upon the emancipation of the Estonian peasants under the rental system? Most of them accepted it as a necessary evil and, with the exception of a more liberal minority, the nobility looked upon the rental system as sufficient reform for future generations.[7]

How ironical that a Baron Hahn—cousin to the Senator in Tiflis who annoyed Rozen so much in the same year—should in 1839 have introduced monetary rent to the Baltic area! There are several salient points here: the fact of the Estonians' mistrust of all reform begun by German landlords; the fact of agricultural inefficiency; the landowners' unwillingness to lose control over the native peasantry. As Nodel says, matters were bad for the Estonians, many of whom had, in the early 'forties, not yet adapted to the changed conditions introduced by the abolition of serfdom a generation earlier. Still thousands held that, if they had a farm or plot (whether on long lease or by hereditary tenure), they controlled that land; but now, it seemed, they could be banished from their "own" land at the landlord's will. That being so, most peasants in the area of Narva had asked for short leases, of two or three years at the most, and exploited the land to the utmost for that period. The land grew less productive year by year, of course, but that had small significance. What mattered was to make prompt, regular payments, to fight off the landlord's efforts to increase one's burden in dues or, occasionally, labour. Some peasants, armed with passports and new surnames (one whole estate of peasant families had been given names of characters in Scott's Waverley novels), might go off to seek a better life; but most remained perforce and, in some areas, continued to be human beasts of burden. Now, in the 'forties, German landlords recognized no obligations to the peasantry surrounding them, yet still exercised various rights. Now, nothing stood between the peasants and starvation in late winter, when stocks were running down. Children died by dozens every March, when scarlet fever struck and when resistances were low.[8] And the Russian treasury demanded a poll-tax of 4·6 roubles for each non-noble man and male child. And year by year, the military authorities arrived to seize Estonian peasants, shave them, give them uniforms, and take them for a period of twenty-five years. Should they ever return to the village of their birth, they would be forgotten strangers. (Soldiers were drawn by lot from each estate from able-bodied men between the ages of twenty and thirty-five; once chosen, a peasant knew that his sons, too, would be at the disposal of the army.)

The Estonians suffered at the hands of the Imperial Government. Most of their anger was reserved, however, for the German nobles in their midst. Indeed, the peasants often viewed Russia as a kind of promised land, and Nicholas as a *grand seigneur* under whose rule they could live in peace and plenty, could they only rid themselves of German landlords. The Orthodox peasants of Russia, some were told, were all allowed to own a piece of land: their faith gave them that right. The rumour would bear bitter fruit (see Chapter 10).

So, hoping to find land in Russia, landless peasants left Estonian estates. Many returned dissatisfied, but restlessness continued in the villages. In the

1830s, many turned to small trade in the country; hundreds became wandering tradesmen, petty merchants, tinkers. They sold goods on credit to their fellow-countrymen, having bought them cheaper in a town. Extended credit sometimes led to ruin for these peasant-traders, but more commonly they flourished, and annoyed the German merchants in the towns. Some even became wealthy, paid their debts to former masters, and departed from their villages for ever, so avoiding certain taxes, likely military impressment, and the need to tug their forelock to a landlord.[9]

These, then, were some facets of the peasant problem in Estonia confronting Rozen. But while pondering on various lines of action, Rozen was not idle: in the summer of 1841 he supervised the building of a bath-house, servants' hall, stable, cellar, new cattle-yard, and better barn. Anna had given birth to her fifth and last son, Andrey, on May 7, and was much preoccupied with him, seldom leaving the house. Another winter came and went; and in April 1842 Rozen was informed that he and Anna were required to appear before the Civil Governor on April 16, the day of the Tsarevich's marriage, to hear a new Imperial pardon proclaimed; he was to regain his lost rights of nobility. Anna was ill and Rozen himself was feeling weak on the appointed day; but he travelled to Revel' nonetheless, and there met the new Governor, I. E. Grinval'd. Grinval'd showed him the text of the decree of pardon: Rozen's sons were to attend State colleges or schools and, *if* they behaved satisfactorily in them and studied well, were to be given noble rank. In that event, however, they were not to use their father's surname, but should use their patronymic as a surname.[10] Rozen was shocked, then enraged. He could not know that the same stipulation was applied to the children of Decembrists everywhere: in Siberia, Prince Volkonsky's children were supposedly to be renamed Sergeyev, Nikita Murav'yov's—Nikitin. But even had he known, the situation would have been as horrible. No one Decembrist, one suspects on reading letters of the period, was more deeply or painfully affected by the terms of Nicholas's "pardon" of March 28, 1842 than Rozen. What, he demanded of himself, was a man if not the guardian of his forebears' name? Where did the fruits of honour lie if not in honourable names? And what more precious thing could a man pass on to sons? It was horrible:

Having returned to the hotel, I placed the paper and some quills on a table and once more read the fateful missive, or proposal, or condition, or sentence, or temptation, or . . . I dipped a quill in ink, but could write nothing. I did not feel well. For a long time I paced the room, knowing what to write about, but not knowing how to write it. The most powerful monarch in the world makes a proposal to a private soldier, wishing to benefit him, but the private takes the good deed as a disgrace and the cruellest of punishments. I admit, I was insulted, I was outraged, and still I paced the room. Suddenly I heard a single drawn-out note, a chime from the cathedral belfry; a few minutes later there were two chimes, a quarter of an hour later, three; and I remembered that in Orthodox churches they were reading the twelve lessons on the sufferings of Jesus Christ. It was the day before Good Friday. My thoughts tore themselves away from earthly matters and passions, from the insults and the injuries of this life ...

For me, and probably for any man of common sense, it was incomprehensible, this mania, this absurdity of taking away a family name, one's patrimonial property. Could there be any benefit to the Sovereign, or to society, or to the State, in doing so? Was it the intention to wound the father or the children or posterity? But that would contradict the manifesto published after our conviction, in which the Emperor announced that no one should presume to blame a kinsman for a kinsman's crime. But if this was being done without forethought, then was it worth even thinking about? And if I took it as personal vengeance, what relationship could there exist between me and the most powerful autocrat?[11]

Rozen was affronted and bemused. Of course there was no question of agreeing to the terms. Faster than the exiles in Siberia, all of whom, after discussion and fully realizing that they would most certainly be charged with egoism, wrote letters declining Nicholas's terms, Rozen declined on behalf of all his sons. In Russia only illegitimate children were given surnames derived from their patronymics: and were his children, the descendants of Teutonic Knights, to be classed with these? The notion was outrageous and incomprehensible. Again Rozen turned the question over in his mind. What possible motive could Nicholas have had in issuing such an affronting decree? In vain Grinval'd assured him that his sons would understand, in later years, that he had acted for their own good in renaming them. More than anything that he had done in 1826, this decree of "clemency" regarding the Decembrists' children and their upbringing earned Nicholas the scorn of Baron Rozen. The wound was deep and lasting. However, something practical had to be done, and Benkendorf expected a reply. If Yevgeniy, Rozen's eldest son, were to enter a State institution, as he himself had done, he would effectively be taken from his parents; only at Christmas, Easter, and for brief summer vacations would he visit them. Was he now to be sent off to the capital or to some other town where his father's very name might do him harm, and where he might be mocked by fellow-pupils? Distressed by such a thought, Rozen applied to Benkendorf for permission to keep Yevgeniy with him, and to educate him personally: also to allow his sons to bear his ancient name. Grinval'd sent the letter on. Rozen returned to Bol'sháya Sóldina. After a month, Benkendorf replied. The Emperor had "deigned to command that Rozen's four young sons remain with him until they reach the age of fourteen."[12] On the question of the surname, not a word. Rozen brooded on the silence; could he *tolerate* such a disastrous situation? He must protest. He must point out that Rozens had been faithful servants of Ivan III two centuries before Estonia had been annexed by Russia; and that statesmen of the present day, Count Osterman and Prince A. Menshikov, for instance, were descendants of men once banished and disgraced; and that all the many exiles of the reign of Catherine had kept their family names, no matter what their faults. Driven to act by his vexation, Rozen mentioned all these points in a letter to the Grand Duke Alexander, the

Tsarevich, who had previously helped him. He wrote at length, and with unwonted heat. But protest was in vain: on June 26, a copy of a letter to General Yur'yevich from Benkendorf reached him from Grinval'd's private chancery. Benkendorf had seen Rozen's appeal to the Tsarevich. In his view, and that of Count Bludov and of Count Panin, Minister of Justice, it was right that sons of State convicts attending military schools should not bear their fathers' tainted names; moreover, the Emperor's decision had been taken long before, was firm, and could not now be questioned. There was nothing to be done. Prudent, after this rash correspondence with the Third Department and the future Tsar, Rozen decided to say nothing more, but to await events. Meanwhile he would continue with his children's education.

Continue he did, with great thoroughness and regularity; and it was now, with four small pupils in his charge, that he began to take an active interest in the theory and practice of teaching. His younger sons were to be officers: that much was obvious. How plain, therefore, that they should not receive a wholly academic training, but should be educated as if they were already in a military school. He would need help. There was in the neighbourhood a section of a regiment of Grenadiers, Friedrich Wilhelm III's Own Regiment. He asked one of the under-officers if he would care to teach his elder sons the elements of marksmanship and drill. The man agreed. He himself would teach them Latin, French and German, whilst Anna taught them English. And they would spend some time each day outside, learning the rudiments of farming. Once having formed a general plan, Rozen adhered to it. Month after month he taught his sons, including Yevgeniy, his eldest, paying attention to their physical development as well as to their intellectual and moral training.[13] He himself enjoyed the challenge; but how did the maturest of the four recipients of this systematic daily training feel about it? Yevgeniy, after all, was entering his nineteenth year in 1844—a time of life when discipline of any kind can seem outrageous. Yevgeniy found the endless intellectual tasks imposed upon him by his father burdensome: so much we can infer from the increasing openness and frequency of disagreement between Rozen and his first son on the question of careers.

Not that Yevgeniy's future seemed unpromising in 1844, given his past. On the contrary, it appeared likely that he would manage very well in the Novgorod Battalion's military *cantonistes*, to which, he was informed by Perovsky, Minister of Internal Affairs, he would shortly be attached. It was merely that he lacked his father's steadiness of purpose. Earlier, we saw, it had been planned that he should enter the School of Jurisprudence in St Petersburg. That he had not, in the event, studied the law could not be held to be his fault; yet, to his father, his failure to have done so was, in some obscure way, rankling. Rozen did not care for altered plans. And with Yevgeniy, plans were ever being changed and modified. Never, however, had Rozen had occasion to imagine that his son would hesitate to enter on a *military* career: since he was ten, Yevgeniy had idealized the life of the Uhlans. But hesitate he did, at the last moment.

For Rozen, who abhorred all fickleness, such conduct was unbearable. His own son not only did not know his mind but was deficient in that greatest of all Rozen qualities—self-discipline. Little allowance could he make, given his own past, for Yevgeniy's youthfulness. True, the boy was not yet twenty; but when *he* was twenty, he had been an ensign charged with regimental duties and no small responsibility. Yevgeniy had responsibilities to his family alone, that was, to Rozen and to Anna; how well he would discharge them would be seen. Rozen's expectations of his eldest son were great.

Not waiting for his son's doubts to grow stronger, he struck a swift blow for tradition and for discipline. All the world, he emphasized in private to Yevgeniy, thought poorly of the youth who was a butterfly. (What he meant, of course, was that he personally thought changeability a sorry quality in junior officers.) Nothing, he stressed, was to be gained by always changing one's intentions or ambitions (nothing, more specifically, in military service). He spoke, not with Yevgeniy, but at him. He insisted that he serve, and long enough to reach the rank of ensign (with which rank, he probably tried not to recollect too often, so painful was the thought, Yevgeniy would have started his career—had it not been for him). Ensigns, after all, could honourably retire as officers; and no Rozen had in seven hundred years ever retired in any other way. Yevgeniy would become an officer: it was important. Under pressure, Yevgeniy acquiesced. So began, in 1844, the time of most unnecessary, most predictable and open tension between Rozen and his eldest son—a son whom, partially in consequence of their long separation in the early, vital years, but more especially because of his own failure to communicate with one so very different from himself, he had failed to come to know. Yevgeniy was a semi-stranger still in 1845. His strengths and weaknesses alike remained half hidden from his father's eyes. The fact was in itself a source of tension.

Very soon Yevgeniy found that all his doubts as to the suitability of army life for him had good foundations. In barracks, life was dull indeed. Week followed week with horrible monotony. His father would, he knew, have borne the challenge patiently, perhaps even enjoyed the regularity. His father would have found a way of drawing the attention of the military authorities towards his own skills. His father . . . But Yevgeniy was not Andrey, and the thought of serving several wretched years merely to reach a rank that was itself inferior, oppressed him like a prospect of imprisonment. Why should he waste his youth to reach the rank of ensign? There were other things in life, no doubt, if he could only find them. He must break his bonds, purchase his freedom. But in any walk of life, his surname would, together with his patronymic, be a heavy liability. The son of Andrey Rozen, convict, criminal, would dog his steps. So, animated by the dazzling idea of change, no longer thinking systematically, he reached a decision: he would change his name or, at the least, employ another name from time to time, to gain new freedom. Glorious his father's name might be, but it was also a great burden. As an aspect of the history of Decembrism, such consciousness of the *unfairness* of their fates among children of Decembrists has been sorrily neglected, and deserves more detailed study. Most felt pride, of course, and feelings of their own separateness. But separateness had its disadvantages, for, as Riverol has said, *qui s'élève s'isole*. To Yevgeniy, as to other sons of exiles, a paternal sense of honour seemed a heavy load to bear.

Having come to the decision, he resolved to act at once. To change his name, it struck him, would have various delightful consequences: he could be another person and do things that earlier, and now especially, were quite impossible. For instance, he could act in plays. He liked the theatre just as much as Rozen scorned it (as unsuitable for the nobility). Again, the Emperor would certainly approve of such an action. His career might even benefit from it. In short, it would be prudent to assume another name, make a fresh start, throw off his father's shadow. His father would be grieved. But he would surely see the desirable results that might follow such a change, and the soundness of his own filial motives, when the situation was explained to him in full. Yevgeniy became positively gay, carried away by the prospect of release from barrack duties. Soon, he ceased to question the advisability of taking such a step; he presupposed his father's acquiescence, even pleasure at his common-sensical approach.

But how best could he present his new persona to the world, and give evidence of freedom? His unit was, in April 1845, stationed near Oryol, in central Russia. He decided, either with permission from his military superiors or, what seems probable, without it, to remove himself from camp and spend a few days in the town. We do not know exactly what he did, having arrived there. Apparently he took some part in a dramatic, even comical, performance. He did not use his own name, but devised another for the hour and circumstances— Karlushka, or Little Karl. He enjoyed himself. But retribution was at hand; his father came to hear of his performance in Oryol. That a Rozen could behave in such a histrionic, uncontrolled, and shameful way!

What correspondence passed between Yevgeniy and his father on the subject of a stage career, or any other future way of life, we do not know. Most probably something was said, perhaps in anger, in the days immediately following the Karlushka adventure: so much we may infer from the few letters of the period that survive. One letter in particular throws fascinating light both on the incident itself and on the strain in the relationship between Rozen and his son. It is to be regretted that the letter from Yevgeniy to his father which provoked the outburst given in entirety below, has not survived. Rozen's response to what appeared to him a sorry and disgraceful situation is, however, of the greatest clarity:

My son! I do not know how otherwise to call you. Whosoever *voluntarily* disowns his father's name is an apostate. Whosoever breaks his given word is a scoundrel. For what reason do you persecute me, poisoning my life? Your actions in Oryol can by no means be excused by your insanity, as you yourself now claim. You knew my way of thinking; you knew that I can honour every calling, even that of an actor. I begged you, I ordered you to serve until you reach the rank of officer, in order to give you more time and more maturity to reflect on your intention; only when you had achieved that rank would I have left your choice of field to you. You gave me your word—I organized everything in accordance with that fact; and you basely broke your word. You have acted like a little child who, shutting his eyes during the day, believes himself in darkness and supposes no one sees him.

In our State, the police are strict; everywhere people of dubious appearance, like tramps, are apprehended. Consequently, in Oryol they knew of your identity, and the Oryol public knows who Karlushka was. Thus your action was a public one—even little Narva knows about it. But that action can in no way blemish any other Rozen but yourself; of that, you have the best and most manifold proof in the fact that my State crime in no way affected you. Setting aside considerations as to duty or propriety or honour (of which you have none), only tell me: could your conduct be consoling or pleasant for me? Why do you insult me and persecute me when even ill-wishers did not persecute me or insult me when I was a convict and in chains? With Christian humility I bore my burden, but you, Enny, are placing an intolerable load on me. Apparently you have not read my letters to you, which you received at Aleksandr Ivanovich's. Otherwise you would be caring for me, you know for whose sake.

What more am I to write to you when you disregard my advice and do not even keep your word? In your letter, you show not openness but insolent raillery in writing, "if you do not wish this, my duty is to execute your will". You knew and *know* what I desire from you. In your letter as in your conduct there is neither common sense nor logic.

1. It is better to sit on a stable-roof, by way of service, then just to play the buffoon.

2. A player in his motley rags risks his health more, in winter-time, than a private soldier who is warmly dressed.

3. Do you really think a player who is coarse will not be dragged to the police and beaten with a whip or fists to boot?

You say you have a strange character—you have no character, because for two years in a row now you have been behaving like a schoolboy, unaccountable in words and actions. You are simply crammed full of futility and folly; you yourself do not know what you are doing. I tell you the truth, my son: the man who so impertinently, insolently tramples under foot those blessings with which you have been born (and which all the worthiest people seek to attain with industry and toil), that man assumes an infinite responsibility before people and before his God. To joke about this is impossible: turn back while there is time. For while castigating your behaviour, I do not condemn you or disown you, as you repudiated me. The Apostle Peter disavowed his Lord, but was exonerated. Exonerate yourself, give me your hand, and do not snatch away my last strength, which the family still needs.

Your father,
A. Rozen.

Tournez le fausse nom que vous vous êtes donné, et vous lirez ce que vous avez fait: les premières trois lettres vous le diront, car vous savez comment on appelle un homme qui jette ce qui ne lui appartient pas—ce qui était sacré pour ses aïeuls.[14]

Gone, for once, is Rozen's customary calm. Indeed, the letter shows another, not particularly admirable side of Rozen's character: that of the self-satisfied, self-justifying patriarch. Hard indeed it must have been for Yevgeniy to read that his father's "State crime" had "in no way affected" himself; his very situation proved the contrary. And as for the equation made so casually by Rozen between St Peter and his son, the Lord God and himself, perhaps it would be charitable to say nothing of it: certainly the last lines of the letter do not bring him credit.

But Rozen was passing through a time of trials in 1845, even if not so grave a time as to justify this painful and pedantic letter to his son. It was, indeed, a wretched year. His youngest son and namesake, Andrey, died aged barely four, of ataxy. The child had never known good health. Rozen buried him beside a waterfall, on a high bank of the River Narova. But even death, and Anna's sickness for a month, could not engross him absolutely: he had quite enough to occupy his mind and heart, starting with Yevgeniy in Oryol. Vladimir was eleven now, in 1845, Vasiliy thirteen, Kondratiy fourteen, and his daughter Anna, nine. The house, it seemed, was full of future soldiers. The family tradition of the Rozens had survived intact. His sons would all be officers; and in 1846 Kondratiy and Vasiliy, now impatient to leave home and taste the pleasures of the capital and start their own careers, sat an examination for the officers of the Regiment of Nobles. Both did well and were accepted.[15] So, as Rozen had himself left Mehntack for the First Cadet Corps thirty years before, Kondratiy and Vasiliy, Siberians by birth, now left for St Petersburg in their turn. But Rozen could not take them there: forbidden even to go seven miles, to Narva, he could only watch them leave in company with his own elderly aunt, Aleksandra Samborskaya, herself so soon to die. Two years later they were followed by Vladimir. The brothers took their military careers extremely seriously. So diligently did Vasiliy, in particular, take to his books that he fell ill and spent six months in convalescence. Assiduous by nature, but lacking in the flair needed to win the hearts of troops, Vasiliy's would be a long but (to his sorrow) a commendable rather than brilliant career. In 1876 he would retire with the rank of Lieutenant-Colonel—a rank attained by many men of thirty-five, not forty-five like himself—to become a small landowner in Izyum, Province of Khar'kov. Together in their later years (Yevgeniy and Kondratiy, too, would become landowners in the district of Izyum, where their late mother's and uncle's huge estate lay, and where Rozens were beginning to proliferate by 1860), the brothers had been close to one another in the 1850s, too. By 1851, in fact, Kondratiy and Vasiliy had contrived to be appointed to the same artillery battery, having finally, by an Imperial ukase, been reinstated in their proper social station as hereditary gentry. They continued to be close— closer, one thinks, than Rozen was to any of his own brothers: with Vladimir, fourteen years his senior, it was patently unlikely that Rozen would be intimate till both were middle-aged at least, and by then Rozen was living far away in the Ukraine; with Otto, we have seen, Rozen was on affectionate, close terms during the 'forties as in 1820–24, yet the two appear to have neglected corre-spondence afterwards. As for Rozen's youngest brother, Yuliy, again affection and regard failed to result in lasting closeness. Why did the brothers, unlike Rozen's sons, go their own ways, sometimes losing contact with each other for an interval of years? Perhaps for two main reasons: each in his way, the brothers were extremely occupied. Indeed if there is any one family trait to be perceived in Eugen Octave's sons, it is an almost constitutional business. Vladimir, retired Lieutenant-Colonel of Artillery, was busy on his land near Dorpat with his son Mikhail (born in his own fifty-third year, in 1838); Otto was busy with two sons in Mehntack; and Yuliy, though childless, was a career officer, busy with the training of new troops. But such things alone do not account for Rozen's separateness from his brothers. It was above all, one suspects, consciousness of his past—of the experience of exile in Siberia and the Caucasus—that, in a way unseen even by Rozen, kept him apart from Yuliy and Otto, and maintained a certain distance, even wariness, between Vladimir and himself. That Vladimir, who was forty by the time his younger brother was arrested, was in sympathy with the Decembrist rising, is by no means evident; but even if he *had* been sympathetic, and had approved of constitutional reforms, what had he now in common with the former prisoner and exile? And how could Yuliy and Otto appreciate what Rozen had experienced? Not for nothing did the former prisoner Rozen form closer links, after the 'forties, with his wife's family, the Malinovskys, than with his own: the Malinovskys, like himself, had personal experience of conflict with the Emperor, and of the long trials of disgrace. Not for nothing did he carefully maintain his friendships with his comrades in Siberia: they, at least, could understand what it was like to live under perpetual police surveillance, and could share a common memory.

But to return to Rozen's efforts on the land, and with the peasantry: the Estonians on the estate of Sóldina demanded his attention in their wretchedness. Here, nothing seemed to have improved since 1820. Every factor worked against the peasant: some landlords in the area had introduced merino sheep, appreciat-ing that the animals required but little labour, lived the whole winter in a simple barn, produced dung to spread over the fields in spring, were practically im-pervious to disease, and gave a high-priced wool. The landlords prospered. Though there was talk of large-scale sheep-farming in central Russian pro-vinces, Estonia still enjoyed a favoured, even privileged position in the St Petersburg and, to a certain point, the Moscow market. And the peasants suffered: they were quite unnecessary, for a dozen men sufficed to run a sheep-farm. The peasants' problems with their German pastors, and with earlier tenants of Bol'sháya Sóldina, have been mentioned. Finally, there was the complication of the four-field system of crop rotation. For the peasantry, the system meant more work. The rotation was so complicated and, to them, so profitless. What was the point of the enormous fields of fodder crops? And why should *they* toil using iron machinery that, though new-fangled, would not change their lot, though it might well bring greater income for the landlord?

Little wonder that the peasants of Estonia seemed to contemporaries improvident, feckless, and idle—though cheerful enough.[16] Illiterate they might be, but they could understand that this work could not benefit them. So the peasants around Rozen idled. Even their appearance was suggestive of decline: as in earlier days, many wore trailing, dirty coats of undyed black wool, and bast sandals or shoes. Long fair hair, glazed eyes—such were the features that impressed a traveller in the Province.[17] (If the eyes were glazed, it was a consequence of the perpetually smoky atmosphere inside the peasants' huts.) Spiritual indifference and economic ruin, landlessness and apathy—or anger with the landlords of the district: the issues facing Rozen were not small ones. What should he do first? He might agitate to have the school constructed which, by the terms of a decree of 1819, every settlement and village was required to have—twenty years too late for children in Bol'sháya Sóldina. But parish schools which had been founded in effect only in villages with populations of 2,000, would do nothing to improve the present situation. Biblical history, reading, and arithmetic, the singing of religious songs, were all, certainly, splendid things, but were investments in the future, not solutions for the present.[18] Again, he might attempt to bring some influence to bear on the local "church-lord". A few liberal pastors had considered renting church land to the peasants, or even, in exceptional cases, leasing land for life at only ten per cent of its true value—the rest of the debt would remain "in the land", making the peasants lifelong renters. But such plans were seldom carried out, though frequently and carefully discussed in *Baltische Monatschrift* and other periodicals;[19] besides, the local clergy were not promising as liberal material. No, rather than make others lease their land to the Estonians, he himself must do so. Such was Rozen's conclusion, having passed no more than three months in the Province. The peasants prized the land. Only on their own land or, at least, to their demonstrable advantage, would they labour. *Corvée* must therefore end in practice as in law, and a new system of rents in kind or money be established. To introduce the new system was logical, given the peasants' attitude and needs, and more appropriate to the modern age than *corvée*—a mediaeval institution. Hired workers on the lord's fields would work better than before, knowing that they were to be paid. It was, in all respects, the sensible approach.

But Nicholas himself, Rozen must certainly have known, had vainly striven to adopt such an approach for fifteen years. "As early as 1826," as Pares remarks,

> he instituted the first commission for the study of practical reforms. It was followed in the course of his reign by five others, which of itself is evidence both of the Emperor's insistence and of the opposition of his nearest counsellors . . . Nicholas made more than one attempt to give further effect to Alexander's law of 1803–4, authorizing and regulating agreements between squires and their peasants, by which the serfs obtained freedom with land.[20]

And Nicholas had failed in that attempt, baulked by the landowners themselves and the bureaucracy. Arguing that such agreements must be absolutely free on

the peasants' part, officials had established such a "system of verification",
generally involving the Minister for Internal Affairs himself, that agreements
were indefinitely delayed in many cases. The will was there: the Emperor had
first appointed Kiselyov, in 1834, to improve the economic welfare of Crown
peasants, then himself examined the peasant situation. He had no wish, he
claimed in all sincerity, to leave this problem for his son. But though the will was
present, means for the enforcing of that will were not. The gentry would not
see their influence over the peasantry diminished. And as in Great and White
Russia, so in the Baltic Provinces. By systematically raising the economic level
of his peasants, and renting his *own* land to them,[21] Rozen would be a pioneer
in Vyru *uyezd*, and would forestall the Tsar's decree of April 2, 1842, abolishing
corvée and striving to establish a new system of quit-rent agreements and
voluntary contracts between landowners and peasants. First, let us see what
practical steps he took to realize his aim of "taking on himself the improvement
of the peasants' material conditions":

On April 3, 1841, I found six peasant farmsteads already in a good state of repair;
on the remaining eight, there was not a single horse. In four, insolvency reigned—
bankruptcy. The members of these households remained serfs, and were numbered with the *batraki*, or landless peasants. In the face of such a feeble and
unreliable work force, I found myself obliged to retain annual hired workers and
horses and to keep my own agricultural implements. But it was not possible to
embark on any radical reorganization without a basic knowledge of the soil and all
component parts of the entire estate. For this purpose, we set about a special land-
survey the next year, and undertook some levelling, after which we could proceed
with the dividing up of fields and pastures and the drying out of parts of the
extensive bogs ... Everything was calculated to bring the peasants out of *corvée*
or obligatory personal labour, and into quit-rent farming. In the autumn of 1842,
three of the peasant masters agreed immediately to my terms. To demand
monetary security from them was impossible, since they had no capital. So, in
order to protect myself and obviate all lawsuits, complaints and litigation, I put
into the contracts that the annual payment of the rent should be made on three
fixed dates: St Yuriy's Day, St Michael's Day, and the Feast of Candlemas,[22]
and in advance in every case. Whoever did not make his payment by the day
appointed would transfer his parcel to another farmer from the same village or, if
no one should be found to take it on, to an outsider; the insolvent man could either
find himself a position elsewhere, or return to *corvée*. A fourth peasant joined the
leaseholders in 1843, and by 1845 twelve of the old inhabitants of the place had
become independent farmers. As a further enticement I made the leaseholds
hereditary, and above that not liable to changed rent-rates. Such a system of farming, not only with hereditary leases but also with fixed rents, was introduced into
Bol'sháya Sóldina earlier than to any of the other landowners' estates nearby ...
The changeover from *corvée* to quit-rent admittedly entailed expenses for the
landowner: it was necessary, for a few years, to change the hired day-workers
and labourers every year. The peasants paid their rents with regularity, however,
and their well-being improved with every summer. Proximity to a town, a large
road and new factories, the carrier's trade from St Petersburg, the nearness of a

seaport, all gave permanent employment opportunities. All my peasants got horses; in farmsteads where there had not been a single one in 1841, there were three in 1855 . . .[23]

Rozen was not merely abreast of, but ahead of the reform movement throughout the Baltic provinces. After five years of successful experiment with renting at Bol'sháya Sóldina, he had the mixed pleasure of seeing Nicholas attempt and fail to institute a comparable agrarian system by force of law. The edict of April 2, 1842, it was said, had abolished *corvée* and given peasants and their landlords every possibility of making mutually advantageous contracts; but whole societies and outlooks were not to be transformed simply by Nicholas's signing several papers. The edict was still-born, for Nicholas neglected to state clearly in the edict by what date *corvée* was to have vanished from the face of Russia. It was Rozen's view that a ten- or twelve-year deadline would have secured the Tsar's supposed first step towards general emancipation—and averted the Crimean War.[24] But the landowners had no reason to hurry. Even if they had not finished thinking out the consequences of a changeover to quit-rents after fifteen years, no authority could force their hand; the contracts with their peasants must be voluntary. A few great landowners, therefore, like M. S. Vorontsov, might quickly introduce quit-rent farming to their lands; most did not. Of 21,400 Russian landowners controlling estates with a hundred peasants or more, Rozen informs us, only ten followed Vorontsov's example. Seeing his plan frustrated, Nicholas issued a further edict on April 3, 1843: peasants should, in certain circumstances, be permitted to acquire land which a landowner, because he had not paid his taxes, had legally forfeited. The second edict, like the first, remained a dead letter, and was cancelled by the Tsar himself in 1845. On Bol'sháya Sóldina, meanwhile, where Rozen's terms were truly advantageous to the peasants (though not, for some years, to himself), matters went ahead smoothly. At last, in 1849, Nicholas confirmed a decree of the Livonian Diet making *corvée* illegal in the Baltic provinces (though, of course, the law was one thing, enforcing it another, especially where landowners and judges were the same men, or related). The essence of the reform, writes J. H. Jackson,

> was the division of each estate into two categories of land, the demesne and the peasants' land. On the former, the lord could do as he liked, but on the latter the permanent rights of the tenants were recognized. The idea was that rents in labour should give way to rents in kind, that all forms of *corvée* should be abolished, and that in time the peasant should be allowed to buy his holding. During the period of transition one-sixth of the peasants' land in Estonia was to be annexed to the demesne, ostensibly to provide cottage-plots for the lord's servants. It was, in more ways than one, a revolutionary change. Not only did it envisage a change from a feudal to a monetary economy, but it accepted the entirely new principle that a peasant might become a landlord. Nothing but lack of money now stood between the Estonian and his age-long dream of becoming the owner of the fields he worked.[25]

But on Rozen's land such revolutionary changes had occurred some years before. He had not chosen to "annex" land then; nor did he do so now, though he might legally have done so. On the contrary, he was thinking of providing the Estonian peasantry with larger plots by renting part of what was, by the terms of the decree of 1849, "the demesne". The more he pondered on the matter, the more he felt inclined to rent more land. Finally, in 1851, he acted:

> The working of the landlord's fields was done by free labour. Wastage of agricultural implements and harnesses was very considerable, especially because of the carelessness of the workers, so that only in a bumper-crop year did the land worked by hired labourers prove profitable. For this reason, I separated four lots off from the demesne land in 1851 and rented them—but only temporarily, for twelve years, and withholding for myself the right to increase the area before twelve years if I so chose. That separated land remains in the hands of peasants, in perpetuity, and they have the right to make it their own personal property, by purchase [in 1867—G.B.].[26]

As to the peasants, so also to Rozen, the new renting arrangement seemed desirable. The peasants, notoriously careless, broke their own tools; what, then, would they do with other men's? And why should he, Rozen, trouble with barely profitable land if, by renting it, he could both help a peasant family and assure himself a steady income from it? As always with Rozen, common sense blended with liberal ideas, and prudence with a genuine desire to help the peasants. Fortunate indeed were the Estonians who lived near him: elsewhere in the Baltic provinces, the landowners were hurrying slowly to implement the terms of the decree of 1849. Though *morally* required to take immediate steps to end *corvée*, indeed (for such, it was quite plain from the decree, was Nicholas's wish for the whole Empire), the German Balts were stalling. Not until 1856 did the Revel' *Landrat* pass its version of the edict passed in Riga seven years before. Small wonder that the peasants were impatient and suspicious by that year. And then they were assured that, by a special clause, the decree was to be valid in Estonia only in 1858![27] As so often in the past, violence erupted. In Mahtra men refused to perform carting service; troops were sent, the local landlord's manor burnt; a fight ensued, and there were deaths. More violence broke out on an estate in Harju, and the *Ritterschaft* reacted savagely. So began another time of hopelessness and, with the advent of Johann Leinberg, also known as Maltsvet the Seer, of religious revivalism. Pray and fast, urged Maltsvet, who taught a variation of Mosaic Law, and a land of Canaan shall be yours in the Crimea. Alexander II having granted them permission, Maltsvet and a horde of followers actually arrived in the Crimea in 1861 to found a settlement; but his departure was itself a cause of tragedy among Estonians: a white ship, it was rumoured, would arrive in the small bay beside Mount Lasna in the neighbourhood of Tallinn on St George's Eve, and bear off faithful Estonians to their special Land of Canaan. Great crowds assembled on the hill and waited pitifully, day by day. St George's Eve came, and no ship arrived.

They stayed, and starved. At last, the survivors were dispersed by the police.[28] Not until the seventh decade would the long-promised reforms be put into effect throughout Estonia, the right to inflict corporal punishment be taken from the landlords, and the last of the ancient strip-fields be divided into new and compact farms. By then, Rozen would be far away in the Ukraine.

But to return to 1853, the year in which the lives of two of the Decembrist's children, Anna and Yevgeniy, at last "arranged themselves" (in Stiva Obolensky's phrase). Anna became engaged to a civil servant, Nikolay Bobrov; and Yevgeniy became a landowner in the Ukraine. By good fortune, a "Description of All Goods Conceded to His Excellency Staff-Captain Yevgeniy Andreyevich Rozen in the Hamlet of Stratilatovka" has survived.[29] It was, we see from the sixty-four items there listed, a rather *small* estate. Still, it contained among other useful things:

> One wooden manor-house, of five main rooms.
> One orchard of mixed fruit trees, 285 yards long, 120 feet wide.
> One kitchen-garden, 187 yards long, 75 feet wide.
> One brick factory.
> 58 rams, 50 ewes of the first grade, 844 of the second.
> 15 pigs, including two boar.

Not too large an undertaking, one might think, to be handled by an army man of almost twenty-nine, yet a sufficient one to enable him to try his hand at running an estate. Yevgeniy left for the Ukraine.

For his own part, Rozen was well occupied on his estate. His peasants prospered now, and land experiments were answering as he had hoped. Financially, Anna and he were sound. His children gone from home, he had no stimulus to take a further interest in schooling and his interest duly lapsed—soon, however, to revive in an even keener form. Yet he was far from idle intellectually. After an interval of eight years, he again took up his memoirs. Deliberately, he pondered how to change them or improve them. Translation, too, was an old occupation now revived. A copy of Macaulay's *The History of England*, volumes one and two presumably, made their belated way into his hands. He read the work with care, and was again prompted to write a history of Estonia.

Other, less satisfactory elements of his past life returned, too, in the 'fifties; and of these, ill-health was the worst. For ten years he had been in admirable health, considering his earlier trials. Suddenly, he felt himself physically weaker. He coughed incessantly and had chest pains. He foresaw the end. He wished to take Communion but was not allowed to go to Narva, where the nearest Lutheran church was situated; perforce, he made his way to the parish church of Vayvor. It was early April and the roads were wet. The church proved cold and damp. All augured ill. But at the very moment that he went up to the altar, the cough left him. It was, physicians told him afterwards, because the crisis had been reached; for his own part, Rozen was not sure. In all events the illness had most beneficial consequences: hearing of his sorry state, Anna's sister, then in St Petersburg, approached Prince A. A. Suvorov, grandson of the Marshal and Governor-General of Livonia, to ask if he could not secure permission for her sick brother-in-law to hear Mass in a church in Narva. Suvorov, who had just arranged for Tizengauzen to return to the Baltic from Siberia, proved highly sympathetic; and so Rozen went to Narva. The church, the pews, the organ, all was as he recollected it. Only the faces in the church were unfamiliar; his friends of 1811, if not dead, were aged now. Two years later and again through the good offices of General Suvorov, Rozen was at last freed of police surveillance. The clouds of 1825, it seemed, were finally receding. That same winter he was visited in Sóldina by Tizengauzen's brother, who came with messages and with an urge to beat his host at boston; they played cheerfully—Rozen for the first time since 1823—and B. K. Tizengauzen, who had served for ten years as an aide to A. A. Arakcheyev, told anecdotes about the former favourite. Rozen noted them down. Other comrades came: first M. M. Naryshkin and his wife, then the Nazimovs. The friends of his childhood were either dead or strangers, but here, more than four thousand miles from the scene of their internment, were the comrades of his 'twenties. To Rozen, the exchange seemed good enough. The Decembrists, it grew plain to them as time passed, formed a circle or society (and by no means a clandestine one), membership of which could lapse only with death. These were his true companions; with these men, he could talk more openly than with his own brothers, and they understood his every word and hint. Other events might have arisen to push those of December 14, 1825 out of the public mind—in January 1855 Rozen heard a distant roar of English naval guns, and saw a huge three-decker of Admiral Seymour's squadron carefully bombarding Narva harbour—but in their minds, those hours by Senate Square were very clear still. Now, in the middle 'fifties, while Russia was at war for no good purpose that Rozen could perceive; now, as the military machine on which the Emperor prided himself was proving as corrupt as his enormous retrograde bureaucracy, Rozen began to understand his own position *vis-à-vis* that Emperor, and in relation to his own and his companions' past. He would record their aspirations and halffailure. Formed in Estonia where, a generation earlier, his own liberal ideals had taken shape, that resolution only grew in strength as he grew older (see Chapter 12), and as, during the months after the new Tsar's amnesty to the Decembrists, of August 1856, other ageing comrades found their ways back home.

Before that amnesty was proclaimed, however, and while Nicholas still lived, yet another major change occurred in Rozen's life. In the spring of 1855, Yevgeniy became seriously ill in Stratilatovka. The illness was less physical than psychological. Yevgeniy's nerves, it seemed, were strained; he could not sleep; he was continually on edge, and growing weaker. For the third time, General Suvorov interceded. Rozen had permission to stay with his son in the Ukraine— if he did not stay in either capital. But it was virtually impossible to reach Khar'kov without passing through St Petersburg or Moscow! Rozen decided that to travel through a town was not to visit it; he left. Having ascertained that Yevgeniy could not, and should not, continue to run Stratilatovka unaided; that to sell would not be sensible, his son having begun large undertakings there; and that he must himself move to the south, he returned to Sóldina, again by rail. (How smooth and fast the trains were! In the silence, one could ponder on the news of the surrender of Sevastopol', and on the awful casualties.) On April 23, 1856, he and Anna left Estonia for good. Seventeen years had passed since his return from Georgia. Now, at the age of fifty-six, he was moving for the fifth and final time.

Rozen left Estonia with uncertain feelings: it was necessary, of course, that someone manage Anna's own interests and land, and care for the distraught Yevgeniy, who had palpitation of the heart, insomnia, and dizzy spells; but matters had been well arranged at Sóldina. The climate in the south would be superior, no doubt, and the soil richer by far than that by Narva, "sandy or boggy, with flints, cobblestones, flagstones in it";[30] but he himself, the fact remained, was an Estonian, not a Ukrainian. Certainly they would prosper, unless unforeseen disaster struck, for he himself had seen the large-scale grain- and sheep-farming in Khar'kov Province. But he had no personal attachment to Izyum, save that gained through his love for Anna and her family. He left with sadness. In Estonia lay buried both his parents and his forebears; in Estonia lived his brothers and his sisters; there, he was known, and felt at home even under surveillance. In Estonia, finally, during the last ten years, he had seen his agricultural reforms come to fruition, and had developed interests in sheep-farming and schooling which, together with his earlier interest in history, would keep him occupied in the Ukraine. By 1856, indeed, the main pastimes and interests of Rozen's later life were present and developed: the pursuit of history, agriculture, and the theory of education. His memoirs, started in exile and continued intermittently, would perhaps be brought to a conclusion in the south —it was in Kamenka that he would put the final touches to his manuscript in 1866–68; but it was in Estonia, during the 'fifties, that he recast his earlier jottings and decided to compose a major work of reminiscences (see Chapter 12). There, the groundwork was begun, the pruning started, that would lead to the appearance, in 1869, of the most lucid, factual record of Decembrist exile life. And of course it was in Vyru district, near his birthplace, that he managed in his middle years to bring into effect so many plans that he had formed either in exile in Siberia or in his adolescence, in Mehntack. Here, he paid his personal dues to liberalism; small wonder that he always viewed the district with affection and recalled it with nostalgia. Rozen left Estonia physically in 1856; but Estonian concerns would never leave him. Fourteen years after his parting with the Baltic, when he was almost seventy years old, he could still carefully follow the developments in local government where he had passed his youth—and well enough appreciate the niceties of economic problems in the Province to compose a lengthy, closely-argued "Personal Opinion of an Estonian Land-owner on a Public Question". Part of that essay will be cited later (see Chapter

11). Still in 1870 Rozen had legal rights over the property of Sóldina. He had not hesitated to dispose of it for fear of losing profits in the future; never had his land in Sóldina or, more specifically, that portion of it under lease to peasants, produced a more than reasonable yearly return (and that only since 1845). There was no fortune to be made from such a property. Rather had he not disposed of Sóldina because he did not wish to break a link of deep emotional significance to him: his own, tangible link with the district of his birth and heritage. When finally, in 1874, he did sell Sóldina, it comes as no surprise to learn, it was to a favourite nephew, Konstantin. Always the Decembrist was intensely conscious of ancestral connections with the Province of Estonia and, more noteworthy by far, with the inhabitants of that ill-fated Province. It was in this respect that he differed from his ancestors and parents: first of the Rozens, he regarded the Estonians as fellow-countrymen, invested the Estonian with dignity, and *acted* on his highest principles. Such attitudes and conduct led him necessarily to come to terms with other questions commonly ignored by his contemporaries and, as we saw, even by the Decembrist federalists: what, he asked on his return from Georgia (where, we also saw, he viewed the government's attempts to russify Circassians and other "native peoples" with alarm and great distaste), did Estonian nationality imply? Indeed, was there such a thing as an Estonian identity, Estonian nationality? The questions were brought home to him in no uncertain manner in the years immediately after his return, in 1839: in that year began the movement of Estonian landless peasants into Riga to demand land from the Governor-General, Pahlen, and the Orthodox Bishop Irinarkh—a movement which in turn resulted in tribunals and, in 1841–43, mass forced conversions of Lutheran peasantry to Russian Orthodoxy. In those years began the pressure from the capital and not, as earlier, from the German Balts themselves, to check the further spread of the Estonian tongue and cause Estonian culture to decay and atrophy. Could Rozen, though a German Balt himself, observe that process passively?

IO

NATIONALISM AND ESTONIAN IDENTITY

Alone of the Decembrists, the Baltic Germans, Tizengauzen, Rozen, and the brothers Kyukhel'beker, were highly conscious of non-Russian-ness. Alone of these, Rozen expressed that consciousness in writing. Tizengauzen was in all events too old and tired by 1853, when he at last returned to Narva, to take a more than passive interest in Baltic matters; associated in his middle years with the Ukraine, Colonel of the Poltava Foot and a member of Pestel's Southern Society, he was an ailing man of four and seventy when Prince Suvorov brought his influence to bear to bring him home. Within weeks of his arrival by the Baltic, he was dead. V. K. Kyukhel'beker, we have seen, had passed his childhood on his father's small estate near Avinorm, in Vyru district; but the Kyukhel'bekers were not Baltic Germans—the Decembrist-poet's grandfather had come from Saxony and, having made his mark in St Petersburg, had bought land in Estonia because it was so near, lay in the general direction of Berlin and Magdeburg, and was a German-speaking province. Rozen alone of the Decembrists, it followed, was by blood and heritage and inclination qualified to give expression to the Baltic German's sense of separateness from Great Russians, Little Russians, indeed, from slavdom as a whole. The fact makes him unique among Decembrists and of special interest to students of the origins of the Estonian nationalist movement, as of comparable movements in the other Baltic provinces. Several Decembrists, to be sure, could boast of foreign and non-Slavic ancestry: Igel'strom (Ygelström) had Swedish origins, the Poggios, Italian, while N. I. Lorer, the most brilliant of the Decembrist raconteurs, was of mixed Muscovite, German, French, and Georgian blood—a bizarre and heady mixture.[1] But these three, like Sub-Lieutenants Fock and Lappa (Finns by ancestry) and Dr F. B. Vol'f (Wolff), had become wholly russified and could (or rather, wished to) identify only with Russia. Rozen alone was highly conscious, not precisely of his German-ness, but of his *special* German-ness—of his Baltic antecedents and ancestral links with the Estonians. Again, many Decembrists deeply sympathized with Polish national aspirations and, like Lunin and Pestel', accepted (with misgivings) the logical necessity, assuming a happy outcome to a Russian revolution, of granting independence to the Poles. (In April 1824, Murav'yov-Apostol could even go so far as to declare that the Southern Society "offered Poland the restoration of her former independence and was ready by all means to assist in the eradication of the mutual antipathy between the Polish and the Russian peoples";[2] but few could go as far as this.[3]) Yet the fact remains that Poles were not Decembrists; nor, far more significantly in our present context, was any one Decembrist either Polish or incapable, because of Polish links or antecedents, of sympathizing with Russian aims, identifying with Russian arms. They might be *friendly* towards individual Poles and to the cause of Polish freedom in an abstract way; but this, intense though friendliness becomes in Lunin's letter-pamphlet of November 1839, "The Poles", was a rather different feeling from the love that Rozen felt for his Estonian "native land". Rozen, too, it may be said in passing, entertained ambivalent feelings towards the Polish Liberals. While in Peter-and-Paul Fortress, we have seen, Colonel Worzel was incarcerated in the cell opposite no. 13, in which Rozen was attempting to keep fit and cheerful by singing. Worzel was a Pole, and a friend of Pestel'; plainly he deserved respect. So, too, did those of his compatriots "who knew so well—better than us—how to conduct their affairs and to keep secret all the workings of the Polish Secret Society" (that is, of Lukasinsky's group). "Only a few of them," remarks Rozen, "including Count Moschinsky, Kryschanowsky, and Janush-Kewitsch [*sic*], were banished to Siberia . . ."[4] One senses lack of warmth in the remark. So, too, in Siberia and in the Caucasus: again Rozen encounters Polish exiles, worthy men with high ideals. He hears their singing, and enjoys the "Polish national airs"; but he avoids them, and never makes close personal contact with them. Was it the memory of his eighteen months in Lithuania "among landowners distinguished for their haughty insolence towards the poor, and for their flattery of rich men and superiors",[5] that had resulted in such coolness? One inclines to think so; the Polish gentry around Vil'no, Rozen noted as a junior officer in 1823, treated their peasantry like slaves. Early contact with the Polish ruling class made an unfavourable impression which, it seems, never left Rozen. But to return to the Estonians and his special link with them . . .

Rozen was a German–Estonian Decembrist—an officer of German ancestry serving the Russian Government. In his leisure hours he read French novels. His wife spoke English and his elder sons wrote tolerable Latin. He had relatives in Sweden. Small wonder that he could not totally identify himself with Holy Russia, though he served the Tsars both loyally and well. But what was he or, more precisely, what did it imply to be "Estonian"? That he loved the region of his birth was natural enough; most of us eventually view the place where we have passed our first years with a special tenderness and, frequently, through rose-tinted spectacles. On leaving for Siberia he took with him a "packet" containing soil from Mehntack. Whenever he had contact with a fellow-countryman, his brother Yuliy in his cell in St Petersburg, for instance, or Fyódorov the astronomer from Dorpat in Kurgan, his spirits rose. It was very natural. But what did it *mean* to him to be Estonian? And by extension did he sympathize with the ideals and aspirations of German-speaking Esthland, or those of the Estonian populace, or both? If both (as was transparently the case—it was the sight of the Estonians themselves, no less than of familiar trees and faces, that first delighted him on his return from exile), what were his attitudes towards Estonian political and cultural identity (two very different matters in the context of the fifth decade)? The questions, to which Rozen gives long answers in his memoirs having pondered on the meanings of both "race" and "nationalism", "independence" and "identity", are best answered separately. First, we may usefully establish the connection between economic ruin and religion in Estonia during the early 'forties; it was essentially against the troubled background of decay and opportunism in both spheres that Rozen came to terms with his particular identity as an Estonian-German, and saw where his true obligations lay.

1839, 1840, and 1841 brought three consecutive bad harvests in most parts of Estonia. The root problem was drought, not a familiar threat beside the Baltic Sea and Lake Peipus. Peasants went hungry; then, instead of breaking out in Jacqueries in the old and hopeless manner, began the drift to Riga mentioned earlier. Outside the city they established huge encampments, annoyed the officials whom they saw, and demanded that their names be placed on some obscure list for eventual allotment of land parcels in their Province. The officials denied that any list existed, or was now to be compiled; but the Estonians, some of whom had walked from Vyru, were not willing to believe this. The rumour persisted seven days and nights. The crowd grew larger.[6] The police tried to disperse the watchful peasants, but failed. And now occurred a fateful thing: certain peasants, knowing that a Russian Orthodox bishop as well as a Russian governor resided in the city, made their way into the town itself, searching out first the bishop, then any Russian clergy, and demanding their assistance and protection against German landowners. Aware of growing rivalry between the Lutheran and Russian Orthodox churches, they attempted to make use of it. In his turn the Russian bishop, Irinarkh, made a mistake (though possibly a calculated one): waylaid by several dozen hungry peasants, he took down their names. Conviction that a list indeed existed grew amazingly —and logically: for how could it be otherwise, the peasants asked, when some among them had already had their names taken by Irinarkh himself? Finally matters went too far even for the Imperial authorities who, in 1840, had observed the Baltic Germans' troubles with their peasants with amusement or detachment.[7] Troops were dispatched to Riga. A fight developed, in which many lost their lives. Several hundred were arrested, many tried, beaten, and sent off to the army. But far from changing their belief that the Russian Government and Church would end by helping them against their German masters, this appalling incident only intensified it among Estonians. The troops, the peasants thought, had been dispatched at the request of anxious German landowners, not by the Emperor. So, in 1841, a new movement began and other rumours spread; and this time, although the movement had begun not in Estonia but in Livonia, a general exodus ensued from areas of south and west Estonia. The authorities became alarmed when, in September and by Puhajärv, peasants offered serious resistance to the military. Repression followed rapidly, with more tribunals, greater floggings. Irinarkh was hurriedly recalled, then Baron Pahlen. Their successors, as the government intended, took a different attitude towards the troubles of the region: Filaret did not hesitate to do his best to undermine the Lutheran Church by accepting Latvian peasants into Russian Orthodoxy, while the new Governor-General, E. A. Golovin, far from sympathizing with the Baltic gentry as had Pahlen (who was himself a local landowner), made his distrust for all things German evident. Rozen takes up the sorry tale:

In the 'forties a new Governor-General, Golovin, was appointed to replace Pahlen, and a new Archbishop, Filaret, to the see of Irinarkh. The Press was silent on the subject of the conversions begun in Riga, but when it proved necessary to move several Cossack squadrons to Livonia, verbal accounts of the reasons and events there spread considerably faster than the printed word.

The first cause of the whole affair has remained all but unnoticed; at least, it is little referred to, though the main reason for the switch from one church to another is concealed in it. The Government made no attempt whatever to hide its aim of unifying the two churches. It merely lost sight of the basic pre-conditions for such unity. For their part, the clergy paid no heed to the Apostle Paul's admonitions to the Corinthians in the First Epistle, chapter 1, verses 12–13 ["Each one says, 'I belong to Paul', or 'I belong to Cephas', or 'I belong to Christ'. Was Christ divided?"—G.B.] or were carried away by the hope that the time had come indeed for there to be a single Church and single pastor . . .

Several thousand apostates abandoned their church, family ties, and former co-religionaries, yet received no reward of earthly goods. Two years after their conversion, so many requitals and formalities were demanded of the new converts, during religious rites, at burials, marriages, and christenings, that they had started to complain. But the spirit of conversion was already blowing on Estonia now . . . Near the borders of the Province, outside Dorpat, my elder brother Vladimir, an old mounted artilleryman of 1812, then lived in retirement. He saw all the preparations going on beyond Dorpat, the Church Militant, the bull-headed conversions, the agitation of the populace, and called the peasants on his estate to a meeting. "Just wait," he said; "if they give land away free, then glory and blessing to the apostates, and I'll be the first to be converted, and you can all follow me!" This had more effect on them than a sermon or long argument.

The Emperor Nicholas was in Palermo at this time, with the ailing Empress. The Estonian nobility took the part of their co-religionaries and petitioned for the preservation of freedom of conscience. The Sovereign replied from Palermo that the process of conversion had been started without his knowledge, and the whole matter ceased therewith. All grew calm and tranquil when the Governor-General and Bishop Filaret were removed; the first phase of the conversions of Letts and Ests in Livonia, begun under the Most Blessed Irinarkh, ended in October 1841. Irinarkh testified that the majority of these Letts and Ests had asked to be received into the Orthodox Church in the hope of receiving, in return, some non-existent land . . .[8]

It was however, as Rozen remarks, only the initial phase of this misguided movement of conversion, or "conversion", that was ended in October 1841. Filaret the proselytizer might have gone; his work remained unfinished. Peasants continued to seek land by being converts to the Russian Church, and were received with open arms. The Lutherans retaliated, preaching the sinfulness, not just the inadvisability, of trading old beliefs for new. Nothing, however, checked the movement: between 1845 and 1847, conversions were occurring in all regions of Estonia, though most especially in Tartumaa, Vyrumaa and Valgamaa, the southern areas.[9] By the latter year, Jackson informs us, "there were 65,000 members of the Orthodox Church in Estonia".[10] But conversion brought no land; and the movement, which continued until 1849, and later on a minor scale, brought only trouble and frustration to the lives of the Estonian peasantry. This, Rozen could not ignore, any more than the outrageous implications of official blessing for the proselytizing movement under Filaret and Golovin: the government, he saw, would not be sad to see a spread of Orthodoxy in the Baltic Provinces at the direct expense of (German) Lutheranism. Indeed, the government appeared to view the possibility with favour, and some interest. Such circumstances, Rozen understood only too well having observed the government's colonial policy in Georgia seven years before, did not bode well for the Estonian populace or for Estonian identity. It was, above all, the *complicity* between the government and Orthodox Church leaders—a complicity apparent in the Russian clergy's very attitude towards their converts in Estonia—that annoyed him. And, as his narrative concerning the conversions progresses, a note of indignation grows more audible:

In the reign of the Emperor Nicholas, between one-ninth and one-tenth of the whole population of Livonia were among the converted Letts and Ests. But just as quickly as conversion had occurred on a mass scale (and without preliminary preparation or instruction), a reverse movement began back to the earlier Church —also on a mass scale, although a smaller one. The new converts to Orthodoxy soon saw the severity of that clergy towards certain individuals who had expressed a wish to revert to their former adherence; and when they saw the forced baptism of infants whose parents wished them to remain in the evangelical Church, and saw that young people who had stayed in their own Church, but whose parents had accepted the other, were being summoned now by the police; and when they saw that converts were conducted to Communion by the police and threatened with a birching should they not fulfil their Christian duties, then indifference towards the new Church was transformed into manifest hatred for that Church and for its servants. The hastily built churches became empty, and hostilities began between the Greco-Russian clergy and most of their rural parishioners. The threats of the Orthodox clergy were unavailing, however, as were the repudiations of the Lutheran pastors: the converts effectively belonged to no Church. Priests demanded written testimonies (of adherence) before performing marriages . . ., while pastors did not dare to celebrate "mixed marriages" because they were not viewed as valid, so there remained only one course for those who wished to enter into matrimony—concubinage. The Emperor, having been given a report on these disturbances and movements, sent Count Bobrinsky to investigate them on the spot. And Bobrinsky announced that "of all the petitioners heard, only ten or fifteen men expressed the wish to remain Orthodox Christians; the remainder in general ask only for material improvements in their lot."

All will unquestionably agree that it is a sorry thing even to have to look into such matters, and to pursue an object that so manifestly contradicts the spirit of true Christianity. But in Russia, too, there are voices which demand freedom of conscience; and not only the Government itself, but also publicists of the (Russian) nationalist party—most notably, and notwithstanding all his zeal for Orthodoxy, I. S. Aksakov—have expressed the view that such a state of bondage as that in which the converts found themselves fails to conform with the Church's dignity; all are agreed, too, that their state was incompatible, as is restriction of free conscience, with the honour and the dignity of the Orthodox Church, as with the honour of Russia. The Count's report produced a powerful impression . . .[11]

Powerful, too, was Rozen's indignation with the Russian Government for having countenanced such an unchristian situation for so long. He saw to what end such trends must lead; yet he was impotent. Deprived of a voice in the *Landrat*, forbidden to leave Bol'sháya Sóldina without permission, he could do nothing to oppose the proselytizing save use his influence on the Estonians around him. But now he was alert to all the danger of the swift russification of the area where German-speaking Lutherans had lived for centuries. He saw Baltic-Russian links in a new light. The persecutions of the 1840s, Nodel writes, taught the Estonian peasantry that neither German landlord nor Russian Government would serve their true nationalist, cultural, or economic ends. ("The first truth the Estonians knew from the experience of six centuries. The second they learned during the upheaval of the 1840s."[12]) But Rozen, too, learned much from the disturbances and politic "conversions" of that decade. Alert to the potential, even probable, fragility of what had seemed so solid only months before—the dominance of Baltic-German culture in Estonia and the Lutheranism of the peasantry—he gave deep thought to the vexed question of Estonian identity. So, in his early fifties, he was led to study modern nationalism. He read Madame de Staël, Cochut, Buchet, John Stuart Mill, and Herder on the subject. Herder's *Die Stimmen der Völke*, in particular, impressed him: here was something more satisfying than Mill's dry discourses on "communalty of past political events", something more closely reasoned than the abstract, ever eloquent, verbal pastiches of *De l'Allemagne*! Herder, it was evident, had considered nationalism from all aspects; indeed, it seemed to Rozen that the German had *begun* an international controversy on the meaning and significance of nationhood:

Herder first provoked this question, and stimulated our taste for popular poetry and simple peasant ways, customs, and songs; he first laid the foundation for the study of national peculiarities. But on the other hand he, together with all the first minds of his age, adhered to cosmopolitanism, to universal citizenship, to the followers of which all the most recent commentaries on nationality would have seemed childish, even harmful (if they show the least hostility towards Culture). One of the most recent German professors of history, in this connection, defines the word "nationality" as *Borniertheit*, not in the sense of intellectual limitedness, but rather in the sense of "enclosure", "separateness", "isolation" when a nation does not leave its own orbit, but prefers its own mediocrity to all that is good but alien . . .[13]

Here was food for thought. Were the Baltic Provinces "enclosed" and "isolated" to the point of actually preferring what was Baltic, and indifferent to the sparkling innovations of the world outside? Nowhere does Rozen say so; yet the fact of his choosing to quote Herder at length, in such a context, surely demonstrates that he was well aware of such a possibility. Certainly he was admirably placed, having spent some years in Georgia, some in Eastern, and some in Western Siberia, as well as lengthy periods in St Petersburg and Lithuania, to see the Baltic Provinces in true perspective. By 1839, when he arrived there to present himself to Pavel Benkendorf, the Civil Governor, Revel' had a population of some 15,000 persons and was a thriving city thanks essentially to the large naval dockyard; but St Petersburg, where he had lived and served, was a city of a quarter of a million long before,[14] and in Kronstadt had the largest naval depot in the Empire! Compared even with Moscow, he perceived, the social life of Revel', of which he had taken brief draughts in 1839 and 1842, was fearsomely stiff. For foreign visitors, indeed, the very fascination of the Domberg, the centre of polite Revel' society, lay in its stuffiness and love of etiquette. There, everyone knew everyone's domestic crises but exchanged only civilities; there, no bourgeois ever penetrated the close circle of the Baltic aristocracy—it was the most exclusive on the continent by 1840, and yearly growing narrower and duller. "None but the Germans", exclaimed one weary English visitor, Elizabeth Rigby, "could have *formed* such a state of society . . . Be a machine, give up all interest, repress all emotion, move only in the set Estonian drill, be everything for show and nothing for reality, and they will hold you up for a pattern."[15] Mercifully for him, Rozen saw little or nothing of this aspect of Estonian life. Still, he was well aware of it through Otto and Vladimir, both of whom played active rôles among the *Ritterschaft* and by the gas-lights of the Domberg. Like most landowners, his brothers lived a life quite unimaginable to the bulk of the Estonian population.

And here, of course, lay the essence of the problem of defining "nationality" in an Estonian context. Ethnically, it was clear, his peasants were Estonian; but was he? Legally, psychologically, historically, yes, of course. But ethnically, no. Necessarily he found himself considering the meanings of more words: "ethnic" and "racial". He was of German ancestry. So were most landowners throughout the Province. But they formed a fractional minority of all Estonians —if they could be viewed as such. Why, then, should they control the Province's and, more, the whole Estonian race's, political development and future? Racial, political, and cultural considerations blended in the forming of an answer to the question:

Each individual ethnic group cannot possess its own political order. Nor can the word "nationality" be taken as the same as the word "race", that is, the origin of a people. Are not the Alsatians and Lotharingians of German origin, and the Corsicans, Italian? Yet no one can doubt that the citizens of Strasbourg, Nancy, and Ajaccio are French. That neither unity of language nor community of faith comprises the necessary condition for nationality we see fully proved in trilingual Switzerland, with its three Churches. In North America, there are innumerable peculiarities and differences of every kind among the people; yet the most powerful and solid sense of nationality exists there. Indeed, if we follow the first principle mentioned above to its conclusion, we see that there is not a single European State which ought not to be divided up and torn asunder—and then any durability in a State would be impossible.

Though logically questionable (why *cannot* every ethnic group have its own political order? The axiom is not proved, nor even discussed), Rozen's remarks are clear, at least. True, race and nationality are demonstrably different; true, to divide the races up exactly would result in the destruction of the major European States; but what is the implication of these cool remarks in the Estonian context? Rozen gives the impression of preparing, at some length, a case against Estonian independence. Suddenly, the root cause of such reasoning grows plain: it is separatism, not nationality, that brings Rozen to discuss the citizens of Nancy and Ajaccio:

When these dark and intricate concepts of nationality arose, part of the Russian Press began to charge the inhabitants of the Baltic Provinces with leanings towards Separatism, and to suspect them of treason. Now, the Ests and Letts were long ago germanized in all respects save that of language. As to the Germans, they were basically romanized two thousand years ago. On these changes and transformations is based Europeanism; it is not based on race, that is, on the origins of tribes. Not since 1710 has any inhabitant of the Baltic Provinces thought of separating; on the contrary, all the individuals in those Provinces have unanimously, and with glory, defended Russian interests together with the Russians.[16]

"Dark concepts", "treason", "glory": the discussion of involved, abstract ideas has become emotionally charged. But Rozen, it grows plainer as the argument develops, felt intensely on the separatism question—a question fundamentally connected, as he saw, with the whole issue of non-Slavic identity of Latvians, Estonians, and Germans. Now, after lengthy passages of calmly reasoned prose, we seem to have entered a new region where a sharper, even faintly propagandist tone prevails. All is more personal, less cool. Can one accept at face value the comment that "not since 1710 had any inhabitant of the Baltic Provinces thought of separating"? Of course not; and Rozen was himself familiar with the work and attitudes of the Latvian educator Jānis Cimze (1814–81), in whose seminary, where German *and* Estonian were spoken, as well as Lettish and Russian, was formed what Nodel grandly terms "the advance guard of the renaissance of Estonian national consciousness".[17] Again, how many peasants from Estonia "defended Russian interests" voluntarily? Thousands were drafted into the army, and served their inhumanly long term; but did thoughts of glory trouble them, or notions of their brotherhood with Russian troops? Rozen was writing *à thèse*—something he did extremely rarely. So were his invisible, faceless interlocutors, the Moscow paper *Moscow News* (*Moskovskiye vedomosti*) and the St Petersburg quasi-official publication *Russian Veteran* (*Russkiy invalid*). Before considering his attitude towards (Estonian) separatism further, let us rapidly survey the very different accusations brought against the Baltic peoples by those papers. They were unquestionably, we shall see, of a nature calculated to enrage a loyal subject of the Emperor who happened to speak German (or Estonian), and whose forebears were not Russian.

First, *Russkiy invalid*, responding sympathetically to charges of pan-Baltic separatist leanings made, in 1863, by *Moskovskiye vedomosti*: "There is no doubt, of course, that the Baltic Provinces now represent the remnants of rotting, aristocratic institutions, most rigidly adhering to their privileges, most decidedly opposing every sign of contemporary progress . . ."[18] Why had the ruling classes of those Provinces clung so long and with such prudence to Russia? Because they knew that were their Provinces a part of any other European State, they would see their precious privileges clipped! Expediency alone brought Baltic-German nobles to adhere to Russia. And, of course, the readers of *Russkiy invalid* should not forget the recent lessons of the Polish rising. What the Polish nationalists had done, to their eternal shame and ignominy, the Estonian and Latvian nationalists and separatists could also do in the near future . . .

Far more substantial and distressing (how could the Polish–Baltic analogy be taken seriously by any reasonable Russian with some knowledge of Polish history?) were the rumblings of *Moskovskiye vedomosti*. In the demands for "unity" and "equalization" of all sectors of the Empire expressed in *this* paper, Rozen saw a threat; for what if Russian readers in large numbers formed a wrong impression of the Baltic privileges then being discussed, and failed to understand the Code (*Ulozheniye*) proclaimed by Nicholas himself for the Baltic peoples? Then, alarmed by phantoms of their own creation, even educated Russians might take steps against their Baltic fellow-subjects, with incalculable consequences for Estonia:

Moskovskiye vedomosti preaches unity alone, unity of any kind, unity and equality *in abstracto*. And with this proclamation it has succeeded in touching a sensitive nerve of the Russians. But to us it would appear that, in consequence of passions recently aroused, most of the readers of *Moskovskiye vedomosti* have not taken its exhortations in the sense intended by its Editor-in-Chief . . . The paper desires unity and equality of institutions; it has positively and on more than one occasion explained that differences of language and religion may be accepted, most especially in Russia where, in these respects, there is always and everywhere a homogeneous nucleus of the population—a great majority. We even feel that *Moskovskiye vedomosti* would not be averse to the establishing of equal rights for all religions in the State . . . But never has this paper told its readers (what is true), that a too urgent striving for unity may actually be of harm.

The unity and indivisibility, greatness and might of the Russian State! That is splendid—and we Courlanders, Livonians, and Estonians would be the last to question the great, manifest destiny of Russia, or to deviate from solidarity with her task and with her honour; we have the reputation of not having ceased, from time immemorial, to participate and collaborate in *all* the deeds of war and peace of the *whole* land . . .

Only one thing, in fact, do we demand of *Moskovskiye vedomosti*: that it not merely judge us by its own abstract tenets of State unity and separatism, but examine in more depth and with more care the essence, significance and, above all, legal and historical foundations of our Baltic institutions. That these institutions stand in the most urgent need of change and of correction, and that on comparing them with various aspects of the Russian statutes one does not always find that the advantage lies on our side of Lake Chudskoye, we long ago conceded. But we affirm, first: that one still finds in the Baltic Provinces, because of the principle of self-government that is so powerfully developed in them, great strengths that must not be destroyed wilfully and forcibly; and, second, that *Moskovskiye vedomosti* will recall that . . . there is another, no less important, reason for leaving our institutions untouched, namely, legality—the Law.

Many chords are struck here: the pride of German Balts in their participation in past Russian victories, for instance, and the absolute conviction of legality in working through the *Landrat* (the main Baltic institution tilted at by Russian nationalists during the 1860s, as twenty years before and twenty later).[19] Both ideas are developed further in a later section of the memoirs. And one can only sympathize with Rozen's irritation with the charge that Baltic Germans always served their own ends, and only German ends. As he remarks, Estonian and Baltic-German blood indeed was shed, under the Russian banners, many times during the previous century and more. As to the contribution made to Russian civic life, Baltic Germans had indeed, as he observes, been active in the work of the whole land; still in the 1860s, German names predominated in the higher echelons of the State service. No doubt the argument that Nicholas himself proclaimed the Code on which Estonia's German bureaucracy based its right to operate, was practically of more significance by far than the emotional, historical and vague consideration of fused loyalty and valour; yet it was the latter argument, and its dismissal by Great Russian nationalists, that most upset and irritated Rozen, as this *cri de coeur* makes plain:

Until now we have always regarded ourselves as true Russians in the political context, although of German origin, and as citizens with full rights like the Russians. But now they teach us something different; now they say that we are aliens and intruding newcomers and that we are a people with no fatherland, a tribe without a country.

Such opinions might well wound us and insult us, and deprive us of that
gratifying feeling with which we are prepared always to serve our Fatherland,
were we not of the firm conviction that, through common struggles over many
years, as through common labouring for the good of the whole State, we have
gained for ourselves equality of rights in the Russian land.[20]

Rozen, in particular, might justifiably take umbrage at the claim that German
Balts were "aliens and intruding newcomers": quite apart from the unbroken
presence of the Rozens in Estonia for six full centuries, there remained the fact
that, as he proudly notes, there were seven Russian generals named Rozen in
1814. Was *he* to be regarded as an alien in Mehntack or in Sóldina? The
suggestion was ridiculous to him.

But what, it may be asked, prompted these Slavophile attacks upon the
German Balts (rather, it must be noted, than on the peasantry), and on their
ancient privileges? Part of the answer lies in the word "Slavophile" itself.
Another part lies in the Polish rising of 1863. Yet it is curious at first glance that
now, in the 1860s and not twenty years before, should have begun such steady
onslaughts on the Baltic-Germans' rights and powers and on possible Estonian
separatism. The Slavophiles, it may be said, had failed and still failed to
appreciate the interplay of German and Estonian elements within the Province
of Estonia. Of the controversy between F. R. Fählman, K. J. Peterson and
Friedrich Kreutzwald, Estonian nationalists and founders of Estonia's intel-
ligentsia, and the historian Carl Schirren, a believer in the hopelessness of all
Estonian national aspirations,[21] Aksakov seems to have known nothing. But
even granted the Slavophiles' failure to appreciate the true political and cultural position in Estonia in the 'sixties, why should Estonian separatism have
rung alarums now? After all, the Estophiles of Pastor Johann Rosenplänter's
group—von Luce, von Frey, Knüpffer, and Otto Masing[22] (whose intense love
for Estonia, its language and its people, might well have worried Russian
bureaucrats had they troubled to peruse the pastor's monumental *Beiträge zur
genauern Kenntniss der estnischen Sprache*),[23] had all been dead some twenty
years by 1860! And other likely causes for alarm among the Russian nationalists
had yet to come: Woldemar Jannsen's Song Festival of 1869,[24] the founding of
the Alexander School in Viljandimaa in 1870—all lay in the future still. (*Here*,
certainly, the Slavophiles would have good reason for dismay; for the *Alexandri-
Kool* "was to be a seminary in which the hearts and minds of young Estonians
would be developed to assume the leadership of their persecuted race. The
collection of money—which reached 72,000 roubles by 1885—was undertaken
by 130 local committees: they ventilated the whole nationalist question, and the
opposition they met from the Balts fanned the flame to a blaze."[25]) But it was
opposition from reactionary German Balts, we see, not from the Russian
Government, which in the early 'seventies prompted the rapid growth both of
the Alexander School and of contemporaneous Estophile societies—the Society
of Estonian Writers and the Estonian Students' Society, both bulwarks against

further germanization of Estonian urban youth! (And though only half the population of Tallinn was Estonian in 1871, by 1897 only 12 per cent was German—an extraordinary change of ethnic character in any town.[26]) Of the Estonian–German conflict in the fields of education, commerce, and literature, the Slavophiles and journalists either knew nothing or had heard too much already! Let us, therefore, quite disregarding this unending conflict—like the editors of *Russkiy invalid* and *Moskovskiye vedomosti*—consider what could have provoked Muscovite fears on the Estonians' account in the years 1861–64.

Again we are faced by the imminence, not the consequences, of events. Thanks in large measure to the completion of the St Petersburg–Paldiski railway in 1870 (a line which ran very near Bol'sháya Sóldina, and still does), Estonians would emigrate by masses, taking their grievance against Baltic-German noble and Russian Government alike to the Ukraine; between 1881 and 1897, we are told, 426,000 left Estonia.[27] Again, Estonians *would become* skilled workers, clerks, even small businessmen during the 'seventies, to the consternation of reactionary German Balts. There were, in fact, only two demonstrable causes of alarm from the Great Russian viewpoint in the Estonia of 1861–64. Of these, one has been mentioned: the religious movement led by Johann Leinberg, or Maltsvet the Seer, whose disciples starved by Tallinn when the white ship failed to come to bear them all off to a land of milk and honey (the Crimea). The other was the publication, in Finnish and in German, then in Tallinn and Estonian, in 1862, of the epic poem *Kalevipoeg*, by Friedrich Kreutzwald—a pseudonym of Vidri Rei Rstimets (1803–82). That the appearance of *Kalevipoeg* was of cardinal importance in the fostering of a proud Estonian spirit and of nationalistic sentiment, there can be no question.[28] A literary conglomerate, combining German, Finnish, French, and Estonian elements (and possibly Italian as well), its very printing was a massive task. Yet it is foolish to imagine that Aksakov, Khomyakov, or any other leading Slavophile, was familiar with a long Estonian epic, not available in Russian, French or even, unless one had connections with the Estonian Learned Society or had bought a copy promptly, German paraphrase. So we are brought to two conclusions: that the Slavophiles were generally ignorant of the intensifying conflict between German and Estonian in Estonia; and that, so far from having speedily reacted to developments beside the Baltic, Rozen's interlocutors were, in fact, judging the whole separatist issue in Estonia either theoretically or, worse, in the light of racial strife elsewhere in the huge patchwork of the Empire. But to return to Rozen's deeply-felt rebuttal of the charges laid against the German Balts (and *he*, at least, understood perfectly that the Germans, not Estonian nationalists or intellectuals of any hue, were the targets of the articles published in *Moskovskiye vedomosti*): he denied, first, that the German Balts felt any animosity towards the Russian Government, or Russian might; second, that Baltic institutions should be speedily abolished in the interests of uniformity, equality, or unity; that those institutions, third, rested on any but the soundest legal base; and, fourth, that German Balts did not have full rights, like all subjects of the Emperor and their Russian-speaking fellow-citizens, "on the Russian land"—rights *earned* by loyal service both in peacetime and in war. So far, so good; but the Slavophiles had one more charge to lay against unspecified German Balts in Courland, Estonia, and Livonia; that they hoped to fuse the three provinces into one State:

Moskovskiye vedomosti fears lest the three (Baltic) Provinces merge and form a State within the State, and one whose elements would be harmful and dangerous to the whole Russian State. While not dealing here with this project for union, we must admit that, perceiving this fear on the paper's part, we could not restrain an involuntary smile; for in the very same article we are called "a vanishing apparition" in comparison with the Russian nation... If the merging and unifying of the Baltic Provinces *has* occasionally been written of in the Press, this has been only in relation to the wish of the Emperor Nicholas, in accordance with which wish the Government itself hoped (once) to bring about more uniformity in the institutions of all three. Among ourselves, some have thought to oblige the Government in this way by removing problems of the administration and legal procedure that have arisen *from* the differences in the three Provinces' institutions. To us, in fact, such a merging, on the terms mentioned, would bring various inconveniences...[29]

So, systematically but with unusual heat in several passages, Rozen refutes the "accusations" of the Slavophiles. He writes, we note, on behalf of Baltic Germans, not for the entire Estonian population; but, as was observed, the Slavophiles took little note, in 1861–64, of Estonian nationalism proper. What, then, did he demand for his Estonia, as opposed to Jannsen's, or Carl Jakobson's? (Of his attitude towards their aspirations we shall speak within the context of linguistic controversy.) Three things, essentially: freedom to practise "Lutheran Christianity"; the right to speak German and to use it, in Canadian terminology, as the working language of the province; and the guaranteed, continuing right to a measure of self-government. Rozen makes the demands in these terms:

We hold fast to our Evangelical–Lutheran creed; and no Russian patriot will reproach us with this, since whoever reveres his faith will revere the genuine religiosity of every heterodox.

We hold fast to our language—this is just; and we hold fast to it with a certain pride. If we ever sink to the extent of feeling ashamed of our tongue, then the time will have come when, with full justice, our intentions may be suspected and our services despised.

We hold fast, finally, to our elective institutions, our everyday customs, our justice, and the small measure of self-government which we have, and which affords us more internal freedom than other Provinces of Russia have enjoyed until now...

The Baltic Provinces demand nothing for themselves save what the law of nature and of reason also demand: they do not wish to rot alive. It is a foolish

16

wisdom that would cut off healthy limbs, hoping to save a body. For us, the following lesson may be deduced from what has been said: we must fulfil our duty, and bide our time until an end comes. We do not pursue phantoms and have no need of childish symbols. We wish to be of service to ourselves and to the State.[30]

Once more the temperature of the discussion rises as Rozen, in conclusion. returns to the question of Estonians' non-Russian identity—and so to prevalent misunderstandings of the difference between "race" and "nationality", and "nationality" and "unity". And once again, though speaking of Estonians in a general sense, he speaks essentially of the small Baltic-German ruling class. Nationalism, he remarks, is in the air: the world awaits developments in Italy and Germany, where states are being fused. But many writers use the word "nationality" (*natsional'nost'*) to suggest a political state; some, indeed, claim that "German" has political rather than ethnic significance.

As if ethnographic terms depend on an individual's caprice, or on political whims! *I* never had occasion to hear of a Dutch Englishman, or a French Italian; yet Russian Germans and German Russians are often written about in the newspapers. By "Russian Germans", the papers mean the nobility of the Baltic Provinces. But these Provinces comprise an inseparable part of Russia, and the services of this gentry are recorded in Russian history, and have often prompted the emulation, even the envy, of Great Russian landowners, writers, and civil servants—who have recently begun to reproach their Baltic fellow-countrymen and to demand that they be made their absolute equals, despite their different faith and special privileges.[31]

Of course the Baltic Estonians are not Slavs! Yet they are fellow-citizens of every Great or Little Russian. Rozen was a realist: cultural, linguistic, even economic independence for Estonia, yes; but political, under no circumstances. On the folly and *naïveté* of aspirations for full nationhood, he stood in full agreement with Carl Schirren.[32] Ethnically, the Baltic Provinces could never be regarded as Russian, unless the population mix were to change drastically. But *politically*, how could they ever be regarded as non-Russian? Yet *Moskovskiye vedomosti* dared to describe the Baltic subjects of the Emperor, loyal for 150 years, brothers and parents of the Lievens, Pahlens, Nesselrods, Ostermanns, Barclay de Tollys, Benckendorffs, as "aliens and intruding newcomers"! Now, all non-Slavs were to be thrown out of the Russian body politic! (Happy for Rozen that he did not live to see the Estonia of Shakhovskoy and the Pan-Slavism of the 'eighties.)

Yet every foreigner who has lived five years in the United States or in one of the European States receives full rights of citizenship. Five generations of Baltic nobility have been born and lived in Russia, served her loyally and truly, and to try their loyalty over 160 years they are still called Germans, foreigners, on a level with those newcomers who settle here from abroad only temporarily and in search of a living! Such injustice brought one of the most glorious of Russia's sons to exclaim, with a feeling of deep outrage: "No matter what I may have done in the Napoleonic War, and in Turkey, and at the taking of Warsaw, everyone in Russia calls me a German." ...[33]

So much, then, for Rozen's refutations of the charges of the Slavophiles. As was said, he was a realist. But this, as is made plain by the real indignation in his refutations, by no means meant that he did not have patriotic feelings for Estonia. He liked the people, and the countryside, traditions, and peculiarities; in short, he was proud of Estonia:

> Always, in all important patriotic undertakings, Estonia has been in the forefront. When the Northern War was causing shifts in the boundaries of the northern States, *Estlyandiya* did not wait on the decisions of her neighbours in *Liflyandiya* and Courland, who went over to Poland, but decided by herself to remain subject to her previous rulers, the Kings of Sweden. When the idea arose of emancipating the Baltic serfs, *Estlyandiya* did not ask the opinion of her neighbours, but resolved to free them a year before *Liflyandiya*—and two before Courland. In a time of external and internal wars, she bore sacrifices to her utmost limit and without preparatory consultations with her neighbours...And when the nobilities of Courland and Livonia were usually seeking to serve in the chanceries of embassies and ministries, the Estonian nobility were toiling in the State system for the most meagre salaries, and were the most reliable defenders of the soldier and protectors of the Fatherland.[34]

Well Rozen might be proud of his own family's service to Russia as, in more recent years, of his own record of service to the peasantry of Sóldina. But always, we have seen, he spoke primarily for the Germans of Estonia in answering the charges of the Slavophiles. The time has come to consider his attitude towards the aspirations, cultural, linguistic, and political, of the other Estonia— that of the Ests.

Rozen, it quickly grows apparent in this context, was a man of the 1830s. Not that his appreciation of Estonians' economic, and even cultural, needs did not grow wonderfully during the 1850s; yet the fact remains that, necessarily perhaps, as he was born in 1800, his understanding of Estonians' political and cultural destiny—sooner or later to be germanized—was that of J. G. Kohl's generation. Legal and economic change in the Province, in the years of his late adolescence, had been followed by a cultural emancipation tending towards general germanization. And how could any Balt, in 1820, have supposed that there would come both an Estonian cultural renaissance and a powerful sense of ethnic pride, all within two generations? In the first place, the Province's educational system did not provide for higher education in the native language; and this was the deliberate policy of the *Landrat*. No German, even were he as enlightened as Jannau or Merkel, thought of the emancipation of Estonian peasants in terms of the renaissance of Estonian culture.[35] Literacy in the native tongue was to be used only as a first step towards germanization; eventually, it was supposed and hoped, the Estonians would become a part of the German people, or at least an indistinguishable part of the German Baltic State. In the second place, it was apparent during Rozen's early years that Estonian villagers were, indeed, doing their best to assimilate Estonian–German culture, and were learning German.[36] Those hoping to advance themselves had little choice in the matter: everyone in a superior position to the peasant, from the cobbler to the clergyman, the bailiff to the landlord, used German; and the road towards complete germanization was smooth, especially in towns. What, thirdly, had the Estonians to gain by resisting German culture (even if it were not too late, as Kohl believed, to elevate Estonian into a modern literary language, so forming a specifically Est culture)? Certainly the evidence of backwardness seemed overwhelming to conservatives, and to all but eccentric liberals, in Rozen's early manhood. Even in the 'thirties, Kohl records, living conditions in Estonian peasant households were appalling:

> Here is the extreme of poverty, filth, disorder and want, and there is nothing comparable to it in the whole of Europe . . . During the winter, the living-area is also a yard for chickens; the benches, tables, and chairs of the Estonians look as though they had grown in a forest . . . and it is obvious that, of the outstanding progress which the rest of Europe has made in the arts and crafts, not a particle has reached *this* people, who remain in the same prehistoric condition as their ancestors in ancient epochs.[37]

Of course it was the destiny of the Estonians to be germanized; and the quicker that process went on (here Rozen differed radically from Ungern-Sternberg and his party), the better it would be for all. Yet, Rozen saw, primary education in the native tongue was vital; so, throughout his life, he actively supported parish schools. Estonian parish schools offered a stepping-stone to peasants wishing to advance themselves, and, besides, were always supervised by pastors. Biblical history, the Catechism, reading, writing, and religious songs—there was nothing here to which a liberal or Christian could object. Rozen's attitude towards the training of Estonians, in short, was essentially that of the religious educator Friedrich August Hollmann (1833–1900). Hollmann's aim, in his Tartu school for primary teachers, was in the first place to preserve the Baltic-German tradition and political system; nor had he any sympathy with national aspirations of a practical, political variety. Yet, Hollmann saw, Estonians could not be stopped from being, like their ancestors, Estonians—and perhaps the effort to transform them was misguided.[38] But Estonian culture as distinct from German? Like Hollmann, Rozen failed to understand the possibility. Ignorant of the peasants' tongue and unacquainted with Estonian *intelligenty* such as Kreutzwald and F. R. Fählman, Rozen, it must be said in fairness to the latter, did not give an incipient Estonian literature the chance to interest him or impress him. Did he know of the Romantic poetry of Kristian Jaak Peterson (1801–22)? Had he a copy of *Kalevipoeg* in translation? Almost certainly not; for Rozen, it was seen, greatly respected poetry and was by no means ignorant of contemporary French and Russian verse. If he had read *Kalevipoeg*, we may reasonably think, the fact would have appeared somewhere in his articles, memoirs, or correspondence.

Rozen, then, was culturally and politically—but not in his economic views—a German of the 'thirties. By his last months in Estonia, in 1855, Fählman and Rosenplänter, Knüpffer and Masing, the founding fathers of the Estonian Learned Society, whose outlook on such matters in so many ways echoed his own, were all dead. Another generation had replaced the earlier German Estophiles, and theirs was quite a different outlook. No longer were the Estophiles content to save a seemingly doomed culture or, indeed, to take an academic attitude towards Estonia's past, present, and future, as during the 1830s and 1840s; no longer was it generally supposed that Estonian culture, or as much of it as had survived six centuries of German domination, would die a quiet death by 1900. Now, the peasantry wished to speak German but in no event at the expense of their own tongue, and Estonian *intelligenty* in Tartu and, a little later, Tallinn, were beginning to perceive that, although German culture still attracted *them*, it was losing its appeal to the masses. How, we may ask, did Rozen's attitude towards the destiny of the Estonians (to be germanized, but to retain their language and their place within the Empire) compare with that of the new German liberals—the Baltic liberals of the 'sixties? The question is best answered by contrasting his approach towards that destiny (or "destiny"), with that taken by the historian Carl Schirren (1826–1910), the leader of the liberals within the changed Estonian Learned Society, in his celebrated *Livländische Antwort an Herrn Juri Samarin* (1869).

Samarin's attack on the Baltic Germans, it must first be said, *Okrainy Rossii* (*Russia's Borderlands*),[39] produced a far greater effect upon its targets than had any previous attack by Slavophile propagandists; for it was no propagandist tract, but a detailed account of the position of "the Germans in the Baltic", of their cultural monopoly in some regions, their political oppression of Estonians and Letts in others, by a serious historian. Samarin, to summarize, accused the Germans of misusing the Articles of Capitulation of the Baltic *Ritterschaften* in order to perpetuate their ancient privileges; of encouraging the Lutheran Church to suppress the peasants' efforts to join the Russian Orthodox community; of pretending to improve the peasants' economic status, while actually controlling credit banks for their own ends; of germanizing only those Estonians who would become "good" Balts and help them in their various tasks; and, finally, of clinging desperately to their mediaeval, feudal powers over the native populace.

Schirren's reply, published in Leipzig within weeks of Rozen's memoirs, was comprehensive and sarcastic. The privileges, he pointed out, had had a good effect within the Baltic Provinces; nor could the Russians justifiably complain of shaky loyalty from German landowners. The Russian Government, however, had wilfully hampered the development of all three Baltic provinces by superimposing alien laws, organizations, and reforms.[40] The Baltic Germans, he insisted, were the only legal heirs to their provinces, and their right rested on law. The Capitulations of 1710 must be the sole basis of all future development and policy within the area.

But where did Rozen stand in this heated controversy? The answer is: a little to Carl Schirren's left. To take concrete points: Schirren had a strong belief in the mission of the Germans in Estonia, Livonia, and Courland—a mission that consisted in the preservation of the German way of life in all three Provinces. So too did Rozen; but Rozen's was a pride in German culture tempered with humility, and with awareness of the Estonians' own virtues: cheerfulness and industry. Again, Schirren held that no Tsar had a moral *or* a legal right to change the basic structure of the Provinces. Rozen, we saw, could argue passionately on the grounds of legal right and moral rightness that the government should leave the Baltic Provinces their measure of self-government, language, faith, and institutions; but he also saw that, as he puts it, "nothing is eternal in this world . . . and all the sacredness of State treaties must be taken only *cum grano salis*".[41] His reasoning, though as committed, was never as intensely partisan as Schirren's, nor his tone as high. Finally, on the question of reform: Schirren accepted the necessity and justness of reform within the frame of the existing socio-political establishment beside the Baltic. Politically and socially, in other words, the position of the Germans should be seen as totally inviolable. Rozen agreed, although he never put the matter in so crisp a form. Culturally, reform should bring Estonians into contact with a higher (German) culture. Once more Rozen agreed implicitly, although not explicitly. But here, the two ceased to agree: for Schirren, it was folly to construct a single secondary school in which Estonian would be spoken. Effort would be squandered pointlessly in writing textbooks. Teachers would be well advised not to think of learning Estonian—for was there not a culture and a language already available? Estonians, in fact, would be well advised to turn their gaze away from *Kalevipoeg* and to speak German. The attitude was widespread among Baltic landowners. Here, to complement Schirren's view, is an extract from remarks published anonymously in *Baltische Monatsschrifte* in 1864:

> We do not have sufficient able teachers to change from a German to an Estonian form of education without damaging the very store of knowledge. For there is not even an Estonian scientific language. Our teacher, whether of German or Estonian origin, is always German-educated . . . If today we wanted first an Estonian literature, and then a corresponding teaching force to educate by means of it, we should hold back our general education for decades.[42]

For Rozen, this was too much. Does not every people have the right to speak its language and develop it? Granted, Estonian was to be subordinate to German in the field of government; but in trade, many Estonians were managing quite well in their own tongue by the 1860s. Legal cases, at the district level, were invariably heard in the defendant's language. Dammed up, the liberalism that had brought him to abolish *corvée* before any of his neighbours and to help his peasants at his own expense, overflowed at the suggestion that all peoples should not freely speak their native tongue. Of course the Baltic Germans would learn Russian. And of course many Estonians would learn German, for their own material advantage. But to *require* that an Estonian not speak Estonian, or even to expect it, was a different and unpleasant matter. Tolerance and consistency of policy: these were the keys, in Rozen's view, to the defusing of the heated argument still raging when, in 1869, his own memoirs appeared. Language, he had no need to be told, was ever an emotionally-charged question. And since Estonia was to be always in the Empire and Estonians fellow-citizens of Muscovites, how could the government gain anything but enmity, resentment, and rebellion by oppressing the Estonian and German peoples, languages, and customs in the Province?

In general, we must be less severe towards our fellow-countrymen of different races. No one will prevent the Englishman from treasuring his nationality and being ready to lay down his life for a Jew, a Don Pacifico, or an Indian who has become an English subject; yet he was not affronted when French became the official language in courts and offices in what had been the French part of Canada, or when the Italian tongue prevailed in Malta, or the German tongue in Heligoland. Nor does the Dutchman take affront because the official language in Luxemberg is French, or the Frenchman when German is to be heard in Alsace and Lotharingia! So, too, the Estonian and Livonian noble feels no anger because Estonian or Lettish, and not German, prevails in the villages around him. Let the Tartars speak Tartar, the Georgians, Georgian, and the Baltic Russians, German, Estonian, or Lettish . . .[43]

Rozen's was a common-sensical, liberal stance. His sojourn in the Caucasus, we see again, made a profound impression on him. Conceivably he sensed even during the 'sixties that, faced by the threat of an intensified russification programme in the Baltic Provinces, Estonian and German stood together—and might even fall together. It was a threat that he saw realized during his lifetime, for the 1880s marked the start of a new chapter in the history of Estonia. Since their conquest of the Province, Russians had, with one short lapse during the governorship of General E. A. Golovin, dealt with the Baltic Germans tenderly. The Rozens and their fellows formed a German-speaking enclave in the Empire. But by 1880, Russia had its own administrative corps, and the *chinovniki* had less need of the assistance of the Baltic civil servant. Moreover, the conviction that German culture was superior to Russian had been fading for at least one generation. Thus two great checks to the advance of anti-German and Pan-Slavic imperialism, so chillingly embodied in the person of K. Pobedonostsev, Procurator of the Holy Synod, had crumbled by the last two years of Rozen's life. But Rozen was himself an aged man by 1882, when, with the introduction of the Russian Municipal Constitution to Estonia, Estonians of peasant origin suddenly found themselves with an unshakable majority on almost all town councils. As in the south, russification had begun in earnest with administrative reform. At least he did not live to see the day when, in 1885, the Balt *Landesgymnasia* collapsed, and Russian priests were offered decorations for impressive numbers of Estonian converts to the Orthodox (and Nationalist and Tsarist) faith.

II

AMNESTY AND EMANCIPATION

Rozen arrived in the Ukraine, in May 1856, not only with two concrete tasks—
the organizing of his son's affairs and the management of Kamenka—but also
with the skills required to do so. He was logical, and tactful, and above all
competent as a farmer. Once more the lessons learned at Mehntack and
Petrovsky and Kurgan were to prove useful; once more his steadiness of
temperament would help others in their troubles.[1] He was received by his
sister-in-law Mar'ya and her daughter Ina, for whom he always felt the greatest
affection. Yevgeniy, he immediately saw, had allowed his estate accounts to
grow chaotic; for the last two years there had been deficits, and his son had been
too ill to make a search of all his books. First, something was to be done about
Yevgeniy. So hateful had Stratilatovka become to him that he was anxious to
move out, leaving the property in his father's hands; and move he did, to the
hamlet of Mar'yansk, where many of his wife's peasants and servants settled
in four cramped huts. Rozen visited his son, and found him much improved,
calmer and healthier, after two months. Next, he turned his attention to his
own new house and land, and set to work:

On May 20, I settled down to work on the new farm; the sowing was over. The
former functionaries—the ataman, clerk, and threshing-master or granary-keeper
—had all been transferred to Mar'yansk, so I had to start on the new farm with
new people, though in the old manner until they and the climate and the soil
should have proved themselves. For three days I was present from morning until
evening while they sheared the sheep, noting down and marking off the weight of
every fleece, and marking the best ewes with a brand. It was evident that my
brother-in-law [Andrey Malinovsky—G.B.] had been trying to improve the stock
and not sparing money in purchasing breeding rams and ewes: I found a mix of
the most fine-fleeced Spanish, Saxon, and Bergam sheep, but the wool was not
profitable because it was too light.[2]

Around Bol'sháya Sóldina, too, sheep-farming had been widespread, although
not on the scale to be encountered in Khar'kov Province. But there, Rozen had
merely watched. Now, he had to learn the basics of a new branch of husbandry,
and he did so with a will. Fleeces were marketed, he found, at the Trinity fair in
Khar'kov; he went there, and spoke to shareholders in joint-stock companies

with interests in wool. Increasingly, he was informed, local landowners were sending washed wool straight to Moscow. He had a wash-trough built, and studied market trends. Both natural and treated fleeces, he saw, had doubled in price over eight years, since 1848; now, the former sold in Khar'kov at 8 roubles on average, the latter at 13.[3] Financially, too, he committed himself to his new enterprise. Why should he not, since the market prospects, like the soil and climate in the area, were so good? The climate, in particular, delighted Rozen, though its changeability at first caused him surprise. But thirty years before, the peasants told him, it had been yet better:

> The climate of the Ukraine, in fact, has changed completely since the first quarter of the century. Old-timers recalled well the most marvellous fruit-gardens with the tenderest of fruits, and the mildest, shortest of open winters.[4] They would lay in enough hay in two and a half months at most, and cattle and horses had pasturage enough almost the whole year round. The cheapness of bread and food supplies had been almost fabulous—a quarter of wheat had cost two roubles in notes, a quarter of rye, one rouble, and of oats, 60 kopeks; for a turkey they had paid 15 kopeks, for a goose—10, and for a chicken—5 . . .
>
> Why such a change in such a short time? In cold Siberia, on the southern slopes of hills, we see whole woods of wild apricot and peaches; and on the icy tundra of the Yenisey and in the forests of Yakutsk district are still found bones and parts of the skeletons of mammoths and of animals and beasts flourishing now only in the torrid zones of Southern Asia and of Africa. But this climatic change has come about gradually, over thousands of years, over eras . . . and from the changing tilt of the earth's axis and its rotation. The visible change that has occurred in the Ukraine almost, so to speak, before our eyes, *I* ascribe to the destruction of the rich forests which once shielded the south of Russia from the north.[5]

Rozen's supposition was well founded. But he had informed himself on the subject of the weather, as on so many other topics, with thoroughness and method. And not content merely to note the sudden temperature changes in 1856, he recorded them. So, too, with the price of wool in Khar'kov fairs from 1848 to 1867,[6] and with the national debt from 1828 to 1856.[7] There was little carelessness, or carefreeness, in his approach to life in later middle age.

So, having assessed the land and market, he set to work to reorganize the whole system of farming. But even to redistribute the land on a different field-plan, he discovered, would be to run against the peasants, whose conservatism on the matter was matched only by their insistence that each mower be allotted three full tumblers of vodka every morning during hay-making. Change was regarded with suspicion:

> I divided the fields into *desyatins*, placed chalky stones at the corners of four-*desyatin* plots, drew furrows, and made field-plans for each wedge; and in that same year, the stones were dragged about and the peasants ploughed over and distorted the furrows so that the division of the fields remained on paper only,

and fresh measurement was necessary annually . . . The custom had been
introduced of giving the hay-makers three tumblers of vodka per man per day.
This generosity, however, did not ruin the landowner, since it gave the worker a
taste for the bottle and obliged him, on festivals, to repay the landowner's
kindness generously—by punctual carouses in the latter's drinking houses. In
four years I managed to put an end to this local custom, having proved to the
peasants by other privileges that *this* innovation was not made out of meanness . . .

The black earth (*chornozem'*) of the Ukraine has earned and kept its fame
because, although it does not yield a harvest of twenty-fold, as it once did, but
only of three-fold to six-fold, still it does this on soil that has had no natural or
artificial fertilizer since the world began. You plough only once before sowing and
sow on the same field several years in a row, and still the soil produces grain, even
abundantly when the rain comes in time. The Little Russian plough is a good one,
but requires three pairs of oxen, while the Little Russians' wooden and
extremely poor harrows do not penetrate arable land, but merely make cloud
designs on it; yet still the earth produces. In a word, agriculture is in its infancy.
There are no drying rooms for grain nor good farm implements, yet nonetheless
agriculture has brought wealth to the landowner here because labour is gratuitous.
Plough as you like, sow, reap, and thresh as you like, still you'll have a clear profit
without trouble or anxieties. But for the experienced farmer such a situation
cannot be satisfactory . . .[8]

Here, Rozen found peasants unwilling to exert themselves not because, as in
Estonia, they saw no point in toiling on the landlord's land, but because, as in
some valleys of the Caucasus, the needlessness of extra toil was so apparent; as
he remarks, "labour was gratuitous" once the necessities had been secured, and
around Khar'kov, grain and vegetables and fruit abounded almost every
summer. It was, in short, a southern situation, comparable to that which had
frustrated him in Georgia where, even more than here, the peasant was happy
to sit idly by a sun-baked wall with a loaf and glass of wine. In the winter, of
course, matters were different; then there could be no *dolce far niente* in Izyum,
where cold winds blew. But now the peasants claimed that their axle was
broken, or their oxen indisposed; they did not plough the corners of a field; and
they were used to receiving gifts, which were almost bribes, of horses from their
master.[9] Rozen struggled with the peasants. He could not adapt to semi-
indolence, though the local peasants' songs were wonderfully harmonious, and
the Ukrainians themselves cheerful and amiable. True, the local peasants were
both healthier and cleaner than Estonian *batraki*: they ate pork or beef, melons
and honey, and washed regularly. True, they were physically more pleasing
than Estonians and better dressed, though the women's working clothes struck
him as ugly.[10] But many years would pass before, at last, he ceased to feel a
stranger in their midst. In the meantime he resisted peasant idleness, rising early
and going out into the fields before the workers had arrived. Lack of sleep,
combined with chalk-dust from the roads along which he rode each morning,
soon resulted in an inflammation of the eye—an old complaint. Hours spent in
dark rooms, lotions, nothing helped. Fortunately a physician in the district

hospital, one K. N. Koversky, proved more competent than had Malinin in Kurgan. Ointment dealt with the problem and it passed away once more, only to trouble him again during the 'seventies.

Now, in August 1856, there occurred an event beside which all his small preoccupations with his health and land paled into insignificance: Alexander II, long haunted by the memory of the Decembrists he had seen in the church of Kurgan, proclaimed a general amnesty. The edict was timed to coincide with the day of his coronation, August 26. A copy reached Izyum on September 3, sent by a local merchant with whom Rozen had had dealings. Only sixteen months before, on April 11, 1855, Rozen had been refused permission to return to, and reside in, St Petersburg. Now, it seemed, the penalty for his participation in the rising on December 14, 1825 had been paid in full. But how could one be sure? Even under the terms of "general amnesty", ex-prisoners of the first category were forbidden to use titles they had borne, though their children might now do so. Thus Obolensky, as I. I. Pushchin remarked in jest, had performed a miracle: not being a prince, he had nonetheless produced small princes.[11] So, after thirty years, the return of the Decembrists started: Trubetskoy, Pushchin, Volkonsky and twelve more returned to European Russia in 1856. But time was running out for charity towards these exiles. Amnesty came late. Amnesty itself, indeed, brought extra worries to some exiles, for it meant that they could leave for a Russia which, they knew, would be a strange country to them. Still, for most of them the temptation was irresistible; only ten, including A. V. Poggio, Mikhail Bestuzhev, and M. K. Kyukhel'beker, chose to remain in Siberia. Of the fifteen who returned in 1856, only four were alive in January 1870.[12] Age was advancing on them all.

What was Rozen's attitude by now towards his own and his companions' past? Certainly it was less simple than that of Yakushkin, or of Pushchin, both of whom remained anti-tsarist diehards; nor could he, like Basargin, say that his happiest days had been passed in a secret political society—for Rozen, the years of his return to Estonia had proved happier than 1823–25. The question is perhaps best answered in connection with his final summing up of Nicholas I, the man responsible for his disgracing thirty years before.

Towards Nicholas, Rozen adopted a deliberately charitable attitude. The Emperor, he knew, had died well, his health and spirits broken at the age of fifty-nine by the disasters of the war in the Crimea and the knowledge of disorder and corruption in his army. He had died a Christian death, begging forgiveness of his entourage, speaking kindly to his servants. But the Emperor's death alone does not account for the arresting quality of Rozen's précis of his life and character; Rozen, we see, had by his middle years become a staunch believer in the value of autocracy in Russia. If there was everywhere corruption and abuse, he could claim, the trouble lay not in autocracy itself, but in the willingness of many to abuse it. Not the system, but corruption of the system, was to blame. Yet, we have seen, he was a liberal in economic and in cultural matters—a believer in the wrongness of *corvée* and slavery. Rozen, in short, could separate the notions of autocracy and serfdom, helping the peasantries of Khar'kov and Estonia to greater economic independence and prosperity, and simultaneously supporting tsardom. Always a gradualist, he was by 1856 far less disposed than he had ever been to jolt the State's foundations. Why was he liberal in his attitude towards peasants in Izyum? For two reasons: because a liberal, charitable attitude came naturally to him; and because common sense and reason both *demanded* that the peasants' well-being be cared for. If they prospered and were satisfied, the landowner would benefit, and so also the State; if they lived wretchedly, in hunger and oppressed, as was the case during his childhood in Estonia, the landowner would feel the consequences—as, too, would the State. Practically, economically, and morally, it was so evident that to mistreat one's fellows was to court one's own (moral *and* economic) downfall: as in Kurgan and in Bol'sháya Sóldina, so here, in Kamenka, Rozen pursued a policy of reasonable charity and charitable common sense. As a younger man, perhaps, moral considerations had had greater weight with him than economic factors; now, as he approached his sixtieth year, practical considerations more than held their own, where a policy towards his idle peasants was concerned. Magnanimous in tone, measured in style, here is a part of his obituary of Nicholas I:

The Emperor Nicholas I was generously endowed by nature both in physical appearance and in intellectual abilities. No one will question his decisiveness or bravery. By temperament, he was highly energetic, but had great strength of self-control also, with which he would often overcome an innately hot temper. He sought the love of no man; he was content to inspire fear, and the man whom he had terrified he always treated kindly, or with condescension. But self-sufficiency and self-confidence, tolerable qualities, and sometimes even useful ones, in a private individual, become a shortcoming in a monarch, and especially in an autocrat. Nicholas I listened to no one, tolerated no advice and, indeed, would not be advised. He had submissive, zealous servants, and they flattered him and even praised his errors at the outsets of the Hungarian and Crimean Wars; how, then, was he to restrain himself from self-sufficiency?

Among us, everything flows from the will of one man, the autocratic Sovereign. And this Sovereign, be he a Trajan or a Caligula, will care faithfully for his subjects—if not out of love for the Fatherland or mankind, at least for present glory and for glory in posterity. Why, then, do his helpful ukases not achieve their ends? Because there are those persons who find injustices and oppression to their advantage. Neither the cudgel of Peter, nor the kindness of Catherine, nor Alexander's wishes nor Nicholas's threats have yet removed abuses.

All Nicholas's educated contemporaries unanimously called him a tyrant. He ruined his own glory, it seems, crushed by the weight of his unlimited power. Yet notwithstanding all this, many people of all classes and conditions bless his memory and praise his name – all those who made fortunes and acquired estates, pensions, high ranks, and orders, and all those who, in their own domains, in crown settlements, and in towns, were acting the despot just as energetically and unaccountably as he . . . Nicholas, there is no doubt, sincerely wished for the good of the Fatherland; but he was mistaken in his main end and his choice of means for reaching it, so that in several respects he became the representative of another century, and the successor to that Tsar who affirmed: "It is not fitting for us to introduce what we did not have before!" . . .[13]

It is a complex passage. Before one's eyes, irreconcilable approaches and contrasting moods strive to predominate. Rozen, it is apparent, found much that was admirable in Nicholas: his decisiveness (becoming in a senior officer, as in a ruler), his courage, and his self-control. (So, too, we may note, did another Decembrist of German antecedents—Baron Shteyngel'.[14]) Yet at the same time he deplored the late Tsar's inability to listen to advice. In Rozen's summary of the effects of Nicholas's policy also, ambivalence prevails: not autocracy itself, he claims, but grave abuse results in evils. But those evils, he can see, were prevalent in 1720, and peasants suffered just as much under the countless petty tyrants of his own day as two centuries before! With the *core* of his assessment: that Nicholas was sincere and well-intentioned, but misguided in his "main end and means for reaching it", there can be no arguing. But why, one wonders at the end of the assessment, does Rozen, having pointed out that in the main Nicholas's merits and achievements could not outweigh his shortcomings, not say so very clearly? Nowhere else can one complain of lack of clarity in Rozen's writings; yet here the issue is, if not precisely blurred, at least left vague. Rozen hesitates to weigh the late Emperor and find him lacking. And the phenomenon is not peculiar to him alone: Sergey Volkonsky, whose life was dislocated by the man, sobbed bitterly on hearing news of Nicholas's death. Seldom would Obolensky miss an opportunity, in his last years, to champion autocracy, while simultaneously adducing evidence of its corrupting influence on the national life! Why so? Because, we must conclude, Rozen, Volkonsky, and Obolensky, like a handful of other Decembrists including Gorbachevsky, Falenberg, Frolov and Kryukov (all of whom, perhaps significantly, chose to remain in Siberia after 1856), entertained double feelings on the subject of their own rebelliousness, so many years before, and of their treatment by the Tsar. On the one hand, they deprecated the adventure. Rozen, in particular, would emphasize the youthfulness of the insurgents, their lack of organization and true leadership, their naïve idealism. ("They . . . had a political impossibility in view, and had only themselves to thank if they proved the victims of their own imprudence."[15]) The whole rising was unfortunate, of course. But on the other hand, they felt a sense of pride in their participation in what was, after all, a noble and idealistic, if impractical, adventure. They had "held it to be a point of honour to share danger with men whom they had known to be devoted, noble champions of modern ideas . . . they had worked with the best of their time."[16] Similarly in their attitude towards Nicholas, their former master now swept from the earth by death. (And how death preyed on their minds by 1860 is apparent from contemporaneous letters by Pushchin, Gorbachevsky, Zavalishin, Obolensky, and Yakushkin. In 1859 alone D. A. Shchepin-Rostovsky, F. M. Bashmakov, V. A.

Beschasnov, A. F. von der Briggen, V. M. Golitsyn, and Mikhail Kyukhel'beker had all followed Nicholas into the grave[17]—surely enough cause for survivors to think apprehensively about their own coming demise. Faced by death, convicts and judges stood together.) Nicholas had been a tyrant, certainly; but not an evil man. For Rozen, too, the link remained unbroken between Russia's glory and the Tsar's, Russia's honour and the Tsar's. Army officers in the Imperial service swore loyalty and allegiance to the Tsar, and so to Russia——not to the Government or to the General Staff. It was a curiously personal patriotism he had shared, in earlier years, with his brother-officers in the Finland Lifeguards; and for the Russian peasantry, similarly, the ideas of Holy Russia and "the little father" were inseparably linked. Such feelings were not soon to be cast off. But in Rozen this duality of outlook grew apparent only when the *motives* of his comrades and their judges were discussed; and, though this became quite frequent in the 'seventies, with the appearance of the memoirs of his comrades,[18] he in general avoided controversy—likely, in his opinion, to create unnecessary ill feeling among friends—and concentrated on the simple statement of attested facts (see Chapter 12). Far more evident was that duality in E. P. Obolensky. Ever hounded by a hyperactive conscience, Obolensky, we have seen, proved something of a menace to his comrades in 1826, providing Nicholas with detailed lists of members of the Northern Society, present and past, and baring his breast because his conscience made him do so. Now, as Zetlin notes, "he would invariably defend his views in such a manner as to make his listeners arrive at diametrically opposite conclusions: thus . . . he would condemn the secret societies by stressing the nobility of their motives."[19]

Rozen's sympathy with Obolensky, and his heavy correspondence with him from the fifth to seventh decades, are of special interest. In the first place, that sympathy and correspondence kept him in close contact with his comrades in Siberia until the amnesty was proclaimed: together with Yakushkin, Pushchin, and Gorbachevsky, Obolensky played a major rôle in the maintaining of friendships between exiles scattered over the enormous Empire. Thus, Rozen was included in the periodic roll-call, mentioned in long letters (from N. I. Lorer to von der Briggen and M. M. Naryshkin in 1841–47, for example,[20] and from Gorbachevsky to Zavalishin in 1857–63),[21] and remembered by his comrades still in settlements. In the second place, it serves as a reminder that Rozen always felt at ease with men of simple Christian outlook. In Petrovsky Zavod, it was seen, he was on close terms with P. S. Bobrishchev-Pushkin; now, more than twenty years later, he was still in contact with him, and admired him even more. So, too, with N. I. Lorer. Lorer, though a cheerfully erratic individual, was also a straightforward man. Rozen liked him for that quality, and, while Lorer was in Tiflis still, in 1848–49, took a practical interest in his sons.[22] But Obolensky, Rozen knew from personal experience having been his fellow subaltern in 1823, had an almost childlike honesty and lack of affectation. Even in exile, conscience did not cease to drive him. Many Decembrists, including Mikhail Bestuzhev, Frolov, and Falenberg, had married Siberian peasant girls;

but only Obolensky had done so from motives of contrition and deliberate self-abasement. In adolescence, he had dreamed of an ideally pure woman of unearthly beauty—a creature of the Schellingian hinterland. Now, in Siberia, he perceived the possibility of self-perfection only in terms of marriage with an ugly, virtuous woman. First, he proposed to an aged chambermaid of Princess Trubetskaya, and was speedily rejected. Later he was accepted, half-willingly, by a young peasant nurse hired by I. I. Pushchin, his neighbour in the township of Yalutorovsk. The girl had been employed to suckle Pushchin's own illegitimate daughter. Even marriage to the girl, which seems to have proved tolerably happy, afforded him another moral challenge: he had to pardon friends for their hostility, overt or veiled, towards that marriage. "My wife", he declared defiantly, "is not from the higher circles, but is a simple, illiterate girl. Honourably and unselfishly did I seek her hand, and she has given herself to me unselfishly and honourably."[23] Here were ideals with which Rozen could entirely sympathize. Obolensky's attitude, it soon transpired, was too straightforward for his theoretically egalitarian friends; but Rozen, who believed in keeping the political and social *status quo*, at least in his own Province of Estonia, said nothing. And how could he chastise a man who viewed all things from an unflinchingly religious standpoint, that is, whose life was governed by his conscience and his duty, as he saw it, to the Church Invisible? Virtuous and honourable, Obolensky spoke to Rozen's heart, not to his mind. As he put it in a letter to the prince on March 23, 1849: "There are those happy persons (like yourself) whose letters and conversation produce on the listener or reader the most comforting impression, inclining him to kindness, tolerance, and a striving for the good."[24]

Above all, Obolensky formed a human link between Rozen, in Estonia or the Ukraine, and Decembrists still three thousand miles away in settlements scattered throughout Eastern Siberia. With the proclamation of Imperial amnesty towards the exiles, Rozen could take his part, first in reunions, then in the writing of the long Decembrist record: for, than him, no one Decembrist was more thoroughly acquainted with all phases of that movement known *post facto* as Decembrism, or with its main participants. Prompted to do so by the reappearance of his comrades "from space", as Volkonsky put it, but more especially by the mortality among those ageing comrades, he again took up his memoirs. The idea of offering his children and their children a complete, factually accurate account of the Decembrist movement seized him. Suddenly, time seemed to press. Siberia was a Decembrist necropolis; several had died of wounds or fever in the Caucasus; I. B. Avramov and N. F. Lisovsky were both killed by bandits in January 1856, on the very eve of amnesty. Rozen rewrote the earlier sections, on the rise of liberalism and clandestine groups in Russia, and began to add new chapters on more recent years.

The present called, however, and the wool-markets of Khar'kov. It was unlikely, he saw, that he would ever have occasion to spend more than days or weeks in Estonia; and, although he had permission now to do so, he felt no urge to live in St Petersburg or Moscow. So, on October 10, 1856, he laid the stone foundations of a new house in the neighbourhood of Kamenka, in the hamlet of Viknino. It was the third time he had done so; but here he would remain twenty-eight years, longer than in Kurgan, or Sóldina, or even in Mehntack. He bred sheep, and wrote his memoirs, and made contact with more comrades from Siberia—P. N. Svistunov, A. N. Sutgof, and S. I. Krivtsov.

So dawned the age of great reforms; and men closely connected with the rising of December 14, 1825 played their part in introducing those reforms. First, there was P. D. Kiselyov (1788–1872), by 1857 a General-Adjutant and Count. So far as had been possible under Nicholas I, he had done his best to soften the rigours of serfdom, proposing measures to improve the peasants' economic situation both in Great and Little Russia and in Rumania, during the Russian occupation. Finally, Kiselyov had been dispatched into honorary exile, as Ambassador to France; but now Alexander II had consulted him, while abroad, on his notion of creating "obligatory peasants"—peasants under definite obligations to their masters until they should succeed in redeeming their land. Next, there was Yakov Rostovtsev who, having informed Ryleyev that he was about to do so, had on December 12, 1825, presented a report to Nicholas, warning him of the plans of the Northern Society and advising him "for the sake of his own glory" not to accept the crown until Constantine came to the capital.[25] Now, in middle age, Rostovtsev more than redeemed his sins—which were exaggerated at the time, it may be added, by overwrought conspirators[26]— towards the Liberals of his youth. From the first, Rostovtsev was a member of Alexander II's Private Committee, established in January 1857 to consider projects for emancipation that had been already made; from the first, too, he opposed Orlov, reactionary chairman of that same Committee, and won Alexander's confidence. Though not a highly cultivated individual, Rostovtsev had much common sense. Studying the peasant question while on holiday in Germany, he quickly grasped the main points, and wrote letters to the Tsar showing that peasants should not only have freedom with land, but should retain the plots that they already held—while the gentry should be compensated not only for the land itself but also for the labour, which would cost the State a high price.[27] Others, too, whose lives had once been overcast by their complicity, real or supposed, in the Decembrist rising, now played their parts in the reform process: S. S. Lanskoy, for example, the recently appointed liberal Minister of Internal Affairs. Once, Lanskoy had been connected with the Union of Welfare. Now, as Minister, he read the new Tsar's comment, "It is better to abolish serfdom from above than to wait till it begins to abolish itself from below", and the Tsar's appeal to the gentry "to consider the proper way in which this can be done", with amazement. For thirty years, N. I. Turgenev had been working for the liberal cause from Paris, where in 1847–48 had appeared his weighty onslaught on autocracy (and on his former comrades who recanted under questioning), *La Russie et les Russes*. But for Turgenev, most Decembrists felt no warmth; if some of them were *vauriens* to him, they

17

regarded him as a deserter. His brother Aleksandr having succeeded in trans-
ferring abroad the proceeds of the sale of their estate before the government
could seize them, he had lived the life in Paris of a well-to-do expatriate. Not
for him the pleasures of Petrovsky or the joys of Chita. Lastly, there was the
Governor of Nizhniy-Novgorod, A. N. Murav'yov. Here, too, many Decembrists felt confused, even occasionally hostile, feelings. Aleksandr Murav'yov
had been among the founders of the Union of Salvation; he, if anyone, could be
held guilty. Yet he had been exiled with no loss of noble status and, from Civil
Governor of Irkutsk in 1828, had risen to be Governor of a major Russian city
by 1856. True, he had not escaped the events of 1825 scot-free like Mikhail
Orlov (who, although celebrated throughout Russia for his part in the taking of
Paris, nevertheless fought with his conscience for two decades and, it seems,
knew little peace);[28] yet *ought* he not to have suffered with his comrades, though
exonerated by a court? Many thought so, while believing that they should not
think so.

The movement towards reform, once started by the Emperor himself, went
ahead inexorably. "In an autocratic country," as Pares observes, "no one can
so effectively launch a movement of reform as the sovereign himself."[29] Yet
opposition was considerable and ubiquitous. "May everyone", the Emperor
had said at the conclusion of peace with France and Britain on March 30, 1856,
"enjoy, in peace, the fruits of honest toil under the shelter of laws equally just
to all, equally protecting all". Had arch-conservatives not reason to be nervous,
hearing such phrases? No time had been lost before Count A. A. Zakrevsky,
Governor-General of Moscow, had begged Alexander to reassure the conservative nobility; but Alexander had been firm. Something had to be done.
Next came opposition from Lithuania, where the Governor-General was a
relation of Nazimov the Decembrist. The landowners, General Nazimov saw,
would have to protect their own interests; therefore he brought suggestions to
the capital for emancipation on the 1804 Estonian model, that is, without land.
In December 1857, thanks to the obduracy of Orlov and his supporters, these
proposals were approved by the Private Committee. But the Emperor, morally
aided by the Grand Duchess Yelena, once a Princess of Württemberg and a
woman of humanitarian outlook, would not be satisfied by them, and demanded
better plans. That same month came support of his own rescript, which
appointed provincial and district committees to draft details of emancipation
with land, from A. N. Murav'yov and the nobility of Nizhniy-Novgorod.
Peasants, it was proposed by Alexander through S. S. Lanskoy, should redeem
their own dwellings and plots at favourable rates, and occupy other land in
return for defined obligations of labour or rent. Fifteen years had passed since
Rozen had himself put such a plan into effect in Bol'sháya Sóldina.

Of the renaming of the Tsar's Private Committee as the Main Committee in
January 1858, or of Alexander's efforts with the help of N. Milyutin, Rostovtsev,
and Lanskoy to produce specific, realizable, and rational plans of action, no
more will be said here. The work of the drafting committee, the arrival in the

capital of seven delegations of disturbed landowners, all the ebb and flow of liberal sentiment—such matters have been dealt with, in considerable detail, by historians of many hues.[30] The persistence of the Emperor, the deporting of Unkovsky (a Liberal reckless enough to seek elective self-government for every Province in the Empire, with independent law courts and freedom of the Press), even the efforts of reactionaries, in Khar'kov as in St Petersburg, to nullify reform, failed to bear visibly on Rozen's life. He worked on his estate; Liberals worked in their committees; neither could help the other, even had they wished to do so. Suffice it to remark, then, that the emancipating edict, signed by Alexander on March 3, 1860, was published on March 17.

Though far from St Petersburg, however, and powerless to help or hinder the reformers in their work, Rozen followed events closely. And he had his own opinion on the question of emancipation throughout Russia; indeed, it would have been bizarre had he, a Baltic *dvoryanin* with personal memories of the reforms of 1804 and 1816–19 and experience of removing *corvée* among peasants used to nothing else, not kept himself informed on such a matter. He was, of course, in favour of emancipation as outlined by S. S. Lanskoy, with peasants redeeming land on reasonable terms; after all, most had no capital. Versed in the development of serfdom under Boris Godunov and Vasiliy Shuysky, and in each phase of its history[31] (he had lectured on the subject twenty-nine years before the forming of the Tsar-Liberator's Private Committee), he saw the economic harm done to the State by an irrational system actually forbidding the movement of labour. He himself had seen the cheerfulness and wealth of peasant farmers in Siberia, where few bureaucrats hindered what seemed a natural balancing of the demand and the supply.[32] There, peasants had money, so they spent it; and in spending it and working steadily for their own good, they benefited others. Rozen was a capitalist. To own a plot of land; to toil and prosper, buy and sell whenever advantageous to oneself and to one's family; to seek employment at the highest going rate—such objectives seemed to him entirely sensible. Who indeed, with knowledge of the peasant's longing to possess the land he worked, in Estonia and the Ukraine alike, could deny the common sense of such ambitions? The free economic system, however, had not developed in Russia; and serfdom had distorted relationships between the various classes of society on every plane—moral, social, economic, and political. Such is the main burden of the ex-convict-historian's assessment of events in 1858–61. Coming to the Ukraine, Rozen tended to concentrate on the economic folly, rather than on the moral heinousness, of serfdom. Five years' experience of wool-farming and grain-growing in Kamenka confirmed him in his view of the ridiculousness, from all pragmatic standpoints, of a system that kept workers chained to villages near which, in many cases, work was lacking, while enterprises in another district suffered from a dire shortage of labour and unnecessarily restricted markets. More than this, five years in the Ukraine showed him the yawning gulfs between *all* Russian classes—gulfs created by, and strengthening, the central fact of serfdom. If only in the cause of national unity, and even had the economic welfare of the State not been involved so fundamentally, Rozen would have endorsed the Sixteen Acts dealing with various aspects of the final settlement of March 3, 1861:

> But every transformation, every new concern entailing difficulties cannot be called an impractical Utopia. If one took such an attitude, it would be easy to postpone or to revoke all useful changes. Only indifference to the improvement of our social structure, only timidity and indolence produced the phrase, "impractical Utopia". Experience, moreover, demonstrates that faith in the possibility of executing what is acknowledged to be just, leads to the fulfilment of a well-planned enterprise.
>
> The main difficulty met in the transformation proposed (in the State) was that, among us, all conditions shun each other, and there is no natural link between them. At the court, the military nobility and the dependent bureaucracy took precedence; the upper gentry class was alien to the people both because of its privileges and in its way of life. The upper gentry imitated English lords and French marquis and for that reason, and in consequence of ignorance of the language of their own people, could not approach the people. Officials, too, were alien to the populace, and comprised another partition; the official's dependence on the Court and Government separated him from the people. Scholars, for their part, formed a completely separate class—a special world with nothing in common with the life of the State and people. And the merchant class found itself in total subjection to the Court and the nobility: in proportion as a merchant abased himself before the latter, so he would put on airs before the peasants . . . There is no middle class among us because of serfdom. For where were free guild craftsmen to be found in towns, and for what purpose were they to be brought in, when landed gentlemen had their own musicians, actors, painters, ballet masters, not to mention carriage-makers, smiths, and joiners?[33]

Never would Rozen advocate a breaking down of social barriers; as we have seen, his economic liberalism went hand in hand with firm support for tsardom. But at least on the pragmatic, economic plane he could accept a certain bending of old practices. Political and economic change, of course, cannot be separated ultimately. But in compartmentalizing change, Rozen was merely following the leading liberal theorists of his day. As for the Emperor himself questions of constitutionalism were distinct from those of economic exploitation, so they were for many liberal and even (unlike Rozen) revolutionary thinkers.

To return to the emancipating edict: the peasants, as the Emperor demanded, were fully emancipated from the gentry. As a class, however, they remained separate from the rest of the population. For one thing, their collective responsibility for taxes and their former passport system made them individuals dependent on their *obshchina*, or village commune; for another, that same commune levied rates from local peasants for religious education, and distributed the land itself—and even when redeemed, land was the property not of an individual peasant, but of a whole community. Peasants admittedly took up more and more land, now having full permission to lease from their own landlords; but this, in Khar'kov as in other areas, was basically because emancipation had resulted in their having less land than before, many having previously been working extra land. And of course the landowner could fix his own price if he did not choose, like many from the south, to collect compensation from the State, sell off what remained of (often marginally profitable) estates, and leave the country for the capitals. Few years would pass before it was apparent that, for ex-serf and ex-landowner alike, matters had progressed from bad to worse in the new, progressive Russia. But at first, even rejoicing was subdued by mental numbness and a grasping at the massive implications of the Sixteen Acts. The emancipating edict, proclaimed before the Senate on March 14, was read out in all the churches of the Empire three days later. Rozen was in the church of Bol'sháya Kamenka when the district police officer rode out from Izyum to announce it to the populace:

The district police officer rode with the Manifesto into the hamlet of Bol'shaya Kamenka and straight into the church, where the whole parish was expecting him. After a thanksgiving service had been held, the priest read the most gracious Manifesto from the ambo; the people listened with strained attention, and crossed themselves when the Tsar's missive touched on hopes for God's aid in the execution of the great, but also difficult and complex, deed. The Manifesto was read through a second time after the priest by the police officer, and the people listened with the same reverence and care as before. On going out of the church, the people thronged in the churchyard, which a cross overshadowed. Then they went off to their homes, and not a single man was later to be found in the drinking-house that day: the peasants honoured the great event reverently, not yet being able to collect themselves and grasp all the importance of this change . . .[34]

It proved complex and difficult to supervise the peaceful distribution of expropriated land among new communes. The actual allotment between peasantry and gentry was entrusted to Arbitrators of the Peace (*mirnyye posredniki*), carefully picked men whose work has been well covered by contemporary students of the period.[35] Once more, Decembrists found themselves in a position to co-operate with the authorities, implementing a reform the magnitude of which was not at first fully apparent to most peasants. Rozen, Obolensky and Svistunov made their contributions to the liberal cause by serving terms as *mirnyye posredniki*. Rozen, in fact, served two three-year terms in the district of Izyum, from 1861–64, and 1864–67. From the first, the work, though onerous, proved sympathetic to him. It was practical and bore immediate and visible effects. It demanded patience and consistency, a knowledge of conditions in the Province, but also a familiarity with the conditions of the edict; in other words, some legal, some political, some economic, and some local knowledge. Rozen was scrupulously regular, predictably impartial, in his work. Necessarily, he came into close contact with hundreds of landowners and peasants in his area, and so became an expert on the workings, needs, and failings of the district of Izyum—knowledge soon to be condensed in an article, "Observations of a Former Arbitrator of the Peace in Izyum District of Khar'kov Province . . ."[36] He worked hard. At the age of sixty-one, indeed, he was embarking on a more exhausting piece of work than any since his youth; but as he aged, so his desire to work, and need of work, increased.

The ukase on the election of Arbitrators of the Peace, and its confirmation by the Senate, was published on March 22, 1861. This new institution was one of the Government's main concerns. The Emperor said, in this connection, that "on the satisfactory selection of Arbitrators depends the success of the transformation and improvement of the peasants' life. The principal function of the Arbitrator will be to be the reconciler and judge of the interests of both classes; in view of this, those persons are to be invited to serve who *are known to have an unquestionable sympathy for the transformation and known for their fair treatment of the peasants.*"

Lists of names were compiled and elections undertaken, in accordance with Articles 13 and 14 of the Statute relating to Provincial and District Institutions concerning peasant affairs. So I had the honour to be appointed to the post of Arbitrator of the Peace for Izyum district. The land area in the district was of 6,123 square versts, the population—132,741 . . .

To introduce the new Statute, there laboured 44 Provincial Representatives, 404 committees of district conciliators, and 1,714 Arbitrators of the Peace.[37]

For months, Rozen immersed himself in the work in hand. In Khar'kov, redistribution of the land went smoothly. (In Penza, there was an open revolt under Anton Petrov, a peasant oppressed by the local police and who claimed to be the Emperor in person.) There, peasants and landowners were, in general, co-operative, and willing to accept the spirit of the Edict of Emancipation. Temporarily, indeed, Rozen saw an end of ancient feuds and grievances. As for his colleagues, F. M. Kovalensky, N. A. Yazykov, V. N. Naumenko, A. S. Levshin and N. M. Stankevich, and their chairman, the District Marshal of Nobility, A. A. Antonov, they were helpful and, for several months at least, as zealous as himself. Even the appointment of a new Governor of Khar'kov, Count A. K. Sievers, helped the Arbitrators in their task: Sievers, a Baltic German, was entirely sympathetic to the cause.[38] Rozen pressed on. Within three years, Khar'kov had overtaken every other province of the Empire in the number of redemption arrangements completed, if not yet executed:

In the number of completed redemption contracts, the Province of Khar'kov occupies the first place in all Russia. The composing of redemption agreements is among the Herculean labours of the Arbitrators of the Peace, for every word and every figure is written out by their hand. The announcement, verdict, agreement, act, and conditions, all this would be sent, countersigned, in two copies to the Provincial Representatives; and on top of this, copies of these documents were given to the landowner and to the peasant commune. And every redemption agreement, of some twenty pages, was sent by mail to Khar'kov, and from there, after a careful check, to the Main Redemption Establishment in St Petersburg . . .[39]

Finally, in 1867, Rozen asked the new Governor of Khar'kov, P. P. Durnovo, to release him from his post. The constant travelling was growing too exhausting for a man with other problems (his eyes and general health) and fresh pre-occupations (the education of the local peasants and the preparation of his memoirs for a publisher). The endless stream of protests to be heard, the interests to be balanced, new arrangements to be studied (after April 1863 *all* work, service and dues could be commuted, if a peasant wished, to money payments), all now kept Rozen from his self-appointed task of writing an account of the Decembrist movement of unquestionable factual accuracy. To serve had been a pleasure, to be honoured—an acceptable surprise (Rozen was awarded the Order of St Stanislav, "for civil services"). But there were so many new ukases to absorb: on corporal punishment, on April 17, 1863; on the *Zemstva*, on January 1, 1864; on popular education, on July 14, 1864; on the Press, on September 1, 1865. Arbitrators of the Peace were expected to be perfectly familiar with the terms of each ukase, for each might bear upon his work. The proper discharge of his functions, Rozen felt, would leave him no spare time; and at the age of sixty-seven, time was precious.

Little will be said here of Rozen's attitudes towards the great reforms, their implementing and the problems met by those who, like himself, were charged with reconciling various interests. He himself covers the subject thoroughly in the article mentioned above. His careful calculations of the cost to a landowner in Khar'kov of a peasant's labour service, in terms of money, quit-rent, and *corvée*; his efforts to suppress the so-called estate police (*votchinnaya politsiya*) by which, even in 1866, some landlords interfered with village communes; his efforts, finally, to have established parish schools for peasant children, with experienced teachers and assistance from the local clergy, all are discussed in detail in his memoirs. Only on the last question, so intimately linked to Rozen's earlier interest in education in Estonia, may brief remarks be added here.

It came as an unpleasant revelation, after Bol'sháya Sóldina, to discover that the peasantry around Izyum was, in the sixth decade, almost totally illiterate. The government had for some time encouraged the establishing of parish schools; but here, it was apparent, the government's desire had not borne consequences. The Orthodox clergy, in Rozen's opinion, were not greatly to blame: priests and deacons serving several churches and communities were naturally obliged to travel every day, or frequently at least. Rozen himself opened a school for peasants in Izyum. At first, there were fourteen local boys. He himself taught them to read Church Slavonic texts, and to read and write (Great) Russian. That something needed to be done to improve literacy among the peasantry was obvious. Rozen made suggestions. First, directors of the district schools that did exist should be requested, by the Governor of the Province, to prepare for village work "such rural teachers as would be capable of teaching only reading, writing, and practical book-keeping". To this end, second, a willing would-be teacher—a sober and literate individual—should be chosen from each rural district (*volost'*). If necessary, the man might be a literate peasant or a former house-serf, preferably single and at least twenty years old. From September 15 until June 15, third, each *volost'* in Izyum should contribute five roubles every month for every man being prepared as a village teacher—three roubles for his maintenance, two roubles for his training. This would cost each individual in a *volost'* of 500 persons one kopek a month. On the completion of his training, lastly, the new teacher should return to his own *volost'* and there, assisted twice a week by the local priest, teach peasants of all ages and both sexes—the women, however, being separated from the men.[40]

Every aspect of the plan shows the pragmatic nature of its elderly creator. It would make use of existing resources and make no demand on the provincial budget. It avoided fanciful theories, dealing directly with an obvious need. It would have useful benefits from a purely administrative viewpoint (for how often had reform been stalled because of the illiteracy of even clever peasants?). Finally, use could be made of the Zalotov spelling system; for all should be made simple and attractive for the pupil, not alarming, as in schools where the Church Slavonic alphabet was used (and from which the pupils fled). Rozen's was a rational and economic project for transforming education on the parish level. Yet it found no favour in the eyes of Durnovo, the Governor of the Province, whose attention was engaged elsewhere. The plan was never implemented. Only by working in his own district, using his own resources, was Rozen able to effect even the best-laid of reforms. Of the Decembrists who had once lived in Siberia, only A. N. Murav'yov and I. A. Annenkov, in 1861 appointed District Marshal of Nobility in Nizhniy-Novgorod, exerted demonstrable influence on the authorities at a provincial level.

But Rozen was about to begin a withdrawal from administrative cares on the district level; to provincial strategy, by 1868, he gave no thought. Not that he intended to break faith or contact with elected Liberals in his area, or to cease to aid the *Zemstva* as he could; nonetheless, the time of his most active personal involvement in provincial public life was ending. And, one senses from his letters, which increasingly from 1869 dwell on the past, he himself felt it correct that it should end. Events were now moving so fast that he questioned his command of them: the violent attacks on Liberals of his generation by D. I. Pisarev in *Russkoye slovo* (*The Russian Word*), and the more constrained, but no less wounding, onslaughts by Herzen in his London-based *Kolokol* (*The Bell*); the Polish rising; the attempt on Alexander II's life, on April 16, 1866, by D. V. Karakozov; the systematic and complete (or seemingly complete) russification, between 1867 and 1870, of all institutions in Poland, including Warsaw University—such things made him feel a stranger in a Russia full of Slavophiles and Nihilists. And, psychologically, he was a stranger in the Khar'kov of the 1870s: he was a Baltic German of the 1820s, and a full-grown man two decades before Pisarev was born. Ever more consciously, his thoughts turned to the fateful insurrection, forty-five years earlier, and to its full significance not only in his own life, but also for his fellow countrymen.

To his old friends and relations in Estonia, too, his thoughts turned often now, in 1868–70; for the province of his birth was in a state of turmoil. Not until 1858, we may recall, had *corvée* been declared illegal in Estonia, but this was not the greatest of the changes, economic and political, that had shaken the foundation of agrarian society in all three Baltic provinces. Now, Estonians had passports and could move about. Huge numbers did so, thousands travelling to the Ukraine in search of well-paid work.[41] Thousands more toiled desperately on their holdings, struggling to amass the capital required to buy those holdings outright. On Crown-owned lands (one-tenth of Estonia only), rents had been fixed at 4 per cent of the land's capital value, instalments towards purchase at 5·5 per cent over forty-nine years. Very different, alas, were the conditions enforced by many noble landowners. But a veritable passion for proprietorship had set in. Landlords, it was reported, were commonly demanding four times the price asked for rich land in the central Russian provinces, and often for poor, swampy soil. But the peasants found the money. But while some were rising on the social scale by virtue of their purchase of allotments of consider-able size, others were swiftly sinking. Cottagers who held a hut and tiny patch on the landowner's demesne, tenants who failed to make a payment, ex-servants of the Baltic-German families now wandering as seasonal labourers—such men knew desperate straits in a hard winter. What could be done to ease the problem, halt mass emigration, stave off ruin or continuing oppression at new hands? For a last time, on the very point of leaving current crises to those younger or more qualified to face them, Rozen turned to the disturbances, the social, economic and political alarums of Estonia.

There is no more concise or illuminating summary of Rozen's attitudes towards Estonian needs and problems than that published in *Russkiy arkhiv* in 1885 by M. Galkin-Vraskoy, Governor of the Province in 1868–70, and headed "The Private View of an Estonian Landlord on a Public Matter".[42] It is, in two respects, a *tour de force*: first, it is encyclopaedic in its scope, though short enough to occupy a mere three printed pages; second, it synthesizes Rozen's views on four interconnected facets of the Province's continuing problem: the legal, the political, the economic, and the cultural. It synthesizes; it does not merely unite, or collate. For many years Rozen had been aware of the capitalist instinct of Estonian peasants—an instinct now, he saw, working against the interests of large sectors of the Estonian population; since his sojourn in the south, he had been conscious of the dangers posed to Estonia's identity by shrewd russification of the Province's industrial, political, and legal life. Now, as an old man, he reconciled freedom to purchase through redemption with the growing presence of the landless peasantry, Russian fears of German power with German rights, liberty with order and stability. It was a final statement of the liberal, rational outlook of a German Balt young in the 1820s, but who, better by far than most contemporaries, had come to terms with the demands on, and new menaces towards, the Baltic Provinces from a much changed Imperial Government. But the article speaks eloquently for itself:

Not entering into any arguments whatever as to the reasons for the disturbances and restlessness of peasants in the Province of Estonia, I shall permit myself to set forth the chief means by which the authorities might set about the urgent *removal* of those same disturbances:

1. By affirming freedom of conscience and religion for all classes in the Province.

2. By affirming the right of property for all conditions in the Province.

3. By introducing, for all classes in the Province, the common legal procedure accepted throughout the Empire—a measure that will conduce not only to the fusion of all classes in the Province, but also to the strengthening of links between the Province and the Russian State. The present state of the peasant district courts I find unsatisfactory as a result of the inadequate development of those same courts; of the absence of proper supervision of their verdicts by courts of higher instance; of the lack of necessary police support in implementing the courts' sentences. In consequence of the above, the law remains a dead letter and serves not as a shield but, on the contrary, to increase disorder and dissatisfaction. Attention should be given, in the first instance, to the majority of the population, that is, to the peasantry, and chiefly to the organization of *volosti* and to district government.

4. As soon as possible, an end should be put to the perplexities and false expectations of Estonian peasants, who hope to get land free of charge either from a landowner or from the Exchequer in areas where there are no landowners. The introduction of general Russian regulations governing redemptions to the peasants of Estonia, however, I consider inappropriate: for the Estonians have never known communal government nor communal property, have never known industrial enterprise in the form of the *artel'*, and have never known a whole community's guaranteeing an individual member. On the contrary, they have always prized their private property and district or separate economy. Besides the reasons adduced here, there remains one more, insuperable hindrance to the introduction of those regulations, namely: in all the Baltic Provinces, one sector of the peasantry has already acquired part of the peasant land by voluntary contract with landowners. These deeds of purchase, confirmed in due legal form, cannot be destroyed. So it remains to grant to peasants the right to purchase, through voluntary contracts, lands that have already been marked off from those belonging to estates. These lands, marked off by red lines on land surveyors' plans, which are deposited in circuit courtrooms for safe-keeping, must be for the perpetual use of the peasants. But in order that hired hands or poor landless peasants shall not remain quite destitute, and without a scrap of soil, a redemption loan should be requested from the Government, so that the remainder of the peasants' lands might be acquired for these poor peasants—and so that these might be enabled to use this land according to commune or individual customs, or as most find convenient. Then, all obligatory relations between landowners and peasants will have ceased once and for all. In the event of insolvency among this category of poor peasants, the Government will have, in the redeemed land, a sound security for the loan made earlier.

5. The introduction of the Russian language as the general language of the State has until now proved difficult because it has been introduced by ukase, and when there has prevailed an insufficiency of experienced teachers for the higher classes and no public schools for the peasantry. Railways, service, commercial and

industrial links with both capitals and the internal Provinces will, of course, absolutely demand a knowledge of Russian and will easily remove all difficulties flowing from trilingualism in the Province of Estonia.

6. The Government may utterly rely on the loyalty and honour of Estonia's nobility, which is not German, and not Swedish, but since 1710 Russian. As far as the privileges of that nobility are concerned—the privileges of a special caste since the days of ancient knighthood: those privileges, which are incompatible with the spirit of this age, are disappearing of themselves and have already vanished in part, through the determination of the nobility itself, which has acknowledged in its general assemblies that those privileges are now, with the removal of serfdom throughout the Empire and the introduction of the new conditions, no longer in conformity with their ancient purpose.

12

ROZEN AS THE RECORDER
OF DECEMBRISM

Rozen had his last personal contact with the Imperial family unexpectedly in August 1861. It brought about a reconciliation. The Empress, daughter-in-law to Nicholas I, passed through Izyum on her way to Livadiya, on the southern shore of the Crimea. Alexander II, who was accompanying his wife, was attending a review of troops in Chuguyev on the 9th, when the Empress came to Izyum and the Svyatogorsky Monastery. Rozen had been advised of her arrival:

I had sent for the village elders in advance, in order to present them at a suitable opportunity; and with them I was awaiting the arrival of the train at Teplyanskaya station, where the inhabitants of the surrounding villages and estates had gathered. Ahead in a courier's troika flew the Provincial Postmaster, Menzenkamf, an old man with a wounded head who had served with the Grodnensky Hussars in 1809 ... From him, I learned that the Empress would arrive in the first carriage together with the Grand Duchess Mariya Aleksandrovna ...

I was presented as an Arbitrator of the Peace. I asked permission to present the new village elders of the emancipated peasants to Her Majesty. The Empress kindly gave me her consent. At a given signal from me the elders hurried up, and one of them, Stepan Fedchenko, said solemnly, in the name of his comrades and the peasants, "We welcome Your Majesty, we wish her health and every blessing, and we ask her to inform our Tsar that we are all grateful for his great mercy— for the freedom given us!" The Empress asked them what *volosti* they came from, whether the people in the villages were thriving, and whether they had blessed the Lord for the harvest. Then she turned to me with a question, and asked if my new position was not too onerous for one of my advanced years. "Your Majesty," I replied, "I have in me the strength and striving of 120 comrades who wished to contribute towards the freeing of the peasants, but who were exiled after December 14 and have not survived; others were freed on the coronation day of the Sovereign, your husband, and I myself, and others with me in the settlement of Kurgan, was returned from Siberia at his instances when he was Tsarevich and heir. Since that day, Your Majesty's husband has interceded for me, my children, and comrades constantly. I have had no opportunity to thank him personally, so now I ask you to move his heart in the most effective manner possible and to thank him on behalf of myself and my comrades." The Empress was visibly moved, and said to me in a distinct and sympathizing voice, "I will carry out your request unfailingly, and with great pleasure." All this lasted no more than seven minutes.[1]

The Empress kept her word. Returning through Khar'kov the following spring, she instructed the new Governor, Count Sievers, to tell Rozen that she had fulfilled his request word for word. News of the meeting and its consequence spread through Decembrist circles. Within six weeks of the Empress's return and comment to Sievers, I. I. Gorbachevsky, still in Petrovsky Zavod, had come to hear of it. (Like Mikhail Bestuzhev, Gorbachevsky sometimes longed to return to Russia, but was too wise to do so: he gave no credence to the slogans of "progress" and "freedom of speech", and besides had no relations left in the Ukraine.) On July 5, 1862 he wrote to D. I. Zavalishin:

... "Surely you haven't the strength for this work, and how did you come to take it up?" she asked. "Your Majesty," Rozen replied, "I undertook this position in memory of my living and departed comrades and friends, and am happy now that their sacred aims are being realized." Having said this, he looked at her, and all saw how touched she was. So you see, Dmitriy Irinarkhovich, Rozen is always having adventures—though I myself am surprised that he ever took it upon himself to be an Arbitrator. For what mediation can there be between oppressors and oppressed?[2]

Other comrades, too, looked askance at Rozen's willingness to work with the new Liberals under the aegis of the Tsarist Government; but most, judging by letters of the period, were glad of the encounter with the Empress. Certainly Zavalishin, though always an irascible and prickly individual, and liable to imagine insults from his wealthier aristocratic comrades, was happy to meet Rozen when the latter came to Moscow in the late 'sixties,[3] and to discuss his work in Khar'kov. Once again, Rozen showed his ability to handle men of every temperament and win acceptance: there was no one Decembrist in more striking contrast with himself than Zavalishin, ever striving to be prominent, ever complaining that due recognition of his talents and position was denied him by his comrades (who were now distorting the true story of their common years of exile in their memoirs, and accusing *him* of twisting it!).

But Rozen, we have seen, made contact with many former comrades in the years immediately following their return to European Russia, and strengthened his links with others. With some, like M. M. Naryshkin and M. A. Nazimov, his neighbours in Kurgan, he had indeed been always in close contact;[4] others, like Obolensky and Lorer, he had come to know as well through steady correspondence between 1839 and 1855 as, in Siberia, he had through private talks; others again he came to know as intimately as he ever would in January 1858, in Moscow: N. V. Basargin, for example, and A. N. Sutgof. Also in Moscow, for the casual reunion of that month (the nobility had been assembled to elect its representatives to the Moscow Provincial Committee for the Improvement of the Peasants' Life),[5] was I. I. Pushchin, now married to the widow of M. A.

Fonvizin, who had died in 1854. And Pushchin *insisted* that he meet P. N. Svistunov. Rozen went to the Pushchin apartment, and found there Obolensky.[6] Through Obolensky, he immediately made contact with S. I. Krivtsov; and Krivtsov told him that, near Julius Rozen's manor in Tver', Matvey Murav'yov-Apostol might be seen—if he made haste. With the death of Tizengauzen, Murav'yov-Apostol had become the *doyen d'age* of the Decembrists, and he was ailing. Rozen hastened to Tver', and found Murav'yov-Apostol in splendid health. So the process of re-forming or improving links with comrades went ahead. It was, indeed, with a complete society that Rozen found himself establishing connections between 1858 and 1863: three-year-old children he had last seen in Petrovsky Zavod were now married and had children of their own; and these children, bound by their childhood in Siberia, showed no urge to cast off links with the revitalized Decembrist world.[7] There had been marriages between Decembrists' widows and Decembrists. Year by year, dozens of families, in Moscow and Siberia, the central Russian provinces and even France and Italy (Poggio, married to a Siberian schoolteacher, had first gone with his wife and infant daughter to his native land, only to feel insuperable nostalgia for the north), were kept linked by a great mesh of correspondence. And this, Rozen appreciated as old age crept on him, was his own society.

Old age: this, too, was a factor in the eagerness with which those Decembrists who were never personally close while in Siberia now corresponded or met regularly. For who could tell when death would make all further contact impossible? It was in the years 1859–60 that thoughts of death seem first to have loomed ominously large for the Decembrists as a group—not just for individuals. (Lunin, for one, was pondering on death at the age of twenty-one.[8]) Suddenly, death was a reality, not an oppressive idea. 1859 took a great toll: seven Decembrists died. In 1861, Basargin died; in 1862—Zakhar Chernyshev, in Rome; and in 1863—M. M. Naryshkin, G. S. Batenkov, and A. N. Murav'yov. Once established, such a rhythm of mortality could not be changed, for the Decembrists were not young. And now, in 1865, death cast its shadow over Rozen's life by claiming Obolensky—and, for good measure, the kindly Pavel Bobrishchev-Pushkin, Volkonsky, and P. P. Belyayev. I. V. Kireyev, Rozen's fellow-officer N. R. Tsebrikov, A. A. Arbuzov, Baron Shteyngel', Count Igel'strom, V. N. Solov'yov, Rudkevich, Mazalevsky and Kolesnikov of the Society of United Slavs, all nine were buried in the course of 1866. And Pushchin, dead since April 1859, had planned to keep a record of Decembrist deaths. The plan had proved presumptuous, Pushchin himself falling under the scythe.

It was significant that Pushchin's list should come to Rozen. Tacitly, Rozen was accepted by some comrades, at least, as the official historiographer of the Decembrists. Certainly he was well suited to keep the record started conscientiously by Pushchin, and which appeared, in the 1870 text of his memoirs, as "A Necrologue of Comrades Who Died in Exile, Were Killed in the Caucasus, or Expired on Returning to the Fatherland".[9] The date and place of death are carefully inserted by each name. So, too, with the "Necrologue of Wives Who Followed their Husbands into Exile . . .", begun and completed by Rozen. (Eight wives died by 1870, including two, Aleksandra Murav'yova and Camille Ivasheva, daughter of the governess in the Ivashevs' Moscow household,[10] who died by 1840.[11]) Year by year Rozen kept the account, compiling notes on each new victim for eventual use, perhaps, in full obituaries. Year by year he spoke or wrote to those who had been personally closest to the dead, building a store of information, proof as far as possible against false emphasis and slander. And he worked on his own reminiscences.

Even in Kurgan and in the Caucasus, "in confinement, in exile, during transfer from one prison to another, during the time of journeying from one land of exile to another",[12] Rozen had made a habit of keeping diaries and making jottings on events and individuals that crossed his path. Later, in Bol'sháya Sóldina, he had revised those notes. But even then, in the mid-'fifties, he "had not had in mind a large public, but children, relatives, and the comrades with whom the author passed the most remarkable part of his life—his years of banishment in Siberia and the Caucasus". Amnesty in August 1856 had changed much; and the passage of so many years since 1825 changed more. Now, to lend urgency to the recording of his comrades' histories, came death. Rozen worked steadily and without interruption on his memoirs in 1858–61, and again, on the completion of his work as district Arbitrator of the Peace in Izyum, in 1867–68. By this last year, even more had changed in Russia:

> Times and events, indeed, have changed so swiftly and so widely that these pages may present some interest even for the general reader. Those who were our judges are all already dead; of the 121 comrades sentenced because of the conspiracy of 1825, only 14 now remain alive. That event itself is of only historical interest now, and its recollecting can seem neither reprehensible to the Government, nor revolutionary or dangerous to the public. Now, it is only a matter of truthfully recording the essence of an historical fact and affording readers sympathetic towards the Decembrists' fate with certain reliable information regarding their characters and destinies.
>
> Most of my comrades could have recorded all the happenings of those times far more circumstantially and entertainingly than I; but they have long been dead; and of the small number of those who *are* alive still, will anyone succeed in doing that? I do not know. Such circumstances have obliged me to devote my few remaining days in conveying conscientiously what I myself have been through, seen, and heard, and what I have gathered from the most reliable sources. I advise my readers that I have tried to be impartial, have nurtured no bitterness or enmity for the trials endured, but recall with gratitude all the kindness shown me and my comrades in the course of all that sad, difficult time.[13]

The message, and indeed the whole introduction to the 1869 German and 1870 Russian texts, is plain enough: Rozen published his memoirs for three major reasons. First, he wished posterity, and specially those "sympathetic to the Decembrists' fate" and his own children, to know about his past. Second, he did so because time was pressing hard, and no other Decembrist seemed about to undertake the task. (He was to be proved extremely pessimistic on this score. The eighth decade was to see the publication of a spate of reminiscences of Decembrists and others connected with their fate.[14]) Third, and most important, he wished the record to be straight. Repeatedly, he stresses his main hope and aim: to present the known facts honestly and fully:

What happened on December 14, 1825 has been distorted practically beyond belief. As proof of this, I adduce the letter from State Secretary A. N. Olenin to his daughter of December 24, 1825, from St Petersburg. This letter was printed in *Russkiy arkhiv* for 1869, no. 4. If a man worthy of general respect and who once held such an important post could send completely false information about those events, what is to be expected from those who give out as the truth what was being passed on, then and afterwards, in gossip and as rumours?

Among foreign writers who were then, or about then, in Russia and St Petersburg specifically, J. H. Schnitzler—who had acquainted himself well with Russia—described the workings of the secret societies most accurately and fully in his work, *The Secret History of Russia in the Reigns of Alexander I and Nicholas I*. The author both establishes the broad march of events with tolerable accuracy, and draws a fair conclusion from the whole issue. Less satisfactory, however, are the comments of other writers, such as Ancelot, in *Dix mois en Russie*; Lesure, in *Annuaire de 1825*; Dupré de St-Maur, in *Pétersbourg, Moscou, les Provinces* . . .; an anonymous Englishman, in *Revelations of Russia*; and Custine, in *La Russie en 1832*. This last author confuses the circumstances surrounding the rising of 1825 with the disturbance on Sennaya Square when there was cholera in St Petersburg and with the rising in Staraya Russa in 1832, in the military colonies . . .

I wish here to refute *all* false opinions concerning the Decembrists *and* concerning their opponents. Especially now, in days that are witnessing the most profound political and administrative changes—changes that have been occurring in Russia since 1856—should it be diverting to read of a curious passage in the history of the previous age, in all its separate parts. And readers will easily convince themselves that the compiler of these Memoirs had in view nothing but the furnishing of *true* information on the strivings and destiny of his comrades and his friends.[15]

It pained Rozen to see facts mistreated, over-emphasized, omitted, or in any way abused. That instinct serves us well, for of Decembrist memoirs, none is more reliable or detailed than his. However, he had one more solid reason for wishing to refute the accusation that he was in any way using facts to suit his case, or that he had an axe of any kind to grind: the memoirs were first published not in Russian, but in German, and abroad.

We do not know when Rozen first resolved to have his memoirs published. It is even arguable whether he needed to be urged to do so, or whether, with the changing atmosphere after the death of Nicholas, he meant to see his reminiscences in print despite the disclaimer that they had been intended for his children and relations. Most probably, he had indeed thought earlier of leaving notes for the perusal of his children, but saw, soon after 1856, that publication might prove possible if he were careful, and excluded passages likely to meet rebuttal from the censors. Such passages, it must be said, are few. Rozen was, as he proposed to be, even-handed in his treatment of his judges and his allies: his assessment of the reign and character of Nicholas I well illustrates the point. As we saw, he concentrated on his memoirs in 1858–61. With the new decade, he began to add chapters, keeping the record up to date. Chapter XXIII, for instance, on the introduction of the Statutes of 1861–67, could not have been begun before 1867, was almost certainly begun in 1868 (for among the most recent events mentioned in it was his own attendance at the first session of the Izyum Circuit Court, on March 19 of that year), and was probably not finished until early 1869.[16]

But however that may be, one thing is clear: Rozen was in contact with two men with influence in Russian publishing during the 'sixties—the novelist and liberal administrator G. P. Danilevsky (1829–90), and the editor and publicist M. N. Katkov (1818–87). The relationships, which were as different as might be, are noteworthy.

With Danilevsky, his neighbour in Khar'kov Province since 1857, Rozen seemed to have everything in common except age. Danilevsky, who had received a Master of Jurisprudence degree from Moscow University (something that Rozen had once had in mind for his own first son, Yevgeniy), had been falsely charged with complicity in the Petrashevsky affair, and had spent two miserable months in Peter-and-Paul Fortress. Like Rozen, he had been on the fringe of a liberal movement, and had paid a heavy price. Again, as a young civil servant, Danilevsky had been sent to work in monastery archives in the south of Russia; he had there acquired a taste for Russian history.[17] And like Rozen, whom he honestly admired, Danilevsky took an active part in the public life of Khar'kov Province, in 1857–62: a member both of the district Committee for the Improvement of the Peasants' Life and of the Khar'kov Educational Council (like Rozen, he approved of the dissemination of basic education through the parish school), he shared the latter's local interests. Finally, there was the fact of Danilevsky's authorship of several tales of Little Russian life, a dozen ballads and, in 1862, a nationally successful novel, *Fugitives in New Russia* (*Beglyye v Novorossii*).[18] Rozen respected writers. Danilevsky's temperament he found most sympathetic. The two men grew close. Several letters survive from the period 1863–64. Some deal with regional administrative questions and with Rozen's work as Arbitrator of the Peace; others have a literary colouring, and deal with recent books and articles.[19] Here, Rozen had a firm link with the world of publishing, specifically, with publishing in Moscow.

It was not through Danilevsky, however, that he came into formal and rather distant contact with Katkov in 1868. He himself, it seems, wrote to that former colleague of Stankevich, now the editor of the increasingly reactionary periodical *Moscow News* (*Moskovskiye vedomosti*).[20] The two were very different in temper and, it quickly proved, unsympathetic to each other. Once, Katkov had made translations from the German Romantics, had been a Liberal, and had slapped the anarchist Bakunin in the face. But all this, alas, was many years before. Now, in 1868, his reactionary position made Rozen feel uncomfortable. However, Rozen seemingly made a proposal that Katkov consider publishing long extracts from his, Rozen's, memoirs, and Katkov declined to do so. Immediately afterwards, we learn from N. M. Chentsov,[21] copies of the memoirs, or lengthy extracts from them, were in fact published in Moscow—without the censor's permission—and were seized by the police. The affair remains obscure. Only one thing is plain: discouraged by Katkov's refusal, Rozen came to the decision not to try to publish the complete text of his memoirs in Russia. In no event would he amend *his* manuscripts to meet a censor's whims. Better to express himself, in full, abroad. So, unexpectedly, there came about his links with the writer Julius von Eckhardt and the city of his father's early manhood (and probably the greatest centre of Russian expatriate publishing during the 'sixties): Leipzig.

Rozen travelled to Leipzig in the autumn of 1868. Within days of his arrival, he had made contact with two major figures in the liberal literary *milieu* of that city: Gustav Freytag, editor, poet and novelist (1816–95) and Karl Geibel (1806–84), bookseller and owner of the publishing house Duncker und Humblot. Whether it was Geibel or Freytag who introduced him to his German publisher-to-be, Solomon Hirzel (1804–77), the Goethe scholar, is unclear. One thing is evident, however: it was through a letter from Karl Geibel that, in late September, Rozen came to meet the writer Julius von Eckhardt. For both men, the meeting was to prove of interest.

Eckhardt, born in 1836, was a man half Rozen's age. His chief preoccupations, moreover, hardly seemed to coincide with the Decembrist's. He, there could be no mistake, was neither farmer, officer, nor teacher. Instead, he was an elegant, polyglot journalist, one of whose main pleasures in life was travelling abroad. (Later, in 1885–89, he would serve as German Consul in Tunis.) First impressions soon proved false, however. The pair discovered three mutual interests. First, both were Liberals by temperament—believers in reform and in free, open institutions; both took an interest in the creation of such open institutions. Second, Eckhardt, like Danilevsky, had once studied jurisprudence. He had studied it, moreover, at the University of Dorpat, in Estonia, and knew that Province well. Both men, third, had a deep interest in foreign countries, attitudes, and manners. As Rozen warmed to Eckhardt, in that autumn of 1868, so Eckhardt warmed to Rozen, and listened sympathetically both to his tales of trial and exile in Siberia—a trial that had occurred ten years before he had himself been born—and to his wish to see his memoirs published, promptly and in Germany. Later, in his own memoirs (*Lebenserinnerungen*) Eckhardt would describe his link with Rozen in 1868–69 and the latter's appearance, hopes, and plans during his Leipzig visit:

Introduced by a letter from my friend, the publisher K. Geibel, an old but still stately-looking gentleman entered my rooms one dull autumn day and introduced himself as "Andrey, Baron Rozen, one of the last surviving Decembrists." His pronounced Russian diction revealed that he had become Russian...As a 24-year-old Guards lieutenant, I learned, he had joined the so-called "Northern Society", to which belonged the cream of the Russian aristocracy with whom he, Estonian-born and a Protestant, had nothing more in common than enthusiasm for the "new ideas". Since he had been directly involved in the events of the day of the revolt, Rozen had had to expiate this passing ecstasy by several months' detention, the loss of his title and nobility, and four years' hard labour in Eastern Siberia. He had had to settle subsequently in Western Siberia, in the town of Kurgan (the place of exile of Kotzebue)—until the accession of Alexander II when he had been completely reprieved. Even now, the old gentleman could make it clear enough that he was by nature an idealist. With flashing eyes, he would declare that consciousness of having suffered for a high goal in the company of the noblest of men had made the hardships of his exile easy, and that he would return most willingly to the prison of ice-cold Chita if there he could find his old, now mostly long-dead friends. "Never", he added in a moved tone, "have I been in better company."

Rozen wrote the tale of the conspiracy and of his own enforced sojourn in Siberia and Transcaucasia in German–Russian. He had, thanks to his being in exclusively Russian surroundings, so much lost the command of his native tongue that his really excellently written book was not, properly speaking, a German work, but a Russian work written with German words. A Russian version was to be prepared later in Moscow; a German version was to be revised by me and published in Leipzig. This was to be joined by a French edition, which the author wished to work at with the help of a Frenchman then living in Leipzig. Since I liked the old gentleman and his book seemed to provoke a lot of interest, I accepted the proposal under the condition that the main sections appear in *Die Grenzboten*. The somewhat wordy manuscript was shortened by a third and rewritten, sentence by sentence. The success was unexpectedly great. The extracts published in the "green pages" turned out to be of valuable service to the swelling of our list of subscribers. The book itself was published by S. Hirzel under the title *Memoirs of a Russian Dekabrist*, and was printed twice... Rozen represented a strange type, long dead now, of the Russian Liberal of the time of Alexander I; strict religiousness and loyalty towards the person of the monarch were united, in those men of aristocratic temper, with a passionate cult of democratic ideas.[22]

Eckhardt, who so usefully explains how the innumerable minor variants between the German (1869) and Russian (1870) texts came about, and whose comments on Rozen's "German–Russian" are particularly interesting, first because unique among contemporaries, second because by a born German, had his reason for proposing that the memoirs appear in the weekly periodical *Die Grenzboten*: he himself was an assistant editor, and had a stake in it. Still, it was as suitable a vehicle for extracts from those memoirs as any periodical then coming out in Germany. As its full title implied (*Die Grenzboten:*

Zeitschrift für Politik, Literatur und Kunst), its scope was wide enough to ensure that many readers, of many disparate interests, would come to hear of Rozen and Chita.[23] And, as though to seal the matter, there was the periodical's fine record for liberal (or, to be strictly accurate, liberal–bourgeois) editorial policy; editor-in-chief in 1868 was the writer Gustav Freytag, whose acquaintance, we have seen, Rozen had made that summer. So it was settled. Extracts from the visitor's memoirs duly appeared; for such memoirs, with their emphasis on truthfulness and strong liberal aura, were precisely what the shrewd Freytag required. Rozen was asked to give more; and he agreed to do so. Arrangements, meanwhile, were made with a book publisher, also in Leipzig, S. Hirzel; and in the early summer of 1869 appeared the first volume by a Decembrist on his exile, to be published outside Russia: *Aus den Memoiren eines russischen Dekabristen: Beiträge zur Geschichte des St.-Petersburger Militäraufstandes vom 14(26) December 1825 und seiner Theilnehmer.*

The publication of the memoirs, in a language accessible to countless German, French, and English readers, was an event of cardinal importance in the growth of Western Europeans' consciousness that there had, indeed, been a Russian rebellion in 1825, and that its well-born instigators had, indeed, suffered great tribulations. Rozen's, it must be said at once, are the only Decembrist memoirs to have been prepared and published with the author's active help in a Western European language, for both Western and Russian readerships. As Eckhardt says, the impression made in Leipzig was considerable. Within weeks, an English version had been started by a senior army officer with close personal contacts with Germany and time, thanks to a staff appointment, to undertake such work: Colonel Edmond St-John Mildmay. Suffice it to remark here that, although by no means literal, it was to be a competent translation or, more accurately, a first-rate paraphrase of Rozen's book. Of course, well-informed Western readers were aware that there had been an insurrection in the Russian capital in 1825. But, then, well-informed readers were in a fractional minority; as Rozen emphasizes, Lesure, Dupré de St-Maur, Ancelot, and Custine left much to be desired as faithful annalists. And only fragments of the memoirs of Decembrists had been printed, by the year in which Rozen's appeared in book form, in periodicals: a few pages by Obolensky on Ryleyev; a few comments by Pushchin on the Lyceum of Tsarskoye Selo, and by Yakushkin on the work of the Committee of Enquiry in 1826; remarks by Lunin on the growth of secret political societies in Russia; a few vague paragraphs by Trubetskoy. But these, in any case, had been published in Russian; few outside Russia read Russian, and it was with some justification that Rozen observed to the English, in St-John Mildmay's text: "The subject of this book will be new to many of its readers. The rising of the soldiers in St Petersburg in 1825 is but little known or remembered . . ."[24] Rozen's reminiscences themselves did much to change that.

Predictably, the publication of Decembrist memoirs abroad provoked much interest in Russia. And in November 1869, in nos. 269 and 274 of *Exchange*

News (*Birzhevyye vedomosti*), there appeared two chapters of the Leipzig text, translated into Russian. The version was printed without Rozen's knowledge or consent. True, the chapters dealt with "safe" topics—his early years and service, the last few years of Alexander I's reign; but they also touched on the formation of the Northern Society and the interrogations of 1826. Rozen was not pleased. But, of course, such was the price of having overcome the Russian censors and increased the Russian reader's appetite. There would be other translations or "translations", notably in *Notes of the Fatherland* (*Otechestvennyye zapiski*), nos. 2–11 for 1876. But by then Rozen would be too much embroiled in the polemics that arose from the 1870 Russian-text edition published, *with* his permission, by Duncker and Humblot in Leipzig,[25] as also from his several articles in the historical journal *Russian Old Times* (*Russkaya starina*), to engage in litigation or in any other way waste energy.

One critic to whom he did feel it essential to respond, however, was P. N. Svistunov, who, in a lengthy article entitled "Certain Observations in Connection with the Latest Books and Articles on the Events of December 14, 1825",[26] found fault with him for failing in his memoirs to discuss in proper detail the causes of the fateful insurrection. Rozen, Svistunov objected, merely treated the events on Senate Square as a set of episodes in his own life; the causes ought to have been treated separately and far more exhaustively—after all, the memoirs were entitled *The Memoirs of a Decembrist* (*Zapiski Dekabrista*). Why, then, did Rozen dwell so lovingly on details of his childhood in Estonia, and on his agricultural activities in Khar'kov in the 1860s? Such issues were irrelevant to the Decembrist question. Rozen's reply, which was controlled and even somewhat tense in tone, was not long delayed.[27] In it he pointed out, first, that the introduction to the memoirs both in Russian and German made it plain that they were in three parts, the second dealing with Estonian history, the third—with "the most important contemporary questions, and the latest tremendous happenings and enormous changes in the Fatherland"; and, second, that Decembrists' childhoods and, indeed, the whole mesh of their personal and social circumstances bore directly on their conduct in December 1825. That, too, had been suggested in the general introduction to the memoirs: "The spirit of a time, the degree of education, the strength of convictions and of circumstances, all these factors, separately and together, strongly influence the acts and conduct of the best of men—and must remove the stain of reproach from their memory."[28] As to the factual accuracy of his memoirs, he defied his critics to disprove it, or rather, would gladly amend any detail that was *shown* to be inaccurate or biased.

One other consequence of the appearance of Rozen's memoirs outside Russia may be mentioned here: D. I. Zavalishin, who by 1869 had begun his own long reminiscences with a view to publication and to vindicating his "true" position as a "prominent" figure in Petrovsky Zavod, was effectively dissuaded from so doing for another fourteen years. Discouraged by the fate of Rozen's memoirs, which appeared in Russian periodicals only in extracts, Zavalishin, wishing his own to appear in full and uncensored (how else could the whole country know how the wealthy, haughty grandees at Petrovsky had affronted him?), declined an offer of money to publish in Germany.[29] Not until 1884, in the event, would even one brief section of his memoirs appear in Russia, in the journal *The Russian Messenger* (*Russkiy vestnik*).[30] And only in 1904, twelve years after his death and twenty after Rozen's, would their full text finally appear, in Russian, but in Munich. Yet the very fact of Rozen's reminiscences having been published, there can be no doubt, encouraged several other of his comrades to prepare their own: A. F. Frolov and A. P. Belyayev, for example, both of whose accounts of the Decembrists' life in prisons in the capital and in Siberia were published in 1882,[31] wrote those accounts during the 'seventies. As Zavalishin's case suggests, however, *Aus den Memoiren eines russischen Dekabristen* bore its negative, as well as its more positive, results. We may be happy that, of all Decembrist memoirs, none proved more steeped in prejudice and bitterness than D. I. Zavalishin's: little was lost to those hoping to learn the truth about "a curious passage in the history of a previous age" by the fact of their delay.

So much for the circumstances of the publication of Rozen's memoirs. (Only in 1907, we may note in conclusion, did their full and annotated text appear in Russia, in the series *Obshchestvennaya Pol'za*, edited by P. E. Shchegolev.) It is time to consider the memoirs themselves, and their claims on our attention.

Rozen's memoirs are among the most reliable of all Decembrist memoirs. He himself, it cannot well be over-emphasized, was of a careful temperament, methodical and diligent in outlook; his reminiscences mirror an un-impassioned nature. His prose style, as seems fitting, is even and unhurried, tending to the dispassionate, always avoiding garish ornament. It is a style, in short, in keeping with his outlook. No flights of fantasy distract the reader from the narrative; only detailed lists—of all Decembrists exiled to Siberia, of wool prices in Khar'kov markets, of reforms passed by the Government between 1861 and 1867—for a moment interrupt the measured flow of Rozen's prose. First the revolt, then the arrest, then the interrogation and the exile, then the years spent in the south—all is controlled and logical. Of course, there *are* peculiar elements: the inclusion of obituaries at frequent intervals throughout the later sections, for example, and the citing of whole poems by A. I. Odoyevsky, P. S. Bobrishchev-Pushkin, by Ryleyev and by Lermontov. But these aspects, from which would grow a dozen articles in 1870–83, somehow blend with the whole so that only if one consciously seeks out idiosyncrasies or individualistic traits do they become apparent. Nothing, in general terms, disturbs the measured rhythm of a calm man's prose. Consider, for example, his approach towards the radicalism of the pre-Decembrist years—a subject which might justifiably make his heart accelerate a trifle, since it brought about his exile and disgrace—as reflected in the following two statements. It is inconceivable that the Bestuzhevs, or Lorer, or Yakushkin, all of whom use brighter colours to present *their* pictures of events on Senate Square or in their cell in Peter-and-Paul Fortress, should have made them:

> I know well enough that men's characters and actions are very much determined by the spirit of the times and by the circumstances in which they chance to be—a fact that may make us bitter towards individuals who have acted harshly towards ourselves . . .
>
> So it may be seen that the conspirators and rebels of 1825 were young enthusiasts who should be judged by other than strictly political standards. The cruel fate they were obliged to suffer for their crime atoned for that crime; and now it is possible for those who read their history to take a kindly and compassionate interest in the first attempt to draw Russia along the path of Western European liberalism.[32]

Is it to his own past and his own comrades that Rozen is alluding here? At first one wonders, so complete is the lack of *engagement*. What a gulf appears to separate the ageing author of the 'sixties from the youthful subaltern who, as a "young enthusiast", ruined his military career! Yet even as one looks, the gulf becomes illusory. Rozen did not change fundamentally during those thirty years that fell between the rising and the amnesty; that we have seen already. True, the feeling lingers that the author of this passage, by some powerful act of will or by the action of his temperament, *almost* disassociates himself from the realities of his own earlier life, standing aside and watching as his youthful wraith performs. Yet that same Lieutenant Rozen drove and shadowed Baron Rozen all his life, bringing him first to Transbaikalia, then to Kurgan, then to the Caucasus, and so back to Estonia. For fifty years Rozen sustained an interest in agriculture, history, and music; for fifty years he took regular physical exercise, and remained faithful to the Lutheran Church. And *can* character change after the age of twenty-five? Now it is commonly accepted that it cannot change, though it may well be coloured by experience or circumstance, after the age of two. Deliberate and cautious in 1869, he was cautious and deliberate in 1825; balanced in outlook in his middle years, he was hardly less so as a youthful officer. He took no foolish risks in later life, nor did he do so on "the day" in 1825. So we come to a vital point in an assessment of the value of the memoirs: it is precisely the deliberate, methodical approach to life characteristic of the man which gives those memoirs their peculiar merit, and which, in 1825, resulted in his loss to the Decembrists in the hour of crisis. That very absence of the wild, erratic element so prominent in Zavalishin's memoirs, and which makes Rozen's reminiscences so pleasantly consistent and reliable, also resulted in his loss to the Decembrists when his aid was most desperately needed.

The description of events on December 14, 1825 occupies a central position in the first part of *Zapiski dekabrista*. Together with the sections on secret societies, the Committee of Enquiry and the "trial" and sentencing, indeed, it forms a key passage, balanced on one side by description of his youth and early service, on the other by accounts of life in Chita and Petrovsky. And Rozen, it was seen from his introduction, intended that the chapter should comprise a focal point and be a fulcrum. From the first he meant to emphasize it, conscious that "what happened on December 14, 1825" had been "distorted practically beyond belief" and that there were few men alive, by 1869, better qualified than he by force of circumstance to present a factually accurate account of one aspect, at least, of the *joli commencement de règne*. He was right; and the chapter constitutes one of the most essential records of events on that day.[33] How paradoxical, this being so, that his written style lent itself less to the recording of dramatic events than to sustained narration and description. We may be thankful, harmful though his standing on St Isaac's Bridge was finally to be for his comrades on the Senate Square, that he at least was stationary and able to absorb the situation and the words and deeds of others rather as if they all comprised a vast, jerkingly animated, grim *tableau vivant*.

Unquestionably, he was admirably situated on the bridge over the ice to observe events as they unfolded. To his left was the yellow mass of the Admiralty, by the far corner of which the Emperor appeared; to his right was the Senate building, by which onlookers had gathered by the hundred; and before him, on the other side of troops loyal to Nicholas, was the rebellion itself. Many who later wrote their recollections of the day—Obolensky, for example, and Mikhail Bestuzhev—certainly *did* more; but they also rushed about far more, and there is, in consequence, a hurried quality and tension in Bestuzhev's recollections of the day that is wholly missing from Rozen's calm account. At times, indeed, the sense of *Ordnung* in those sections of the latter's work which deal, supposedly, with passion, blood and death, can be oppressive. Rozen may "hurriedly return" to his regiment, and troops may even "cross the ice at a charge" while cannon-balls bounce near them, but still events unfold with easy dignity. Only by reading other eye-witness accounts of the same, hectic afternoon can we appreciate that many things were happening simultaneously, and that confusion reigned supreme.

This very shortcoming, however, if shortcoming it is, is transformed into a virtue in the later parts of Rozen's narrative. Not all was drama, after all, and hours of feverish activity were followed, for most rebels, by long months of incarceration which in turn gave way to years of exile. Not always happy when describing sudden turns of circumstance, quick movements and volte-faces, Rozen came into his own as a narrator when sustained description was required. And it is, perhaps, his numerous and finely drawn descriptions of Siberian life and of the climate and geography, peoples, commerce and industry of Transbaikalia and the Caucasus, that constitute the greatest single merit of the later passages of reminiscence. But are his detailed word pictures of Kurgan main street as it appeared in mid-September 1832, for instance, or of the tawdry, pilgrim-thronged interior of the church of St Mitrofan in Voronezh in September 1837, in fact reminiscences? Not in the true sense of the word, for Rozen made extensive use of notes made at the time, and sometimes on the spot. Merely to glance over his descriptions, of towns between Tyumen' and Chita for example, or of the rock-faces by Lake Baykal, is to be sure of that. Again, conversation is conspicuously missing. The fact is reassuring: for could Rozen truly have recalled what was said by anyone three decades earlier, unless he had made notes at the time? Natural and physical description, of towns, rivers, mountains and buildings; accounts of the dress, appearance, and activity of groups or individuals met; brief retellings of the histories of exiles, colonists, soldiers, and even jails (only Rozen tells us that the prison at Petrovsky Zavod was utterly destroyed by fire on April 15, 1866): these are the precious elements in *Zapiski dekabrista* and are Rozen's most enduring contribution to the history of the Decembrists in Siberia. Memoirists give, axiomatically, according to their means. Thus, Nikolay Bestuzhev has no more valuable offering to the contemporary student of the period than his aquarelles showing the jails in Chita and Petrovsky Zavod, the surrounding countryside, Decembrists, and their wives.[34] Thus Obolensky makes his contribution, not by giving detailed information of a factual kind, but by casting light on his emotional and psychological condition in 1825 and subsequently, and on the moods and hopes of other men.[35] For Rozen, there was nothing more deplorable than distortion of the truth as it appeared to honest eyes; at the core of his descriptions lay hard fact. *Im Anfang war die Tat* . . . Several Decembrists note in passing the splendour of the River Selenga, with its high cliffs and lazy waves; only Rozen presents a virtual colour photograph: "Picture to yourself a broad river, whose right bank was formed of high rocks of various-coloured strata, red, yellow, grey and black granite, mixed with spar, slate, sand, lime, gravel, and chalk; this bank was sixty feet high, and in clear weather the perpendicular wall of rock shone with a thousand hues . . ."[36] The rocks, we see, were granite, spar, slate, lime, and chalk; and the wall was sixty feet high, not forty. Again, let us consider Rozen's comments on the subject of the Buriats' "brick-tea"—something mentioned by no other memoirist:

> The chief luxury of every class, and a principal support of those who can afford it, is a particular kind of tea, a mixture of decayed and spoilt tea-leaves, which is pressed into cakes with cherry-tree gum or some other sticky substance—cakes which look like smooth bricks one or two feet long, seven inches wide, and three inches thick: from this resemblance the tea is called in Siberia "brick-tea". The Buriats would break off little bits from these lumps with their hatchets, ground or pound them in mortars, boil the powder in a kettle, add some flour, milk or butter, and fat, and drink this brew with great relish from wooden lacquered bowls, rather deeper and larger than our saucers.[37]

No doubt such details do not add to our understanding of the final phase of the Decembrist *movement*; yet they tell us much, not only about Buriat life, but also about intellectual activity among the exiles. Several Decembrists, notably M. Murav'yov-Apostol, Shteyngel', M. K. Kyukhel'beker, I. I. Gorbachevsky, and Nikolay Bestuzhev, took an informed and lasting interest in the customs of Siberian native peoples. Gorbachevsky in time became an expert on shamanism in Eastern Siberia. Kyukhel'beker gathered local folklore —a task in which Princess Trubetskaya aided him—while Nikolay Bestuzhev, a self-trained ethnographer, compiled a little Buriat–Russian dictionary.[38] When, in 1829, the German scientist G.-A. Erman visited Siberia with an expedition which was part of that led by the celebrated Humboldt, he found several Decembrists and their wives only too willing to inform him on such matters. "From no one", he recorded,[39] "had I ever heard a juster appreciation of Siberian character. Their representation of the pantomimic dances with which the natives accompany their songs, was given with such impressive grace as to surpass every performance I had hitherto witnessed in Russia." But Erman died; and the Decembrists died; and how are *we* to appreciate the grace of their representations of the Buriat and Tungus dances? Nikolay Bestuzhev's aquarelles, and Rozen's word-pictures, remain. From them, as from the work of other keen-eyed visitors at the same time such as Charles Cottrell, in *Recollections of Siberia in the Years 1840–1841*, I. Boulitchoff (Bulichov), in *Voyage dans la Sibérie orientale* . . . (St Petersburg, 1856), and, of course, Baron A. Haxthausen,[40] we may form a sound impression of conditions, physical and social, economic and political, in Transbaikalia in the latter part of Nicholas's reign. With Baron Haxthausen-Abbenberg's work on the Russian Empire and its peoples, in particular, Rozen's account of life in exile may with justness be compared: both are the works of cool, rational Germans; both show expertise in various fields, from botany to farming, literature to commerce; both are of interest to the social scientist and the anthropologist, as well as the historian of Russian (and Siberian) liberalism, trade and commerce. Both, essentially, rest on a solid foundation of fact.

Rozen's memoirs are a treasure-house of factual information. He alone of the Decembrists, it was noted earlier, saw fit to provide a complete list of all Decembrist exiles in Petrovsky Zavod; but he does more than this: in his memoirs we are offered a plan of the prison itself showing the cells of sixty-four men in relation one to another. (Rozen occupied no. 11, between Trubetskoy and Obolensky.)[41] He alone gives, in their categories, those sentenced on July 9, 1826. He alone provides a "necrologue" of his companions, and obituaries of comrades as reliable in detail as controlled in tone. Always one is aware of the pervasive sense of balance in *Zapiski dekabrista*—of the quest for proper emphasis. Always one is reminded of the author's sense of honour, of respect for comrades' memories, of duty to himself.

It was, above all else, that growing feeling of respect, which false accounts and slanted or perverse interpretations outraged, that led Rozen to embark upon a period of intensive journalism at the age of seventy. He was, as he himself knew well, an old man by the year of publication of his first brief article dealing with the Decembrists, "Corrections to The Memoirs of M. A. Bestuzhev" (in 1870, in *Russkaya starina*).[42] Awareness of encroaching age had made him hasten to complete his memoirs and submit them to a publisher; now, that awareness made him publish such "corrections" to the works of others as seemed fitting, and while he still had strength to do so. But strength, the passing years showed, was not deserting him. Indeed, his eighth decade covered a period of activity unequalled by any since his first years as an Arbitrator of the Peace, in 1861–63. At last, it seemed, those energies denied an outlet in his late twenties and thirties, when to have toiled would have been natural, were finding full expression. And how better, after all, to serve the cause of truth where the Decembrists were concerned, and to honour his companions' memory, than to correct such errors as he found, and to publish comments on his own account?

Rozen published eleven articles on individual Decembrists and their families, Decembrists' reminiscences, Decembrist verse, and exiles in the Caucasus, in the journal *Russkaya starina* between 1870 and his death in 1884. In addition he wrote two, on his work as an Arbitrator of the Peace in Izyum and on Estonian affairs, which were published posthumously in 1885,[43] and completed *An Outline of the Family History of the Barons von Rozen*, published in St Petersburg in 1876 and translated into German shortly afterwards.[44] No other Decembrist contributed so munificently to a periodical or almanac. No Decembrist took more care over his sources, or published with a greater sense of need (to Russian readers) and responsibility (to comrades). Rozen's articles in *Russkaya starina* were, chronologically:

"Corrections to The Memoirs of M. A. Bestuzhev" ("Popravki k Zapiskam Bestuzheva"), 1870, vol. II, 56–9.

"Verses by Pavel Sergeyevich Bobrishchev-Pushkin" ("Stikhotvoreniya Pavla Sergeyevicha Bobrishcheva-Pushkina"), 1871, vol. III, 534–6.

"Aleksandr Ivanovich Odoyevsky", 1871, vol. III, 635.

"Nikolay Nikolayevich Rayevsky",[45] 1873, vol. VII, 372.

"Nekrolog Yeleny Aleksandrovny Bestuzhevoy", 1874, vol. IX, 577–8.

"Ivan Aleksandrovich Annenkov", 1878, vol. XXII, 525–6.

"Remarks on The Memoirs of A. P. Belyayev" ("Zametki k Zapiskam A. P. Belyayeva"), 1881, vol. XXX, 452–4.

"P. Falenberg: A Tale From the Era of 1826" ("P. Falenberg: Rasskaz iz epokhi 1826 goda"), 1883, vol. XXXVIII, 573–92.

"M. N. Murav'yov and His Participation in a Secret Society from 1816 to 1821" ("M. N. Murav'yov i yego uchastiye v taynom obshchestve 1816–1821"), 1884, vol. XLI, 61–70.

"Decembrists in the Caucasus" ("Dekabristy na Kavkaze"), 1884, vol. LXI, 303–38.

"P. I. Pestel' ", 1884, vol. LXII, 79–83.

His articles published posthumously, in *Russkiy arkhiv* and *Russkaya mysl'* respectively, were:

"An Opinion on Estonian Affairs" ("Chastnoye mneniye estlyandskogo pomeshchika po delu obshchestvennomu"), *RA*, vol. IV, 641–3.

"An Outline of the Activity of an Arbitrator of the Peace in Khar'kov Province, District of Izyum, Section 2" ("Ocherk deystviy mirovogo posrednika Khar'kovskoy gub., Izyumskogo uyezda, 2-ogo uchastka"), *RM*, bk. 9.

By itself, Rozen's history of his family since A.D. 992 would have been testimony enough of a remarkable activity, and one more noteworthy, because of his advanced age, than either Gorbachevsky's ethnographic work during the 'sixties or Zavalishin's passionate polemic, ended with his forced departure from Chita in August 1863, with N. N. Murav'yov-Amursky, Governor-General of Eastern Siberia (and another expert on Pacific and Far Eastern affairs).[46] The simultaneous preparation of three articles, all to appear in their author's eighty-fifth year, is surely proof of an extraordinary, not merely noteworthy, last flare of energy. But the demise of the majority of those who even recollected Alexander I and the events of the Napoleonic Wars served only to increase the strength and vigour of survivors. Now, in the 1880s, even the amnesty of 1856 was long before—a quasi-historical event. Then, there had been thirty-four Decembrists in Siberia to respond to Alexander's act of clemency—twenty-one in the east, thirteen in the west—and perhaps a dozen more in European Russia. By 1884, only eight Decembrists lived, including Rozen. They were, starting with the youngest: A. F. Frolov, aged 80; Svistunov and A. P. Belyayev, aged 81; Zavalishin, aged 82; M. A. Nazimov, aged 85; N. A. Zagoretsky, aged 88; and Matvey Murav'yov-Apostol, aged 91. Of the eight survivors, two worked for the pleasure and the inner need of it: Rozen and Frolov. Two others, Zavalishin and Svistunov, worked of necessity. Financially, both men were insecure. Svistunov gave French lessons in a school for girls in Kaluga, where Prince Obolensky (or rather, Yevgeniy Kaluzhsky, as he could not use his title) had died in 1865. Zavalishin acted as a private tutor to the sons of wealthy merchants in Moscow, and detested it. Murav'yov-Apostol, Zagoretsky, and Nazimov were too frail to work or travel, and rarely left their homes.

What, then, of Rozen's articles? Five are obituaries or, in Odoyevsky's case, remarks on certain aspects of the life of a man dead thirty years. Three are literary in content—those concerning Odoyevsky, Bobrishchev-Pushkin, and Falenberg. On these, brief comments may be useful, since the titles are not wholly self-explanatory.

With Pavel Bobrishchev-Pushkin, we have seen, Rozen was on friendly terms in Chita and Petrovsky Zavod, where Pushkin was the leading figure in "the Congregation" (see Chapter 6). Pushkin, like Odoyevsky, wrote verses while in exile; and, as for Odoyevsky, Rozen served as private archivist for him. The verses in question, "An Imitation of the Thirteenth Chapter of the First Epistle of St Paul to the Corinthians", were touched on earlier.[47] Suffice it to observe here that those verses, written in Chita in 1829, were in Rozen's possession for some forty years.

Odoyevsky's poems, too, Rozen treated with an archivist's respect. Extracts from some, including the "Epistle to My Father" which, it is held by some historians, so pleased the Emperor that he hastened Odoyevsky's death by approving his prompt transfer to the Caucasus, were included in Rozen's memoirs in the Russian text of 1870.[48] As for the piece around which he composed the article on Odoyevsky of 1871, "To One Arrived From Kurgan . . ." ("Priyezzhemu iz Kurgana . . ."), it, too, was known by that year.[49] Merely to present a poem rescued from oblivion, however, was not Rozen's object in his article: rather was it to offer to the public, which already had before it one version of the fifteen-line epistle, the *correct* version. How could Rozen be sure of the correctness? Because the poem, written by Odoyevsky in the village of Ishim, in the Province of Tobol'sk, on October 3, 1836, had been personally checked by him at Rozen's own request. Odoyevsky, we learn, rarely wrote down verses unless urged to do so. Rozen thus prompted the unhurried poet to commit the piece to paper, or saw that someone else did so, and proceeded to ensure its textual accuracy! Literary historians, as well as their political and social counterparts, have reason to be grateful for the method and precision so amusing to the friends and fellow-exiles of Kuno von Kyburg.

Finally, Falenberg's tale, and the résumé of the Decembrist exiles in the Caucasus: Falenberg entrusted Rozen with his "tale", a manuscript concerning his relations with Prince A. I. Baryatinsky, ardent member of the Southern Society and supporter of Pestel', immediately before his death in 1873. Possibly because Nekrasov asked him for it with a view to publication in his *Notes of the Fatherland* (*Otechestvennyye zapiski*, which he had edited with Saltykov and G. Z. Yelizeyev since January 1868), Rozen forwarded it to Nekrasov. However, the tale failed to appear; and Rozen suspected that it was because of certain references to Benkendorf, Chernyshev, and Levashev, members of the Committee of Enquiry of 1826. Rozen was indignant, decided to publish the tale himself, in *Russkaya starina*, and did so, with the full approval of its editor, Mikhail Semevsky, with a note alluding to the recent Nekrasov incident—and to Alexander II's comment, cited earlier, that Rozen would (the Emperor knew well) "never write or publish anything harmful". For Rozen, it was intolerable either that his own intentions in offering manuscripts for publication should be questioned, or that the whole truth of the Decembrists' trial, imprisonment, exile and scattering should not be told. It was, as always, with the object of presenting the complete facts of the matter that he gave Semevsky his last considerable essay, "Decembrists in the Caucasus", three months before he died. The essay shows the qualities in evidence in Rozen's memoirs: method, thoroughness, a sense of balance. The exiles are divided into five groups: members of the Northern or Southern Society who, not having been sentenced to exile, distinguished themselves in the Persian and Turkish wars of 1827–28; those reduced to the ranks and dispatched to the Caucasus to serve; those transferred to the Caucasus from Siberia at the request of others in Russia; the 1837 group, including himself, Naryshkin, Lorer, Nazimov, and V. N. Likharyov; and those Decembrists killed in the south. The essay is, essentially, a factual compilation. No detail was too small for Rozen to have checked it, or so obvious as to invite omission. For the historian of the Decembrist movement, such statistics are of the most obvious value.

It was a wish to honour his companions' memory, then, together with his irritation at the publication of inaccurate accounts and anger with perverse interpretations of his comrades' aims and actions, that brought Rozen to write with such devotion and persistence in his last few years. Had there not been a suitable outlet for his articles, however, he could not have become, so indisputably, the most authoritative and most diligent recorder of Decembrism. In fairness to its editor and founder, therefore, something must be said here of the early years of the greatest historical journal to appear in Russia in the later nineteenth century: *Russkaya starina*.

Russkaya starina, founded in 1870 by M. I. Semevsky (1837–92), historian, teacher and journalist, was a journalistic reincarnation.[50] A. O. Kornilovich had published an almanac of the same title almost fifty years before, in which he had placed, *inter alia*, his own works on the reigns of Anna Ivanovna, Elizabeth, and Peter the Great.[51] Semevsky thus exploited an established, though by 1870 half-forgotten, name. He gambled on sufficient interest in recent Russian history among a wide public to justify a personal investment of 5,000 roubles. It was a calculated risk, and one that paid off handsomely. The time, it was apparent by the spring of 1876, by when the circulation of the periodical had trebled,[52] was right for the appearance of a quarterly or monthly on post-Petrine Russian history. Many would gladly read about the wars against Napoleon or yet more recent happenings—and Semevsky had no fears of publishing the reminiscences of men still living, and on subjects that might justifiably have been regarded as extremely sensitive. The Crimean War, for instance, still aroused deep passions after twenty years. Semevsky did not shy away from it, if he thought the manuscript in question sound and of interest to the public. And his instinct in such matters seemed infallible. At his request, T. P. Passek and the ageing actor P. A. Karatygin wrote their memoirs *for* him and his periodical.[53] In 1871, 3,500 persons subscribed to *Russkaya starina*, which meant that perhaps 20,000 read it. By 1876, the circulation had passed 10,000; at least 60,000 Russians might be presumed to glance through it each month. Encouraged, Semevsky redoubled his efforts to seek out arresting manuscripts; and, more than ever, he resolved to concentrate not on the eighteenth, but on the nineteenth century, and on purely historical themes. Competition had intensified between his journal and *Russkiy arkhiv*. The latter was a literary as much as an historical journal; Semevsky saw the need to avoid duplication, and to improve the printed quality and the appearance of *Russkaya starina*. Profits were on principle ploughed back into the journal; and profits were considerable by 1878. So in 1879 Semevsky introduced finely engraved portraits in every issue. And always he sought manuscripts to satisfy his readers, whose appetites were growing year by year. Already, with Karatygin and P. M. Daragan, whose memoirs of court life in 1817–20 had appeared in 1875 (Daragan had been a sharp-eyed page-in-waiting, or *kamer-pazh*, as a child), he had had success enough to encourage him to publish memoirs separately, as books—those of Prince Ya. Shakhovskoy in 1872, for example.[54] More coups would follow in the 1880s: the memoirs of S. A. Poroshin, for instance, once tutor to the Grand Duke Pavel Petrovich, later Paul I (in 1881); and of Ya. I. de Sanglen, chief of secret police under Alexander I (in 1882–83). But now, with *Russkaya starina* firmly established and in its first maturity, he struck the richest vein of reminiscences imaginable: the Decembrists'. Five decades having passed since the rebellion on Senate Square, the very word *dekabrist* had an attractive ring. And the survivors (the survivors! What romantic overtones the word evoked, what visions of Siberian wilderness!) had been pardoned by the Emperor. Even physically, the aged men struck chords of sympathy among their Liberal admirers of another age: and some, like Prince Volkonsky, whose nose was too beak-like for true beauty and whose hanging lower lip had once distressed him, had actually been transformed by their long trials. "With his tall figure and his long silvery locks," as Zetlin puts it in appropriately wide-eyed style, "he combined the aristocratic distinction of an Old Testament patriarch with something soil-bound and typically Russian."[55] So it seemed to Nekrasov, too, whose interest in the Decembrists, provoked by Rozen's memoirs, had already resulted in the poems "The Grandfather" (1870), "Princess Trubetskaya" (1871), and "Princess Volkonskaya" (1872). Encouraged by the obvious approval of young radicals connected with the journal *Novosti* (though I. S. Turgenev found "Princess Volkonskaya" flat and tedious),[56] the poet interviewed Nazimov, asking for more details of General Leparsky and A. G. Murav'yova, soon to be the heroine of a new piece, "Russian Women". (But, of course, although Nekrasov was acquainted personally with Rozen[57] and had read his memoirs carefully, it was not the bare truth about exile life that he either sought or found; for Nekrasov, with his notion of "the people's happiness" in ownership of land and personal liberty, Tarbagatay had seemed a veritable earthly paradise—a place of laughter, industry, abundance. Rozen, or rather *his* interpretation of the memoirs published recently by Rozen, merely confirmed a vision of Russian happiness which he, Nekrasov, had been nurturing since 1863 and "Moroz Krasnyy-nos" ("Red-Nosed Frost"). For the poet, indeed, Rozen's reminiscences were merely to be used. Nor is one well advised to read through "Russian Women" for a true reflection of the life and work of the Decembrist wives in exile.)

Thus on an emotional as well as intellectual plane, the memory of the Decembrists, their brave attempt, failure and suffering, struck sympathetic chords among young readers born after the amnesty of 1856 had been proclaimed. Throughout the reign of Nicholas, the Russian Press had been forbidden to make any references to the Decembrists or their whereabouts—a fact sufficient in itself to nurture Herzen's grand Decembrist myth. But even by the 'fifties, that myth had become powerful. "I swore", Herzen declared in 1855, "to avenge the murdered men, and dedicated myself to the struggle with that throne, that altar, and those cannon."[58] Now, in the late 'seventies, the myth was stronger still. The Decembrists were exalted, as they had been earlier by Belinsky, Petrashevsky, Chernyshevsky, Ogaryov, and would be by the Bolsheviks and Mensheviks alike, as victims of autocracy and martyrs to the Liberal cause. It was essentially in the creation of their legend that "the young enthusiasts, clinging to highly-gifted but impractical leaders",[59] made their enduring contribution to the cause of liberty in Russia. So Rozen, with his rigorous insistence on the factual truth of the rebellion, its causes and results, stood apart from the contemporary mainstream in its attitude towards "that throne, that altar, those cannon". To read his correspondence with Nekrasov from 1871 to 1875 is to grow acutely conscious of the fact.[60] But others, too, felt that the memory of the Decembrists was best served, not by creating glorious myths, but by publishing the whole, unbiased truth; and one of these was M. I. Semevsky. From the first, he and the ageing Rozen found each other sympathetic; from the first, the two co-operated fully. Like Rozen, Semevsky had connections with the First Cadet Corps, where he had once been an academic coach.[61] Like Rozen he wrote articles on Russian history, and valued the continued publication of such articles to the extent of a deficit for *Russkaya starina*, notwithstanding its immense profitability ten years before, of 38,500 roubles by 1892, when he died. Like Rozen, lastly, he believed intensely that the truth should be recorded, and untruths refuted, while men were still alive who could perform those tasks. So came about Semevsky's personal and journalistic link, first with Rozen, then, through Rozen, with other Decembrists. In *Russkaya starina* appeared reminiscences by Mikhail Bestuzhev in 1870 and again in 1881; V. K. Kyukhel'beker, in 1875, 1883–84, and 1891; A. P. Belyayev, in 1880–81 and 1884–86; D. I. Zavalishin, in 1881–82; and Matvey Murav'yov-Apostol, in 1886. No doubt these and other notices on individual Decembrists and their wives (Annenkova in 1888, for example) would have appeared, in *Russkaya starina* or elsewhere, even had Rozen not unlocked the gates for all Decembrist reminiscences in 1869. There can be little doubt, however, that Rozen's publishing, when, where, and *how* he did (early, abroad, and with unshakeable insistence upon accuracy), exerted a considerable influence not only on Decembrist memoirists over the next two decades, but also on the work of others editing Decembrist reminiscences— Trubetskoy's daughters, for example, and P. E. Shchegolev, Rozen's own Russian editor, both in 1907. A high standard of accuracy had been set; most kept to it. Rozen had showed the sense of publishing while one had both the strength and will to do so, and while others were alive still who might criticize with good results: others[62] followed him—F. F. Vadkovsky (1873), Trubetskoy (1874), A. P. Belyayev (1880), Frolov (1882). The disadvantages of publishing abroad, finally, had been made plain for later writers. Still, if one could not publish in Russia, or chose not to do so . . . Germany was seemingly the place. It was in Berlin and Munich, respectively, that Trubetskoy's and Zavalishin's *zapiski* appeared, in 1903 (Hugo Steinitz Verlag) and 1904.[63] Finally, there was the fact of the connection between memoirs on or by Decembrists and Semevsky's journal—a connection forged by Rozen. By publishing his own memoirs, he had helped to stimulate an interest in the Decembrist movement in the general public (and incidentally, helped by Nekrasov, to embellish the Decembrist myth); by contributing to Semevsky's journal from the outset, in 1870, he had reinforced that interest and disposed Semevsky to accept more reminiscences on the same general topic early in the day—in 1870, not 1880; by writing systematically and steadily about Decembrism himself, lastly, and about men he had personally known, events that he had personally experienced and could verify, he served as the true guardian of the story of his own and his companions' past. He was, *par excellence*, by choice and temperament, the recorder of Decembrism.

These, then, were Baron Rozen's main concerns during his eighth decade. However, it should not be thought that he was weak or failing, mentally or physically, in his last years. To the contrary: he undertook, for instance, a major agricultural project in 1875. Among the Vaksel' papers now preserved in Leningrad, we find various documents relating to the wish of "Andrey Rozen, landowner" to rent, on terms as favourable as possible, the lands adjacent to his own, belonging to Ekaterina Fedoseyevna Malinovskaya. Unfortunately, cousin Katya had no interest in renting land. Anna asked her brother to speak to her on her, Anna's, behalf. Rozen, she knew, would be much disappointed if the land could not be rented. Finally, her nephew Pavel was successful. Ekaterina gave him full authority to represent her in negotiations with her elderly but still extremely energetic relative, the late State convict, Andrey. The text of the agreement reached by Rozen and his wife's nephew reads in part as follows:

Contract of Lease

The parties being, Pavel Ivanovich Malinovsky, representing his mother Ekaterina Fedoseyevna Malinovskaya, proprietress of the farm (*khutor*) of Viknino-Grekov, in Izyum district, and Baron Andrey Yevgen'yevich Rozen. These two have come to the following agreement: I, Pavel Malinovsky, hereby lease to Andrey Rozen the above-named property of my mother, tilth and meadow, suitable and unsuitable land, and wood, all to the extent of 120 *desyatins* and 1,267 square *sazhens*, as shown on the plan decreed by the Chancery of Land Measures, for a term of three years beginning now, in 1875. In the above-named farm are a wooden water-mill with one set of mill-stones and one ancient cottage with no outhouses.

Secondly: I, Andrey Rozen, hereby lease the above-named property for three years and undertake, on the day of this contract's confirmation, to pay the rent for the three years in advance, in one lump sum of a thousand roubles.

Thirdly: The lessee shall be permitted, in order to improve the meadow, to drain flooded water-meadows, to clear fields of bushes and weeds, etc....

Sixthly: I, Pavel Malinovsky, undertake not to hamper the agricultural

19

enterprise of the tenant, and I, Andrey Rozen, undertake to maintain everything in good order.

Seventhly: If metals or coal should be found on the property of Ekaterina Malinovskaya, these shall be inviolably for the owner's use.

Eighthly: Expenses for headed notepaper and notarial expenses shall both, in equal parts, be met by the owner's representative and the lessee. This contract shall be kept solemnly and inviolably by both parties.

(signed)   Andrey Rozen
Pavel Malinovsky[64]

No small undertaking for a man of Rozen's ripe years, we may think. But Rozen carried out his plans for Viknino-Grekov, a property of slightly more than 330 acres, in the following three years. Inundated meadows were, indeed, thoroughly drained; the water-mill, moreover, was repaired, and the whole property was made to show a profit. For good measure, Rozen made a new, accurate survey of that property, the 1847 plan of which (kept in the Chancery of Land Measures) was based, so it transpired, on a faulty survey of 1779. Always, inaccuracy pained Rozen. Always, he had energy enough to see that *he*, at least, avoided it, no matter where or how he was engaged.

These agricultural activities, however, pleasurable though he clearly found them, did not occupy a central place in Rozen's mind or heart by his last years. That place, we see from most of his surviving correspondence, was taken up by family concerns and by his memory of exile in Siberia.

To the last he corresponded with survivors from the time of Alexander I, gathering information, urging them to send him what they wrote. Thus, on January 3, 1883, to Nazimov: "I had letters from Murav'yov-Apostol and Svistunov in Moscow at the end of last week... The first is dictating something on the old Semyonovsky story [the rising of October 1820—G.B.], in connection with which some brochure or other has offended him—by Gorbachevsky, I think, and from *Russkiy arkhiv*."[65] Murav'yov-Apostol, aged ninety, was dictating to a daughter-in-law because he was half-blind; Gorbachevsky's "brochure" which so vexed him had been written twenty years before, and Gorbachevsky had been dead some fourteen years. But Nazimov, like Rozen and Svistunov, was still mentally and physically alert. Every day, Rozen took exercise, as he had since 1827 in Chita; every day, he worked a few hours in his study on the ground floor of the handsome house in Viknino, two hours' ride from Izyum.[66] And to the last he fasted on December 14 every year, and kept his interest in Estonian affairs. What he learned about Estonia, however, was not cheering: the ancient post of Hakenrichter was abolished by the Ministry of Justice, and in higher courts German could not be used. And the Ritter-und-Domschule in Revel' was to close, after five centuries. And the Lutheran Church was under growing pressure from the Baltic agents of the Holy Synod, K. Pobedonostsev, and increased russification in the area. Fortunately he had no desire to see his "native land", which he would evidently scarcely now have recognized. Common sense kept him in Viknino, and it was there, on April 19, 1884, his wedding day, and four months after Anna, that he died in his sleep. Semevsky, with whom he had been corresponding days before, himself wrote the obituary published in volume XLII of *Russkaya starina*.[67] Rozen, he emphasized, had been in various respects a happy man: to the end, his mind had been clear, his memory superb, his health steady enough; to the end, he had pursued his chosen interest. He had lived to see the freeing of the serfs, the great reforms, and he had even, as an Arbitrator of the Peace, played his own part in the full realization of the moderate Liberals' dreams. The full realization? One might question whether N. M. Murav'yov, or any of the constitutionalists of 1825, would have found a grain of pleasure in the spectacle of Grinevetsky's Russia, effective though his bomb had been, and grim the death of Nicholas's son. The spirit of Kakhovsky, would-be regicide, was plainly flourishing two generations later; but was autocracy not as apparently a vital limb of the Russian body politic as sixty years before, and just as "fatal to both rulers and society", as Murav'yov had put it? But what had Princess M. N. Volkonskaya, activist though she seemed in 1835, in common with a Sof'ya Perovskaya? Or Trubetskaya with a Vera Zasulich? Rozen, too, belonged in another Russia. He did not die too soon. "But under all conditions, everywhere, always he kept his cheerfulness, his faith and inner strength . . . Everywhere he strictly followed the pattern of a high, moral, laborious life—the pattern which he had established for himself."

EPILOGUE

Three of Rozen's sons, it has been seen, settled in Izyum district, Province of Khar'kov, and there, like their now ageing father, became landowners and farmers. Rozen's immediate family thus acquired two centres of emotional and economic gravity—Estonia and Khar'kov. In Revel', relatives continued to represent the ancient line of Rozen in the *Landrat* and in regional affairs; but, it was clear by 1870, Khar'kov had become the major centre of Rozen–Malinovsky interests. Yevgeniy, we have seen, had married an Izyum maiden; the Taranukhins had been settled in the district for a century. Kondratiy and Vasiliy, Rozen's second and third sons, also settled in Izyum on their retirement from the army. Vasiliy, a Lieutenant-Colonel when he left the Artillery in 1876, was financially as well as temperamentally well fitted to strengthen the already firm family grip on that district. Both younger brothers flourished, with their families; nor was Yevgeniy's situation, after the disastrous period of 1853–58, a bad one by the eighth decade. The Rozens occupied impressive manor-houses, and grew tolerably wealthy on their sales of wool and grain.

Several factors combined indeed, in that same decade, to make it seem quite possible that, in the near future, the Rozens of Mehntack might vanish from Estonia. Yevgeniy's eldest son, Vyacheslav, born on February 14, 1855, had in 1875 become a *Beamter* (as his grandfather expressed it), and showed little interest in the damp Baltic littoral. Nor was his wife, Varvara *née* Katayeva, disposed to move to Estonia, with which she had no links of any kind. The couple settled in St Petersburg. There, on January 18, 1892, a son would be born to them—Boris. For their part, Vasiliy and Kondratiy, both childless and in Khar'kov Province, had produced no youthful Rozens to experience the charms and the dynastic magnetism, if any, of Estonia. Rozen himself then died. Another link with the province, Rozen's elder brother Vladimir (Woldemar), had likewise disappeared: having lived in retirement since 1815, half a century before, on an estate near Dorpat, Vladimir had been buried several years by 1870. Nor did his only son Mikhail (born in 1838) object to living in the capital. There Mikhail would remain until his death, in 1911. General-Major Julius, Rozen's younger brother, had never planned to settle in Estonia. Besides, he was on active service still. Finally, the Bobrovs lived far from Revel'. (Rozen's daughter Anna had married Nikolay Bobrov, Collegiate Assessor and servant of a Ministry in St Petersburg.) Even Sonorm, deeded to the family two centuries before, had slipped out of their hands: since the late 'fifties it had been the property of one Friedrich von Baumgarten.[1]

One Estonian property, however, remained in the possession of Rozen's family in 1880, and formed a powerful link between the grandchildren in Khar'kov and the Rozens' native land. Otto Yevgen'yevich (1795–1882), the Decembrist's elder brother, had for years (1821–34) rented the manor-house and the estate of Mehntack from his father. Rozen, we may recall, had stayed with Otto at Mehntack during the early 'twenties, and had found his economic situation parlous. His brother had then lived in straitened circumstances—a result, in Rozen's view, of admirable loyalty to a father (then in Revel'). But Otto had been genuinely and deeply attached to Mehntack. He had persevered with grain farming for fifteen, twenty, thirty years. He had declined to sell, even when land prices had risen so considerably during the sixth decade. Rozen loved him for it; and Otto, we have seen, had fundamentally improved his situation, and with it the manor-house of Mehntack, when Rozen and his family had come, and stayed, in 1839.

> As for my brother Otto, he looked older in the face and was now greying, but in his heart and enterprising nature he remained as I had known him. After many and long wanderings, I was again within those walls where my cradle had once stood; the huge stone house had been rebuilt after a fire and internally arranged quite differently by my brother . . .[2]

Gone, by 1840, were all traces of the former wooden manor-house which had once stood in the immediate vicinity. Otto's was indeed, as Rozen says, an enterprising nature: the house had been transformed since 1820. On the south front, twenty windows faced a much improved, well-tended park of maples, ashes, lime-trees, even little clumps of oak. Five central windows on the upper floor gave out on to a handsome balcony. The house, well stuccoed and well painted, was 85 feet wide and 45 feet deep. Outside there were new out-buildings, barns, a reconstructed carriage-house, a group of store- and lumber-rooms. Inside, "all the conveniences of modern life" were offered: a schoolroom, a large study, three drawing-rooms each with a generous fireplace. And, of course, there were young Rozens, too: Otto, the hero of Leipzig, had married late but happily, and had two sons, Herman (1829–84) and Konstantin (1834–1915).

Otto continued to live in the large manor-house of Mehntack (Maëtaguse) until his death. The estate and house then passed, by right of primogeniture, to Herman; but Herman had not long to live himself. Within two years of his father (and six months of his uncle, the Decembrist) he, too, had been buried in Jõhvi. The estate passed to his younger brother, Konstantin. And Konstantin it was, from 1884 until 1915, who maintained the house and lands of Rozen of Mehntack.

The new century brought troubles to the area. Some cousins might attempt to ignore the repercussions of the revolution of 1905—Eugen, for example, a lover of the theatre, whose works on the stage included *Ruckblicke auf die Pflege der Schauspielkunst in Reval* (1910). Other cousins lived, oblivious to warnings, on the fringe of high society in St Petersburg.[3] But for Konstantin, 1905 brought warnings for the future too clear to be ignored. On January 10, 1906, there arrived in Mehntack a sizeable punitive force (*karatel'nyy otryad*), bent on revenging punishment already meted out to their anti-government companions in other regions of Yarva and Vyru districts.[4] They burnt huts, shot several suspects, lingered by the manor-house a while, then moved on south. Not until the 1950s would north-eastern Estonia be absolutely tranquil. First, campaigns by troops against the Bolsheviks and other dissidents; then local strife between adherents to the Party and the *ancien régime* throughout the Baltic; next, partisan struggles, between nationalists and russophiles, pro-German and pro-Soviet factions, new men and the representatives of feudal decadence.

Many manor-houses (*myzy*) in Estonia fell into disrepair or were deliberately destroyed in the first quarter of this century.[5] In 1917–20, they were viewed as dark memorials to a vanquished master race; local peasantries burnt manors by the dozen in Vyru district. Later, in the time of the Estonian Republic, the often poorly-kept (but seldom empty) houses earned even less approval in official eyes. Baltic-German families began to leave, first in small numbers, then, in 1939–40, in a flood. Many went to northern Germany, and thence to Sweden, Canada, the U.S.A., unless they felt pro-Nazi sympathies. Other manor-houses simply crumbled. Avinorm, for instance, where the Decembrist poet V. K. Kyukhel'beker passed the larger part of his childhood in 1801–8, had become a pile of stones by 1940. Other manor-houses still, like Voka beside Sakgof, where Rozen had a cottage by the Baltic in 1841, were destroyed during the Great Fatherland War. Yet many manor-houses did survive; and those that were intact in 1945 are, with few exceptions, standing now. Uses have been found for most of them. The former *myza* of Kal'vi, also on the Baltic coast, north-west of Kokhtla-Yarva, is a sanatorium; that of Aa, ten miles to the east, is a home for retired soldiers; and that of Ontika, due north of Maëtaguse, a miners' rest home. All three former *myzy*, like a hundred others in the north-east of Estonia, are fine stone structures and are carefully preserved by the Estonian Soviet Republic. But the commonest of all uses for structurally solid manor-houses in Estonia is that of institute or school building. So it is that Otto Rozen's Maëtaguse presents itself today (1975). Like Pjussi *myza*, forty minutes' drive to the north-west (where in 1804 was born the painter Karl Neff), Maëtaguse is an "8-year school" (8-*letnyaya shkola*) for local children. The school-children tend Otto's park, which still covers two full hectares, with its stream and artificial pond, maples and oaks. And on the back wall of the main building, extending to the windows of the upper floor where Rozen and his wife settled so happily in 1840, there grows a giant vine. Rozen's interest in teaching, one need hardly labour, is perpetuated in his birthplace: all Estonian children are acquainted, in their fifteenth year, with the grand Decembrist myth.

Baron A. E. Rozen's line has disappeared, as far as the direct line of descent is concerned, from Soviet Estonia. The Decembrist's grandson Vyacheslav, it was observed, had a son, Boris, in January 1892. Boris maintained the venerable military tradition of the family, and joined the cavalry in 1911, the year of the death of his great-uncle, Mikhail Vladimirovich, then head of the House of Rozen of Mehntack. He thus bore all the military tradition of his family alone, since neither his cousins nor his uncles were then serving. And when Konstantin, his great-uncle and A. E. Rozen's nephew, died at Mehntack in 1915, Boris it was who became *de facto* head of the surviving family. For eight years, he served the Emperor faithfully. At length, however, it grew clear that Nicholas II had lost contact with realities both on the Western Front and in the capital. Still, he remained loyal, having, like his great-grandfather, an abhorrence of the broken word. The Bolsheviks seized power. The Imperial family was exiled. Boris joined the white forces, and found himself a *Garderichtmeister* (captain of cavalry) in Baron Wrangel's army. For some months he fought the Red forces (May–September 1920) under Denikin's successor, first in the Ukraine, then in the Crimea. Finally, it grew apparent that, on Russian soil at least, the White cause had been lost. Boris made his way, by an unknown route, to Berlin. There, by November 1922, he had settled with his wife. There, until the early part of 1934, he lived. There, perhaps a victim of the Nazis, he disappeared without a trace, intestate, leaving neither sons nor daughters.

Several living descendants of cousins of the subject of this book have, intermittently, taken an interest in their exiled forebear. Two of them, Baroness Ingeborg Anna von Rosen (b. 1908), granddaughter of Friedrich Julius of Gross-Roop, and Hans von Grocholin, have published articles on the Decembrist in the family annual bulletin, *Nachrichtenblätte des Rosenschen Familienverbandes* (no. 13, April 1956; and no. 18, April 1959). Both, reflecting recent and not-so-recent attitudes towards Andrey Yevgen'yevich among the twentieth-century Rosens of West Germany, are of intrinsic interest. Here, first, is an extract from Hans von Grocholin's essay of April 1959, "Referat auf dem Familientag 6/7 April in Marburg über Unsere Dekabristen":

Andrey Rozen, the "Dekabrist", is considered by his family to have been something of a black sheep. He was no criminal (or else he would not have been reprieved), although he was admittedly a conspirator against the sacred person of the Sovereign. Unfortunately, not very much is known of the attitude taken towards him by members of his immediate family. However, his brother Otto, of Mehntack, co-founder of the Family Association in 1875, received him kindly after his return from Siberia, and also supported him for several years; this emerged from Andrey's speech for Otto's birthday. It cannot, however, be assumed that the rest of the family, who were very loyal Tsarists, were particularly proud of Andrey. Nor can one blame a Johann Gustav, who lived in Siberia at the same time as Andrey and who rose to be a General in command there, if he did not appreciate the somewhat different life of his cousin. This family reserve would explain why Andrey sold his estate at Klein-Soldina to Otto of Mehntack and retired to his wife's lands in the Province of Khar'kov. Three of his sons had properties there. His great-grandson Boris, who was a Tsarist officer in the World War, lived in Berlin after 1920, but regrettably the family did not make contact with him.

Here, next, is an extract from Ingeborg von Rosen's "Andrey Rozen, der Dekabrist". The father mentioned is Baron Fabian Johann (1868–1943):

"To have a Decembrist in one's family is almost as good as descending from Ryurik." So I was told by an expert on Russia when we mentioned "our" Decembrist, Andrey, Baron Rozen. Although I knew what the rebellion of the Decembrists of 1825 was all about, and that its name was derived from the Russian word *dekabr* meaning December, I had never really concerned myself with it or with Andrey. Yet a volume of Andrey's memoirs had been in my father's bookcase, though unfortunately only in a shortened version. When asked, however, my father did not care to speak about it and would only talk in a vague way about Rozen. He rejected the acts of the Decembrists; they were repugnant to him, the nobleman so strongly attached to tradition and unconditionally devoted to the monarchy. It may well be that, intellectually, my father understood something of what the Decembrists wanted, but did not approve of such acts of violence, thinking of oaths taken and obligations to one's loyalties; but however that may be, he seldom spoke of such things, and never mentioned anything to *me* in connection with the Decembrists. Certainly he never thought of Andrey von Rozen as a hero or a member of the family to whom one might allude with praise. He liked best to speak as little as possible about him, deplored, however, the harsh fate of Andrey, and emphasized with some satisfaction his reprieve and the eventual restitution of all his rights.
   We of the modern day see all these things quite differently—we have seen too many things that were sublime and great, sacred and proud, collapse and disappear—some of them shattered. We have grown more detached . . .
   Rozen's line, alas, has probably died out. We know nothing after 1934 about its last member, Andrey's great-grandson, who was born in 1892 in St Petersburg and whose name was Boris. When last heard of, in 1934, he had had no children, after a marriage of seventeen years.[6]

Rozen's lineal descendants, to conclude, have disappeared from view, though not, perhaps, completely. (Boris had a sister, Ol'ga, of whom virtually nothing is known; and may not the descendants of Andrey Yevgen'yevich's daughter, Anna, be alive today? It is known that she had children by Nikolay Bobrov.)[7] But however that may be, Rozen's memory lives on in several regions of the Soviet Union, as well as in West Germany and Sweden: in Pyatigorsk, for instance, and Edise, outside Kokhtla-Yarva. Like the *myza* of Maëtaguse, the manor-house of Edise (Ets) has survived.[8] In Kurgan, Western Siberia, the house inhabited by Rozen and his family from December 1833 to September 1837 has for the past two years (1974–75) been under the control of the Director of the new Decembrists' Museum in Siberia, Boris Nikolayevich Karsonov.[9] A plaque adorns the building, which is shortly to be opened to the public.

NOTES

ABBREVIATIONS

St P.	St Petersburg
L.	Leningrad
M.	Moscow
Poln. sob. soch.	Polnoye sobraniye sochineniy
SIRIO	Sbornik Imperatorskogo Russkogo Istoricheskogo Obshchestva
TsGIA	Tsentral'nyy Gosudarstvennyy Istoricheskiy Arkhiv
TsGVIA	Tsentral'nyy Gosudarstvennyy Voyenno-Istoricheskiy Arkhiv

1 : The Rozens in Estonia

1. See Princess E. E. Trubetskaya, *Skazaniye o rode knyazey Trubetskikh* (M., 1891), 5.
2. Leipzig, 1876; published simultaneously in St Petersburg as *Ocherk famil'noy istorii baronov i grafov von Rozen*. The work may be used in conjunction with D. M. von Stackelberg's *Genealogisches Handbuch der estländischen Ritterschaft*, 2 pts (Görlitz, 1929), pt 2, 232–6, in which may be found close details of A. E. Rozen's long family history.
3. Sir Bernard Pares, *A History of Russia* (London, 1962), 90.
4. Or Klein-Roph; 50 miles east of Riga.
5. J. H. Jackson, *Estonia* (London, 1941), 51. A lucid but occasionally superficial general study of Estonian history.
6. ibid., 51–2.
7. A. Bilmanis, *Baltic Essays* (Washington, 1945), 96; see also *Litovskaya metrika*, 3 vols (M., 1903–14), vol. 2, on the understanding reached by the von Tiesenhausens, von Ropps, von Siebergs and other German houses in the south-east Latvian province of Latgale with the kings of Poland; and N. Kostomarov, *Posledniye gody Rechi Pospolitoy* (St P., 1870), on German paladins who helped Russia to dismember Poland in the eighteenth century.
8. *Istoriya Estonskoy Sovetskoy Sotsialisticheskoy Respubliki*, 2 vols (Tallinn, 1961), vol. 1, 333.
9. ibid., vol. 1, 480; see also Stackelberg, *Genealogisches Handbuch*, pt 1, 172. Ennobled by the King of Sweden in 1617, Bogislaus von Rosen was granted 10,000 thalers for services rendered to the Swedish Crown. From his two sons, Andreas and Heinrich, sprang the "white" and "red" branches of the Baltic House of Rosen—the Houses of Weinjerwen and Rosenhagen-Kardina respectively. Neither should be confused with the line founded, 350 years before, by Waldemar Rosen of Riga, from which sprang the Decembrist.
10. A. E. Rozen, *Skizze zu einer Familien-Geschichte*, 18. The estate, which included six hamlets, came into the possession of the Baumgartens in the 1850s, and remained in their

hands in this century; for details of the estate, as of Mehntack, see A. Richter, *Baltische Verkehrs-und Adressbücher: band 3; Estland* (Riga, 1913), 398, 333.

11. G. Veskow, *Minne af grefve Gustav Friedrich von Rosen* (Stockholm, 1852).

12. The former specialized in Estonian military history, while the latter painted scenes from Baltic-German and Swedish annals. Count Georg's descendants still live in Stockholm.

13. H. Pearson, *The Life of Oscar Wilde* (London, 1946), 3.

14. Rozen, op. cit., 82.

15. T. B. Macaulay, *The History of England from the Accession of James II*, 5 vols (Boston, 1900), vol. 3, 225–6.

16. Rozen, op. cit., 56.

17. *Istoriya Estonskoy S.S.R.*, vol. 1, 479–80.

18. J. G. Kohl, *Russia and The Russians in 1842*, 2 vols (London, 1843), vol. 2, 200–1.

19. For statistics, see A. Svābe, *Latvju Tiesību Vēsture* (Riga, 1935), 3–4, and M. Skujenieks, *Latvija* (Riga, 1926), 328–31.

20. Rozen, op. cit., *passim*. Rozen's second daughter, Sof'ya (3.4.39–13.4.39) and fifth son, Andrey (1841–45) both died prematurely, however, reducing his family to five children; see *Zapiski dekabrista* (Duncker und Humblot, Leipzig, 1870), 388, 460.

21. Jackson, op. cit., 98. On German cruelty towards the Ests, see H. Kruus, *Grundriss der Geschichte des Estnischen Volkes* (Tartu, 1932), chs 2–3, and, on racial segregation, Aino Julia Kallas's *Eros the Slayer*.

22. *Rossiya v XIX-om veke*, trans. by B. G. Pares as *Russia in the Nineteenth Century* (Ann Arbor, 1953), 74.

23. *Latvian-Russian Relations in Documents* (Washington, 1944), 20; on the *Privilegium Sigismundi Augusti*, its abuse and supposed history, see A. Svābe, "Sigismunda Augusta Livonijas Politika", in *Latvijas Vēstures Institūta Zurnāls* (Riga, 1937), no. 1, 107–10.

24. V. Raud, *An Outline of Estonian History* (New York, 1953), 20.

25. See Evald Uustalu, *The History of Estonian People* (London, 1952), 95–6, and Jackson, op. cit., 69; see also *Istoriya Estonskoy S.S.R.*, vol. 1, 536. The "declaration" was first published only in 1820, by Garlieb Merkel (1769–1850), as *Deklaratsiya barona Rozena*, and provoked a monograph by the Estonian liberal historian J. Vigrabs: *Die Rosensche Deklaration vom Jahre 1739; ein Beitrag zur Geschichte der Leibeigenschaft in Livland und Estland* (Tartu, 1937).

26. Jackson, op. cit., 69.

27. Stackelberg, *Genealogisches Handbuch*, pt 2, 234.

28. Richter, *Baltische Adressbücher*, vol. 3, 333.

29. The letters are now kept in a Rozen family *fond* in the main building of the Estonian Academy of Sciences, Tartu.

30. Cited by N. Polevktov, *Nikolay I* (Petrograd, 1918), 35.

31. S. Monas, *The Third Section* (Harvard, 1961), 11.

32. ibid.; further on Nicholas's exalting of authority, as an idea and an ideal, see Hermann Broch, *The Sleepwalkers* (Boston, 1932), 25–6.

33. See O. Kirss, L. Payos, *Po Obeim Storonam Dorogi* (Tallinn, 1972), 51.

34. The mean precipitation every year (700 mm.) falls now, as in the nineteenth century, as drizzle, not as heavy rain or snow; see E. F. Varep, V. Tarmisto, *Sovetskiy soyuz: Estoniya* (M., 1967), 29, 35. Always the dampness has oppressed the visitor. One thinks of the German publicist Karl Philip Snell (1753–1806), whose sojourn in the Rozens' humid land resulted in *Beschreibung der russischen Provinzen an der Ostsee* (Jena, 1794) and of Elizabeth Jane Rigby, later Lady Eastlake (*Letters from the Baltic*: London, 1841).

35. Estonian: Peipus. On the physical surroundings of the Decembrist's childhood, see *Topographische Nachrichten von Liefland und Ehstland*, 3 vols (Riga, 1774–82), by the judicious August Wilhelm Huppel (1737–1819). How little those surroundings changed over the years is plain from C. H. J. Schlegel's *Reisen in mehrer russische Gouvernements*, Bd. I–X (Meiningen, 1819–34).

36. *Sovetskiy soyuz: Estoniya*, 47.
37. *Istoriya Estonskoy S.S.R.*, vol. 1, 664–70.
38. F. R. Kreutzwald, *Izbrannyye pis'ma* (Tallinn, 1953), for Estonia in the 1830s; V. Severgin, *Zapiski puteshestviya po zapadnym provintsiyam Rossiyskogo Gosudarstva v 1802 godu* (St P., 1803), for 1800–10.
39. See V. V. Doroshenko, "Khozyaystvennaya otchotnost' liflyandskikh imeniy v XVIII veke: myznyy arkhiv v Mazstraupe", in *Istochnikovedcheskiye problemy istorii narodov Pribaltiki* (Riga, 1970), 153–201. Doroshenko makes use of Rozen family materials in TsGIA (LSSR), *fond* 5836, op. 2.
40. *Istoriya Estonskoy S.S.R.*, vol. 1, 670.
41. ibid., vol. 1, 671. On the economic misery of peasants in northern Estonia during the 1780s and, indeed, until the century ended, see *Ehstland und die Ehsten, oder historisch-geographisch-statistisches Gemälde von Ehstland . . .*, 3 pts (Gotha, 1802), by J. C. Petri, an early agitator against serfdom in the province.
42. *Istoriya Estonskoy S.S.R.*, vol. 1, 671–2.
43. Nechkina, op. cit., 77.
44. Yu. F. Samarin (1819–76), *Okrainy Rossii* (Prague, 1868); cited by Nechkina, op. cit., 75.
45. *Istoriya Estonskoy S.S.R.*, vol. 1, 679–81. For a chilling picture of oppression, drudgery and flight, see the *Istoriya rabstva i kharakter krest'yan v Liflyandii i Estlyandii* (1786) of G.-I. Jannau (1753–1821), a reforming pastor and Estophile.
46. A. E. Rozen, *Zapiski dekabrista* (Leipzig, 1870), 6.
47. J. Kruus, *Histoire de l'Estonie* (Paris, 1935), 54–6, on the landlords' economic troubles; J. C. Petri, *Neueste Gemählde von Lief- und Ehstland unter Katherina II und Aleksander I in . . . merkantilischer Ansicht* (Leipzig, 1809), on the Estonian peasantry's wretchedness.
48. Nechkina, op. cit., 77.
49. E. Nodel, *Estonia: Nation on the Anvil* (N.Y., 1963), 41–2. Nodel makes good use of Jüri Uulots's study, *Grundzüge der Agrargeschichte Estlands* (Tartu, 1935), especially pp. 135–43.
50. A. E. Rozen, "A Brief Sketch of the History of My Fatherland."
51. *Istoriya Estonskoy S.S.R.*, vol. 1, 712–13.
52. Nodel, op. cit., 43.
53. Nechkina, op. cit., 83. On the beginning of the peasants' problems *after* reform, see J. P. Ewers, *Provisorische Verfassung des bauernstandes in Ehstland: H. Storch, Russland unter Alexander I . . .* (St P., 1806).

2: Youth and Liberal Circles
 1. A. E. Rozen, *Skizze zu einer Familien-Geschichte*, 81.
 2. See Bibliography, page 301.
 3. i.e. Ofitserskoye uchilishche; see *Entsiklopedicheskiy slovar'* (ed. Brokgauz, Yefron), 60 vols (St P., 1892), vol. 12, 855–6.
 4. In 1760.
 5. Sir Bernard Pares, *A History of Russia* (London, 1962), 323.
 6. A. E. Rozen, *Zapiski dekabrista*, 3–7.
 7. ibid., 4.
 8. Baron Konstantin Nikolayevich Korf(f) married a Rozen; Baron M. A. Korf's *Vosshestviye na prestol imperatora Nikolaya I-ogo* (St P., 1848) was translated as *The Accession of Nicholas I* (John Murray, London, 1857). Perhaps out of regard for his cousins, married to Rozens in their turn, the historian concealed A. E. Rozen's identity in his account of the insurrection of December 14, 1825 (London edn, 249): Rozen became merely "a young lieutenant who . . . had succeeded by secret suggestions in corrupting his platoon."

9. Rozen, *Zapiski dekabrista*, 5–6.
10. ibid., 7; for further information on Otto, the second of Eugen Octave's four sons (b. 1795), see Chapter 9.
11. A. Bilmanis, *Baltic Essays* (Washington, 1945), 98–9.
12. And of 15 Governors of Livonia, from 1790 to 1885, 14 were of German origin.
13. Rozen, *Skizze zu einer Familien-Geschichte*, 69.
14. Note to Lady Emma Hamilton of May 13, 1802; cited by J. Russell, *Nelson and the Hamiltons* (N.Y., 1969), 248.
15. G. Giesemann, *Kotzebue in Russland* (Frankfurt, 1971), 43.
16. A. G. Tseytlin, *Tvorchestvo Ryleyeva* (M., 1955), 20.
17. *Voyennyye postanovleniya* (1869), bk XV, appendix 1; see also *Entsiklopedicheskiy slovar'*, vol. 26, 874.
18. ibid., 874–5.
19. That is, not the Guards.
20. A. Haxthausen, trans. by R. Farie as *The Russian Empire, Its People, Institutions and Resources* (London, 1856; reprinted by Cass, London, 1968), 344–6. For an impression of the number of Rozens in the nineteenth-century Russian Army, see Grand Duke Nikolay Mikhaylovich, *Peterburgskiy nekropol'*, 3 vols (St P., 1912), vol. 3, 608–10.
21. A small selection appears in K. F. Ryleyev, *Polnoye sobraniye sochineniy* (ed. Tseytlin) (L., 1934; reprinted by Mouton, The Hague, 1967), 425–33.
22. See Tseytlin, op. cit., 20–2. Also in the Corps, in Ryleyev's first years there, was the future Decembrist A. M. Bulatov. With Estonia, Ryleyev had a link through his father—a Lieutenant-Colonel in the Estlyandsky Jägers.
23. *Istoriya russkoy arkhitektury* (M., 1956), *passim*. Not until their fourteenth year, it should be added, were boys admitted to this building and the senior part of the Cadet Corps.
24. *Meyers Konversations-Lexikon* (Leipzig, Vienna, 1908), vol. 11, 142.
25. Tseytlin, op. cit., 20.
26. Rozen, *Zapiski dekabrista*, 12–13.
27. A. E. Rozen, *Aus den Memoiren eines russischen Dekabristen* (Leipzig, 1874), 194–5. Compare with the English text, based on the first (1869) German edition, by E. St-John Mildmay, *Russian Conspirators in Siberia: A Personal Narrative by Baron R.* (Smith and Elder, London, 1872), 130–1.
28. A. P. Belyayev, "Vospominaniya", in *Russkaya starina*, vol. XXX (1881), 812.
29. Tseytlin, op. cit., 20. Also, "Iz pis'ma A. M. Bulatova k Nikolayu I", in *Literaturnoye nasledstovo*, vol. 59 (1954), 213.
30. "Zapiski M. I. Pushchina", in *Russkiy arkhiv*, 1908, no. 11, 412.
31. See note 15.
32. I. D. Yakushkin, *Zapiski* (M., 1925), 13.
33. See *Vosstaniye dekabristov: materialy po istorii* ... (ed. M. N. Pokrovsky), 8 vols (M., 1925–37; hereafter referred to as *Materialy*), I, 298; II, 203–4; III, 42, 55; IV, 100, 273–4.
34. *Aus den Memoiren* ..., 1874 text (hereafter referred to as *Memoiren 1874*), 3–6.
35. *Zapiski dekabrista*, 1870 Russian text (hereafter referred to as *Zapiski 1870*), 11.
36. See V. T-V, "Andrey Yevgen'yevich Rozen", in *Russkiy biograficheskiy slovar'*, 26 vols (St P., 1912), vol. 17, 378.
37. *Zapiski 1870*, 28–9.
38. J. D. Clarkson, *A History of Russia* (London, 1962), 290–1.
39. *Zapiski 1870*, 33–5.
40. ibid., 37.
41. ibid., 40.
42. ibid., 44.
43. ibid., 45.
44. ibid., 50; on V. F. Malinovsky (1765–1814), one of Rozen's human links with the Decembrist I. I. Pushchin, see V. Seleznev, *Istoriya Imperatorskogo Aleksandrovskogo*

Litseya (St P., 1861). Malinovsky's son Andrey would be deeply implicated in the Decembrist conspiracy; see "Dekabristy-Literatory", in *Lit. nasl.*, vol. 60, bk 1, 187. Rozen and Anna Vasil'yevna were betrothed by an Orthodox priest, N. V. Muzovsky, on February 19; three days later, Rozen left for Revel' to seek his parents' blessing. The marriage ceremony, it appears, was also Orthodox, not Lutheran, and Rozen's children were brought up as Orthodox believers; see V. T-V, "Andrey Yevgen'yevich Rozen", *Russikiy biograficheskiy slovar'*, 26 vols (St P., 1896–1913), vol. 17, 378–9.

45. *Zapiski 1870*, 49.
46. I am indebted to the Director of the Manuscript Department (*Rukopisnyy otdel*), Saltykov-Shchedrin Public Library, Leningrad, for permission to publish this and other letters relating to A. E. and A. F. Rozen. Together with an earlier note to P. F. Malinovsky, dated August 22, 1822, this note, written in a small, sloping hand on a single sheet of paper, is now kept under archive ref.: Sobraniye P. L. Vakselya, *fond* 124, no. 3697.
47. ibid., *fond* 124, no. 3696.
48. M. A. Fonvizin, in *Obshchestvennyye dvizheniya v Rossii v pervuyu polovinu XIX veka* (ed. V. Semevsky, P. Shchegolev), 2 vols (St P., 1905), vol. 1, 183.
49. *Russkaya starina*, vol. XI (1874), 466.
50. ibid., vol. CIII (1900), 642–3.
51. *Materialy*, II, 145; IV, 45–6.
52. *Obshchestvennyye dvizheniya v Rossii . . .*, 1, 15.
53. *Minuvshiye gody*, vol. III (1908), 309–11.
54. Rozen returned to Mehntack from the Caucasus, in 1839, to be reminded of the fact: "Finally the white walls of the Mehntack buildings became visible through the groves; two verst posts flashed by—posts looking like broken columns, the symbolic sign of Masonry—which had been set up by my father . . ."; *Zapiski 1870*, 448.
55. On Rozen's pursuit of history, see Chapters 5 and 12.
56. *Zapiski 1870*, 61.
57. ibid., 299.
58. *Memoiren 1874*, 145.
59. Specifically, Rozen's attitude towards the peasantry both in Estonia and, in the sixth decade, in the Ukraine shows traces of the influence of Jean-Baptiste Say's *Traité d'économie politique, ou simple exposition de la manière dont se forment, se distribuent, et se consomment les richesses* (Paris, 1803). In particular, it seems, he felt the cogency of bk 1, ch. XIV ("Du droit de propriété"), and bk 2, ch. IX ("Des revenus territoriaux: du Fermage"), wherein Say argues the inefficiency of the *métayage* system by which landlords provide capital, as well as land, for would-be tenant-farmers. For centuries, Say held (and Rozen also), *le gros de la nation était misérable* for lack of prudent capital investment. Such was the pragmatic, reasoned shell of Rozen's liberalism.
60. *Zapiski 1870*, 442.
61. ibid., 79.
62. *Memoiren 1874*, 99.
63. ibid., 278–9.
64. A. G. Mazour, *The First Russian Revolution, 1825* (Stanford, 1962; 2nd printing), 42.
65. *Entsiklopedicheskiy slovar'*, vol. 71, 7.
66. For money, at least; see *Zapiski 1870*, 60, 469.
67. Haxthausen, op. cit., 344.
68. K. F. Ryleyev, *Poln. sob. soch.* (L., 1934), 428.
69. *Dekabristy: sbornik otryvok iz istochnikov*, compiled by Yu. G. Oksman, N. F. Lavrov, B. L. Modzalevsky (M., 1926), 60–3; *Materialy*, V, 42–3, 406–7.
70. Mazour, op. cit., 58.
71. *Russkaya starina*, vol. XXXVIII (1883), 83.
72. The actions of the Finland Lifeguards may be traced through the service records of its

officers—Col. M. F. Mit'kov, for example, in *Materialy*, III, 189. On the Semyonovsky Regiment, see *Russkiy arkhiv*, vol. XI (1902), 410–11.

73. Mazour, op. cit., 59.
74. *Russkiy arkhiv*, vol. XI (1902), 417–19.
75. Cited by Mazour, op. cit., 62.
76. *Materialy*, IV, 307–8.
77. ibid., 107; see also *Zapiski 1870*, 14–15. Through P. I. Grech, a fellow-officer with whom Rozen shared quarters in the spring of 1820, he came to know A. A. Bestuzhev(-Marlinsky) and A. A. Del'vig well, and N. I. Gnedich and V. A. Zhukovsky slightly. Rozen enjoyed literary company, later growing intimate with another poet, Prince A. I. Odoyevsky; see Chapter 12.
78. Posted ensign on April 20, 1818 (*Materialy*, VIII, 388), he was promoted the following summer (*Zapiski 1870*, 13), remaining in the rank of *podporuchik* until 1824.
79. See my compilation, *Voices in Exile: The Decembrist Memoirs* (Montreal, 1974), ch. 1.
80. *Materialy*, vol. I, 284.
81. ibid., vol. I, 209.
82. ibid.; see also I. D. Yakushkin, *Zapiski* (M., 1925), 131–2.
83. See note 79.
84. V. Nabokov, *Eugene Onegin*, 4 vols (N.Y., 1964), vol. 2, 446.
85. Pestel' devoted a section of *Russkaya Pravda* (first published in a careless edition by P. E. Shchegolev, St P., 1906; see *Byloye*, vol. V (1906), 278–83) to the Baltic provinces.
86. *Zapiski 1870*, 443.
87. I deal with this briefly in "A Note on N. A. Bestuzhev and the Academy of Chita", in *Canadian Slavonic Papers*, vol. XII (1970), no. 1, 47–59.
88. *Memoiren 1874*, 194.
89. A. I. Odoyevsky, *Polnoye sobraniye stikhotvoreniy* (St P., 1883), 11–12. Not only did Rozen write a "biographical sketch" of Odoyevsky, which was published with his poems; he also persuaded the Decembrists K. Igel'strom and N. A. Zagoretsky to do the same, and incorporated their (in some parts contradictory) recollections of the poet in that work; Rozen to Nazimov, September 11, 1881, MS. in Pushkinsky Dom, r1, op. 24, no. 49.
90. *Zapiski 1870*, 441.
91. J. H. Jackson, *Estonia* (London, 1941), 97–8.

3: December 1825
1. *Memoiren 1874*, 35.
2. See the author's *M. S. Lunin: Catholic Decembrist* (Mouton, The Hague, 1976), ch. 4.
3. A. G. Mazour, *The First Russian Revolution, 1825* (Stanford, 1962; 2nd printing), 155.
4. "Passers-by clustered in front of them, paying attention mostly to the physiognomy, which recalled that of Paul I. And sarcastic comments were not lacking from the candid . . .", *Obshchestvennyye dvizheniya v Rossii . . .*, vol. 1, 435.
5. p. 2, col. 3.
6. S. P. Trubetskoy, *Zapiski* (St P., 1907), 33.
7. See M. A. Korf, *Vosshestviye na prestol Imperatora Nikolaya I*, 17–30.
8. *Memoiren 1874*, 38.
9. Still among the most readable accounts of events during this period is N. K. Shil'der's *Imperator Nikolay I, yego zhizn' i tsarstvovaniye* (St P., 1903); see esp. 1, 205–7.
10. *Russkaya starina*, vol. XXX (1880), 493–4.
11. *Materialy*, I, 248.
12. Mazour, op. cit., 161–2.
13. ibid., 157; *Memoiren 1874*, 40–1.
14. *Memoiren 1874*, 42, 44; also *Vospominaniya Bestuzhevykh* (ed. M. K. Azadovsky) (M., 1931), 82.

15. See Chapter 12.
16. *Memoiren 1874*, 32–3.
17. "In Moscow alone, of 250,000 inhabitants, 90,000 were serfs, ready to go for their knives and abandon themselves to every passion"; Shteyngel' in *Obshchestvennyye dvizheniya v Rossii . . .*, vol. 1, 436.
18. *Materialy*, I, 23–4.
19. *Vospominaniya Bestuzhevykh*, 138.
20. Cited in full in the author's *Voices in Exile* (Montreal, 1974), ch. 2.
21. *Materialy*, I, 187, 452.
22. A. Kotlyarevsky, *Dekabristy: Odoyevsky i Bestuzhev* (St P., 1909), 17.
23. Glynn R. Barratt, *Voices In Exile: The Decembrist Memoirs* (Montreal, McGill-Queen's University Press, 1974), 9–10.
24. A. E. Presnyakov, in *14 dekabrya 1825 goda* (M., 1926, 129), accepts the remark as authentic; see also *Russkiy vestnik*, vol. III (1893), 161–2.
25. *Voices In Exile*, ch. 2 (Introduction to A. E. Rozen).
26. For a bibliography, see Mazour, op. cit., 300–20. Further to enhance the usefulness of Rozen's memoirs, it may be observed, we have detailed comments on them by V. S. Tolstoy, his fellow-rebel; see "Zamechaniya V. S. Tolstogo na polyakh i v tekste knigi A. E. Rozena, Zapiski dekabrista", in *Dekabristy: novyye materialy* (ed. M. K. Azadovsky) (M., 1955), 33–95.
27. *Memoiren 1874*, viii.
28. R. Payne, *The Fortress* (N.Y., 1967), 25.
29. Mazour, op. cit., 169–80, and Presnyakov, op. cit., 3–170, are both more factually reliable than M. A. Korf, J. H. Schnitzler or, indeed, any nineteenth-century historian, Russian or otherwise.
30. The bridge is no longer extant. It was replaced by a temporary Dvortsovyy (Palace) Bridge, also spanning the Neva from the First Cadet Corps building to the Senate, which itself gave way to the present Dvortsovyy Bridge, crossing from the Exchange to the Winter Palace. Later in the century, most of the Vasil'yevsky Island traffic used the Nicholas Bridge 300 yards upstream, built by Kierbedz in 1842–50. Near *this* bridge there was, in 1825, "a wooden foot-bridge laid across the ice"; Korf, op. cit., 248. See K. Baedeker, *Russia: A Handbook for Travelers* (N.Y., Arno Press reprint of 1914 edn), 111.
31. *Memoiren 1874*, 48; see E. St-John Mildmay, *Russian Conspirators in Siberia: A Personal Narrative by Baron R.* (London, 1872), 12.
32. *Memoiren 1874*, 87.
33. *Zapiski, stat'i, pis'ma dekabrista I. D. Yakushkina* (M., 1951), 154.
34. *Memoiren 1874*, 53, 55.
35. The fact is emphasized, with a touch of irritation, in the memoirs of Mikhail Bestuzhev: "Then men of the Preobrazhensky Regiment appeared, advancing from Palace Square with artillery ahead (for which they had forgotten or had not managed to get any ammunition, and which was sent on after them. Still towards evening they were bringing up ammunition!)." cited from *Voices In Exile*, ch. 2.
36. *Materialy*, III, 370–1.
37. Rozen would have further dealings with the former Brigade Commander: in 1842, E. A. Golovin would be Governor-General of Livonia, and pursue a briskly anti-Lutheran policy in the Baltic area; see Chapter 10.
38. *Memoiren 1874*, 56.
39. *Vospominaniya Bestuzhevykh*, 149–50; also *Pamyati dekabristov: sbornik materialov*, 3 vols (L., 1926), vol. 1, 243–4.
40. *Vospominaniya Bestuzhevykh*, 149.
41. *Materialy*, II, 359.
42. B. Pushkin, "Arest dekabristov", in *Dekabristy i ikh vremya* (M., 1927), 402.
43. T. G. Masaryk, *The Spirit of Russia*, 2 vols (London, 1919), vol. 1, 105.

44. On this, see S. S. Tatishchev, *Imperator Nikolay I i inostrannyye dvory* (St P., 1889), 49.
45. Shil'der, op. cit., 1, 204; also F. F. Vigel', *Zapiski*, 7 vols (M., 1892), vol. 5, 70.
46. The writings of A. I. Herzen are available in English, in the sometimes erratic but fluid translation of Constance Garnett (Chatto and Windus, London, 1924); for further information on Nicholas's cold beauty, see C. de Grunwald, *La vie de Nicholas I-er* (Paris, 1946), 156.
47. *Memoiren 1874*, 73.
48. P. I. Falenberg, for example; see Mazour, op. cit., 217–19.
49. See P. E. Shchegolev, *Dekabristy: sbornik statey* (L., 1926), 266–7.
50. Some thirty letters, dated from September 13, 1819 to March 5, 1828, written by Baron Otto Johann to close relatives, are to be found in the Historical Museum of the Estonian Academy of Sciences in Tallinn, archive ref. *Fond* 28, *opis'* 1, *ed. kr.* 87.iv.9. I am indebted to Sirje Annist for permission to inspect this correspondence and to publish the brief extract given here.
51. *Memoiren 1874*, 72–3; for Nicholas's impressions of this and other interviews, see *Mezhdutsarstviye 1825 goda i vosstaniye dekabristov v memuarakh i perepiske chlenov tsarskoy sem'i* (comp. B. E. Syroyechkovsky) (M., 1926), 31–3.
52. *Memoiren 1874*, 101.
53. S. P. Trubetskoy, *Zapiski* (Berlin, 1903), 17.
54. J. H. Schnitzler, *L'Histoire intime de la Russie sous les empereurs Alexandre I et Nicholas I*, 2 vols (Paris, 1847), vol. 2, 299.
55. Shchegolev, op. cit., 200–1.
56. See I. K. Luppol. *Istoriko-filosofskiye etyudy* (M., 1935), 252–4.
57. *Obshchestvennyye dvizheniya v Rossii . . .*, vol. 1, 197–8.
58. *Memoiren 1874*, 82–5.
59. M. Fonvizin, in *Obshchestvennyye dvizheniya v Rossii . . .*, vol. 1, 198.
60. ibid., 1, 271.

4: Trial and Imprisonment
 1. *Istorichesky vestnik*, vol. VII (1916), 108.
 2. A. M. Murav'yov, D. I. Zavalishin, N. V. Basargin and I. D. Yakushkin, among other Decembrist memoirists, dwell on the rôle and true feelings of the Orthodox priest P. N. Myslovsky; some felt he was sincere in his desire to mitigate their fate, while most regarded him with some suspicion. As Lutherans, Rozen and Pestel' were visited by Pastor Reinboth, whose sympathy towards the prisoners was never in question.
 3. *Memoiren 1874*, 86–90.
 4. N. K. Shil'der, *Imperator Nikolay I, yego zhizn' i tsarstvovaniye* (St P., 1903), vol. 1, 696.
 5. No. 58, supplement p. 12; cited by J. H. Schnitzler, *L'Histoire intime de la Russie sous les empereurs Alexandre I et Nicholas I*, 2 vols (Paris, 1847), vol. 1, 237.
 6. *Materialy*, II, 358.
 7. *Memoiren 1874*, 94. In the Russian text (*Zapiski 1870*, 121), Rozen tells us that, besides walking, he took more violent exercise: "I would mark time on one spot, turn around, spin, and leap about as best I could." No other Decembrist records having so conscientiously taken physical exercise in his casemate.
 8. *Materialy*, II, 371.
 9. *Literaturnoye nasledstvo*, vol. 60 (1956), bk 1, 228.
10. ibid.; Rozen expands the theme of the visit to the indisposed Ryleyev in *Zapiski 1870*, 85.
11. *Materialy*, II, 270.
12. ibid., I, 447.
13. ibid., II, 363.
14. ibid., I, 236.

15. *Literaturnoye nasledstvo*, vol. 60, bk 1, 196.
16. *Materialy*, I, 284.
17. ibid., II, 369.
18. A. G. Mazour, *The First Russian Revolution, 1825* (Stanford, 1962; 2nd printing), 210.
19. *Memoiren 1874*, 103–5, 108.
20. Mazour, op. cit., 220.
21. *Memoiren 1874*, 108–11.
22. See, on Lunin's intransigence, the author's *M. S. Lunin: Catholic Decembrist* (The Hague, 1976).
23. Mazour, op. cit., 221.
24. ibid., 213.
25. *Memoiren 1874*, 113–17.
26. ibid., 125–6.
27. *Zapiski 1870*, 8.
28. *Memoiren 1874*, 190.
29. ibid., 209.
30. ibid., 211.
31. ibid., 79.
32. ibid., 172.
33. ibid., 251–7.
34. *Zapiski 1870*, 199: "It became evident that I had scurvy; my gums became swollen, turned white, and my teeth ached and began to fall out." This is all Rozen has to say of twelve months of deprivations, in so far as they affected him physically.
35. *Memoiren 1874*, 149–50.
36. N. V. Basargin, *Zapiski* (Petrograd, 1917), 47–8.
37. *Memoiren 1874*, 144.
38. ibid.; other prisoners, including N. V. Basargin, whom the noisome damp air reduced to a physical shell within two months (he spat blood and had constant chest pains), had to be removed to (relatively) dry casemates; Basargin, op. cit., 56. Rozen was at least spared the Alekseyev Ravelin, in which Yakushkin, Lorer, and Obolensky suffered silently; see *Voices In Exile*, ch. 5.
39. *Memoiren 1874*, 232.
40. ibid., 94.
41. ibid., 219.
42. ibid., 140, 143, 146–7.
43. ibid., 151–2. As he crossed the river, we read in the Russian text (*Zapiski 1870*, 205), Rozen thought of his wife, praying for him, he knew. Informing her father-in-law of Rozen's imminent departure for Siberia, she had quoted Pascal: "Il n'y a rien de plus beau dans le monde que le ciel étoilé et le sentiment du devoir dans le coeur de l'homme."

5: The First Years in Siberia: 1827–30
  1. See *Mezhdutsarstviye 1825 goda i vosstaniye dekabristov v memuarakh i perepiske chlenov tsarskoy sem'i* (compiled by B. E. Syroyechkovsky) (M., 1926); also "Perepiska Imperatora Nikolaya s Velikim Knyazem Konstantinom Pavlovichem, 1825–1829", in *SIRIO*, vol. 131 (St P., 1910), esp. 51.
  2. *Mezhdutsarstviye*, 30–6; also *Materialy*, IV, 272, 289–90, and Yu. G. Oksman (ed.), *Bunt dekabristov: yubileynyy sbornik, 1825–1925* (L., 1926), 283–4.
  3. S. Maksimov, *Sibir' i katorga*, 3 pts (St P., 1871), pt. 1, 10.
  4. ibid., 12.
  5. ibid., 5.
  6. ibid., 17.
  7. See M. Raeff, *Siberia and the Reforms of 1822* (Washington, 1956).

20

8. S. B. Okun', *Dekabrist M. S. Lunin* (L., 1962), 256–7.

9. *Mezhdutsarstviye*, 32–4.

10. *Zapiski 1907*, 159.

11. *Gosudarstvennyye prestupleniya v Rossii v XIX veke* . . . (compiled by V. Bogucharsky), 2 vols (Stuttgart, 1903), vol. 1, 24.

12. *Obshchestvennyye dvizheniya v Rossii v pervuyu polovinu XIX veka*, 2 vols (St P., 1905) vol. 1, 250.

13. *Mezhdutsarstviye*, 207; also F. F. Vigel, *Zapiski*, 7 vols (St P., 1893), vol. 5, 66.

14. A. I. Dmitriyev-Mamonov, *Dekabristy v zapadnoy Sibiri* (St P., 1905), 2.

15. On this, see P. E. Shchegolev, *Dekabristy: sbornik statey* (L., 1926), 267.

16. I. D. Yakushkin, *Zapiski*, 96–7; N. V. Basargin, *Zapiski*, 90.

17. Yakushkin, op. cit., 95.

18. D. Lanskoy surrendered his own nephew with an eye to his own career in the Admiralty.

19. See S. Monas, *The Third Section* (Harvard, 1961), 95.

20. Yakushkin, op. cit., 110–11; Basargin, op. cit., 91.

21. *Zapiski 1907*, 132.

22. V. Timoshchuk, "Stanislav Romanovich Leparsky, kommendant Nerchinskikh rudnikov i Chitinskogo Ostroga", in *Russkaya starina*, VII (1892), 153–4.

23. Did Bestuzhev not understand, asked Nicholas, that he, the Tsar, could save him with one word? That, replied Bestuzhev, was precisely the trouble.

24. *Mezhdutsarstviye*, 196.

25. Basargin, op. cit., 95.

26. ibid., 91.

27. ibid., 92–3.

28. Mazour, op. cit., 227.

29. *Memoiren 1874*, 145.

30. ibid., and *Zapiski 1870*, 200.

31. M. O. Gershenzon, *Dekabrist Krivtsov* (Berlin, 1923; 2nd edn), 244.

32. P. E. Shchegolev, *Istoricheskiye etyudy* (M., 1913), 392–3; also *Sbornik statey, posvyashchonnykh S. F. Platonovu* (Petrograd, 1922), 405–8.

33. Basargin, op. cit., 94; M. K. Azadovsky (ed.), *Vospominaniya Bestuzhevykh* (M.-L., 1951), 168–9; Maksimov, op. cit., pt 1, 12–21.

34. *Memoiren 1874*, 226.

35. ibid., 158–60, 162–4.

36. ibid., 167–8.

37. Letter of July 17 (no. 1253) cited by M. N. Kuchayev, "Stanislav Romanovich Leparsky, kommendant Nerchinskikh rudnikov s 1826 po 1837 god", in *Russkaya starina*, VIII (1880), 718–19.

38. For details, see V. Timoshchuk, "Stanislav Romanovich Leparsky . . .", in *Russkaya starina*, VII (1892), 156–8.

39. See Kuchayev, "Stanislav Romanovich Leparsky . . .", 711–13.

40. S. N. Malkov, "K prebyvaniyu dekabristov v Sibiri", in *Sibirskiy vestnik*, no. 46 (Tomsk, 1887), 2–3. (Malkov was appointed deacon to Gromov in Chita, in 1829.)

41. *Zapiski 1870*, 466.

42. Yet Leparsky would never reach a higher rank than General-Lieutenant (January 1833).

43. Mazour, op. cit., 224.

44. Zavalishin, *Zapiski*, 259.

45. ibid., 258–9.

46. Mazour, op. cit., 249–51.

47. A. V. Kharchevnikov (ed.), *Dekabristy v Zabaykale: neizdannyye materialy* (Chita, 1925), 60–6.

48. V. I. Shunkov (ed.), *Ekonomika, upravleniye i kul'tura Sibiri XVI–XIX vekov* (Novosibirsk, 1965), ch. 2.

49. See *Bol'shaya Sovetskaya entsiklopediya*, 51 vols (M., 1957), vol. 47, 407; also *Vospominaniya Bestuzhevykh*, 163–4.
50. See *Dekabristy v Buryatii* (Verkhnyeudinsk, 1927), *passim*.
51. For a clear map, see M. Gilbert's *Russian History Atlas* (London, 1972), 33.
52. See note 49. The arrival of the Trans-Siberian Railway at Chita in 1899 brought an influx of settlers in 1900–12.
53. On this, Rozen insists.
54. *Vospominaniya Bestuzhevykh*, 164.
55. *Zapiski 1870*, 266.
56. Basargin, op. cit., 129.
57. N. I. Lorer, *Zapiski dekabrista* (M., 1931), 110.
58. ibid., 111.
59. See ch. 7.
60. I. Golovin, *Russia Under the Autocrat Nicholas the First*, 2 vols (London, 1846; reprinted by Praeger, N.Y., 1971), vol. 2, 204.
61. See *Lit. nasl.*, vol. 56 (1960), bk II, pt 2, 88; also pt 1, 278–80.
62. Barratt, "A Note on N. A. Bestuzhev and the Academy of Chita", in *Canadian Slavonic Papers*, XII (1970), no. 1, 47–53.
63. Yakushkin, op. cit., 120–1.
64. The growth of the Decembrist myths merits a special study; it is to be hoped that one may soon be written.
65. Basargin, op. cit., 131.
66. *Memoiren 1874*, 174.
67. Basargin, op. cit., 110.
68. See note 2 to ch. 3.
69. P. Annenkova, *Vospominaniya* (M., 1929), 166–7.
70. *Memoiren 1874*, 169–70.
71. *Zapiski 1870*, 236.
72. *Vospominaniya Bestuzhevykh*, 145–6.
73. *Memoiren 1874*, 172–8.
74. *Zapiski, Stat'i, pis'ma dekabrista I. D. Yakushkina* (M., 1951), 116.
75. A. P. Belyayev, "Vospominaniya", in *Russkaya starina*, vol. XXX (1881), 812, 815. Rozen's soubriquet poses a problem: for the eponymous hero of Heinrich Zschokke's early novel *Kuno von Kyburg* (1795–99, appallingly translated into Russian by Ivan Kuzikov in 1809 as *Kino von Kiburg Took the Silver Locket of the Decapitated Man and Destroyed the Inquisition's Secret Court*), is a daemonic character, systematic only in his nastiness. But perhaps this was the point of the joke. The novel had been imitated during Rozen's youth, it may be added out of interest, as a play, *The Consequences of Ardent and Unadvised Passions* (St P., anon., 1811; see *Sankt-Peterburgskiy vestnik*, 1812, vol. 1, no. 2). Again, the inappropriateness to Rozen's case is striking—even droll.
76. Yakushkin, op. cit., 117.
77. *Memoiren 1874*, 192.
78. ibid., 199–200.
79. *Sibir' i dekabristy* (ed. M. K. Azadovsky) (Irkutsk, 1925), 141.
80. That is, private's pay; these men were also issued with clothing; see A. I. Dmitriyev-Mamonov, *Dekabristy v zapadnoy Sibiri* (St P., 1905), introduction.
81. Basargin, op. cit., 138.
82. Figures cited by M. Zetlin (trans. by G. Panin), *The Decembrists* (N.Y., 1958), 298. Deplorably, Zetlin gives no sources. His figures, however, tally with those given by M. N. Kuchayev—see note 37.
83. *Memoiren 1874*, 191.
84. George Kennan, *Siberia and the Exile System*, 2 vols (N.Y., 1891), vol. 2, 335–42 on Chita; vol. 2, 278–318 on the Nerchinsk Mines and, in particular, Akatui.

85. *Vospominaniya Bestuzhevykh*, 230–1; also G.-A. Erman, *Reise um die Erde* (Berlin, 1838):
English trans. of 1848, *Travels in Siberia*, vol. 2, 184.
86. *Memoiren 1874*, 194–5.
87. N. I. Lorer, *Zapiski dekabrista* (M., 1931), 154.
88. For a basic bibliography, see K. Muratova (ed.), *Istoriya russkoy literatury XIX-ogo veka: Bibliograficheskiy ukazatel'* (M., 1962), 27–8.
89. Mazour, op. cit., 244.
90. Basargin, op. cit., 178–86.
91. *Obshchestvennyye dvizheniya v Rossii . . .*, vol. 1, 276.
92. Rozen became close to Torson and the latter's intimate friend, Nikolay Bestuzhev, in 1829–30. After Torson's death, in 1851, Rozen was privileged to inspect his private papers, and found an interesting set of "Notes on Agriculture" (*Zapiski o zemledelii*); see V. V. Danilov, "Dekabristskiye materialy v Pushkinskom Dome", in *Dekabristy i ikh vremya* (M., 1951), 277. Torson was equally well versed in national finance, North American trade, Ukrainian grain-farming, and the arcane skills of ship-building. Always Rozen liked the company of those (Odoyevsky, Kornilovich, Torson) able to teach him.
93. *Memoiren 1874*, 95.
94. ibid., 100–1. Some impression of the sad appropriateness of Zschokke's work to the Decembrists situation in their cells is to be had from its full title, as translated ten years later by Charles Monard: *Méditations religieuses, en forme de discours pour toutes les époques, circonstances et situations de la vie domestique et civile* (Paris, 1836, 8 vols). Though stripped of his commission, Rozen enjoyed no civil rights; nor could he boast of a domestic life. He stood in need of *méditations religieuses*—and would later make his own, Russian, translation of the work (see Chapter 6).
95. Basargin, op. cit., 117.
96. *Memoiren 1874*, 144–5.
97. ibid., 194–5.
98. Cited from *Voices In Exile*, ch. 8.
99. There were also, we see, "several Polish and Italian papers" in the library: a group of Polish revolutionaries, participants in the Warsaw rising of November 28–30, 1830, arrived in Petrovsky Zavod early in 1831. As Rozen ordered German-language papers through Anna, A. V. Poggio ordered Italian ones.
100. On Anna's arrival in Siberia, see *Zapiski 1870*, 246–7, and *Dekabristy: neizdannyye materialy i stat'i* (ed. B. L. Modzalevsky, Yu. G. Oksman) (M., 1925), 141 (Shteyngel''s account).
101. *Memoiren 1874*, 279–81.
102. Baron V. I. Shteyngel', "Dnevnik dostopamyatnogo nashego puteshestviya iz Chity v Petrovsky Zavod v 1830 godu", *Dekabristy: neizdannyye materialy i stat'i*, 135 ff.; Basargin, op. cit., 130–2.
103. *Memoiren 1874*, 206–7.
104. See note 100.
105. *Memoiren 1874*, 211–12.

6: Petrovsky Zavod

1. S. Maksimov, *Sibir' i katorga*, 3 pts (St P., 1871), pt 3, 217–20, for a survey of the prison facilities.
2. Or, more accurately, no longer did they choose to trouble to gather.
3. See L. Chukovskaya, *Dekabristy—issledovateli Sibiri* (M., 1954); A. V. Kharchevnikov (ed.), *Dekabristy v Zabaykal'ye* (Chita, 1925), 25–30; N. A. Belogolovyy, *Vospominaniya i drugiye stat'i* (M., 1897), 21–9, 40–8.

4. Maksimov, op. cit., pt 3, 253–4. Repin left Petrovsky in June, and was burned to death in September 1831, together with A. N. Andreyevich.
5. S. B. Okun', *Dekabrist M. S. Lunin*, 134–5; *Vospominaniya i rasskazy deyateley*, 2, 292–4.
6. A. I. Dmitriyev-Mamonov, *Dekabristy v zapadnoy Sibiri*, 16–20.
7. *Zapiski 1870*, 277, provides a useful list of dates of Decembrists' and their wives' deaths.
8. N. V. Basargin, *Zapiski*, 162; *Vosp. Bestuzhevykh*, 736–7.
9. See S. D. Watrous's fine introduction to *John Ledyard's Journey Through Russia and Siberia, 1787–88* (Madison, 1966), 59–60.
10. ibid., 63, 67–8.
11. Basargin, op. cit., 94; Martin Sauer, *An Account of a Geographical and Astronomical Expedition to the Northern Parts of Russia . . .* (London, 1802), 15–18; W. Kirchner, *Eine Reise durch Sibirien im achtzehnten Jahrhundert . . . Doktors Jakob Fries* (Isar Verlag, Munich, 1955), 75–8.
12. On the "outcast tribe" of factory workers in Siberia, see *Vosp. Bestuzhevykh*, 168–9, and A. P. Shchapov, "Sibirskoye obshchestvo do Speranskogo", *Sochineniya A. P. Shchapova* (St P., 1908), vol. 3, 643–717.
13. Sauer, op. cit., 9.
14. See A. N. Radishchev, *Polnoye sobraniye sochineniy* (M.-L., 1952), 3, 389.
15. D. I. Zavalishin, *Zapiski*, 301.
16. ibid., 300.
17. See Maksimov, op. cit., pt 3, 218.
18. Basargin, op. cit., 135–6.
19. Zavalishin, op. cit., 299–300.
20. I. D. Yakushkin, *Zapiski*, 128.
21. *Memoiren 1874*, 219. Anna received permission to join her husband in Siberian exile on September 23, 1829. An awareness that the exiles would soon leave Chita, however, coupled with the need to make arrangements for Yevgeniy's future, delayed her departure for nine months; see *Materialy*, VIII, 388.
22. Letter dated June 19, 1830 and written by Kalinovo, near Pernau; now kept in a Russian copy (the French original is lost) in Saltykov-Shchedrin Public Library, *fond* 124, *ed. kr.* 3698.
23. *Memoiren 1874*, 227–8.
24. ibid., 232–3.
25. ibid., 94–5.
26. ibid., 178.
27. ibid., 192.
28. ibid., 199.
29. A. P. Belyayev, "Vospominaniya", in *Russkaya Starina*, vol. XXX (1881), 813.
30. ibid., 196.
31. However, he seems not to have played it in Siberia. "It was a shame to torment the ears of one's comrades, and for that reason I chose for myself that most modest and soft, but also most ungrateful of instruments, the *czakan*; with the aid of a printed teach-yourself manual, I sorted out the notes . . ."; *Zapiski 1870*, 231.
32. Basargin, op. cit., 118.
33. See Chapter 12.
34. *Zapiski 1870*, 3–4.
35. *Memoiren 1874*, 103.
36. ibid., 108.
37. Rozen, *Skizze zu einer Familien-Geschichte*, 82.
38. *Memoiren 1874*, 150.
39. Yakushkin, op. cit., 111.
40. *Memoiren 1874*, 240; see also note 2 to Chapter 3.
41. ibid., 309–10.

42. ibid., 221–2, 225.
43. Belyayev, op. cit., 813; see also N. I. Lorer, *Zapiski dekabrista* (M., 1931), 145.
44. *Memoiren 1874*, 193.
45. *Russkaya starina*, vol. III (1871), 534.
46. For further information on this, see Chapter 12.
47. Belyayev, op. cit., 452–4.
48. Vol. XLII (1884), 658.
49. *Memoiren 1874*, 258. Basargin (op. cit., 94) and I. I. Pushchin (*Zapiski o Pushkine* (M., 1934), 178) make similar comments and comparisons between Siberia and America.
50. See "O vinokurenii i otkarmlivanii domashnego skota" in *Trudy Vol'nogo Ekonomicheskogo Obshchestva*, pt LXIX (St P., 1818), 200–25, by "Baron Rozen".
51. *Memoiren 1874*, 104, 106.
52. ibid., 265.
53. ibid., 141.
54. ibid., 305–6.
55. Basargin, op. cit., 110. Significantly, neither Basargin (op. cit., 104–6) nor Yakushkin (op. cit., 105–7) nor Lorer (op. cit., 134–7), in their accounts of their first impressions of Chita, stress the physical charms of the area, its healthy climate and rich soil. Only Lorer, indeed, mentions the relative mildness of the local climate (op. cit., 134). Rozen, too, was acutely conscious of the cramped conditions in the prison, in 1827–28; unlike most memoirists, however, he could appreciate the topographical and natural beauty of the Ingoda Valley to the full.
56. *Memoiren 1874*, 174–5.
57. *Pis'ma iz Sibiri dekabristov M. i N. Bestuzhevykh* (Irkutsk, 1929), bk 1, 17. In fairness to him, Bestuzhev spoke, more specifically, of the views around Nizhnye-Udinsk.
58. R. J. Kerner, "Russian Expansion to America", in *The Papers of the Bibliographical Society of America*, vol. XXV (1931), 114–15.
59. M. I. Murav'yov-Apostol, *Vospominaniya i pis'ma* (Petrograd, 1922), 63.
60. P. Annenkova, *Vospominaniya* (M., 1929), 151–2; *Sibir' i dekabristy*, 154.
61. See note 2.
62. *Dekabristy v Zabaykale*, 26.
63. *Memoiren 1874*, 303.
64. *Sibir' i dekabristy*, 16, 29–31; also Maksimov, op. cit., 390–2.
65. Yakushkin, op. cit., 128.
66. *Zapiski 1870*, 250–1.
67. *Memoiren 1874*, 258.
68. A. I. Dmitriyev-Mamonov, *Dekabristy v zapadnoy Sibiri* (St P., 1905), 141–2.
69. *Memoiren 1874*, 247, 248–50.
70. ibid., 252–4.
71. A humorous allusion to Yevgeniy's (Enny's) loss of noble rights, in consequence of his, Rozen's, position.
72. I thank Baron Kersten von Rosen of Flensburg, in whose possession the French original now is, for permission to quote from this letter.
73. *Zapiski 1870*, 273.
74. *Memoiren 1874*, 257, 259–60.
75. ibid., 266–7.

7: Kurgan
1. A. von Kotzebue, *Das merkwürdigste Jahr meines Lebens* (Kösel, Munich, 1965), 174.
2. *Memoiren 1874*, 268–9.
3. M. I. Murav'yov-Apostol, *Vospominaniya i pis'ma* (Petrograd, 1922), 61.
4. N. I. Lorer, *Zapiski dekabrista* (M., 1931), 168.

5. Cited by A. I. Dmitriyev-Mamonov, *Dekabristy v zapadnoy Sibiri* (St P., 1905), 142.
6. ibid., 143.
7. A. G. Mazour, *The First Russian Revolution, 1825* (Stanford, 1962; 2nd printing), 243.
8. *Memoiren 1874*, 272–4.
9. ibid., 270. For details of the exiles' social life in Kurgan, musical dinners at the Naryshkins, friendly contact with Poles, Fokht's illuminating Kurgan's main street with 500 "lampions" the night before the Tsarevich's arrival—aspects of exile life missing from Rozen's account—see Lorer, op. cit., 171–3.
10. Dmitriyev-Mamonov, op. cit., 144.
11. Lorer, op. cit., 167–8.
12. See Mazour, op. cit., 240.
13. *Memoiren 1874*, 271–2.
14. Dmitriyev-Mamonov, op. cit., 145. V. D. Vol'khovsky (1798–1841) had been a friend of the Malinovskys since his time at the Lyceum of Tsarskoye Selo. Like A. V. Malinovsky, he formed a link between Rozen and the *lycéens* I. I. Pushchin and V. K. Kyukhel'beker.
15. M. Zetlin (trans. by G. Panin), *The Decembrists* (N.Y., 1958), 323.
16. *Sibir' i dekabristy*, 56. Most Decembrists, however, felt appeals to Nicholas too humiliating to be made; see Mazour, op. cit., 237–8.
17. *Memoiren 1874*, 282–3.
18. *Vospominaniya Bestuzhevykh*, 246.
19. *Sibir' i dekabristy*, 142.
20. Lorer, op. cit., 172.
21. *Memoiren 1874*, 283–4.
22. ibid., 285.
23. *Pis'ma i sochineniya M. S. Lunina* (ed. S. Ya. Shtraykh) (L., 1926), 37.
24. Lorer, op. cit., 177.
25. *Memoiren 1874*, 289–91.
26. ibid., 295–6.
27. Dmitriyev-Mamonov, op. cit., 146–7.
28. *Memoiren 1874*, 298.
29. ibid., 299–300; see also Lorer, op. cit., 174.
30. Dmitriyev-Mamonov, op. cit., 147.
31. Zetlin, op. cit., 313–14.
32. *Zapiski 1870*, 316.
33. ibid., 317.
34. Dmitriyev-Mamonov, op. cit., 148.
35. See Lorer, op. cit., 177.
36. *Memoiren 1874*, 304–5.
37. ibid., 307.
38. ibid., 308.
39. ibid., 311.
40. ibid., 313–14.
41. On the delectable weather in this region, see Dr Robert Lee, *The Last Days of Alexander and the First Days of Nicholas* (R. Bentley, London, 1854), 25–6. Lee also, interestingly, noted the increasing number of Lutherans in Simferopol' and in the Crimea, by 1826, although the Governor-General of Novorossiya, M. S. Vorontsov, chose to be ignorant of the fact (32–3).

8: Rozen in the Caucasus
1. D. M. Lang, *A Modern History of Georgia* (London, 1962), 49.
2. Cited by J. F. Baddeley, *The Russian Conquest of the Caucasus* (London, 1908), 97.
3. Lang, op. cit., 56.

4. See Barratt, "A Note on the Russian Conquest of Armenia, 1827", in *Slavonic and East European Review* (1972), 386–409.
5. L. Blanch, *The Sabres of Paradise* (London, 1957), 4–5.
6. Lang, op. cit., 72–4.
7. *Memoiren 1874*, 315–18.
8. ibid., 320.
9. *Meyers Konversations-Lexikon*, vol. 17, 147; see also de St Aubin, *Trente-neuf portraits, 1808–1815* (St P., 1902).
10. A. Berzhe, *Baron Rozen i yego upravleniye Kavkazom* (St P., 1874), 90–6.
11. TsGVIA, *fond* 395, op. 268, no. 856, packet 192.
12. *Zapiski 1870*, 344; *Memoiren 1874*, 323.
13. The question of Lermontov's meetings with Decembrists is treated thoroughly by D. Gireyev and S. Nedumov in "K istorii znakomstva Lermontova s dekabristami", in *Lit. nasl.*, vol. 60 (1956), bk 2, 507–14.
14. See note 11.
15. TsGVIA, *fond* 395, op. 268, no. 856, packet 195.
16. *Memoiren 1874*, 333–5.
17. ibid., 338–9.
18. *Zapiski 1870*, 386–8.
19. *Memoiren 1874*, 328–9.
20. *Zapiski 1870*, 392–3; Lang, op. cit., chs 2 & 3.
21. *Materialy*, I, 209.
22. Cited by M. Raeff, *The Decembrist Movement* (Englewood Cliffs, N.J., 1966), 133–5.
23. ibid., 142 (from Pestel's Section VI: "The Lettish Race").
24. *Zapiski 1870*, 350–1.
25. ibid., 391–2.
26. ibid., 400–1, 416.

9: The Return to Estonia
1. *Zapiski 1870*, 447–53. At this point, the 1874 German text ceases.
2. For Pushchin–Obolensky correspondence, see *Pamyati dekabristov: sbornik materialov*, 3 vols (L., 1926), vol. 3, 26, 36; on the Imperial School of Jurisprudence, see *Pyatidesyatiletnyy yubiley Imp. Uchilishcha Pravovedeniya* (St P., 1886), 7–41.
3. *Zapiski 1870*, 452–3.
4. A. Buchholtz, *Fünfzig Jahre russischer Verwaltung in den Baltischen Provinzen* (Leipzig 1883), 238–9. To appreciate how the Estonian peasantry had advanced in farming technique and literacy, since the 1770s, see I. Georgi, *Opisaniye vsekh v Rossiyskom gosudarstve obitayushchikh narodov: o narodakh finskogo plemeni* (St P., 1776), pt 1. On Bol'sháya Sóldina, see Richter, *Baltische Adressbücher*, vol. 3, 381.
5. Julius Eckardt, *Die Baltischen Provinzen Russlands* (Leipzig, 1869), 423–5.
6. See Chapter 12.
7. E. Nodel, *Estonia: Nation on the Anvil* (N.Y., 1963), 50–1, 53.
8. J. H. Jackson, *Estonia* (London, 1941), 92.
9. H. A. von Bock, "Uber den Handel auf dem Lande in Livland", in *Das Inland*, vol. 1 (December 16, 1836), Dorpat, 842–5.
10. *Zapiski 1870*, 455.
11. ibid., 456, 463.
12. ibid., 457.
13. ibid., 459–60.
14. Letter preserved in the *rukopisnyy otdel* of Saltykov-Shchedrin Public Library, Leningrad, under archive ref. *sobraniye* P. L. Vakselya, *fond* 124, no. 3693.
15. *Zapiski 1870*, 461.

16. Elizabeth Rigby, *Letters from the Baltic* (London, 1841), ch. 2, and, especially, Johann Georg Kohl (1808–78), *Die Deutsch-Russischen Ostseeprovinzen*, 2 pts (Dresden, Leipzig, 1841), pt 2, 193–201, stress these qualities. Yet within three decades, a traveller could emphasize the general lack of indolence among the Estonians: Paul Hunfalvy, *Reise in den Ostseeprovinzen Russlands* (Leipzig, 1874). It may be noted that Eckhardt, Kohl, Buchholtz and Hunfalvy all published their volumes treating different aspects of Estonian life and history in Leipzig. Between the Baltic-German nobility and Leipzig there existed strong cultural and literary links—links further strengthened by the Rozen family: the Decembrist published his memoirs there; Friedrich August Rosen (1805–37) and Viktor Romanovich Rozen (1849–1919), Sanskrit specialist and Arabist respectively, both studied at Leipzig University (in 1822–24, 1868–71), as did the former's brilliant nephew, the German diplomat Friedrich Rosen (in 1879–80), the Decembrist's father, and several other members of (three branches of) the family.

17. Notably Miss Rigby (1809–93), whose distaste for the backward Ests is more than balanced, however, by antipathy towards the Baltic Germans.

18. Nodel, op. cit., 47, 75.

19. ibid., 53.

20. B. Pares, *A History of Russia* (London, 1962), 371.

21. That is, demesne land by the classification of 1842.

22. i.e. February 2/15.

23. *Zapiski 1870*, 464–6.

24. ibid., 466.

25. Jackson, op. cit., 96–7.

26. *Zapiski 1870*, 466.

27. Jackson, op. cit., 97.

28. See Aino Julia Kallas, *née* Krohn, *The White Ship* (London, 1924), *passim*.

29. Saltykov-Shchedrin Public Library, *Fond 124, ed. kh.* 3691. Yevgeniy signed the paper on February 10, 1853; by it, his mother's estate of Stratilatovka passed to him irreversibly.

30. *Zapiski 1870*, 517–19.

10: Nationalism and Estonian Identity

1. See *Voices In Exile*, ch. 3.

2. *Materialy*, IV, 107, 283.

3. See the author's paper "M. S. Lunin and the Question of Polish Sovereignty", in *East European Quarterly*, vol. V (1970), no. 1, 1–3.

4. *Zapiski 1870*, 202.

5. ibid., 28–9.

6. E. Nodel, *Estonia: Nation on the Anvil* (N.Y., 1963), 42.

7. ibid., 43, and J. H. Jackson, *Estonia* (London, 1941), 94.

8. *Zapiski 1870*, 471–2, 473.

9. Reinhard Wittram, *Baltische Geschichte* (Munich, 1954), 185–6. Also, on the question of forced conversions and conflict between the Orthodox and Lutheran Churches, see G. J. Kohl, *Die Deutsch-Russischen Ostseeprovinzen*, pt 2, 336–56; P. Hunfalvy, *Reise in den Ostseeprovinzen Russlands* (Leipzig, 1874), 108–9; and A. Buddeus, *Halbrussisches*, 2 vols (Leipzig, 1847), vol. 2, 47–64.

10. Jackson, op. cit., 94. Jackson does not give his source, unfortunately.

11. *Zapiski 1870*, 474–5.

12. Nodel, op. cit., 44.

13. *Zapiski 1870*, 477.

14. By 1832, we see from R. Pinkerton's *Russia, or, Miscellaneous Observations on the Past and Present State of that Country . . .* (Seeley, London, 1833, 8), it had a population of

330,000, compared with Moscow's 250,000, and 30,000 in both Kiev and Riga. Pinkerton gives many interesting statistics: in 1832, for instance, the total population of the Russian Empire was estimated at 54 million, 3 million persons being Finnish, Estonian, Livonian or "German Lutheran", and 2 million Moslems.

15. Cited by Jackson, op. cit., 85.
16. *Zapiski 1870*, 478.
17. Nodel, op. cit., 48.
18. *Zapiski 1870*, 478.
19. See T. Pfeil, *Livlands Erlebnisse seit 50 Jahren* (Tartu, 1906), 8–10; also R. Wittram, *Baltische Geschichte* ... (Munich, 1954), 217–20; and *Zapiski 1870*, 479–82.
20. *Zapiski 1870*, 484.
21. Nodel, op. cit., 66.
22. Otto Wilhelm Masing (1763–1832) was of mixed Swedish and Estonian origin.
23. Pärnu, 1813–32; 20 vols.
24. H. Rosenthal, *Kulturbestrebungen des estnischen Volkes während eines Menschenalters (1869–1900)* (Revel', 1912), 48–58.
25. Jackson, op. cit., 107.
26. ibid., 101.
27. ibid., 100.
28. Hunfalvy, op. cit., 138–9.
29. *Zapiski 1870*, 487.
30. ibid., 485.
31. ibid., 489.
32. Nodel, op. cit., 65–6.
33. *Zapiski 1870*, 490.
34. ibid., 494.
35. Wittram, op. cit., 192–8; also "Die Nationalitätenfrage", in *Baltische Monatsschrift*, vol. XIII (1864), 568–75.
36. Rosenthal, op. cit., 14–15; also Kohl, op. cit., vol. 2, 311–13.
37. Kohl, op. cit., vol. 2, 207.
38. Nodel, op. cit., 48.
39. Prague, 1868.
40. *Livländische Antwort an Herrn Juri Samarin* (Leipzig, 1919; reprint from the 1869 Leipzig edn), 48–9.
41. *Zapiski 1870*, 481.
42. "Die Nationalitätenfrage", vol. IX (1864), 606.
43. *Zapiski 1870*, 495–6.

11: Amnesty and Emancipation
 1. *Zapiski 1870*, 524–5.
 2. ibid., 528.
 3. ibid., 529.
 4. That is, when all roads remained passable.
 5. *Zapiski 1870*, 529–30.
 6. See note 3.
 7. *Zapiski 1870*, 507.
 8. ibid., 531, 533.
 9. ibid., 533–4.
10. ibid., 535.
11. ibid., 537.
12. Of the Decembrists who had returned to European Russia earlier, however, at least twelve survived in that year; and even with the death of I. A. Annenkov in 1878 (A. E.

Rozen, "I. A. Annenkov: nekrolog", in *Russkaya starina*, vol. XXII, 1878, 526), there remained eight survivors: M. Murav'yov-Apostol, Zagoretsky, Nazimov, Rozen, Frolov, Svistunov, A. P. Belyayev, and Zavalishin.

13. *Zapiski 1870*, 510, 516.
14. *Obshchestvennyye dvizheniya v Rossii...*, vol. 1, 442.
15. *Memoiren 1874*, 33.
16. ibid., 34.
17. *Zapiski 1870*, 421.
18. See Chapter. 12.
19. M. Zetlin (trans. by G. Panin), *The Decembrists* (N.Y., 1958), 347–8.
20. N. I. Lorer, *Zapiski dekabrista* (M., 1931), 378 (Lorer to Briggen, December 5, 1841: "Our arch-methodologist is living quietly in his hamlet"); 383 (Lorer to Naryshkin, February 22, 1845: "I am in constant correspondence with... the Rozens"); 387 (Lorer to Naryshkin, February 10, 1847: "The main trouble is that I can't find a nurse for the children; and it's hard for my wife, with her poor health, to be never away from the children... with never a free moment. She reminds me of Madame Rozen—do you remember in Kurgan?—*Toujours les enfants*. I know from a letter that you have visited those devout people—Rozen wrote to me, and with such joy...").
21. See I. I. Gorbachevsky, *Zapiski i pis'ma* (M., 1925). Especially valuable are Gorbachevsky's letters to Obolensky.
22. Lorer, op. cit., 390.
23. *Sibir' i dekabristy*, 28.
24. *Dekabristy: neizdannyye materialy i stat'i*, 238.
25. B. Pares, *A History of Russia* (London, 1962), 400–1.
26. In the first fit of wrath, according to Shteyngel' (*Obshchestvennyye dvizheniya v Rossii...*, vol. 1, 437–8), Ryleyev "proposed that Rostovtsev be killed". Others who, like Yakushkin, had been equally enraged by Rostovtsev's actions, came eventually to view him as an overwrought, slightly unbalanced youth; see I. D. Yakushkin, *Zapiski*, 147.
27. Pares, op. cit., 401. For details, see T. Emmons, *The Emancipation of the Russian Serfs* (N.Y., 1970) and, of course, the excellent study of P. A. Zayonchkovsky, *Otmena krepostnogo prava v Rossii* (M., 1954). Pares's précis of events of 1857–59, though dated now, is sound enough in broad outline.
28. "One thing that puzzles me," wrote Constantine to Nicholas I in August 1826, "is the conduct of Orlov, and how *he* came out of the water dry..."; *Mezhdutsarstviye...*, 196. Several Decembrists held the opinion, expressed most forcefully by Lorer perhaps (op. cit., 107–8), that Orlov *ought* not to have accepted full pardon; but Lorer, who felt strongly on such matters, like Zavalishin, also thought that A. N. Murav'yov, Decembrist Governor of Tobol'sk, "would have acted more honourably in the moral sense, had he redeemed his error—if error it was—by the same punishment as his comrades" (op. cit., 167). Rozen passes no judgement.
29. Pares, op. cit., 397.
30. But scarcely, it is interesting to note, over the past ten years.
31. *Zapiski 1870*, 543–5.
32. ibid., 248–52.
33. ibid., 558–9.
34. ibid., 560.
35. The most recent general survey of their work is that of H. Seton-Watson, *The Russian Empire, 1801–1917* (London, 1967), 342–54.
36. Based on Chapter XXIV of the 1870 Russian edition ("Observations of a Former Arbitrator of the Peace on the New Order"), the article appeared in slightly altered form in *Russkaya mysl'*, 1885, bk, 9.
37. *Zapiski 1870*, 567–8.
38. ibid., 574–5.

39. ibid., 578.
40. ibid., 600–3.
41. Also, more especially after 1880, to North America; see H. Kruus (trans. by A.-D. Toledano), *Histoire de l'Estonie* (Paris, 1935), 125–7. Between the censuses of 1881 and 1897, the population of the province increased by 45,498; but in that period, 26,386 left Estonia officially. Unofficially, no doubt more than this number emigrated.
42. The paper was given to Galkin-Vraskoy, in March of that year, by Baron N. A. Korf; see *Russky arkhiv*, no. IV (1885), 641.

12: Rozen as the Recorder of Decembrism
1. *Zapisky 1870*, 573–4.
2. I. I. Gorbachevsky, *Zapiski i pis'ma* (M., 1963), 202.
3. *Vospominaniya i rasskazy deyateley taynykh obshchestv 1820-kh godov* (M., 1933), 366.
4. Since 1824.
5. *Zapiski 1870*, 553.
6. ibid., 539.
7. ibid., 539–40. In Moscow, Rozen met Nikita Murav'yov's daughter Sof'ya (Nonushka; 1826–92), now married to a nephew of Matvey Murav'yov-Apostol and the mother of four boys.
8. See note 2 to Chapter 3.
9. "I am including Baten'kov in the general list of our dead fellow-exiles, which Ivan Pushchin began . . ."; Rozen to Obolensky, letter of November 22, 1863, now in Institut Russkoy Literatury i Iskusstv, *fond* 606/21, 1.153.
10. On Camille Le Dentu (1804–39), daughter of a French republican émigré, see I. D. Yakushkin, *Zapiski*, 172–6; N. V. Basargin, *Zapiski*, 125–9; and a work by V. P. Ivashev's own granddaughter, Ol'ga Bulanova, *Roman dekabrista: dekabrist V. P. Ivashev i yego sem'ya: iz semeynogo arkhiva* (M., 1933, 3rd edn).
11. *Zapiski 1870*, 422.
12. ibid., v.
13. ibid., v–vi, viii.
14. See *Voices In Exile*, Appendix D.
15. *Zapiski 1870*, vii–ix.
16. ibid., 591.
17. *Entsiklopedicheskiy slovar'*, vol. 19, 75–7.
18. Published under the pseudonym A. Skavronsky.
19. See D. I. Balagey, *Materialy dlya biografiy yuzhno-russkikh nauchno-literaturnykh deyateley XIX-ogo veka* (Kiev, 1903), in which two letters from Danilevsky to Rozen of 1864 appear; and *Russkaya starina*, 1904, no. 6, 621–5, for a letter from Rozen to Danilevsky of January 18, 1863.
20. *Vospominaniya i rasskazy deyateley taynykh obshchestv 1820-kh godov*, 353.
21. N. M. Chentsov, *Bibliografiya: vosstaniye dekabristov* (M., 1929), no. 2731.
22. J. W. von Eckhardt, *Lebenserinnerungen*, 2 vols (Leipzig, 1910), vol. 1, 156–7.
23. Founded by I. Kuranda in Brussels, the periodical moved to Leipzig within twelve months, in 1842, and continued to appear there until 1922.
24. E. St-John Mildmay, *Russian Conspirators in Siberia: A Personal Narrative by Baron R.* (London, 1872), v.
25. See note 16 to Chapter 9.
26. *Vospominaniya i rasskazy deyateley taynykh obshchestv 1820-kh godov*, 249–56; Rozen's rebuttal is also given here (272–5).
27. It was, however, his sole excursion into controversy in the press. Privately, he engaged in civil arguments with many correspondents in 1870–80.
28. *Zapiski 1870*, ix.

29. *Dekabristy: neizdannyye materialy i stat'i*, 186.
30. Bk 2, 834–6.
31. *Russkaya starina*, XXXV, 465–82, and XXIX, 1–42, XXX, 811–17, respectively.
32. *Memoiren 1874*, 33–4.
33. Others, in the view of this writer, are those of M. A. and N. A. Bestuzhev, I. D. Yakushkin, and Baron Shteyngel'; see *Voices In Exile*, ch. 2.
34. *Literaturnoye nasledstvo*, vol. 60, bk 2.
35. "Vospominaniya knyazya E. P. Obolenskogo", in *Obshchestvennyye dvizheniya v Rossii . . .*, vol. 1, 231–81.
36. *Memoiren 1874*, 220.
37. St-John Mildmay, op. cit., 144.
38. *Vospominaniya Bestuzhevykh*, 317–18; also N. Kotlyarevsky, *Dekabristy: knyaz' A. Odoyevsky i A. Bestuzhev* (St P., 1909), 234–5.
39. G.-A. Erman, *Reise um die Erde* (Berlin, 1838); English trans. of 1848, *Travels in Siberia* vol. 2, 180–1.
40. See note 20 to Chapter 2.
41. *Zapiski 1870*, 417.
42. Vol. II.
43. On the former, see note 36 to Chapter 11.
44. The Russian edition, in full *Ocherk famil'noy istorii baronov fon Rozen iz domov Roop, Gokhrozen, Shonangern, Rozengof, Moyan, 992–1876*, is now a bibliographical rarity outside the U.S.S.R.
45. Not, of course, a Decembrist; on the Rayevsky–Volkonsky–Pushkin nexus, see V. Nabokov, *Eugene Onegin*, 4 vols (N.Y., 1964), vol. 2, 120–4.
46. A. G. Mazour, *The First Russian Revolution, 1825* (Stanford, 1962; 2nd printing), 249–51.
47. See Chapter 5.
48. pp. 365–6.
49. Rozen also kept for thirty years the manuscript of a "Russian Grammar" by Odoyevsky (see *Lit. nasl.*, vol. 60, bk 2, 729). His "Biographical Sketch of Prince A. I. Odoyevsky: The Last Days", published in the *Poln. sob. stikh.* (St P., 1883) is touched upon in an interesting anonymous review of that edition; see *Otechestvennyye zapiski*, vol. CCLXI (1883), no. 2, 213–15. The poem "To One Arrived From Kurgan . . .", which Rozen published in *Russ. star.* in 1871 (vol. II, 635), was in his keeping at least thirty-three years.
50. *Russkaya starina: karmannaya knizhka dlya lyubiteley otechestvennogo, na 1825 god* (St P., 1825) was, properly speaking, a booklet, not a periodical; it contained a collection of tales and articles of various kinds and by several authors, so might loosely be termed an almanac.
51. Kornilovich (1800–34) was returned to Peter-and-Paul Fortress in February 1828 as a consequence of a denunciation by the journalist–agent, F. V. Bulgarin; see also *Memoiren 1874*, 194.
52. Vol. XV (1876, dated 1875), 635.
53. V. Timoshchuk, *Semevsky, osnovatel' istoricheskogo zhurnala "Russkaya starina"* (St P., 1895).
54. In 1891, Semevsky would publish separately the memoirs of Count Ernst Johann Münnich. Rozen himself took an interest in the more famous General Burkhard Christoph Münnich (1683–1767), Anna's powerful favourite; see *Memoiren 1874*, 280–1.
55. M. Zetlin (trans. by G. Panin), *The Decembrists* (N.Y., 1958), 344.
56. C. Corbet, *Nekrasoff: l'homme et le poète* (Paris, 1948), 393.
57. N. S. Ashukin, *Letopis' zhizni i tvorchestva N. A. Nekrasova* (M., 1935), 168. On Nekrasov's deliberate use of Rozen's memoirs, see Corbet, op. cit., 391–5; and K. Chukovsky's "Zhizn' Nekrasova" in the *Poln. sob. soch.* (L., 1934, 7th edn), 524.
58. Note 46 to ch. 3.

59. *Memoiren 1874*, 33.
60. See *Arkhiv sela Karabichi* (M., 1916), 164–6. Edited by K. Nekrasov, the work contains two letters from Rozen to Nekrasov of 1875. Karabichi, an estate bought by Nekrasov in December 1861, was 15 kms from Yaroslavl' on the Moscow railway line.
61. *Repetitor*; in 1857, at the age of twenty; *Entsiklopedicheskiy slovar'*, vol. 27, 321–2.
62. And their literary executors.
63. Russian editions appeared in 1907 and 1906 respectively (St P.).
64. Saltykov-Shchedrin, *fond* 124, *ed. kh.* 3691.
65. IRLI, P1, op. 24, *ed. khr.* 49, 1.132.
66. Part of that work, in his last years, became the protection of Decembrists' families, some of which were in want; see, for example, the conclusion of his obituary of E. A. Bestuzheva (*Russ. star.*, vol. IX (1874), 578): "During the past decade I have called on the Bestuzhev sisters every time I have passed through Moscow, so have been able personally to appreciate that sad picture of moribund old age, with all its attendant ailments: exhaustion of the body's strength, failure of the eyes, hardness of hearing. But one had only to touch upon the memory of the departed brothers, or upon the futures of brother Mikhail's orphans, Mar'ya and Aleksandra, and for an instant half-dimmed eyes would be lit up . . ." In the same piece, Rozen also speaks for A. A. Bestuzhev's son, whose career prospects were uncertain.
67. No. 6, 657–8. Obituary notices also appeared, in 1884, in *Novoye vremya*, no. 2936 (May 2), "khronika", 3, and *Istoricheskiy vestnik*, VII, "smes' ", 223–4; while D. D. Yazykov referred respectfully to him in an "Obzor zhizni i trudov pokoynykh russkikh pisateley, umershikh v 1884 godu", ibid., 1887, XII. See also E. Veydenbaum "Dekabristy na Kavkaze", *Russkaya starina*, VI (1903), 481–502; V. Timiryazev, "Pionery prosveshcheniya v Zapadnoy Sibiri", *Istoricheskiy vestnik*, 1896, V, 629–47; VI, 961–84; and N. M. Chentsov, *Vosstaniye dekabristov: bibliografiya* (M.-L., 1929), 480–9 (items 2729–2756 on A. E. Rozen).

Epilogue
1. See A. Richter, *Baltische Verkehrs- und Adressbücher: band 3: Estland* (Riga, 1913), 398.
2. *Zapiski 1870*, 447.
3. The photograph of one (unspecified) Baroness Rozen appears in *Russian Court Memoirs 1914–1916*, by B.W. (N.Y., 1916), 120.
4. See *Istoriya Estonskoy S.S.R.*, 2 vols (Tallinn, 1961), vol. 2, 464.
5. See O. Kirss, L. Payos, *Po obeim storonam dorogi* (Tallinn, 1972), I am much indebted to Dr Waldemar Miller, Head Archivist, Library of the Estonian Academy of Sciences (Lenini Puiestee 10, Tallinn), for his generous assistance in this matter.
6. *Nachrichtenblatt des Rosenschen Familienverbandes*, no. 18, 2, and no. 13, 8, respectively.
7. Since writing the above, I have learned that a grandson of Anna Andreyevna still lives in Moscow.
8. Thanks, in no small measure, to the care lavished on it by two sisters, Sophie Yermolova, *née* Rozen, and Catherine von Baer, *née* Rozen, who together purchased it on April 23, 1912; see Richter, *Baltische Verkehrs- und Adressbücher*, 329.
9. I thank Dr August Martin of Kokhtla-Yarva for this information. (The former Rozen house in Kurgan is now known as 67 Ulitsa Sovetskaya.)

SELECTIVE BIBLIOGRAPHY

TOPICAL BIBLIOGRAPHIES

On Estonian History
Istoriya Estonskoy S.S.R. (ed. A. Vassar, G. Naan), 2 vols (Tallinn, 1961), 897–918.

On the Decembrist Movement
Chentsov, N. M., *Vosstaniye dekabristov: bibliografiya* (M.-L., 1929), 4451 items.
Pereselenkov, S., "Dnevniki i memuary dekabristov: bibliografichesky ukazatel", in *Byloye* (1925), no. 5, 240–62; 235 items.

ON THE ROZEN FAMILY

Doroshenko, V. V., *Istochnikovedcheskiye problemy istorii narodov Pribaltiki* (Riga, 1970), 153–201. (On the estate of Baroness Anna Rosen, Klein-Roph, 1705–42.)
Lenz, W. (ed.), *Deutsch-Baltisches Biographisches Lexikon, 1710–1960* (Cologne, Vienna, 1970), 643–4.
Lyubarsky, A., "Glashatai vol'nosti", in *Slovo druzhby* (Tallinn, 1956). (Decembrist links with Estonia.)
Meyers Grosses Konversations-Lexikon, 24 vols (Leipzig, Vienna, 1909), vol. 17, 147.
Rozen, A. E., *Skizze zu einer Familien-Geschichte der Freiherren und Grafen von Rosen* (St P., 1876).
Russkaya starina (1884), vols 41, 94–99; 43, 390–3. (On the career of General G. V. Rozen in the south and in Warsaw.)
Svābe, A., *Latvju Tiesību Vēsture* (*A History of Latvian Law*) (Riga, 1935). (On the nobility of Baltic-German families.)
Vassar, A. (ed.), *Istoriya Estonskoy S.S.R.*, 2 vols (Tallinn, 1961), esp. vol. 1.
Veskow, G., *Minne af grefve Gustav Friedrich von Rosen* (Stockholm, 1852). (Swedish Gov.-Gen. of Finland, 1747–51.)
Vigrabs, G. M., *Pribaltiyskiye nemtsy: ikh otnosheniye k russkoy gosudarstvennosti i k korennomu naseleniyu kraya* (Yur'yev, 1916). (Rozen attitudes towards the Ests.)
Vigrabs, J., *Die Rosensche Deklaration vom Jahre 1739 . . .* (Tartu, 1937).
Vosstaniye dekabristov: materialy po istorii vosstaniya dekabristov . . ., 13 vols (ed. M. N. Pokrovsky) (L., 1925–37), esp. vol. 8, 388. (This "*alfavit dekabristov*", compiled by B. L. Modzalevsky and A. Sivers, concentrates all the biographical data on A. E. Rozen in the *Vosstaniye . . .*)

ON THE HISTORY OF ESTONIA UP TO 1800

Bilmanis, A., *Baltic Essays* (Washington, D.C., 1945).
Bunge, F. G. von, *Arkhiv für die Geschichte Liv-, Esth-, und Curlands*, 8 pts (Dorpat, Reval, 1842–61).

Gadebusch, F. K., *Livländische Jahrbücher*, 4 pts (Riga, 1780–83).
Mikkola, J., *Berührungen zwischen den Westfinnen und den Slaven* (Helsingfors, 1894).
Richter, A. von, *Geschichte der deutschen Ostseeprovinzen*, 2 pts (Riga, 1858), pt 2.
Ruswurm, H. C., *Shvedy na beregakh Estlyandii* (Reval, 1885).
Schirren, C., *Scriptores rerum Livonicarum: Sammlung der wichtigsten Chroniken und Geschichtsdenkmale von Liv-, Esth- und Kurland* (Riga, Leipzig, 1848–53).
Soom, A., *Der Herrenhof in Estland im 17 Jahrhundert* (Lund, 1954).
Winckelmann, E., *Die Capitulationen der estländischen Ritterschaft und der Stadt Reval vom Jahre 1710* ... (Reval, 1865).
Zutis, Ya., *Ostzeysky vopros v XVIII veke* (Riga, 1946).

LUTHERANISM AND ORTHODOXY IN ESTONIA

Hunfalvy, P., *Reise in den Ostseeprovinzen Russlands* (Leipzig, 1874).
Passir, G., *Iz istorii pravoslaviya v pribaltiyskom kraye* (Riga, 1892).
Scherwinzky, C. F., *Etwas über Ehsten, besonders über ihren Aberglauben* (Leipzig, 1788).
Trusman, Yu., *Vvedeniye khristianstva v Liflyandiyu* (St P., 1884).
Wittram, R., *Baltische Geschichte, Die Ostseelands ... 1180–1918* (Munich, 1954).

A. E. ROZEN'S EARLY LIFE: THE ESTONIAN SETTING

Bestuzhev(-Marlinsky), A. A., *Poyezdka v Revel'* (St P., 1821).
Ewers, J. P. G., *Provisorische Verfassung des Bauernstandes in Ehstland* ... (St P., 1806).
Hansen, C., *Geschichte der Stadt Narwa* (Dorpat, 1858).
Jordan, P., *Ergebnisse der Ehstland. Volkszählung* (Reval, 1883–84).
Jordan, P., *Sbornik svedeniy po geografii i statistike Estlyandskoy gubernii* (Reval, 1889), (Interesting appendix on ancient town sites, Ets, etc.)
Kotzebue, A., *Bedenklichkeiten über die neue Bauerverfassung in Ehstland* (Berlin, 1805).
Petri, J. C., *Neuestes Gemälde von Lief- und Ehstland unter Katherina II und Aleksander I, in historischer, statistischer, politischer, und merkantilischer Ansicht* (Leipzig, 1809).
Petri, J. C., *Ehstland und die Ehsten, oder historisch-geographisch-statistisches Gemälde von Ehstland* (Gotha, 1802).
Petrov, A. V., *Gorod Narva: yego proshloye i dostoprimechatel'nosti* ... (St P., 1901).
Severgin, V., *Zapiski puteshestviya po zapadnym provintsiyam Rossiyskogo gosudarstva v 1802 godu* (St P., 1803).
Tooke, W., *A View of the Russian Empire*, 3 vols (London, 1799), vol. 3, 564–7. (On commerce in the Baltic, from Revel' and Narva.)
Tseytlin, A. G., *Tvorchestvo Ryleyeva* (M., 1955), 20–4. (On the First Cadet Corps in 1812–16.)

ON NINETEENTH-CENTURY ESTONIA:
SOCIAL, AGRICULTURAL, POLITICAL CONDITIONS

Alexander, Capt. J. E., *Travels to the Seat of War in the East*, 2 vols (London, 1830), vol. 2, 19–27. (Revel' in 1829.)
Brevern, G., *Meine Erinnerungen an die Anfänge der zweiten Agrarreform in Estland, 1839 bis 1842* (Berlin, 1892). (Conditions in the Province on Rozen's return from the Caucasus.)
Brieflade, Est- und Livländische (ed. R. Toll, F. Bunge), 4 pts (Reval, 1856–87).
Eckhardt, J., *Die baltischen Provinzen Russlands* (Leipzig, 1869).
Gernet, A., *Geschichte und System des bäuerlichen Agrarrechts in Ehstland* (Reval, 1901).
Guk, A., *Issledovaniye sel'sko-khozyaystvennykh usloviy v Estlyandii, Liflyandii, i Kurlyandii* (Leipzig, 1845).
Himmelstierna, R. J. L. von, *Historischer Versuch über die Aufhebung der Leibeingenschaft in den Ostseeprovinzen* (Riga, 1838).

Jackson, J. H., *Estonia* (London, 1941). (Superficial in parts, but clear.)

Jannau, H. J., *Geschichte der Sklaverey und Charakter der Bauern in Lief- und Ehstland . . .* (Dorpat, 1786).

Kohl, J. G., *Die deutsch-russischen Ostseeprovinzen, oder Natur und Volk-erleben in Kur-, Liv- und Estland* (Dresden, Leipzig, 1841).

Kreutzwald, F. R., *Izbrannyye pis'ma* (Tallinn, 1953).

Kruus, H., *Grundriss der Geschichte des estnischen Volkes* (Tartu, 1932). (A classic general survey, well translated by A.-D. Toledano as *Histoire de l'Estonie* (Paris, 1935); splendid on the economic background.)

Linkov, Ya. I., *Ocherki istorii krest'yanskogo dvizheniya v Rossii v 1825–1861 gg.* (M., 1952). (Comparison of the Baltic and Great Russian situations.)

Loone, L. A., "Iz istorii promyshlennogo perevorota v Estonii", in *Voprosy istorii* (1952), no. 5, 77–96.

Maidel, G. von, "Sovremennoye sostoyaniye sel'skogo khozyaystva v Estlyandii", in *Trudy Vol. Ekonomicheskogo Obshchestva*, vol. 4 (1852), sect. 3, 16–23.

Nodel, E., *Estonia: Nation on the Anvil* (N.Y., 1963). (Useful on the origins of national consciousness, and on the cultural–economic osmosis, 1840–70.)

Rigby, E., *Letters From the Baltic* (London, 1841). (On the state of German-Baltic society.)

Rozin-Azis, F. (trans. A. Klyavs-Klyavin), *Stranitsy iz istorii krest'yanstva: istoriko-ekonomicheskoye issledovaniye agrarnykh otnosheniy v Pribaltike* (L., 1925).

Samarin, Yu. F., *Okrainy Rossii* (Praha, 1868). (A well-written and well-documented attack on Baltic Germans' privileges.)

Wiedermann, F. J., *Aus dem inneren und ausseren Leben des Esten* (St P., 1876).

Winckelmann, E., *Biblioteca Livoniae Historica: systematisches Verzeichniss der Quellen und Hülfsmittel zur Geschichte Ehstlands . . .* (Berlin, 1878).

ON THE DECEMBRIST MOVEMENT

Rozen in Contemporary Memoirs
Basargin, N. V., *Zapiski* (Petrograd, 1917).

Belyayev, A. P., *Vospominaniya dekabrista o perezhitom . . .* (St P., 1882). (Invaluable on Rozen in Petrovsky Zavod.)

Gorbachevsky, I. I., *Zapiski i pis'ma dekabrista* (M., 1925).

Lorer, N. I., *Zapiski dekabrista* (M., 1931).

Nicholas I, *Mezhdutsarstviye 1825 goda i vosstaniye dekabristov v memuarakh i perepiske chlenov tsarskoy sem'i*, compiled by B. E. Syroyechkovsky (M., 1926).

Obshchestvennyye dvizheniya v Rossii v pervuyu polovinu XIX-ogo veka, 2 vols, compiled by V. Semevsky, P. E. Shchegolev (St P., 1905); vol. 1, 443 (Memoirs of Baron V. I. Shteyngel'.)

Pushchin, I. I., *Zapiski o Pushkine i pis'ma iz Sibiri* (M., 1925).

Shteyngel', V. I., "Dnevnik dostopamyatnogo nashego puteshestviya iz Chity v Petrovsky Zavod 1830 goda", in *Dekabristy: neizdannyye materialy i stat'i* (M., 1925). (On the arrival of Anna Rozen, and Rozen on the march to the new prison.)

Vospominaniya Bestuzhevykh (ed. M. K. Azadovsky) (M.-L., 1951).

Vospominaniya i rasskazy deyateley taynykh obshchestv 1820-kh godov, 2 vols (ed. Yu. G. Oksman, S. N. Chernov) (M., 1931–32), vol. 1, A. V. Poggio; vol. 2, P. N. Svistunov (on Rozen's memoirs).

Yakushkin, I. D., *Zapiski, stat'i, pis'ma dekabrista I. D. Yakushkina* (M., 1951).

Zavalishin, D. I., *Zapiski dekabrista*, 2 vols (Munich, 1904).

Rozen on December 14/26, 1825
Hennigsen, C. F., *Revelations of Russia in 1846 . . .* (London, 1846), 262–90. (A general account of the rising by an Englishman better informed than most.)

Korf(f), M. A., Baron, *Vosshestviye na prestol Imperatora Nikolaya I* (St P., 1857); published
  simultaneously in London (John Murray) as *The Accession of Nicholas I*; see p. 249 in
  English trans. (on Rozen's conduct on Isaac Bridge).
Presnyakov, A. E., *14 dekabrya, 1825 goda* (M., 1926).
Pushkin, B., "Arest dekabristov", in *Dekabristy i ikh vremya* (M., 1927), 402.
Rozen, A. E., *Zapiski dekabrista* (Leipzig, 1870), 80–102.
Shteyngel', V. I., *Obshchestvennyye dvizheniya . . .*, I, 443.
Schnitzler, J.-H., *Histoire intime de la Russie sous les empereurs Alexandre I-er et Nicholas I-er*,
  2 vols (Paris, 1847).
Vosstaniye dekabristov: materialy, vol. 1, 236 (E. P. Obolensky); vol. 2, 358–9 (N. R. Repin);
  vol. 2, 370–1 (A. E. Golovin).

Rozen in Trial and Siberian Exile
Azadovsky, M. K., "Stranichki krayevedcheskoy deyatel'nosti dekabristov v Sibiri", in
  Sibir' i dekabristy (Irkutsk, 1925).
Barratt, G. R. V., *Voices In Exile: The Decembrist Memoirs* (Montreal, 1974).
Dekabristy: sbornik materialov (L., 1926).
Dekabristy: sbornik otryvkov iz istochnikov (compiled by Yu. G. Oksman, N. F. Lavrov
  B. L. Modzalevsky) (M., 1926).
Dekabristy v Zabaikale: neizdannyye materialy (ed. A. V. Kharchevnikov) (Chita, 1925).
Dmitriyev-Mamonov, A. I., *Dekabristy v Zapadnoy Sibiri* (St P., 1905), 141–8. (Invaluable
  source for Rozen in Kurgan, 1832–37; based on Siberian archive material.)
Ivanova, V., "Dekabristy v Kurgane: dom dekabrista A. E. Rozena", in *Sovet. Zaural'*
  (Kurgan, 1960), 1.
Kovalevsky, E., *Graf Bludov i yego vremya* (St P., 1869). (Useful remarks on the Committee
  of Enquiry's actions in the spring of 1826.)
Kubalov, B., "Sibirskoye obshchestvo i dekabristy", in *Katorga i ssylka*, VIII (1925), 139–72.
Lacroix, F., *Les mystères de la Russie* (Paris, 1845), 83–106. (An entertaining gallic résumé
  of the Decembrist movement.)
Mazour, A. G., *The First Russian Revolution, 1825* (Stanford, 1962; 2nd edn). (On Rozen
  the farmer.)
Nechkina, M. V., *Dvizheniye dekabristov*, 2 vols (M., 1955). (Still the standard Soviet work.)
Obshchestvennyye dvizheniya, vol. I, 197–8 (M. A. Fonvizin on the horror of incarceration
  and interrogation by night).
Paina, S. B., *Deyatel'nost' dekabristov po narodnomu obrazovaniyu . . . (Uchonnyye zapiski
  Glazovskogo Pedag. Instituta*, 1954, no. 1, 3–29; on Decembrist-teachers).
Pamyati dekabristov: sbornik materialov, 3 vols (L., 1926).
Pazhitnov, K. A., *Ekonomicheskiye vozzreniya dekabristov* (ed. I. D. Udal'tsov) (M., 1945).
  (Interesting for its Stalinist tone—a period interpretation.)
Semevsky, V. I., *Politicheskiye i obshchestvennyye idei dekabristov* (St P., 1909).
Shchegolev, P. E., *Dekabristy: sbornik statey* (L., 1926), esp. 199–270. (A fine collection of
  essays, throwing light on Nicholas's attitudes towards his prisoners.)
Volk, S. S., *Istoricheskiye vzglyady dekabristov* (M.-L., 1958).

ON ROZEN IN THE CAUCASUS, AND THE CAUCASIAN SETTING

Baddeley, J. F., *The Russian Conquest of the Caucasus* (London, 1908). (A work on which most
  subsequent works on the subject depend in some measure; a pioneering book.)
Dubrovin, N. T., *Istoriya voyny i vladychestva russkikh na Kavkaze*, 6 vols (St P., 1871–88).
  (No less essential for the period of General G. V. Rozen.)
Fonton, V., *La Russie dans l'Asie Mineure* (Paris, 1840).

Gireyev, D. and Nedumov, S., "K istorii znakomstva Lermontova s dekabristami", in *Literaturnoye nasledstvo*, vol. 60 (1956), bk 1, 508–13. (On Rozen's arrival in Tiflis and his lameness.)

Haxthausen, Baron A. von (trans. J.E.T.), *Transcaucasia . . .* (London, 1854).

Marlinsky, A. A., *Esquisses Circassiennes—Esquisses sur le Caucase* (Paris, 1854). (Romantic treatment of sporadic warfare with tribesmen.)

Montpereux, F. D. de, *Voyage autour du Caucase, chez les Tcherkess . . .*, 6 vols (Paris, 1839).

Spencer, Capt. W., *Travel in the Western Caucasus in 1836* (London, 1838).

Olonetsky, A. A., "Dekabristy v Gruzii", in *Iz istorii velikoy druzhby* (Tbilisi, 1954), 5–38.

ON ROZEN IN KHAR'KOV

Balagey, D. I., *Materialy dlya biografiy yuzhno-russkikh nauchno-literaturnykh deyateley XIX-ogo veka* (Kiev, 1903). (Rozen and G. P. Danilevsky.)

Corbet, C., *Nékrasoff: l'homme et le poète* (Paris, 1948), 391–5. (Nekrasov's use of Rozen's memoirs.)

Nekrasov, K. (ed.), *Arkhiv sela Karabichi* (M., 1916).

Rozen, A. E., *Zapiski dekabrista* (Leipzig, 1870), 517–93.

Russkaya starina (1904), no. 6, 621–5. (Letter of Rozen to G. P. Danilevsky of 18.1.63.)

Zhdanov, V., *Nekrasov* (M., 1971), 435–8. (Nekrasov's use of the Tarbagatay ideal in Rozen's memoirs.)

Zil'bershteyn, I. S. (ed.), letter of N. A. Bestuzhev to Rozen of 31.8.38, in *Literaturnoye nasledstvo*, vol. 60, bk 2.

INDEX